THE REAL JEWISH WORLD

A Rabbi's Second Thoughts

By the same author:

The New Jewish Identity in America (forthcoming)
Great Religions of the Holy Land
The Jewish Community in Canada (Two Volumes)
What Do We Believe? The Stance of Religion in America
 (Co-Author, with Martin E. Marty and Andrew M. Greeley)
To Understand Jews
America Is Different
More Loves Than One
The Bible Is For You
Bridge To Brotherhood: Judaism's Dialogue With Christianity
A Time To Speak
Lines On Life
The Road To Confidence
Man Is Free
The Jewish Community in Rochester
A Humane Society (editor)

THE REAL JEWISH WORLD

A Rabbi's Second Thoughts

by

Stuart E. Rosenberg

Philosophical Library
New York

Library of Congress Cataloging in Publication Data

Rosenberg, Stuart E.
  The real Jewish world.

  1. Rosenberg, Stuart E.   2. Rabbis—Ontario—Toronto—
Biography.   3. Jews—Politics and government—1948-
4. Toronto (Ont.)—Biography.   I. Title.
BM755.R554A37   1984   296.8'3'0924 [B]   83-17455
ISBN 0-8022-2439-3

Copyright 1984 by Philosophical Library, Inc.
200 West 57th Street, New York, N.Y. 10019
All rights reserved
Manufactured in the United States of America

For
Hadassa
Rachelle
Ronni
Elissa
and
Yael and Yonatan

TABLE OF CONTENTS

PART ONE: GROWING UP JEWISH IN NEW YORK

Chapter	1:	Zaydeh	3
Chapter	2:	School Days	23
Chapter	3:	The Decision	42
Chapter	4:	Becoming a Rabbi	61

PART TWO: RABBIS AND CONGREGATIONS

Chapter	5:	Denominations	91
Chapter	6:	The Pulpit	106
Chapter	7:	Bar Mitzvahs, Weddings, and Funerals	135
Chapter	8:	The Corporate Synagogue	
		Part One: How it Happened	174
		Part Two: A Case Study	184

PART THREE: JEWISH LEADERSHIP IN NORTH AMERICA

Chapter	9:	The New Establishment	229
Chapter	10:	The Holocaust and Soviet Jewry	273

PART FOUR: ISRAEL AND THE JEWS

Chapter	11:	A Year of Firsts: 1949	329
Chapter	12:	The Need for Dialogue	368

INDEX   421

PART ONE

GROWING UP JEWISH IN NEW YORK

Chapter 1

ZAYDEH

It was not long after The Crash. In Chicago, Manhattan and other fashionable centers, yesterday's millionaires were killing themselves in a variety of ways. Most seemed to prefer ending it all by jumps off tall buildings. My typical Brooklyn seven-year-old, sadistic, evil mind's eye saw them eagerly lining up to make what could hardly be called their leap of faith. In our middle-class Jewish Flatbush, it was highly doubtful—if in fact possible at all—that there were Jews who could qualify to make the jump.

Today, they tell me, the same, changeless streets of my Jewish Flatbush are populated by many Sephardim of Middle Eastern origin. There were none there in my childhood. Their stately homes, once owned by some of the parents of my classmates, are now regarded as "mansions" and sell at prices ranging high into six figures. Strange irony: by the 1950's, Jewish millionaires in *my* Jewish Flatbush, had become a dime a dozen.

It was soon after the Crash that a man came into my life who changed it forever. I might add that he also helped change Jewish life in America, though I have not read much in learned tomes about him, or listened to scholarly lectures on American Jewish history which have mentioned his name. His name was

Joel Braverman—or *Mahr Brahverman*—as we kids who were to speak only in Hebrew when addressing him, would soon learn.

I wasn't part of the evening conversation between Braverman, then only in his late twenties, and my parents. But on the morning after his visit, I knew that this man, who seemed so much older to me then, must have had some magical potion in his bag.

In those dark and sad days of the Depression, he had to be some kind of a wizard to be able to convince parents to send their children to a costly private school, and an experimental and untried Jewish school, to boot. Thinking of him later, across the years, I became convinced that it was more than wizardry and magic; the man had the infectious convictions of a missionary. You could not easily deny him, even if, like my parents, at the time, you had barely enough to make ends meet.

That morning I was given the news. My mother (not my father) announced to me that I would soon be transferring out of Public School 177, to a new school; so new, in fact, that it had only two classes and met in cramped rented quarters in rooms located in the building of the Young Israel of Flatbush on Coney Island Avenue and Avenue I. Those were light and airy, at least. Soon thereafter the school population quickly bulged—Braverman's door-knocking and ceaseless campaigning were incredibly successful.

Looking back, I find it difficult to believe what Braverman was able to accomplish, in just two or three years. After all, he had only begun in February 1928, with just twenty-two children, four teachers, and two classes—a kindergarten and a first grade. The harder the times, it seemed, the greater the response to his appeals for new enrollments. Additional rooms were rented. Soon, the two oldest classes, one of which was mine, were moved across the street on Coney Island Avenue, to study in the dark and musty schoolrooms of the "Talmud Torah of Flatbush," a traditional synagogue presided over by Rabbi Max Mintz.

Braverman had pioneered his "Yeshivah of Flatbush," an elementary Hebrew Day School, long before the Hebrew Day School was even conceived. A few scattered *yeshivot ketanot*—literally elementary rabbinical academies, but actually full-day parochial Jewish schools—taught a handful of Orthodox-minded and observant *boys* in the Greater New York area. Most of these schools were populated by the sons of rabbis and other religious functionaries. Until Braverman came along, none of them took any serious interest in the need to provide a general education. This they assigned, ironically and euphemistically, to the Secular Departments of their parochial schools. Braverman's was a solo venture in Jewish utopia: the creation of an integrated and cultured Jewish person, at home in the Jewish and all other worlds, not an *American* Jew, or a partisan Jew who belonged in the American world of belongers to a particular religious or secular party or movement.

Braverman was relatively simple and untrained; to my knowledge, he had not completed college nor did he later contribute seriously to the literature of education in America. But without fuss or feathers, without a string of degrees after his name, without higher Jewish scholarship or profound worldly culture, he unswervingly and almost instinctively knew what he wanted: to create in the America to which he had emigrated a Jewish community that could rival all of the great diaspora centers of Jewish learning and culture of the past. And he achieved all that he did in pre-Holocaust days, without the props of post-Hitler Zionism.

I think now of two of our teachers, many of whom were latter-day *maskillim*, enlightened scholars from Russia. Silver-maned Avraham Epstein, masterful teacher of the Prophets (all taught in Hebrew), whose long, lean figure must have suggested his literary pseudonym: *Abba Arikha* ("Big Abe" is the closest translation I can find for this Talmudic rabbinic name Epstein used when publishing his Hebrew sonnets). He surely was a world-class pedagogue. But much more: he was a modern poet and lyricist who romantically declaimed by heart all of Isaiah—and all of the other Prophets he taught us. I'm sure he must have known that none of us eleven- or twelve-year-olds could really fathom what Isaiah was all about or saying so profoundly. Never mind, he must have said to himself, someday you will. But for the present, it is enough if you little tykes get a little of the heavenly rhythms of Isaiah's cosmic, musical sweep in your bones; enough if you learn his language; enough if you set your minds to great and good themes to contend with for the rest of your lives.

Unforgettably too, Eliyahu Rabinowitz (*Mahr Rahbinovitz*) animates my memories of those years. Bulky but handsome, blue-eyed, with carefully barbered white hair, he taught with emphatic, persuasive, yet rational style. He would start a Biblical quotation, or a Rabbinic saying slowly and deliberately and then, with vocal decrescendo, wait for the whole class to finish the phrase, snapping his fingers like a musical conductor until all of us in unison, even the slowest, would sing it along with him to completion. Rabinowitz was a *Litvak*, a Lithuanian-born-and-trained Jew, schooled by the masters of the Hebrew-Zionist enlightenment movement in the old world. Like him they had fashioned themselves into *Maskillim* or "enlightened ones." Fully at home in the classical Jewish literary and religious traditions, they determined to read and interpret the Bible, Talmud and other writings with secular eyes and hearts. In effect, they reconstructed Jewish thought, if not Jewish life, by bringing it into their own turn-of-the-century humanistic universe of discourse, as Mordecai Kaplan, my teacher still later—founder of the Jewish Reconstructionist movement—would say of himself.

Rabinowitz taught us a variety of subjects in Hebrew: Bible, Rabbinic codes, but especially Jewish history as a separate, special subject—an unheard of thing in most Jewish schools of the day, which never got around to thinking about Judaism in historical terms. Throughout, his aim was sure, and he never wavered; he was not so much an iconoclast as a positive and deliberate shaper of still-flexible, open minds. He insisted that we think our way rationally through the Jewish past, and always, his arguments and expositions made the exercise seem so plain, so easy. From him I learned that the past had a past.

He was carefully grounding us in the traditional literary and religious materials, but his ultimate purpose was grander—he sought to make us understand ourselves and the Jewish cultural heritage from a rationalist position. And whatever he did not, or would not, explain in this fashion, seemed to us, therefore, to be irrelevant and inconsequential aspects of Jewish life and thought. Small wonder, I discovered later, that *Litvaks* such as he had already been dubbed, in nineteenth-century East Europe, by other, intellectually timid Jews, as a *Tzelem Kopf* (literally, a "mind tainted by the Crucifix") or a Jew on the brink. For them, he was too close for comfort to the borders that should separate him from the rest of the "Christian" world. These self-ghettoizing Jews considered it dangerous to engage in anything that smacked of flirtation with world culture. But to look at him—and all the other male teachers and pupils—was to see a class studying every day of the week, except Saturday, from 8:30 to noon (our English subjects were taught after lunch on weekdays only) with *kippot*, or skullcaps, almost glued to our heads. Externally, we must have appeared to be typical traditional scholars and masters, despite the fact that as good middle-class folk, we all dressed in the fashions of America—or should I say, of trendy Brooklyn—of the day.

The most significant part of the miracle of the Flatbush Yeshivah, beyond its unique team of principal and teachers was, I believe, the composition and the attitudes of the parent body. Most were, by 1929, Americanized, already middle-class, first generation immigrants; otherwise, they were born to Orthodox parents, on New York's Lower East Side, children of recently arrived East European immigrants. In my case, the two types were combined: my father, Hyman, was born in Jassy, Romania, a fair-sized city, and my mother, in New York.

Father said he had left behind his own "wealthy" father, a successful miller, because of a cruel stepmother. At the age of seventeen he set off in pursuit of a better life with other members of his family in the New World.[1]

Mother was born on Houston Street on the Lower East Side, in 1902, to Abraham and Rachel Weissman, Romanian Jews who had already come in the 1880s from the self-same Jassy, with two babies. Like many another immigrant, my grandparents had worked hard, laboring side by side in their kosher butcher store for many years. Slowly they prospered. Abraham Weissman was a pious and learned Jew and he found the time each daybreak for early morning services at the nearby synagogues; and time, as well, for daily Talmudic study.

During the booming Twenties, he was buying real estate properties for income and investment, including a row of handsome brownstone townhouses on East 97th Street on the Upper East Side near Harlem. As newlyweds, my parents were settled by him into one of these, and it was there that I was born. Our extended family of grandparents, uncles, aunts, and cousins, was typical of many others; from the "area of first settlement" all of us had moved to the "area of second settlement": from downtown Jews, we became what most immigrant New York Jews in those years wanted to be. But soon, it was time to move up again. In 1926, when I was four years old, our entire family—grandparents, parents, uncles, aunts and cousins picked themselves up—virtually at once—from what had been fashionable Jewish Harlem and moved to Brooklyn. My parents, though, were the only ones to move to the "best part of Brooklyn," Flatbush.

Father had been busy "achieving," too, but he had no time for prayers or study. After working hard as a well-paid cutter of ladies' hats, he took a partner—a fellow worker and operator of sewing machines in the same sweat-shop where he

---

[1] On June 29, 1941, Romanian and German soldiers slaughtered the entire Jewish population of Jassy. My grandfather, Joshua Zev Rosenberg, and scores of my father's family were among them. I had never met any of them.

worked. Like many other Jews of the time, the two partners—very few were courageous or pecunious enough to go it alone—were now in business for themselves, running a small millinery factory on the 16th floor, atop a loft building on West 38th Street, in Manhattan.

Typically, the firm—or the "foim," as he called it—was not named after the Jewish-sounding names of the owners. Everyone surely knew that the highly competitive millinery manufacturing industry was almost entirely in the hands of Jews, and was completely situated in a tight little island, a small strip between Fifth and Sixth Avenues, and from West 36th Street to West 39th Street, where the better "houses" were located. It lay hard by the larger ladies' garment district, similarly owned and worked by Jews. Nevertheless, there were the American, "goyish" customers to think about: J.J. Newberry, J.C. Penney, Montgomery Ward, and their likes, and it seemed safer and more fitting to call their company Moran Hat Co. Inc., which they named after their Catholic designer.

In 1929, of course, all my grandfather's houses and properties were lost, and my father's business was tottering on the verge of ruin. Most of my classmates' parents were in the same leaky boat, as a mood of fear and despair came to grip America in those dark days. The Flatbush Yeshivah, an untried and fledgling educational experiment run by immigrant Jews, and a very costly private school, which struggling parents couldn't really afford, should simply have faded away.

But it didn't.

I come back again to those unique and curious, mostly Americanized parents, who defied economic difficulties and enrolled children. My father's friends, unlike my grandfather's, had brought with them from the old country only a smattering of Jewish learning and culture, although, of course, they had imbibed Jewishness with their mothers' milk. None could even come close to the background of a Braverman—not to speak of an Epstein or a Rabinowitz. And once arrived in America, they were devoured by the all-consuming job. They had to learn a new language for the job; new skills for the job; new lifestyles for the job.

My grandfather's cronies, Jews who had arrived in America toward the turn of the century, never did bother to learn too much English—they lived in "the Jewish street," joined *Landsmanschaften* with Old World friends, where they spoke Yiddish, or read Yiddish books, pamphlets, and newspapers. They kept time to a different clock: the Jewish clock of ages past. Their Jewish impulses were never thwarted by any serious concern to accommodate to America in a religious or even cultural way, although, of course, many, like my grandfather, grew interested and active in local American politics. But politics and religious culture remained two different things: you needed the former to help make a living and to protect yourself; the latter was your own business—in Grandfather's time—and you minded your own business, and allowed no one else to mind it, either. What's more, if you really wanted to observe all of the Jewish religious laws without letting America interfere, you did something like what my grandfather did: you opened a kosher butcher store. Because it allowed you to own your business, and because you lived and worked only with Jews, you had no problem keeping the Sabbath and observing the Torah.

But the other Jewish businesses—the New York needle and garment trades of my father's generation—had no such Jewishness in mind, or in sight. They were competing, cut-throat style, with other Jewish manufacturers-jobbers, or workers in the job market, to stay afloat during the Depression years. Many had come, like my father, as very young people, and even if they had had an opportunity to study in European *yeshivot* or Talmud Torahs, would have been overwhelmed by their need to find jobs, and to make a new life in America.

All of them, however, had one thing in common: awe for learning in general, and for the learned Jew, in particular. If there were no *Maskillim* among them, then, like the man who never jumped but enjoys being with paratroopers, they knew and respected a Jewish scholar when they saw one. Out of this urgent feeling—the desire to succeed in America in order to produce children who would know and remember more about their Jewish heritage than they—their devotion to the Flatbush Yeshivah was born and nurtured. It didn't matter that the cost for tuition was an overwhelming $30 a month, times ten school months, plus bus transportation and fees for daily; hot (and "scrumptuous") American-style, but, of course, kosher lunches. "So we'll go without new shoes, or movies, vacations, or whatever," I kept hearing one parent after another say, in mutual support of the same financial difficulties all the parents were in. And propping up this entire enterprise, like some hidden Atlas maintaining our parents' world, were the grandfathers. Since all of the students came from the same kind of extended family that I did—being Jewish after all, was always a *family* matter—the patriarchal *eminence grise* of every grandfather was the strongest influence in the tribal families of our day. Everyone seemed to have a *Zaydeh* (grandfather) who really "pulled the strings"—and set the tone of their lifestyle.

Zaydehs, for the most part, like mine, were pious, Jewish-oriented scholars or near-scholars, whose central presence in the midst of all of these families really made the sacrifice of our parents worthwhile—and, I should add, even necessary.

All of us were loved by our grandfathers. You knew and felt this as soon as you walked into my friends' homes, since many of their *zaydehs* lived in the same house, or upstairs from them, in their two-family house. But none of my friends seemed to love their grandfathers as much as I did mine. They were around too much; they got in your way, asking foolish questions; they either got your messages mixed up or forgot them altogether. They were always pleasant and hospitable, but they were usually boring to talk to. When I thought of them, all I could picture were old, irrelevant people, customarily doing nothing but shuffling around the house; or with a glass of tea in hand, spoons almost poking their eyes out as they drank, reading a Yiddish newspaper. They were always getting last week's news—which Yiddish newspapers specialized in—and never seemed to catch up with what was going on today. And they spoke to you that way: always about stale things, the yesterdays you had already dismissed.

But that was not the way things were with us—my *zaydeh* and me. I knew Abraham Isaac Weissman in a variety of roles: sometimes as a businessman; more often as a scholar, writer, and public speaker; most of all, as a dreamer of Jewish dreams. He had no living sons of his own, and so I had become a surrogate son; he probably saw in me something he must have wished himself to be—young again, in a free land, full of the hopeful Jewish future. Like many other grandchildren, because I was not his child, I enjoyed his unending love without ever having to pay any price for it. I truly loved him: we were made for each other because we needed each other. I needed someone who would listen and understand. He needed someone—even a tyke like me—who could at least listen even if I couldn't always be expected to comprehend. I remember him most because of all the Sabbaths and Festivals I spent at his home.

When we moved to Brooklyn in 1926, we began spending each Sabbath weekend in my grandparents' nearby home. When I was about nine or ten, I vividly recall him becoming, for me, much more than the venerable, saintly grandfather he had always been. Amazingly, we seemed to become colleagues. If you think that we did what some people would call "levelling" with each other, you are mistaken. *He* did not *level* at all—I was invited to climb up to his station; he loved watching me grow taller, week after week. And as I did, he would embrace me with kisses and big bear hugs, patting my head with his warm and large hands, whispering words of affection and encouragement. These friendly feelings were always preceded by the same loving sigh: "*Oy, mein kind, du bist mein liebe*"—Oh, my child, you are my beloved. "*Mein Kind*": I could never forget those words, and those strong, strengthening hugs.

Those were the days before his sickness, when he was still

able to walk. We would go to his *shul* together—just the two of us—every Saturday morning. On arrival, he would unfurl his oversized, white woolen *tallis*, after carefully removing it from a blue velvet bag embroidered with his initials. As he wrapped himself in this lovely prayer shawl, he would quickly draw me close to his body and cover me over with it, too, as he proclaimed aloud the benediction. I waited for that beginning moment every Sabbath at shul; it made me feel secure and warm because I was actually a part of him.

But it was after lunch, and after the Sabbath nap that followed lunch each week, that I came to feel his special powers. He knew, of course, that while he was napping, I had gone four doors down the block, to my aunt's house, to tune in on the weekly college football games. Nobody was ever home there on Saturdays—they worked—and I enjoyed being all alone, with the radio blaring forth its play-by-play descriptions, and no one to tell me to "make it lower, or turn it off, altogether." He did not countenance playing of the radio, or the turning on of any electricity in his own home on the Sabbath, but he would never tell me that it was wrong, or "living in sin" to listen to those Saturday football games at my aunt's house. But he surely expected me back at his side in time for "tea and Torah" at about three-thirty, or so, whether the game was finished, or not. It usually was not.

Tea-time at my grandfather's house on Saturday afternoons was always Torah-time, the time when his *shul* cronies dropped by to study, discuss, and inevitably argue esoteric points of Jewish law or fine shadings of Biblical exegesis. His Rabbi friends were usually there, too, as part of his small circle of intimates. I was expected to be there, to listen and to absorb, though not to participate directly. Yet, it never failed to happen: somehow he managed to keep me engaged during what were clearly adults-only sessions, whether by helping to bring him books from his library shelves that he needed instantly to prove his point, or by merely sitting by, in case one of his guests needed or wished similar assistance. He was training me: I soon came to know virtually all of the books on his shelves; not their contents, of course, but their titles, and in many cases, the names of their learned rabbinic authors. I was drawn to this magnetic man, center of his friends' attention and admiration. I couldn't really know then what he was trying to achieve by having me sit in for tea, each Saturday, the only child at a session of rabbinic scholars. But after he died, not many years later, I began to understand.

It was then that I began to reflect on the unusual combination of influences in his own life which he had, subtly, but effectively, transmitted to me. I came to see in his life more than one man's struggle to integrate his multiple homelands, changing identities, and conflicting loyalties into a single harmonious whole. It was, for me, the unending story of the Jewish people itself that I read into his own search. Of course, neither he—nor we—could ever fully succeed in such an improbable exercise. Yet, the game was worth the candle; the effort itself, I discovered, added new textures and dimensions to his life. Most of the conflicts and inconsistencies could never be fully beaten down, but his unflagging efforts to contend with them, gave his life sparkle and zest. If, despite his best efforts he remained a contradiction, he also remained a lively, full-blooded man, strong and full of ideals and convictions. If he remained Orthodox, he did so in most unorthodox ways.

Such attitudes came much easier to merchant Jews who lived in larger cities and who were exposed to the currents of commerce, than to those who remained in the *shtetl*. By any definition, the Weissman family were already middle-class folk, even in nineteenth century Jassy. Long before Broadway popularized Sholom Aleichem's Tevyeh, my grandfather had often quoted approvingly: It's no sin to be poor; but it is no great blessing, either." He was trained to be future-oriented, optimistic, clear-headed, logical and all this, with one clear purpose in mind: to break out of the binds of life, by making the most of every opportunity. These bourgeois views must have been the motive powers that drove him to leave Jassy in the early 1880s, restless after almost a decade of growing anti-Semitism in Romania. He was ready to accept the challenge of making a new life in America. I suppose you could say, that like many other proto-middle-class European Jews, he had arrived in America long before he even got there.

Some new immigrants believed in defying both time and space; they tried to maintain their Jewish life here as if nothing had changed, as if they were still living in the small towns of East Europe. Abraham Weissman was not one of them. Soon after arriving in New York, he attended night school to learn the new language, which he later wrote impeccably, and spoke almost as well. He believed in the freedom of personal choice, and respected the non-observant Jew. He never tired of warning against withdrawal into our own selves; all forms of education were not to be feared, but sought. He blamed the Orthodox parents of defecting offspring for not realizing that it was their own thoughtless and uncaring rigidities that had boomeranged, and not the children who had really sinned. He was not sure of how Judaism would ultimately fare in America—but he was never prepared to write off its future. If he willed it, we would survive gloriously even in the midst of freedom. "It will be a different kind of Jewishness, but it will still speak to the world, and maybe for the first time since the days of the Prophets, it will even speak without fear." For him, America was different: It was a new version of a promised land.

I could not realize how sick my grandfather had become, until he could no longer work, or walk, or go to *shul* with me. For almost three years, he was in and out of hospitals. Each time they amputated more and more of his gangrene-eaten right leg. Our visits became more frequent—often we'd be at his home, visiting his bedside, almost every afternoon, after school. Then, no one had to tell me: The air of slow death hovered over his room.

But if he sensed this—and I am sure that he did—there was nothing about his demeanor that revealed it to us. On the contrary, day after day he sat uncomplainingly atop his spotless bed, with his bandaged leg raised high. He had work to do; he doggedly continued penning his learned commentary on the Five Books of Moses, in his patient and impeccable Hebrew script, forgetting his pain. He remained equally oblivious to the crying of his daughters, in the back rooms of the house. He couldn't possibly be joyful, but he was never sad or saddening.

I remember some of the conversations we shared during those long, last months.

"Sholomel, some people ask me: 'Avraham Yitzhak, how can you believe in God, when He pains you so?' I tell them, Sholomel, that the world wasn't created for me. The Jewish people have suffered much more, and they will survive as long as they believe in him.... The best proof that there is a God, is the continuing existence of His people...and with His help, even this madman in Germany, may his name be erased, will be destroyed.

"Some day, soon, your turn will come, Sholomel, and with the power of all those words, in all those sacred books that you will learn, you will help prove that there is a God in this world...and that His people still live. You will see: There will be days when you will be tempted to turn away from the world, and maybe, from all these books, too.... But the words...the holy and powerful words...will always draw you back...to Him...to the world...to your people.... You will never be alone in the world, frightened of life, as long as you are part of your people.

"To know, to believe, and to lead...for these things you don't have to be a Rabbi...I am not a Rabbi...but I must never stop studying. Studying is asking questions, even though you don't always get an answer. Sometimes, to have 'answers' that are really no answers, can be very dangerous.... That happens when you stop having questions that are really questions.... But if you never stop studying, you never stop having good questions.

"Be a businessman, a doctor, a lawyer, a teacher—but,

above all, be a learned, loyal Jew. There is no nobler profession than being an intelligent Jew. And the harder it is to remain loyal, the greater the test to your character.... You cannot struggle to be a loyal Jew, without refining your character, at the same time.

"You see Friedman and Margolis here almost every *Shabbos*. Take Rabbi Friedman. He's just arrived from Europe—Poland, I understand—with eight children and a sick wife.... With his learning, he should have stayed in Europe, because he will never be appreciated here as a Rabbi. He shouldn't have become Rabbi of our *shul*.... The *balebatim*, those coarse, unlearned people on the Board, will eat him alive. He should have become a storekeeper, maybe a teacher. In America, they don't need a scholar, a *talmid chocham* for a Rabbi. All they want is *shamosim*, errand boys, who will do what *they* tell them to do, and *when* they tell them; only a slave serving slaves—*eved avodim*—that's what a European Rabbi becomes in America. But Margolis, he's another kind of 'Rabbi.' He gave himself the title in America. In Europe, he'd be a *mohel*, maybe. What does he do for a living? He smiles. He's always smiling. You know why? That's his Rabbi's uniform. Take away his uniform, and there's nothing underneath. He should be in Washington, in the State Department, he's such a diplomat.

"Be a Jewish leader, Sholomel, even when there are no Jewish followers.... Be a *mensch*, especially when nobody else is.... That's what the Mishnah teaches: 'In a place where there are no men, strive to be a man.' "

My grandfather died without my ever telling him what I thought I was going to be.

It was only in the synagogue—his synagogue—at my Bar Mitzvah, when I spoke his words as if I were actually him, that I think he may have surmised that I would not forget what he taught me.

My Bar Mitzvah remains a bittersweet memory. For a year

or so before my thirteenth birthday, my father kept recounting stories of his own unceremonious Bar Mitzvah in Jassy. He was already preparing his own defense against the possibility of a Bar Mitzvah affair, which was just then beginning to become the rage in Flatbush. (Everything good and bad about middle-class American Jewry, as the years followed, seemed to have originated in Flatbush.) My father kept repeating that "in his days," he was already a regular public reader of the Torah at the age of eleven, and so *everybody* knew that he had mastered *that* skill. He was, of course, leading up to his inevitable crushing punch-line: His Bar Mitzvah ceremony was no ceremony at all and need not have been one.

Because he was orphaned of his mother, he was expected to start putting on phylacteries every weekday morning, beginning at the age of twelve, a year earlier than usual. So when the appropriate day came, he was brought into the Beth Ha-Midrash (the small "chapel" used for weekday prayer) on a Monday morning, when the Torah was read briefly. He donned his phylacteries for the first time, and as a mark of his newly conferred maturity, was called to the Torah for the first time as well. That's the way he "became a man," he insisted.

My mother, who had no brothers, feigned other memories. In America, she insisted, we did it differently. "We celebrated, with parties, and a big Kiddush at *shul*, and..." At this point, my father would always go into orbit, like a missile after lift-off. "You did what? *You* did *what we did* in Jassy, *and that was that*. Who ever heard of a Bar Mitzvah on *Saturday morning* anyway? And all that *we* did, was all that '*you*' did—there was a little herring, some *kichel*, and a few drops of *schnapps*, for the immediate family, and *that was that*." And then, in triumphant conclusion, he would add: "And after *that*, I went to work, that same *Monday morning*."

But like most other Jewish males of the time, my father was no match—on any subject whatsoever, for my mother. He knew, and she knew, that what she was after she would get. His preliminary fencing and hedging, for a year before my Bar

Mitzvah, were merely his way of saying: "Look, you're going to do it your way, anyway. Just let me say what I have to say!"

My mother had it her way. Her father was dying, after all, she explained, and *he* deserved a little *nachas*.

For several weeks before my Bar Mitzvah itself—in bed or in a wheelchair—my grandfather was busy preparing my speech—fifteen minutes of learned exegesis, in Biblical and Talmudic Hebrew which I carefully studied and dutifully memorized. It was *his* speech—and I deeply felt it. When I finally declaimed it before my adoring family at my grandfather's synagogue, the Hebrew Alliance of Brighton Beach, that Saturday morning in July, I was crestfallen. Nobody understood a word of all of this ancient mellifluity; bored with it all, they unceremoniously went to sleep, or loudly chatted with their neighbors, throughout my carefully rehearsed, learned discourse. (Par for the synagogue course, I was later to learn.) None of this, of course, stood in the way of their lavish compliments on "my" speech when they shoved by me, as they rushed to devour all in sight on the beautifully set and heavily laden tables, groaning with gefilte fish, herring and assorted Jewish delicacies, at the splendid Kiddush for the congregation, which followed the services, in the basement hall. "You did a good job!" That, again—and for the last time, I hoped—was the way they showed their appreciation to my parents, as they departed, loaded to the gills with good food and drink.

But that was only the beginning. The main event was to follow, that night.

There had been some small soul-searching on my mother's part, about having a "Saturday night affair." There was little money for it; her father might not still be alive by then; and yet, if you wanted one, you had to pay to reserve a hall, and for a band, and buy special party clothes, and all the rest. In the end, she went the way of all Jewish flesh in Flatbush and rented the Casa del Rey on Coney Island Avenue, in the heart of our Flatbush. She had taken the route of neighbors and friends; she *couldn't* disappoint *them*.

That was part of the new style of American Judaism, just then beginning to sweep the continent, and for generations after—and all of it had emanated out of Flatbush, or other sections of middle-class New York. Most of my non-Yeshivah friends, like most of North American thirteen-year-olds today, needed at least one day in their lives to prove that they were still Jewish. More accurately, their parents required it, as a kind of coming-out party for public display and conspicuous consumption. Their reasons had nothing to do with Judaism. As early as 1935, Bar Mitzvah in middle-class America, as some wag had put it, had already become more "Bar" than "Mitzvah." Successful, materialistic Jewish parents, it seems, required at least one day (*and* one *night*, too) for the "Jewish debut" of their children. (Since the mid-fifties, egalitarianism has come into vogue on this score, and thirteen-year-old girls are now given the same treatment on the occasion of their Bat Mitzvah.)

But debuts like this are really finales. Nobody profits, except maybe the caterers, the local department stores, and gift shops. The social pressures that operate in this arena are a useful index of almost every other aspect of Jewish community life in America. The need to "appear"—successful, rich, responsible, dutiful, charitable, religious, or what have you—drives most middle-class Jews. The fellow who wrote the advertisement for Dodge cars in the fifties—"You don't have to be rich to own a Dodge; you only have to look rich"—was either one of these, himself, or was surely thinking of them.

Since it was early July, and Sabbaths did not conclude until close to ten o'clock, the affair had to be pretty much of a midnight-dinner, preceded by cocktails—with blaring music bouncing around the hall for well over an hour. The band had been suggested by my violin teacher, gum-chewing Mr. Frankel, who had already made sure that I would never turn into a lover of the instrument; barring any native talent I may have had, he quickly and successfully prevented any future success I would have with the "fiddle," as he called it. (I gave it up a year, or so, after my Bar Mitzvah; it was either Hebrew High School or violin lessons, I told my mother, knowing full well which way she'd go.) Like Frankel, the band-players doubled or tripled in "brass"; they were harried clerks, or factory workers, trying to earn an extra dollar, on the side. Their music, like his, showed it.

The noisy music they sounded forth provided a splendid backdrop for the motley parade of guests, each couple bashfully sauntering in with neatly packaged gifts to give to the "Bar Mitzvah boy" as if presenting tickets of admission. (It was considered the height of poor taste *not* to bring your present to the "affair." Some had braved the disallowing stares of the more religious among us, and had even brought their gifts earlier—to *shul*, at the Sabbath morning service.)

When we finally were seated at the head table, my mother gave what I clearly and embarrassingly felt was an audible sigh of relief. At last, all the nights of planning, the arguing with the caterer over whether we'd have sweetbreads on a biscuit shell or fruit cocktail as the starter, and the other great decisions, like who would be seated with whom—considering that not all the members of the two families were on speaking terms—had come to a glorious end. (We had sweetbreads, by the way, on my mother's demand, but on the caterer's terms—twenty-five cents more per person.) Course followed course, dance followed dance, and everyone was happy. Everyone but me, it seemed.

In the midst of all of this jollity, I managed to wave to my three friends—that was the quota allowed me—to join me, as I stole my way to a nearby exit sign. I was not about to spend the rest of the tired old evening saying "thank you for the present" to this or that adult cousin or distant relative, whom I barely knew, even by name. We made our way to the checkroom, where there hung a sign, "Tips Have Been Taken Care of by Your Gracious Host," and with the help of the watchful attendant, I hunted up the prize gift of all, from out of a stack of gift packages that I instinctively knew was a pile of fountain pens and cuff links. (This was the era of fountain pens as Bar Mitzvah gifts, later immortalized by Catskill comic Henny Youngman—or was it Milton Berle?—in the routine Bar Mitzvah speech, in which the celebrant begins, "Today, I am a fountain pen." The earlier "Today I am a man" was already passé; the current "Today, I am a calculator" was still unknown.) After some small confusion, I fished it out. It was the tennis racquet I had always wanted.

It was a hot summer night outside. After commiserating over our mutual boredom, the four of us began a "game of tennis" in the parking lot behind the Casa. I had the only racquet, of course, and there were no balls, no net, no court. But for what seemed like the sweetest hour of the night, we "played" on and on, enjoying our phantom match, swapping wisecracks. When I finally re-entered the hall, I had the feeling that if I had walked from there to the Brooklyn Bridge, and fallen off, nobody would have been the wiser. This, like all other Bar Mitzvah affairs, was a very important and busy time for the adults: They were catching up on all the gossip they had missed since the last time they saw each other—at the last family Bar Mitzvah or wedding. They were probably "checking out the house," to see who had *not* been invited, and clucking over the reasons why not.

Sometime in the early hours of the morning the band played its last number, a few brave oldsters stepped onto the still-slippery dance floor for a hasty foxtrot, the lights switched off and on, and we moved out to the street. The ball was over.

A year or so later, my grandfather, who was too sick to attend the evening affair, died. But not all of those who had been invited to the Bar Mitzvah bothered to come to his funeral, heavily attended though it was.

CHAPTER 2

SCHOOL DAYS

For almost six years I had lived in the closed world of the Yeshivah, yet I never felt walled in because we were taught that Jews were citizens of the larger society of men. Our teachers had never failed to remind us that when our Amoses and Isaiahs spoke they were always addressing the world, not only a local audience of neighbors and relatives. The Hebrew prophets were powerful defenders of all the disadvantaged, whoever they were; the railing scourges of tyrants, wherever they were. Jewish minds and hearts focused upon the wider horizons of universal man.

In the wider world we now came upon, however, the only "majority" we could find consisted of the sum of all minorities. New York City, though it was not the whole of America, still pointed the way for the nation. It was, is, and seems forever destined to be, wholly ethnic—a community of parochial communities. There were, we discovered, Great Walls in New York guarding each disparate group from the other: these were euphemistically called neighborhoods. Clearly, they shut out as much light as they kept in.

Chinatown, Harlem, Little Italy, and all the other "little

somewheres" may have caused out-of-town visitors to think of New York as a great cosmopolis, a model of the New World, where the rivalries and hates of Asia and Europe were dissipated by the warm proximities of tolerant and colorful minorities co-existing cheek by jowl. But we who lived there soon came to know better. If John Donne was right and no man is an island wholly of himself, most New Yorkers somehow managed to live on their own religious and cultural peninsulas, connected to the mainland, yet set apart and buttressed by their ethnic churches, foreign-language newspapers and radio programs—and most important—based in their own subcultural neighborhoods. So instead of feeling deprived or sorry for ourselves for having been protected from the world, we actually felt very much part of the scene we were now entering. We had thought that only we had been raised in an envelope, a neatly-packaged, self-contained environment. We soon realized that cultural isolation was the one thing New Yorkers of all backgrounds shared most.

Ironically, the special kind of cloistering we experienced had prepared us to face our environment, in a unique, if also somewhat naive, fashion. Our Yeshivah education had made us into Jewish élites, so naturally rooted in the soil of our own culture that no strange or hostile winds could ever blow us down, or so we believed. We were therefore not reluctant but eager to join the world: to meet new kinds of people, to hear them out and learn from them—all the while we would be speaking up as the cultural ambassadors of our people.

If anything, it was the new Jewish types we would be meeting in our public high school, not our newfound Christian classmates, whom we regarded with doubt and suspicion. To us, they appeared as a breed of vulgar barbarians: The only thing Jewish about them was their common fear of being Jewish, or of appearing "too Jewish" in the sight of others. It was from them that I first heard that anti-Semitism was really not the fault of the Christians, but of Jews themselves—Jews who act like Jews. I had always been taught differently: Anti-Semitism, my rather extravagant teachers had said, is not something Jews should worry about; it's not really a Jewish problem but a Christian problem.

We were not at war with the rest of the world; certainly not on the defensive, either. We knew, of course, that the neighborhood churches and synagogues were not yet open to each others' sympathy and understanding. That was the way of the world, and that was the way it was going to be. But the reason for this built-in impasse, we were taught, had nothing whatever to do with Jews or Judaism, not even with Christianity itself, but only with illiberal Christians. After all, they said, we were not out to convert *them*; nor did *we* call *them* "Christ-killers."

In fact, nobody had ever called me "Christ-killer," nor did anybody seem worried about my obvious total loss to the ranks of new Christendom. Still, my nervous, middle-class Jewish classmates at James Madison High School would be telling "stories" about those other Jewish kids—in neighborhoods far from Flatbush—who always seemed to suffer some humiliation at the hands of the "Church gangs," as they were called. It was only after they had succeeded in transplanting those distant fears into my own heart that I began changing my daily walking route to school: I now crossed to the other side of the street, as I neared the yard of the Irish parochial school of St. Brendan's Catholic Church. Aside from *those* Irish, at the Church—who, by the way, never even came near me—I could not really fathom why so many felt so nervous about being "a Jew in a non-Jewish world." Increasingly, during my years at Madison, I came to regard this view of my middle-class Flatbush schoolmates as the last and only shield left to defensive, self-scorning Jews. It was their lame excuse for opting out of Judaism, blaming their own Jewishness.

That old bedeviling need of middle-class teenagers, which we all were, the urging, pressing need to conform, had been very hard to resist. None of the kids living near me were anywhere else but in the public schools of the area. For years, they had taunted me for going to a "Jewish school." "What, are you going to be, a Rabbi or something?" they kept mocking. "Why aren't you a 'regular guy' like us?" "O.K. So you're Jewish. But for Christ's sake, do you have to be *so Jewish*? Doesn't anything else matter?"

No, I wasn't going to be a Rabbi, I kept telling them, and going to the Yeshivah was lots of fun. Still, in my heart I secretly envied them most of all for their leisure. They had time for movies, picnics, outings—and for games: stickball in the spring and summer, and touch-tackle football in the fall. And as if for spite, all the big neighborhood games always seemed to take place on Avenue O, right in front of my house, before cheering crowds who came from blocks and blocks away and lined the sidewalks on either side of the street. Not only couldn't I join any of the teams, but I usually even missed watching the exciting games themselves; I didn't return home from the Yeshivah until about five in the afternoon. If I went to Madison High, I told myself, I could be like them: still Jewish, but not "too Jewish."

Nor was there any possibility of continuing to study *only* at the Yeshivah, even if I had wanted to, which I did not. This was not yet the hour for a parochial Jewish high school in Flatbush. The tuition costs for such a program would have been far in excess of what most parents could then afford. Unlike the Catholics, Jewish parochial school advocates had not campaigned in favor of their programs on the basis of a war against the "Godless public schools." Jews, in those days, still had a love affair with Horace Mann's concept of public education as a democratizing force for liberal values, and they refused to align themselves with any who consciously sought to weaken the public schools of New York.

A handful of Joel Braverman's first elementary school graduates had agreed to continue their Jewish studies at the Yeshivah three nights a week and on Sunday mornings, on a trial basis. Only about ten of us heeded his admonitions: "If you do not continue now, during your teen years, you will forget everything you learned, and all of your earlier years will have been wasted." He spoke of the time immediately ahead of us as "crucial years": they were not only the "years of forgetfulness"—*yemai shicheha*, as he called them—but also a time of "value-testing." He warned that if we did not continue to deepen our Jewish thought as adults, we would forever remain "childish Jews" who remembered Judaism only in a childish way. "If you do not continue to grow as Jews, your Jewishness will be no match for all the new ideas and glittering knowledge you will soon be acquiring as adults, in adult fashion." He predicted that if we stopped developing and growing in Jewish thought and culture, and grew only as ordinary Americans, "that is precisely what you will always remain: ordinary Americans." "You are too important to the Jewish people, too important to yourselves, to allow that to happen. You have something very special to say to America and the Jewish world."

Since we were born not long after the close of the Great War, we helped make up the heavy Baby Boom that now descended upon New York's high schools. As a result, we had to postpone our arrival at the destination of our deepest Flatbush desires, the stately but overcrowded main building of James Madison High School, located in the heart of our section's most affluent area, on tree-lined Bedford Avenue. High schools were bulging at the seams, but owing to the depressed state of the economy few new buildings or even temporary additions were being erected. But things were dramatically different in the elementary schools; the Depression had caused a sharp drop in the number of children now entering. Accordingly, an ingenious idea was devised involving the use of empty classrooms in nearby public or private elementary schools as temporary "annexes" to the overflowing high schools. I spent the first six months of my high school career at the Annex of Abraham Lincoln High School, located "across the tracks" and paradoxically, housed in the same elementary school building, P.S. 177, I had briefly attended, before entering the Yeshivah. After Lincoln, I was admitted to Madison, but I had to spend a full year at its Annex, where I was greeted with still more irony: It was the vacant quarters of the Sunday School of the area's only Reform congregation, Temple Ahavath Sholom. So, in a way, it was back to Jewish school, but now in a most improbable place, for me—a Reform Temple.

At Lincoln, only a week after graduation from the Yeshivah, I was immediately thrown together with children of Italian working-class immigrants whose parents had arrived from Sicily about a decade earlier. They ate together, bunched together, played together. Worst of all, they spoke Italian together. I suddenly found myself inwardly critical of their apartness, and began wondering about something that had never really bothered me before. Maybe the Jewish kids in my own neigborhood who had always berated me for being "too Jewish" were right. Maybe I looked to them like these Italians now appeared to me.

It didn't take much time before I began to see and read a series of signals that would help me begin to decipher my confusing puzzlements. One half-serious, half-comical incident stands out. "You speak Jewish?" With this lead question, a group of Italians, coming out of their shell and moving toward us, struck up their first serious conversation since we had come to Lincoln. "No, not Jewish," I cracked wise in defensive retreat, "there's no language called Jewish, only a people called Jewish." "Oh, no?" one of them quickly countered, looking at me as if I were completely lacking in intelligence. "My father told me that Jews speak Jewish, so we Italians should speak Italian! If there's no Jewish, what *do* you fellows speak?" We broke into mock laughter at the thought that we were supposed to be setting an example for them, at least according to their fathers. "Well," I finally countered, "can we try this on you? You fellows should recognize it from your Sunday School." And I began to recite, in slow and mock-majestic cadences, the opening verses of the twenty-third Psalm, in Hebrew.

"What are you crazy or something? We never heard that

funny stuff in Sunday School, or in Church! What in the world are you giving us here, Chinese, Turkish, or something?"

"Did you ever hear about lords and shepherds?" I teasingly replied. In a few moments, the Italians were receiving instruction from us in early Church history and listening to interpretations of Jewish-Christian relations they had obviously never heard before. Disbelieving, they told us that they would have "to check out all this new stuff with the Sisters, at Sunday School." Yet it was our facility with the Hebrew language that put them completely off balance, particularly since we explained that our own parents only knew how to read prayers, but never spoke or understood Hebrew; not the way we did. "You mean you fellows speak Hebrew, right out of the Bible, and your own parents don't even know what you're saying? You've got a good deal: You can keep secrets from them by talking right under their noses. And what can they tell you? To stop talking like Jews? Boy, what a set-up!"

The brightest among them, a lean, ascetic-looking boy of about fourteen, now tried to sum it all up, in a practical, yet almost philosophical way. "Now I undertand," he looked exceedingly wise as he spoke, "why your parents don't make you talk this Hebrew—Jewish, or whatever you call your language: They don't want to be kept in the dark. But what beats me is why they'd want you kids to know a language they themselves don't use or understand. Either it's your family language and you use it, or it's not. And if it's not, *forget it*! With us, the whole family speaks Italian. It's our language; we brought it here from our own country; it's part of our whole life. But why in the world would you guys want to speak a language nobody speaks at home; a language that doesn't even have a home itself?"

That closed the discussion, and for the next six months at Lincoln I studiously avoided opening it up again with our Italian classmates. I was just not ready, nor were my Yeshivah friends, to articulate our deepest feelings in the language and accents required. We were no match for our Italian friends, and for a simple reason: They existed as Italians, while we had to create something for ourselves out of our older Jewish roots—something that had not taken form before our eyes, or grasped within our own family experience. My Yeshivah teachers had taught me a melody, and I loved it—but, for me, it was still a stirring song, but one without words: passions without a clear shape or a vivid language.

At Madison, we came upon a much different world, populated by a large number of Anglo-Saxon types and an even bigger group of disconnected, passionless *American* Jews. Even the handful of Italians we found were principally fair-haired. They made certain to remind us that their long-settled families hailed from northern cities like Rome or Milan; that they were born in New York; that they knew no Italian and had no desire to learn it; and that they were definitely not to be confused with those late-arrivals, the Sicilians. While we melded into one big community and boasted of serious-minded teachers and ambitious student achievement, most of Madison's Jewish population was a source of great annoyance to me. I had never met such uninspired, bland and collapsible Jews before: They seemed never to have had a Jewish dream, never to have cherished Jewish heroes. They might just as well have told me that they too came from Rome or Milan; I would probably have believed them.

These other Jews were typical Flatbush people, without Yeshivah education, and most, without any Jewish education worth thinking about. While they reflected the ambition of their middle-class environment and often excelled in their studies, many were also caught up in nothing more significant outside their schooling than the social whirl of the fancy neighborhoods in which they lived. Their mothers were busy playing *Mah Jongg* and they were preoccupied with other indoor sports at their weekly Friday night parties. We, from the Yeshivah, were not quite ready for their boy-girl games. We were still really elementary school babes in high school clothing—I was barely thirteen at the time—and our earlier

School Days 31

friendships were not social-sexual, but an integral part of the true stake each of us had in being "special," when studying at the Yeshivah. We were school friends, who became life-long friends—not "party friends" who just happened to go to the same school.

I began to realize, however, that for all of its universal love of Jews and Judaism, the Yeshivah was a sheltered Jewish society which had not only dealt with the world outside in genteel abstractions, but had also kept me from knowing and understanding the less fortunate, poorer Jews in my own city.

I felt that I had been consciously protected from contact with many of my fellow Jews, and this upset me. How could I dream of a worldwide Jewish People if I did not even have a connection to Jews outside of Flatbush? I knew nothing about those still living on the Lower East Side, except that they were still condemned by their poverty from moving away from those slummy ghettoes. Nor had I ever been exposed to Jews in uptown Manhattan and parts of the Bronx. Even closer to home, in Brooklyn, I had not been encouraged to forge any personal ties to the people living in the poorer sections: in Boro Park, Brownsville, or East New York. Most of those who lived there belonged to the working class, or were petty shopkeepers, and I was fashioned to feel different—both at the Yeshivah and at home.

I began to feel that I had been externally tattooed, against my will, with the tribal marks of the middle class. Though they never spoke of it, I could not avoid the feeling that my parents saw themselves as having "made it": they were no longer "struggling workers." I saw my father then as a bundle of self-deceptions. What I couldn't realize, of course, was that his identification with the "bosses" was only a thin veneer of self-protection in the face of his own doubts and difficulties as a plodding, small businessman. At first, I was close to being angry at him for not seeing what I saw—that small businesspeople and factory workers were all co-strugglers, and that he should not regard himself as if he were the head of General

Motors. Though he considered himself an "American businessman" I was convinced that he really was not a businessman at all. I suggested to him that he was as much a struggling factory worker, enslaved to his new job as the "Boss," as he had been to his older job as cutter, a few years before "graduating" to the presidency of Moran Hat Co. Inc. "Who has been teaching you all this nonsense?" he would reply. "Is this what I sent you to the Yeshivah for? So you can tell me that I should become a cutter again?" I was clearly moving away from the very middle class he had, according to his lights, worked so hard to help me join. And my continuing challenges bothered us both.

Soon my anger turned to a mixture of pity for him and confusion over where my own sympathies should really lie. At the close of every slack summer, in anticipation of the new and crucial fall season, and after full days of work—often, from seven to midnight—he'd be battling with workers' committees setting prices for every new "number," piece by piece, since trimmers were paid as "piece-workers." I had worked in his factory as a shipping clerk during my summer vacations, beginning with my pre-teens, but now I was terribly embarrassed to overhear, throughout long hours waiting for him in the nearby office, the shouts and near hair-pulling bouts of these horrible bargaining sessions. I can still hear his agonizing cries: "You're going to drive me out of business, you and your Roosevelt."

For one full week, or more, at a time, these hectic "price settlement" nights would turn my father into an angry tiger, as he powerfully defended his small strip of territory. He sometimes even came close to cursing Roosevelt's New Deal, which took away, he said, what little control he still had over his tottering business, and placed it squarely in the hands of the workers' price-setting committee. At his factory sales price of $10 per dozen hats, net—if he was lucky—there really wasn't too much room to maneuver, he kept insisting. But now, I also saw myself as a "worker," too. He may have had his problems, but so did "we." I found myself in the uncomfortable position of opposing my father, not because he was harsh, but because he was forgetting who he was—not just a millinery manufacturer, but also the son of the Jewish prophets.

But this was an hour of widespread rebellion against all assorted, accumulated and accepted norms of conventional America—particularly among sensitive young people. After all, what had they to lose? There was little save unemployment awaiting even the most ambitious among them; and if, upon graduation, they wanted to starve as lawyers, accountants, or engineers they were perfectly free to do so. I was surely inhaling some of their exasperations.

In the arts, and among literary people, experimentation was now the vogue, too. And on the stage, people's political theater and music had become the rage, funded by the W.P.A. (Works Progress Administration) and largely the result of Franklin Roosevelt's political support and his wife Eleanor's personal encouragement. "Sing Me A Song Of Social Significance, Anything Else Is Taboo!"—hit tune of the International Ladies Garment Workers Union's off-then-on-Broadway show, *Pins and Needles*—fairly well summed up the new and volatile social mood of the day. It certainly spoke to me: I saw the show five or six times.

The Depression years were coming to a close for some, by that time, but not for my family. The Hebrew education afforded me for the past nine years (my brother was also a student at the Yeshivah of Flatbush, by this time) had simply drained our strained finances. Out-of-town universities were then in vogue among my Madison classmates. Harvard, Yale, and Princeton were reserved for the rich, but there were the state universities, like Michigan and Wisconsin. In the end, as I secretly had known, despite my fleeting flirtation with the idea of studying out-of-town, I would apply to and be accepted at Brooklyn College, where free tuition and easy accessibility to its newly-built Bedford Avenue Campus decided the issue.

As it happened, staying in New York City not only gave me

the chance to continue my higher Jewish education at Herzliah Hebrew Teachers Seminary, on East Broadway, but changed the course of my life, and led me into a career of Jewish service. Had I gone to any of the out-of-town schools I was thinking about, like so many of my Yeshivah schoolmates, I would probably have lost my most serious ties to Jewish life, and become like many of them—just typical middle-class American Jews—who had truly forgotten most of what they had learned as children, as Mr. Braverman had forewarned. Attending a Jewish Day School, by itself, I was to discover, was no guarantor of later allegiances to the Jewish community, or to a continuous, serious commitment to lifestyles that differ substantially from the bland American way of life. Even intensive Jewish education that does not keep up with a growing life slowly recedes into nothing but vague shadows without substance. Like language itself, if not spoken and used, it will even fade from memory.

Yet, staying in New York to attend college had exacted its price. Riding its overcrowded and noisy transportation system to go to school—trolley cars to buses to subway trains—for what seemed like interminable daily stretches of time, was not exactly calculated to make you "the happy-go-luckiest guy in town," at week's end.

This was no pretty, little college town, neatly tucked away atop faraway, picturesque hills—as my mind had always pictured those happy state universities in the carefree Midwest. Nor, to complete my mental picture, did it have many pretty coeds, running around manicured campuses, in their powerful two-seater roadsters. There were probably relatively few raccoon coats to be found on any of the city's campuses: New York was a serious place.

Nor was New York a place where politics and economics could be put on the back burner during your college years, affording you breathing time before catching up with life's harsher realities. For these were not only days of Depression but also a time of even darker worries for young people—they sensed that a world war was only around the corner. There was thus no time for leisurely, unhurried study, or relaxed hours for academic speculation and detached thought. Things were happening too rapidly—mostly not very good things—and though we surely did not know exactly what to expect, or in which direction we should be headed, the environment called for haste and rushed movement—whether or not we had clear or well-examined goals.

Staying in New York surely helped to reinforce my own accumulated seriousness about study, war and peace, the world and its minorities, and it ultimately strengthened my desire to share my life with the Jewish people. But it also robbed me of the youthful playfulness and the sweet years of casual leisure that I consider to be a vital part of the wit and wisdom of the later years. Nor was attendance at Brooklyn College much of a help in this regard. It was not a school that afforded you any opportunities for shedding your boyish tomfooleries and prankishness in slow and easy stages, as life surely requires. It prevented us from taking our time to grow up; on arrival, we were catapulted into grave and worrisome adulthood. Overnight, we were politicized and quickly made into *weltversorgers* overloaded and wracked with *weltschmerz.*

Admission to a college sponsored by the City of New York was only open to the top students of the city's high schools, since tuition was free and the applicants more numerous than the places available. Yet even with our free "scholarships," no student at "Brooklyn" allowed himself the luxury of going "only to school." It was unthinkable not to seek some kind of employment, either before or after classes; some students even worked all night. Brooklyn College was a proletarian, "subway college," which explains why so few Madison High School graduates had chosen to enroll. There was no room here for the snobbism of my high school, where it was considered unstylish— or pitiable, at best—to work while studying. At Brooklyn, work, not play, was deemed the proper adjunct to study. I remember most students complaining of being tired for four solid years. Still, even fatigue and work as students didn't stop us from intense political activities. On the contrary, the experience of being working students in difficult times at a public university fueled and reinforced our student activism.

You were expected to take sides and line up, almost from the first day at school, with at least one of the many organizations on campus. The political spectrum started with left-of-center and from there to the farthest reaches of the left, you could find an ample array of groups, splinters or blocs from which to choose: from the moderate, soft-pink Socialists to those flaming-red warrior-rivals, the Stalinists and the Trotskyites.

The student body was probably three-quarters Jewish, but this was of no special help to "Jewish causes" on campus. In fact, there were virtually no Jewish causes at Brooklyn College, when I arrived there in 1938, despite the fact that Nazism was already understood to be much more than an anti-Communist scourge. It was, to say the least, already perceived to be virulently anti-Jewish; some even said Hitler was bent on Jewish destruction. But this did not cause too many ripples among the majority of the students. If anything, to join a Jewish student organization was considered either a reactionary or a counter-revolutionary step, depending on the degree of your leftward tilt. It was never right, always wrong, to "speak up as a Jew," or even "to think as a Jew." Attending meetings of the single on-campus Jewish club, the Menorah Society, let alone joining it, was enough to get yourself labelled as incurably religious—or what was considered just as bad, inescapably middle-class—for the rest of your campus career.

I soon discovered why it was impossible for us Zionists to conduct logical, dispassionate argumentation with Jewish radicals. It had a great deal to do with the fact that they were disabled Jews. Despite all of their careful rationalizations, they knew that their brand of salvation—an authoritarian internationalism based on bedrock, immovable commitments to the "class struggle"—required the demise of the Jews, their culture and their religion. Jew-scorning they were; but after all they still had loving Jewish parents. There was the rub. While, by day, these budding Socialists, Communists, or fellow-travellers were busy prophesying the coming of the Marxist Messiah, they still had to go home at night, to spend some time with their immigrant families; maybe even, to speak occasionally to their "irrelevant *zaydehs*" and willy-nilly hear a "Jewish word." In short, who were these so-called Jews really despising? Not themselves; *they* were the heroes of the new age. Unlike the Jews of Berlin or Prague, who had disdained "those other Jews"—the *öst-Jüden* of Poland and Russia—these young world-remakers did not have any other Jews in mind. Surely, it was against their own parents—those benighted Jewish immigrants—that they were also rebelling.

But most of all, they took aim against the unwanted part of themselves that they did not care to know or understand—their unreal Jewish selves. This is what they were seeking to jettison, and with it, the whole Jewish people. They could not even be accused of wanton self-destruction; Judaism, in their view, was long dead, and had never reached them alive. Clearly, they were the unintended victims of their own parents' difficult road to Americanization. In an all-out devotion to the job, or to help their children obtain an education, their parents had either neglected or did not know how to transmit their own Jewish heritage. All that perhaps remained now were scattered and stray sentiments, not real feelings: loose ties to quaint words, or smells, or foods—and perhaps the most sinister thing of all, the haunting fear of having to remain Jewish, like their parents, without ever knowing why or wherefore. If their parents had maintained their own Jewish ties, it was only because of inertia, and maybe even Old World ignorance and superstition. *They* were on the march going somewhere else, liberated from all of these meaningless burdens. Where *they* were headed did not require them to be card-carrying members of the Jewish people.

We could not have known about the ultimate disaster that awaited European Jewry. We still had no concrete evidence of the success of Hitler's plans for the "final solution." Dachau, Auschwitz, Buchenwald—and all the rest—had not yet become household names for Jews to curse. Still, Jews knew that something terrible was in the making. And we few Zionists had no viable campus organization with which to silence the daily thunder coming at us from the left. The deep pain we felt was matched only by our gnawing frustrations.

It should have been a time for unity among campus Jews, for the closing of ranks, for standing up together and shouting. Instead, we were confronted with a sad and angering spectacle. Here were these bright but politically naive Jews steadily losing control over their own destiny, cynically hypnotized and bewitched by the opiate of Sovietism, archenemy of the Jewish people from the earliest days of the Revolution. How could they allow themselves to be enslaved to other slaves, the so-called "masses of the world" who themselves were being manipulated—inside and outside of the Soviet Union—by sly and cunning Communist overlords? And if their compassion was so great, enabling them to reach out even to people they did not know, was there no room left for sharing some small feelings of kinship with their own Jewish brothers? Did they not understand from history, these brilliant debaters of history's meaning—these "historical empiricists"—that in the crunch, the Jews were always left friendless; that all they really had to save them from annihilation was "family." Now that the battlelines were clearly drawn for our greatest fight since Rome destroyed Jerusalem how could they dare tell us that salvation was at hand if only we joined our enemies—the very people who had long been jailing and torturing Zionists in Siberia.

My high school classmates at Madison had succeeded in teaching me an unintended lesson: They sharpened my will to fight political indifference and to steer clear of their middle-class self-indulgence and smug apathy while the world was burning. And now there were these world-savers, these self-defeated Jews of Brooklyn College, full of boundless and passionate zeal, scouring the universe in search of underdog causes to espouse and secure power-bases to attack. But their pent-up, free-floating feelings of political outrage would never seek or land on targets of urgent Jewish concern. Once again, I was provided with negative examples by my fellow classmates: Their abject retreat from Jewish responsibility in our gravest hour of need taught me painful political and psychological truths. The world of the Jews was about to be utterly destroyed and blown off the face of the earth. Who would join in the battle to help save the victims of two millennia of accumulated madness?

It was becoming clearer to me that only those who had strong ties to the Jewish past would ever truly care about the Jewish future. My middle-class friends had been infected by a raging disease of social conformity. Their false aspirations to material success could not, of course, find any room for the "encumbrances" of Jewish history. The way to make it, in America, they believed, was to be "all-American": to look, feel, act and believe like everyone else by denying any meaning to group differences and distinctiveness.

The radical Jewish students had reached a strangely similar conclusion via an altogether different route. They were certain that the coming revolution would smash all national differences, in any event. Since Jews had the least amount of "territory" or power to protect, it was their duty to lead the line of march toward a world of equality wherein all peoples would gladly divest themselves of their own national uniqueness for the sake of the universal good. To continue to remain Jewish in the face of these "messianic" hopes and expectations was regarded by them as reactionary and counter-revolutionary. If ever the world needed Jews, it was now: By committing group suicide and giving up their own national ghost, they could help bring Paradise down to earth!

Nor was this their unkindest cut. Worse still was the way they had appropriated the most immoral, if not demonic, characterizations and conclusions about Jews and Judaism, from classical Christian anti-Semites. While Hitler was screaming madly that "all Jews are Communists" these Jewish radicals were busy proclaiming that Jewish Jews were a reactionary and retrograde element in society because they continued to identify with a bourgeois tradition whose "essential authoritarianism was comfortable with the capitalist domination of the struggling working class." All of these—theological anti-Jews, Hitler and his followers, and the radical Jewish students—shared the same horrible sin: They were guilty of blaming the Jew for the ills of the world.

Blaming the victim was their supercilious, self-righteous way of covering over their own destructive designs on him. We were rightless and stateless wanderers, tossed out of one exile after another, and who was to blame? Why Jews, of course—people are not punished for doing nothing! All of these self-haters were hopelessly convinced that Jews were always wrong—just because they were victimized—and justly deserved extinction as a people, to uproot the evil of their very being-in-the-world. Blaming the victim—especially when the accusations pour forth from the mouths of victims themselves—robs any argument of its moral and rational content. This is only one of the reasons why I could no more think of becoming a Communist than I could dream of conversion to Christianity.

My mind kept rejecting all these invitations to Jewish self-destruction. I had not come this far in order to cast aside my newfound political awareness as a Jew in a free America. In a curious way, these radicals served me well: The more self-defeating they were, the more they helped bolster my own sense of Jewish belonging. Unwittingly, their careless and cavalier discarding of a venerable tradition—which had survived empires and onslaughts—only helped to galvanize further the feelings of Jewish pride long nurtured in me by my teachers. They made me resolve then that I would never walk away from Jewish history, or sit idly by, when Jewish survival was threatened. I cared very deeply and not only for my own people and its future, although these were urgent to me. I also cared to live in a world that was safe—because I was safe as a Jew—for all minorities to be confidently themselves. I, the Jew, was the barometer of the universe, measuring the climate of its hates and affections, and something precious would be lost for all others if I lost sight of that. I was going to be just what I was: a living part of a worldwide family, with a classical, cosmic history. I would not be a member of a class or a worshipper of an institution.

More than anyone else—at school or at home—it was my grandfather who had strengthened this resolve. He had passed along, out of his great treasure-trove of folk wisdom, the spiritual and psychological truth distilled in an old but oft-forgotten Yiddish saying: *Az ich vel zein vi yener, ver vet zein vi ich?* "If I would be like someone else, who will be like me?"

Chapter 3

THE DECISION

I thought that I would never imagine myself as a Rabbi in America, certainly not after all the cautions my grandfather had placed in my path. But it was my curiosity about a strange and very different brand of Jews in Brooklyn that first set me thinking—not aloud, or for very long—about the idea. I was only a recent Bar Mitzvah, at the time.

It was ironic that James Madison's Annex should be—of all places—the Religious School of a Reform Temple. During all my years at the Yeshivah I had never met a single Reform Jew, and I vaguely knew about this style of Jewish religious life only from the stray, pejorative comments I had heard, from time to time, from my parents and other adults. I don't think that my own parents knew very much about Reform Judaism, or that they numbered any of its adherents among their friends. I remember that I was not supposed to think too highly of them, since in my parent's words, "'Reformed' Jews live and pray like *goyim*, while making believe that they are still Jews." Never mind that I used to cringe every time I heard any Jew—especially my own parents—refer to Christians as *goyim*, with all the scorn they could politely muster: There was obviously something wrong with being Reform if you had never heard a good word about them from any Jew you knew.

Now, at last, we were close enough to *their* territory—after all, it was our school too—to pierce the veil of mystery that kept us from knowing for ourselves more about these so-called Jews, strangers to us for so long.

We planned visiting the Temple's major weekly service, almost every Friday night after dinner, that fall.

At first, we had some difficulty adjusting to the fact that this was indeed a *Jewish* service. We sat amidst men who were bareheaded as in church; listened to organ music whose melodies reminded us of the Sunday morning Church services we always rapidly tuned out, skipping quickly by on our own radio dials. And where was the Hebrew language? A smidgeon, here and there, in the truncated, translated liturgy that passed itself off as Jewish prayer of *davening*. Far removed, we felt, from the heartfelt, rousing prayer we knew—and almost all of it by heart. Pay no attention, we told ourselves: This is research, or maybe just some "Jewish slumming" to get away from our families after Friday night dinners, to enjoy ourselves "with the boys." We didn't take the services too seriously, and after a couple of months of fall Fridays, we stopped going.

But I had learned enough in those seven or eight weeks to help rid me of negative stereotypes for the rest of my life. It wasn't the services in themselves that had helped. If anything, they turned me off, and still do: Reform liturgy is, at best, an American bastard, illegitimate now, for at least five generations. And how I am annoyed by bastards, of all kinds; especially by those who pretend to be genuine and legitimate.

What opened me up to a new understanding and appreciation of the American Rabbi—if not always a high regard for Reform Judaism—was the Rabbi of that Temple, Alexander Allen Steinbach. True, his Southern American accent made him very folksy, to begin with, and interesting, too: I had never before met or heard a Jew with a southern drawl. But it was really what he was saying, not how he was saying it, that captured my attention, and which gave me real pause. He was talking about real things, real people—real issues! I had never heard *our* Orthodox rabbis speak about very much except the ancient past, or about moral questions in vague and general terms. They always seemed to be answering questions nobody was asking. Inoffensive little men, I thought, as I began comparing them with Steinbach's steady stream of socially and politically focussed preaching: the Civil War in Spain, F.D.R.'s New Deal, the breadlines—and on and on he went, dealing with issues never discussed by my own Rabbis in their sermons. And he didn't forget his own people, either.

For at least a year after hearing him on one of those Friday nights in the fall of 1935, I kept mimicking him at every suitable (or sometimes unsuitable) occasion, purposely doing violence to his quotation of Genesis 37:16—and for laughs, using a broad southern accent in rendering the Hebrew original of: "Mah brethren ah do seek!" My repeated renditions secretly helped to reinforce my identification with him: Obviously I could not forget that sermon, but in public had to find a way to make a Reform Rabbi look ridiculous. In my heart I knew better. Steinbach was telling his *Reform* members that they were not just an "American denomination" but an integral part of the *Jewish* world, in Palestine, Germany or whatever. And like Joseph of old, they must walk about the world, telling themselves and all who would listen: "I will seek my brothers and I will find them." And this, he said, joined to a real concern for the social and political worlds surrounding us as Americans, was the essential goal of being alive as a Jew. We had to reach out to our brothers, everywhere, while not retreating from the world. My grandfather, I was sure, would have vigorously applauded, Reform Rabbi, or not.

We soon became disenchanted with the service, the people who attended, and the theatricality of the Cantor and choir. Nobody seemed to participate but the paid personnel; the congregation, dead-headed, seemed only to be waiting around to be entertained by the players on the "stage": by the Cantor, choir, and finally, by the Rabbi's sermon. I always looked at the congregation's faces during the course of the sermons. I was sure that each person believed that the Rabbi was talking to someone else—not to him. Poor Rabbi. We soon "quit" the Temple, but not the Rabbi.

Still, I had been exposed to a liberating, liberal example: an American Rabbi who had more than mere smiles to offer his congregation, or pleasing platitudes about pies in unreachable skies. He was as much at home in the Jewish world of literature and art as he was in philosophy, history, politics and liberal thought. He had a winning combination of faculties and interests. I was thoroughly impressed: I had never thought that such people were to be found in the ranks of the rabbinate.

In the first few months at college, I was so busy adjusting to my many new obligations that I had no time to think, as many of friends had already done, about what I was preparing myself for at school, or what I wanted to be. I bought an old, beat-up Plymouth for $85 to help speed me around town, in order to give lessons in Hebrew to as many private students as my time would allow. I was paid from fifty cents to a dollar—it depended on the neighborhood—for a full hour's instruction, so I hardly believe that my investment in private rapid transit really paid for itself. But I enjoyed the contact with young people, and relished the joys I had in opening up their minds and hearts to the untapped resources of the Jewish culture. Though I liked the jingle of quarters in my pocket, I would probably have continued teaching even if they couldn't pay.

There was only one part of the work that I did not exactly like: They always called me "Rabbi." "Stephen, your Rabbi is here for your Hebrew lesson," was the way I was usually greeted by sweet mothers, doting on me, amazed that so young a man—and American born, at that—would be capable of making their sons "adore Hebrew." I enjoyed their compliments, their cookies, and their chocolate milk. But "Rabbi"? That was more than I had bargained for.

After lectures and library study at Brooklyn—and at least three Hebrew lessons a day—I made my way to the nearest subway station to take the long and tiring ride and brisk walk to my Lower East Side School. I would attend Moshe Feinstein's Herzliah Hebrew Teachers' Seminary for four years of nights and Sundays, throughout my college career.

At Herzliah, I felt at home. I would never become a Hebrew School teacher. But then again, although it was called Teachers' Seminary, Herzliah was principally a vehicle for continuing our Jewish studies, without pressures of theological persuasion, or the need for a fundamental commitment to a future career. I was doing what I had secretly promised myself, after my grandfather had died: I would be like him, committed to study and leadership, *with no strings attached.*

I had never forgotten my grandfather's own choices in life: You did not have to be a rabbi to do what you had to do, as a Jew. Indeed, considering my own predilections for secular Zionism, and my flirtations with humanist Socialism, I could not imagine anyone ever calling me Rabbi. And when they did, like those Brooklyn mothers of my students, I felt strange; as if I had betrayed my own grandfather, and gone over to the "Margolises" of the world. Nor did I want to become a "Friedman."

I remember all the cafeterias and tiny restaurants that surrounded Herzliah, which was two flights above, but not beyond the non-aromatic intoxications of Birnbaum's Winery, on East Broadway. Except for a few tuna-salad sandwiches in between, I would guess that in the four years I spent having "dinner" in and around East Broadway, I must have consumed at least a thousand *latkes*. I still salivate when I think of them: matzah latkes, with red horseradish—stinging, delicious *chrein*; potato latkes, with thick applesauce, or even thicker sour cream.

Attending Herzliah was a very good thing for us—"Flatbush gangsters"—as our demanding Grammar teacher, the well-known Hebrew humorist and feuilletonist Daniel Persky had playfully dubbed us. (I suppose it was our relatively smart attire, including felt fedora hats, rather than skating toques and the like, which gave us a "dashing" look—on the Lower

East Side, at least.) There were only a few of us from the Yeshivah High School who had remained in New York, and fewer still who had followed Moshe Feinstein to his own school. Herzliah, as the name implied, was a staunchly Zionist, Hebraic-saturated school. There were a few religious types among the students, but most, like Feinstein and his teachers, were Jewish culturalists, secular nationalists, and Hebraists, rather than apostles of the creed. Many were recruited from the immediate neighborhood, and had studied together for four years in Feinstein's Herzliah Evening High School, before entering the Teachers' Seminary or College Division. They were mostly graduates of Seward Park High, and other lower Manhattan schools; a few also came from the poorer sections of Brooklyn—from Brownsville and East New York.

There was also a small handful of vigorous, serious, and exciting young people I would meet for the first time: Jews from Palestine who had come to study at various universities in New York City. They attended Herzliah, at night, in order to qualify as licensed Hebrew teachers in local schools, as a means of paying their way through college. They gave our student body a unique flavor, and opened up our parochial Jewish experiences to a still larger Jewish world. One of them, in particular, caught my eye—and my fancy, too—the moment she entered my senior class in 1940. Her name was Hadassa Agassi. She advanced into this class immediately upon arrival at our school. My friends and I were awed and impressed with the fact that *we* had already spent three long years before becoming seniors, while she simply became our "equal" on coming to New York from Jerusalem. The Faculty, however, was not overgenerous: she was the brightest, most advanced member of the class, though younger than most of us. She helped raise the level of learning in our group because we all tried hard to catch up to her. I confess that in many areas of Jewish learning—especially in biblical studies and modern Hebrew literature—I have still not caught up with her, even after being married to Hadassa for forty years.

Herzliah was located hard by the landmark building of the Socialist Yiddish newspaper the *Jewish Forward*—you always saw the "Forward" when you crossed over the Manhattan Bridge by train from Brooklyn. It was crammed into the upper storeys of a tenement building amidst the sights, sounds—and most important—the smells of what was by now a ghetto community. But it was colorful and wonderful. There was indeed a kind of heroic joy in my heart, every time I came there: My parents had run away from these very streets twenty long years before and gone "up to Flatbush" via Harlem; and here I was, a good, young Flatbusher, now becoming a living and happy part of the very scene of their great escape. *Plus ça change....*

Coming into direct, intimate and regular contact with immigrants' children living on the Lower East Side was exciting; it was like spending four years abroad in a Jewish immersion program. This was not only the East Side; it was more like East Europe. Even then, in those precincts of New York City in the pre-war Thirties, Jewish cultural life was as vibrant and flavorful as any parallel expressions still alive, say, in Warsaw, Poland, or other East-European cities. The "Jewish Way" was still the primary mode of life: Yiddish was spoken in virtually every home, and heard on every street; arguments over this or that Jewish ideology or philosophy still dominated daily discussion; concern over the fate of all the world's Jews—not just those in your own club or neighborhood—intruded itself into almost every thoughtful conversation. It was not only the private-public smells of *gefilte* fish wafting over the streets from Jewish kitchens, or the savory, sweet aroma of *hallah* bread baked in honor of Sabbaths and Festivals, but mostly the feeling of living deep inside Jewish territory—in a kind of transplanted heavenly-earthly Jerusalem—that linked me to Jews in a way Flatbush had never done.

If I had never experienced East Side Jewish life personally, I would have missed a unique and non-recurring source of Jewish vitality—a connection to primary Jewishness most American-born Jews sorely lack. Comprehension and understanding of this special mode of self-expression is simply not available from Jewish book-knowledge alone—even less so when tempered by the cramped views imposed on us by our middle-class American mind-set. In my case, the East Side served as a strong counterbalance to the many banalities that often went by the name of Judaism in the Flatbush of my day.

I hadn't realized it, at first, but obviously most of our classmates had probably never before met a Flatbush Jew; we were like people from a newer and richer planet. I remember Feinstein's very first introduction of us to our class; it had something of the ring of "these Flatbush fellows are *also Jews*" about it. But if they needed orientation lectures about us, we needed these even more, about them. I thought that I had been meeting all of the then extant Jewish types of Brooklyn or Manhattan, during the day, at college. While many looked and dressed alike and came from similar, depressed neighborhoods—at Herzliah, they did not think or sound alike. These were Zionists—*Jewish* Jews, at last! And my new and joyful discovery was duly reciprocated by their warm feelings toward us. *They* had never expected to meet Jews like us, and—of all places—from Flatbush.

Students at Herzliah reflected an entirely different spectrum of Jewish attitudes and positions than I had encountered before. Without exception they were all committed to a philosophy of Jewish nationalism, or Zionism, that placed a rebuilt Palestine at the core of their lives.

Like the other students, I believed strongly in political Zionism. I was regarded as something of a curiosity because I joined with all their factions, "Mizrachi," "Labor," and "General Zionists." But my understanding of the historical design of Zionism took me farther afield than politics, protest meetings, or fund-raising drives, although I was active on all these fronts, as well. For me, Zionism had to be seen as a radical point of personal departure for Jews who wished to lead; it had to have the full force of a new and vital religion.

Looking at Jewish history, I had come to the conclusion that Zionist thinking consistently overlooked one massive, crucial fact: Jews had never constituted a true majority or ever behaved like one—not even long years ago when they lived in relative security on their own land. Conventional Zionist wisdom, however, had always argued differently. The popular view regarded the continuing disabilities and persecutions of diaspora Jews as the product of an interlocking set of abnormal conditions. Homelessness was responsible for turning Jews into a wandering minority; and movable minorities are easy prey for scapegoating attacks by powerful majorities. Zionists seemed to have a love affair with two words: normalcy and majority. In their mind, the only way Jews could return to the course of their own history was for them to become normal again; then, and only then, would they become "just like all the peoples of the earth." Jews would regain title to their land and be restored to their normalcy only by political means. Then all would be set right: from a rejected, pariah-like minority, Jews would become a "majority people" once again—politically respectable and acceptable as a sovereign nation like all others.

My own understanding of history convinced me that "normalcy" was, in fact, the enemy of the Jewish people. For their part, most Jews never seemed to realize this truth; they always needed adamant, strong-minded leaders to teach them otherwise. Despite widely advertised opinions that have lauded the independence and stiff-neckedness of history's Jews, I was now reading our past altogether differently. I saw that the individual members of the Jewish people, whenever or wherever they lived, had shown no special talent or great heroism to take on the burdens of uniqueness, or to act on behalf of a difficult national mission to be unlike the others. Our history was not exactly a tribute to the power of grassroots populism. If we survived it was because of another, more deeply ingrained quality of our national character.

We remained alive as a witness and reminder to the world of the "power of powerlessness" not because we were either a spiritually uncrushable, or a morally stiff-necked people—we were often soft and compliant—but only because we were also an "elitist" people. We possessed one unique and redeeming talent: After every self-defeat, some of us had the wisdom to listen to our own authorities and to follow their example. Always, it was the strength of a minority—a nucleus of leaders and disciples—that gave the people the will and power to survive. These bold and stirring examples of what the prophets had called "a saving remnant" helped us march through history, undefeated despite our many defeats.

I had come to the conclusion that Zionism was really more than what the Zionists themselves had made it out to be. It was nothing less than the vehicle for the creation of a new generation of leaders who would serve as effective role-models in turning back the steady tide of our creeping absorption as de-Judaized Jews into middle-class America. I was not merely a political Zionist like all the others, but even more a cultural Zionist, influenced by the writings of Ahad Ha-Am, the modern Hebrew essayist.

It was not that I rejected the basic tenets of political Zionism, but that I wanted more for my people than their nationalist beacons were pointing to. They correctly realized that historically, anti-Semitism was the natural result of the unnatural Jewish condition: our abnormal patterns of social and economic stratification in the life of the various foreign countries to which we had been exiled. We would be regarded as aliens as long as we persisted in living only in strange lands where we were incapable of being absorbed into the fiber of local society. Organized hatred for the Jews would never vanish in the diaspora because Jews were destined to remain perennial strangers, or at best short-term guests, in all of these lands. The followers of Herzl, father of political Zionism, were right—but only partly so, I believed—in insisting that only by re-establishing our own nation-state in Palestine, where we would be "master" of our own destiny and national character, would we be successful in achieving the desirable goals—the normalization of our social and economic life. Only in our own homeland could we Jews avoid the inevitable discrimination inherent in our anomalous, irregular existence everywhere else.

But what about those other Jews—perhaps even the majority—who would always remain outside of Palestine? Were they to be written off completely? After all, not every diaspora was exile. I was not prepared to accept a Jewish position which based itself on the assumption of "all or nothing at all": either Palestine or else Jewish oblivion. Had not Jews, as a result of their unwavering leaders, continued to build creative communities? Visible monuments to our capacity to grow and aspire spiritually, even outside of the homeland, were to be found in Babylonia, Spain, and even in darkest Poland and Russia.

Asher Ginzberg, or Ahad Ha-Am ("One of the People") as he became known by his *nom de plume*, whose writings had led me to espouse aspects of "Cultural Zionism," did not answer all of my problems, either. His secular reinterpretations of Jewish history went too far afield. Religion, he thought, although one of the most important expressions of the Jewish spirit in the past, was now dispensable altogether, as we re-assumed our national status, in our own land. It had served its function well as a protective shell. It was, however, *only* a means for the preservation of the Jewish people.

To be sure, in many places, Judaism had degenerated to anachronistic levels and was no longer widely palatable as publicly practiced or espoused. But this was beside the point. Historical Judaism had done much more than merely serve as a tool of national survival; it was the creator of our uniqueness and not merely its hapless, mindless creature. Nor did we invent a moral world-view only to preserve our national skins. Our prophets and teachers had fashioned us into a model people—"a light unto the nations," they said—to enlarge our human connections and our universal, international passions, not merely to glorify our own territorial culture. Of course, we now had to become a people again before we could even aspire to become a "model people." But did we need to cast out the broad span and historical structure of our unique religious and philosophical differences and criticisms in order to re-enter the world on a new footing? I was hoping that the national renaissance would produce a religious one; that the 151st Psalm could now be written, because we had returned. And that in our blessing the whole earth would be blessed.

This is probably why I remained in the synagogue long after many of my Zionist friends had left, in search of different Jewish models. It wasn't that I had thought very highly of what I was seeing all around me in the Orthodox *shuls* I frequented. But there, at least, you could be sure to find Jews on a regular basis. Their thoughts were far from mine and my Jewish world surely exceeded their narrow precincts. Still, I instinctively felt that the synagogue was a home for the Jewish spirit that was waiting for renovation and redirection, too. I was willing to secularize Judaism—to bring it back to the real world of Jewish national need and concern—but unwilling to turn away from it, completely. I found myself considering the synagogue as a natural base for the recreation of the national spirit.

It was about this time, too, that I met two magnetic men with great charismatic appeal. Both were Rabbis; dissimilar, yet complementary. Both excited my imagination. Together, they forced me to begin a period of self-examination. For many months I would be agonizing over a crucial question. Here I am, a Zionist in the Synagogue because I believe that it can be recreated to serve the national agenda. Why not the Rabbinate?

There were many questions. Could I keep my own integrity; continue to grow in knowledge and creativity; remain open to the larger universe of men and ideas; stay worldly and flexible; retain my sense of humor, independence and balance? Could I do any of these things—and the many more I knew that time would make me hope for—if I made a commitment now, to follow the two men, Stephen S. Wise and Mordecai M. Kaplan, and prepare to study for the rabbinate? Or would such a step prove emotionally irrevocable, and turn me out as still another Rabbi in America—a Margolis, a Friedman, or some other misfitted, nondescript, what-have-you?

When I went to the Brooklyn College Hillel House on Flatbush Avenue to attend a noon-hour lecture by Dr. Stephen S. Wise, I had known, of course, much about him, from the newspapers and the Jewish press of New York. But I was totally unprepared for his overwhelming personal presence. I was surprised to find only twenty or thirty students in the small meeting hall of the newly opened House. This was one of its first meetings and it was widely publicized, in the hope that the famous Stephen Wise would attract large numbers to the new enterprise. He was introduced very briefly by the Director, Dr. Rabinowitz—there was barely a fifty-minute hour available for lecture and discussion period before we would have to dash back to campus, to attend our next class. As it was, we munched our way through lunch, as the talk progressed.

I can't remember the title of his advertised lecture, but it probably encapsulated some rubric relating to the Jewish condition in the world, at that time. But no matter. It wasn't the subject of his speech that brought us there; it was Wise himself. And from the first moments after his introduction, my heart did not stop pounding. He did not fall one whit short of his great reputation as a spell-binding orator. But much, much more: he was a conscience-stimulator; a provoking voice that reminded me of a prophet—crying out in the wilderness. Rushing to begin immediately after he was introduced, he mounted the small podium, placed his gold watch on the lectern, smoothed down his long, leonine hair, and lost not a single moment in taking us by storm.

There was music—and lamentation, heroism, and urgings to greatness—aloft in the air, all about us. Recollections of grandeur were mixed with weeping over the lost hopes and the tragic, unknown fate of Europe's Jews; sweeping, powerful denunciations of Jews—and others—who were "at ease" while the Jewish world was burning; masterful, verbal lances aimed at fellow-travelers and Communist sympathizers, whose mistaken loyalties would not save them on the day of political reckoning. These were some of the blasts blown on his stirring trumpet by this courageous man, who had all but riveted us to our seats. When he finished, and the questions were over, I determined to cut my next class, and spend as much time as I could talking with Dr. Wise, personally.

He was extremely approachable, warm and eager to talk with me. I cannot remember the exact details of our conversation; I was, I recall, very nervous, and overawed to be so close to the great Dr. Wise. This was the Reform Rabbi who had been called to New York's vaunted Temple Emanu-El in 1906, when it was then regarded as the "Cathedral Synagogue of America." Insisting that the "pulpit must be free," he was told that "the pulpit of Emanu-El has always been and is subject to and under the control of the Board of Trustees." He declined the congregational offer on this matter of principle—something very few others would have done. He wanted to speak his mind—on social causes, Zionism, and all the human things dear to him. He would not be muzzled. Undismayed and undefeated, he came to New York from his former congregation in Portland, Oregon, and founded the Free Synagogue. It became a dazzling forum for his views and leadership.

This was the man whose voice was heard every Sunday morning from 1910 to 1940, in a jammed Carnegie Hall. Other halls would be too small to accommodate the thousands of people—of all religions, and of no religion—who often waited in line, Sunday after Sunday, to hear him lash out, with great force and elegance, against assorted varieties of vested authority and political corruption. He was a household name—but his was also a name feared by those who had reason to be lashed with his fiery scorn.

Could this man also be a "Rabbi in America"?

He was that, and more. He explained some of the reasons why he had to establish his Jewish Institute of Religion. It was a post-graduate school for the training of Rabbis, of all denominations, and if he could really have his way, he said, "of no denominations, at all: not Orthodox, Conservative, or Reform—only Jewish." He "had to" take on whole establishments—rabbinic and lay: the Hebrew Union College in Cincinnati, for its "anti-Zionist, anti-Jewish, 'American Judaism' "; the American Jewish Committee, for "refusing to take the lead and stand up against Nazism, to fight for Jewish rights." He "had to" found the American Jewish Congress as a counterweight against the long-established, self-anointed American Jewish voice of fright and fear, the "Committee," as he called it. "My Yiddish-speaking friends call them, 'Sha-sha Jews,' " he laughed. "You know what *sha-sha* means? Do you know Yiddish, or are you, like me, still catching up with the rest of the Jewish world, trying to learn everything Jewish that was denied me. They thought I'd make a 'better American' that way—without all that European stuff. *Sha* means 'hush' in Yiddish. 'Hush-Hush Jews' think they can be seen as better Americans by keeping quiet. But when the world is ablaze?..."

"Make a big noise. Sound the *shofar*. Wake our people up." He repeated these words, over and over, not as slogans, but as highly visible signals of his own profoundly Jewish stance. He had to.

His powerful sense of "oughtness" appealed very strongly to me. Perhaps, because of my own sensitivity to Jewish learning, it was when he began relating some of the important things he was doing to save European Jewish scholars, that I had fully and completely "fallen in love" with this man. I trembled as he spoke of European Jewish scholars who "had no place to teach, no future, no liberty to grow and discover." Some were already appointed to his Faculty at the "J.I.R."; others, were on the way to some American college or university; there were many others "we have to reach, to save from the jaws of hell." I could never forget the way he had pronounced those last words—so slowly, so forebodingly.

Some months later, as I began to follow Dr. Wise's every move, I found myself sitting high up in the furthest reaches of Madison Square Garden. There he was, far, far away—down below, on the platform, presiding over the rally he had called as President of the American Jewish Congress. There he was, no Sha-Sha Jew, systematically documenting the Nazi horror to an audience now stunned into silence. But the world outside—New York, and its teeming millions of Jews—was cold, quiescent and disbelieving. This would not stop Wise from shaking them up, "sounding the shofar" of alarm, as no other single Jew could, or would. And that night, I knew why. He had to. Right there, in the awesome quiet of the Garden, as Wise went on with his tragic litanies, I began telling myself, over and over again: "You have to."

Professor Mordecai M. Kaplan was different, yet strikingly similar, as he quickly made clear during the course of the lecture he gave at Hillel House, that same season. He was a *Litvak*, a *tzelem kopf*, who honored the traditional Jewish ways, but "honored them more," he explained, "by making them real, viable, and rational—not as a museum-piece to be appreciated, but which never becomes a part of your own living experience." Judaism had to be used—and had to "use you"—or else it was somebody else's Judaism, not yours. This was why, he, like Wise, had to found his own congregation, The Society for the Advancement of Judaism—the S.A.J.—on West 86th Street. The average congregation had no use for him.

To look at him, was to see somebody's wise and knowing grandfather—he was sixtyish, with short, white hair, and a carefully tapered goatee. But to hear him, was to listen to a young and exuberant college professor, warming you to the joys of discovery, as, together, you climbed higher mountains of knowledge. He was professorial: careful, deliberate, appealing to your reason, all the way. Yet, he did not lack in love for his subject. He was no less romantic about the Jewish people or Judaism than Stephen Wise, only more precise, more thorough; devastatingly thorough.

He was more like an architect than a Rabbi, I thought, as he was intently building his structures, detailing how Judaism always reconstructed itself to meet changing conditions and circumstances. It was never orthodox or static. "Static things ossify and soon die. Judaism survived only because it refused to remain what it *was*. In fact, there is no single Judaism—only many Judaisms, for many times, and in many places." He was putting forth some of the ideas I had learned earlier; but stringing them together, systematically.

Like Wise, he preferred talking about Jews—the noun—not the adjectives Orthodox, Conservative, or Reform. There was no room for denominationalism in Jewish life. "It is a form of assimilation to the Christianity of America." And, then, a series of definitions and descriptions:

"A Rabbi is a social engineer, an adult educator, a community leader, a learned layman—never a clergyman with purely congregational interests.

"Congregations as now constituted are the curse of Jewish life. They are private membership clubs, devoted only to their own self-interests. We need to organize Jewish life in America around the community, not the congregation. And intelligent rabbis—who don't just see themselves as employees of a specific congregation—will help, not hinder, this effort.

"What kind of community will we have in America? It depends upon the rabbis we will have. If we continue along our present course, we will be creating ecclesiasts and ecclesiologues—good Jewish churchmen—not Jewish leaders for the Jewish community and the world. We need Rabbis who see themselves as learned laymen, and who will put their worldly skills and their literary and intellectual talents into the service of the whole Jewish people. They will not be parochial, and they will not run away from the world, or regard the social and political issues that plague all men as alien to their concerns or activities."

I began reading everything that Kaplan wrote, including the regular issues of his "Reconstructionist Magazine," and as I did, kept hearing my deceased grandfather whispering to me: "He's my man. He asks my questions. He says *Tomar Verkehrt!*—maybe the 'right way' is really the wrong way; maybe the world's logic should be reversed and placed upside-down."

The Decision 59

It was somewhere around this time, too, that Joel Braverman had telephoned. Now that I was at Herzliah, and no longer at the Flatbush Yeshivah building, he missed seeing me; would I come over to chat? Not long after I had arrived in his spare office, I found myself "elected"—by him—as President of a non-existent Alumni Association of the Yeshivah of Flatbush. "It need not take too much of your time. It is something that must be done, however. Even if the group meets only two or three times a year. There are important things that such an organization can do."

I think what he really wanted, was to see some of the old faces of the first students at the Yeshivah, some of them scattered to the campuses across the country; others, still at colleges in New York, but like myself, preoccupied with other tasks and involvements. I told him that I would think about it, and let him know.

I really did think about it. I discovered that I was now ready to "go public" as a Jewish leader, of sorts.

When I returned to see him, a few weeks later, I put my plans to him, explaining that such a group should be highly visible, as active as possible, and conduct programs for the whole community, not just for ourselves. It should organize a "free synagogue" in which no membership was required, no fees requested; it should be self-led, with our own graduates helping to direct it outward toward the entire community. We should be actively involved as a free educating vehicle for all adults who would be interested, and enlist the help of as many of our graduates as possible, in experimenting with new Jewish programs, Zionist and anti-Nazi activities, community service, and the like—all freely given and on a non-partisan basis. Mahr Brahverman looked up at me strangely and quizzically, after I had rolled off this rather unexpected list of "demands." "Who gave you all of these 'crazy' ideas? You call this an Alumni Association? Who ever heard of an Alumni Association doing things like this—a synagogue without members; a free adult-education forum; community service, on a non-partisan basis? Tell me, Shalom, who gave you all of these ideas?"

I could not tell him that Stephen Wise and Mordecai Kaplan told me these things. I could not tell him that *his own school* had laid the groundwork for my thinking.

I could not tell him—yet—what would I tell him a few years later: I was going to be a Rabbi; but not before I "tried it out" right here. Not before I could see if here, in the very school where Jewish learning began for me, I could discover if there was really a place in America for the kind of Rabbi I would be, if ever I would be.

I gave no answer at all.

"Go ahead, Shalom," he relented. "But if you get hurt, and the bricks start flying don't say I didn't warn you."

I paid no immediate heed to his clear admonition. I just knew that whatever I was going "to be" in life, I would have to be a Jewish leader. Yet, the more I thought of what he had said, the more I thought of my own grandfather. *He* had not recommended that I become a Rabbi; he had even warned me about what happens to Rabbis in America. Why not walk away from the organized community, and if need be, lead from a distance, without standing too close to the line of fire? Why not a professor of Jewish thought at some great university, or a professional writer and lecturer—a Jewish leader "without pay"? Or why not say goodbye altogether to the stresses, strains and taints of American Jewish life and take the real leap of faith, by starting Jewish life clean and fresh, doing almost anything useful in Palestine?

But always, my mind would bring me back to visions of those two men: Rabbi Kaplan and Rabbi Wise. If they could lead as Rabbis, couldn't I? And my grandfather? If he were alive, what would he say? I decided for the hundredth time that he was really a very wise man. He never said that I should *not* be a Rabbi.

Chapter 4

BECOMING A RABBI

In the late Thirties, if one had wished to dissuade any bright young American from considering the rabbinate as a profession, the best preventative would have been to set him down, for only a month of Saturdays, in a typical New York synagogue. Had he been taking notes of his observations—never on Saturdays, of course—he might have drawn up a forbidding little list, possibly along lines such as these:

1. White-haired men all around; many more pews than Jews. Not a young person in sight. Nor many women, for that matter.
2. The Sabbath service is a series of mechanized, ritualistic maneuvers: hardly a learning experience. Nor does much comfort and warmth come from the pulpit: principally, harangues against those who are *not* in attendance; little encouragement or relevant instruction for those who are there.
3. Prayers are not really prayers. Actually, they are a series of run-on Hebrew sentences, spewn forth, on all sides, by indifferent men, who seem to be "racing" the Cantor, right down to the finish line.
4. On weekdays, morning and evening services are even more desperate. You spend a good part of the time waiting for the tenth man. The first eight or nine worshippers are there

only because they are saying *Kaddish*—memorial prayers, recited daily throughout the year following the loss of close kinsmen; or on the anniversary of their death, for *Yahrzeit*. When the tenth man doesn't arrive, you send the *Shammos*, the bedeviled Sexton, to fetch someone—off the streets, if need be—to perform a *mitzvah*, by rounding out the group to ten, the required number for a *minyan* to start its service. (Sometimes, the non-Jewish janitor will poke his head into the prayer room, tantalizing the waiting worshippers with the suggestion that he too can don a *yarmulke*, or skull cap, and pass as the tenth.)

Now the speed session begins: you compress a brace of prayers that should take a full hour to recite into half that time, so that bored and harried worshippers—upon whom you are relying for tomorrow's service—can catch the subway train to get to work on time. But if it fails at everything else, here is where the synagogue is succeeding: as a "service station," or "*Kaddish* factory" for the community's mourners.

5. The rest of the hours of the week, the place is virtually dark and empty, except, maybe, for the occasional committee or board meeting. But don't attend these if you're looking for inspiration, or Jewish spiritual values. One squabble after another. There seems to be no fixed agenda except for a single recurring item that never fails to be heard. It is the unfailing, consistent theme in a series of incoherent, themeless meetings; you might call it the synagogue's *leitmotif*: "For the $1,800 a year we pay him, we can do better. Let's fire the Rabbi."

6. Predictably, the Rabbi looks permanently worried. Save, perhaps, at Sabbath Services, where he's busy fence-mending: patting people on the back, when he's not busy pumping their hands.

7. Conclusion: The synagogue, in America, is apparently on its way out, and no young Jew in his right mind ought now to be on his way in. Certainly, not as a Rabbi.

I could have drawn up such a list myself, judging from the

synagogues that I knew, those days. Why then was I acting as if I had never heard my grandfather's admonitions? Why, I kept asking myself, was I still wasting my energies allowing myself to flirt with the thought of studying for the Rabbinate? The Jewish comics were probably right: Being a Rabbi wasn't a "decent job" for a nice, American Jewish boy.

The Jewish world I knew at college was different. There was, to begin with, no room for nostalgia, no hankering after old worlds lost, and no place for mystical connections to ritualistic vocabularies or languages. These were, for the most part, determined realists, who had measured all religious traditions, including their own, in the scales of history and had found them wanting. The vacuum that was created between their past and present was generally filled by the new gods of socialism, Communism, or, less frequently, of Jewish nationalism.

The synagogue had no place in their lives. It had long been surpassed and now belonged only to the ancients, or at best, to antique-like people. There was no life in it; it could not serve as a vehicle for modern hopes. The radicals scoffed at it, as they did at every other institutional "opiate of the people." But the secular Zionists were not far behind, and if they did not openly scoff, they did something even more disheartening. They ignored the synagogue—discounting it completely.

I could readily dismiss the views of the radicals. They would have lost little sleep if the whole Jewish people had suddenly disappeared from the face of the earth. But it was with the Zionist student position that I had the most difficulty. After all, they were friends. Their dedication to the survival of their people was unquestioned. Yet, to me, they seemed to be making a serious mistake—one that would haunt later generations of American Zionists. In their zealous preoccupation with the plight of European Jews and the precarious nature of the fledgling Zionist enterprise in Palestine, they had no interest in the fate or fabric of Jewish life in America. But even then I felt what I can see more clearly now: The fate of the Jews in Palestine (now Israel) and the quality of American Jewish life were interlocked. A weakened and desiccated Jewish community here could become a liability to vigorous Zionist achievement there.

I could not really fault any of my Zionist friends for their refusal to define themselves in religious terms. They avoided *shuls* like a plague because churches and synagogues, they told themselves and everybody else, were for people who required constant reassurance and external support. The older folks needed either the warmth of human companionship or the protection of a divine providence to bolster their sagging and lackluster conventional lives. Nor was this a normal case of children rebelling against the traditional habits of the parents. Their own parents had already kicked over the traces.

Then, too, far from being an age of "religious return," this was the day of secular rebellion against religious power of all kinds. Their Zionism was such a protest. It was not so much a rejection of non-existent Jewish hierarchy, as it was a repudiation of the Jewish status quo. They were, in effect, protesting against the politically quiescent Jewish establishment, and this inevitably included the synagogue. But they were also seeking authority, including the synagogue. But they were also seeking new Jewish options. Their espousal of Zionism as a national solution to the problem of being Jewish in a non-Jewish world meant that they were voting for self-liberation as well as self-determination. It was not really a vote "against religion"; it was a vote "for themselves," as active players in the drama of Jewish redemption. They simply did not respect those Jews, then in the majority in America, who were complacently willing to continue doing business as usual within the Jewish community.

"Business as usual" was a strikingly accurate way of describing the manner in which most synagogues were still conducting themselves. They were tribal, or familial; small pockets of local vested interests, unwilling or unable to open themselves up to the larger needs of the Jewish world. This was not yet the Fifties or Sixties, when Zionists found it necessary to latch on to the growing prestige and grassroots strength of local synagogues—especially in the suburbs—in order to rally the Jewish community behind large-scale rescue operations or to mount politically oriented public programs. Unlike our own time, in those days community-wide meetings rarely took place in a synagogue—that would have given them a public "kiss of death"—but, principally, in rented halls around the city. The synagogue was simply not an attractive Jewish address for those who regarded themselves as full-time members of a world-wide people, and not merely as infrequent visitors at a neighborhood *shul*. Besides, in Zionist eyes, most synagogues seemed to be oblivious to the really vital, long-term Jewish issues, and were slumbering away while "Jerusalem was burning."

Moreover, the human models offered by the synagogue also played an important role in keeping these young Zionists from coming too close to its touch. Most synagogues were perennially led by the same self-elected people: small-minded, provincial men who woud be horrified to think that the serious and gripping Jewish political issues of the day had any place whatsoever inside their precincts. Synagogues often called their Rabbis "spiritual leaders," but they were kept on very short leashes by their masters—presidents, committee chairmen and such like—the effective heads of the synagogue world. They made certain that "their" rabbis were restricted to supervision of "religious" matters, most of which turned out to be irrelevant to the majority of members, anyway. Any rabbinical wings capable of soaring beyond the earthbound and commonplace concerns of the local "parish" were effectively clipped by lay leaders who "made it their business" to keep their Rabbis in place.

As important as any of these considerations was the clear feeling of most Jewish college students: They simply did not see any signs on the part of the synagogue leadership that they were wanted. Their youthful exuberance and activist enthusiasm were too threatening to most local *shul* lords to permit them to extend any welcoming hands in the direction of the college crowd. I remember one synagogue president explaining to me why he saw no need for a youth room in his congregation: "Who needs the noise? And who will pay for all the broken furniture?" The next Saturday, of course, as at almost every other opportunity for public lament, that congregation's rabbi was still asking the same rhetorical questions during his usually lachrymose sermon: "Where are our young people? Why aren't *they* in the synagogue?"

Unconsciously, I had picked up the same refrain when I visited Mr. Rabinowitz at the Yeshivah, to compare ideas with him before actually embarking on my program to organize the Alumni Association. Casually and playfully, he lobbed the ball right back at me: "If the youth are not in *their* synagogue, why don't you bring them to your synagogue?" My synagogue? Had Braverman jumped the gun and told it all? I let his serve go right over my head, for the moment, and launched into a serious discussion of what I considered to be an important challenge as head of an Alumni Association like ours: the urgent need to find a suitable replacement for the ailing synagogue. "Replacement?" he scoffed, after hearing me out. "Jews don't replace their own history. They change it. But that takes knowledge, wisdom, and even more. It takes courage. Think about that."

We did think about it. Patiently but doggedly, during meetings lasting over the next month or so, he continued to pump wind back into my deflated sails. He took me through two thousand years of Jewish wandering and wondering, losing and winning, always coming back to what I dubbed Rabinowitz's law: "For Jews, nothing is more permanent than change. To survive, we adapted. How? By making a virtue of necessity."

I can still see and feel his piercing blue eyes as he earnestly assured me that before our discussions would conclude, he, a so-called "secular Zionist," would prove that both the synagogue and the rabbinate were themselves innovative—even radical and secular responses to national deprivation, and not merely religious aberrations brought on by the Destruction and the Exile. "These two institutions, never dreamed of in the Bible, were Jewish responses that grew up from the grassroots—not from Him on High—but straight out of the national genius of our people. We had *hutzpah*. We said to God: 'You thought that you would mortally punish us by sending us into Exile. Remember Your covenant. For *You* to be known, *we* must survive. You need us as much as we need You! You lay upon us the necessity of surviving without Your Temple, and without Your priests. But Your Temple and priests are obsolete, archaic, and even more; they are corrupting and corruptible. We will go into Exile, and not be consumed. Wherever we go, we will build synagogues that will surpass your Temple with their devotion to humanism, and replace Your priest-magicians with fearlessly rational, worldly teachers: Rabbis of our own making."

I was sure that the easily frightened, most unworldly Rabbis that I knew would hardly have agreed with his secular defense of the synagogue and the rabbinate, if they were sitting there with me. But they would have been no less intrigued and heartened than I was, with Rabinowitz's ringing call for revising the estimates of their future by reassessing all Jewish values in terms of the national will to survive. For him, even the Jewish religion, in response to Exile, became a new and crucial secular weapon—to help us "live in the world."

He was going to convince me, he said, thumping his pudgy hand on the table, that there was more for the synagogue in America to do, than it could itself have imagined. He saw no other popular vehicle in sight, in the American scheme of things, that could reach Jews at the growing edge of their roots, and help restore their national self-awareness. The problem, he explained, was not the synagogues, as such—after all, it was merely a religious center, like a church—but that it had been reduced to being church-like in America. This was why it had become a refuge principally for the elderly: a kind of "home for the aged," for whom religious rituals and symbols now represented the only clear and visible certainties they could cling to. Or, for their Americanized adult children—the generation of my parents—it now served as a museum of sorts, a place of quaint, archaic memories: it was a "ritualarium" you frequented only when seized by occasional or seasonal fits of mystic need to recall and revive the dead, but unknown, past. But for neither of these was the synagogue part of any real world. It was all make-believe, except for the small handful of true believers.

I was being reminded that of all the groups which make up the Western World, we Jews have had one of the longest continuous experiences in living together as a community. And one did not need to find recourse to mysticism or supernaturalism to account for this. The key to survival of the Jews as a visible community is to be found in their ability to adapt their communal life to the dynamic circumstances of a shifting environment. We are now facing the third important crisis in Jewish history: learning how to live as a distinctive group within a secular democratic state like America, where your citizenship is neither linked to, nor impaired by, your religious affiliation.

"It's important to know something about the other two crises, and how we reacted to them," he emphasized. The first, of course, was the loss of the Temple and the state, when Jerusalem fell just seventy years into the Christian era. This created the de-nationalized diaspora Jewish community. The second crisis is much more recent, and that faced us when the governments of the West began granting us civil rights, and even citizenship for the first time, in the nineteenth century. And it is no coincidence that as a result of both of these challenges, Jewish life underwent a series of far-reaching changes. "The first crisis brought the synagogue and the rabbinate into being; the second brought forth new meanings for the synagogue, and completely changed the role of the Rabbi."

He continued to move his chessmen around the board of history, with precise and preconceived logic. True, Jews had always been basically religious in their outlook on the world, and it was to be expected, therefore, that their views would be deeply colored and influenced by the weight of accumulated religious tradition. Since tradition is a conservative force, Jews were not likely to accommodate to change by eliminating institutions, if they could avoid doing so. Over and over again he would repeat: "We do not eliminate; we do not walk on air; we rebuild and renovate. We give the traditional forms and institutions new meanings, new functions and roles. We make virtues of necessities that confront us. We make sunshine in the middle of the night."

His sweeping review of the history of Jewish social change was, of course, not intended to prove himself a virtuoso, nor to engage in extended and detached academic exercises. Soon enough, what he was really after became clear to me. He was after *me*. "Start a synagogue for young people that would be neither Orthodox, Conservative, or Reform—only Jewish. Make room for those who are not necessarily synagogue-oriented, but who, like me, love to survive." "But what Rabbi would be willing to undertake such an assignment?" I asked, rather naively. He was ready with a rapid reply: "That's just the point. We're not talking about Rabbis. Not yet, at any rate. You don't need a Rabbi. You lead it. Get your friends together, and start changing the Jewish world."

A few weeks later, the "Alumni Association of the Yeshivah of Flatbush" was finally launched, in late 1940. It was established as a "community" with various arms: educational, political, cultural. It immediately shook up all the nearby complacent synagogues, not because we were a synagogue in competition, but because just one of our programs—weekly Sabbath Services—was, to use the language of their complaint, "taking away all of *our* young people, the children of *our own members*." They were shedding crocodile tears, of course, over the same young people they had never seen in their synagogues, anyway, and if they had, would never have abided because of their "noise"—not to speak of all the mythical broken furniture!

In any case, ours was not a service, as much as it was a weekly meeting, which used the language and the setting of the synagogue only as a pretext. Our real purpose was to renovate Jewish life and to extend our welcome to all the young people who would come and help us achieve this. Services were led by us all; it was a collective experience in self-education. The "synagogue" was no longer outside of our real world; it was a rallying center and reporting station of a community at work. We were all Rabbis, none of us members.

Scores of us served as volunteers throughout the community; as youth leaders and Zionist organizers. Some assisted teachers at the Yeshivah on a voluntary basis; others helped write and publish a sharp and topical monthly publication that was widely read by the community's elders. We turned the Yeshivah building into an open Jewish house, keeping its doors regularly ajar, for one educational enterprise, or anti-Nazi protest rally, after another. Hundreds clamored for seats, even in the dead of winter, at our Friday Night Forums devoted to "Jewish Strategies for Survival." Places were freely available, wall-to-wall, and with standing room only; no tickets of admission, no membership cards or fees, no exclusions.

We enjoyed our studied iconoclasm, carefully breaking all of the known rules of organized Jewish life. We blindfolded ourselves to "parties," "movements," "membership organizations." Most of all, we savored our ability to scandalize all of those *grosser kenockers*—the "big shots"—the so-called Jewish leaders who customarily met with no one but themselves, behind closed doors, in board rooms beclouded with the blue haze of their smelly cigars. They were always busy protecting their own organizational coastline. But we were a different target, far out of their range. We really belonged to no organizations because we naively thought that we belonged to all. Maybe we saw ourselves as members of a "super organization" called "the Jewish People."

Overnight, it seemed, we became serious men and women, no longer engaged in innocuous Jewish "youth activities"—the kind of indoor sport our parents would have encouraged. We did not change the world—or even our own community—after all. But we changed ourselves.

Graduation from Brooklyn College was only a year away. There was no way to get to Palestine, the Mediterranean was still inaccessible because of the War. This continuing impasse helped me to clear my last mental hurdle. I scuttled all lingering hopes of taking my doctorate in Jewish history at the Hebrew University.

For almost two years, as head of the Alumni Association, I had been called "Mr. Rabbi," jokingly and affectionately by my friends, and mockingly by some local rabbis and synagogue leaders, who felt themselves threatened by our work. All through this, my mind kept returning to "Rabinowitz's law": to make a virtue of necessity. If I could not help rebuild Jewish life in Jerusalem, just now, I would start on my goal where I was, in New York. If synagogues were forever dark and sunless, I would leave them behind. To be "a Rabbi" was not to be wedded everlastingly to certain buildings, and certain people in certain places. It was a way of knowing, a way of keeping up my love affair with the culture of the Jewish people. It was also a way of transcending the materialistic "isms" of the day: Nazism, Communism, even Capitalism; a peaceful way of fighting all of these forces that carried the seeds of Jewish destruction.

By summer's end, in 1942, I had made up my mind. I would take the road that would lead me to study with Mordecai M. Kaplan.

In a few months, I was busy taking the week-long entrance examinations together with about a hundred others in the beautiful buildings of the Jewish Theological Seminary of America, near Columbia University. Then, in October, 1942, I attended my first class at the Rabbinical School—a day that remains clearly etched in my memory. It was a brisk and clear Monday morning in autumn; the lecture began promptly at 9

A.M. and continued for four solid hours, with only three five-minute breaks. We were seated before a distinguished-looking white-haired and white-goateed lecturer, standing tall on the podium above us, who proceeded to "destroy old worlds in order to build new ones." Some of my new classmates were dismayed; they had never heard such "unrabbinical talk" coming from the lips of a Rabbi. And on their very first day in Rabbinical School! Others were delighted. We stood around in little knots, arguing with each other for an hour, before leaving the lecture hall.

I listened, but did not talk. My heart was pounding too hard. For me, it was something of a vindication of choices; a feeling of being in the right place, and with the right guide. It would be sheer joy to hear this man for almost four hours every Monday morning. At last, at the feet of Mordecai M. Kaplan, and his "unrabbinical rabbinics," I would find out what direction my love of Jewish life should really take.

Or so I thought.

Because it was not their station, millions of New Yorkers, condemned to their daily round of underground shuttling in the city's dank and deafening subways, had probably never ventured above ground to be uplifted by the sights and sounds of Morningside Heights. For me, a provincial Brooklynite, this had to be the spiritual center of the city, and I always experienced a feeling of rising elation as soon as I began climbing up to its special streets, leaving the darker netherworld behind. There were students here from all over the world. Some, at Juilliard School of Music, could be heard playing their instruments, or practicing arias, even through closed windows, in the dead of winter. Others were very busy scurrying seriously about the campus of Columbia University, which took up the lion's share of this small "cultural island." University buildings spilled over into the city's streets, where even the clanging streetcars and hissing buses seemed to be carefully muted, in deference to the Heights. Soon, however, crowded streets disappeared into campus playing fields, terraced lawns, secluded walks, and then—library after library. Brooklyn, I told myself, was not New York; and New York, I was already certain, was surely the Capital of the World.

A block or so to the north, my eyes caught, for the first time, the Union Theological Seminary, the great interdenominational Protestant center, looking very serene and immovable in the midst of busy Broadway. Even strangers to the area pointed me in awe to these quiet, grey buildings; inside, they knew, were to be found some of the giants of modern Christian thought, men like Reinhold Niebuhr and Paul Tillich, whose books were known around the world. A short block to the west, closer to the banks of the Hudson River, and not far from Grant's Tomb, stood the towering Riverside Church, or "Socony Temple," as we later dubbed it, in mock recall of the petro-riches of the founder of Standard Oil of New York, John D. Rockefeller, who had helped build that unique community center. And even more important than the building was the magnificent leader of the congregation, Dr. Harry Emerson Fosdick, whose spiritual voice rang out from its pulpit, clear across America. I would be dropping in to his church, just to thrill to his eloquence, as often as I could, during my student days at the Seminary.

Block after block, and everywhere you traversed, you almost never moved out of sight of stately and imposing buildings—schools, institutes, colleges, libraries—dedicated to the pursuit of truth and beauty, in the service of God and man. Each building conjured up important names; each reminded you of the enduring contributions the scholars, teachers, artists, and leaders of these institutions had made to America and the world. I felt that I was taking a walking tour through the pages of American cultural and intellectual history.

When you reached the northeast corner of Broadway and 122nd Street and looked up at the impressive buildings that occupied a whole city block, you had the feeling that these, too, were either part of Columbia University, or that they housed some other prestigious American college. Those who had erected this pleasant little campus, with its grassy quadrangle and red-brick Colonial architecture, must surely have been old-line Americans, who had blended their school neatly into the cultural landscape of this important part of the great metropolis. Its wrought-iron gates, however, bore an inscription that seemed to give out a different message. This was, you now discovered, The Jewish Theological Seminary *of America*, and a nattily uniformed doorman was there, to lead you through and to announce your arrival.

"America"—this was to be the key word and the focal idea at the Seminary, throughout the years I was in attendance, and for many years thereafter. To be sure, in my freshman class of twenty or so young men, about half did not come from the "real America," but like me, hailed from that peculiarly enclavic community of New York City. But some of my new friends spoke in Yankee accents derived from their native Boston; or in a Midwestern twang reflecting their hometowns of Chicago, Pittsburgh, or Minneapolis; a few even drawled, Southern style, in a manner of speech they had learned at home in places like Baltimore or Atlanta. The colleges and universities we had graduated from reflected our geographical diversity, too; most had studied at state or private universities, at or near their homes: Chicago, Minnesota, Northwestern, Pittsburgh, Harvard, or Yale. A few of us, from the environs of New York, had been enrolled at one of the free schools, like City College or Brooklyn College. The rest of the locals were all graduates of the Orthodox center of higher education, Yeshiva College (now known as a University).

Virtually all of my classmates were sons of pious parents who scrupulously kept the tradition as Orthodox Jews—who never violated the Sabbath and minutely observed all of the commandments. What is more, a goodly number were the sons of Orthodox Rabbis, Cantors, Hebrew teachers, and *shohetim*—ritual slaughterers.

True, a very few entered merely to enjoy the draft deferral granted in wartime to "divinity students": they never intended to serve as Rabbis after graduation, and did not. They became lawyers, university professors, or directors of bureaus of Jewish education, and such like. The fact is, however, that most did want to become practicing Rabbis.

They had come to the Seminary with the blessings and encouragement of their Rabbi-fathers, who by the late 1930s and early 1940s, had fully despaired of the possibility of Orthodox Judaism ever striking deep roots in the America they knew. They confided that their fathers believed that "the future was with Conservative Judaism" and even "with Reform Judaism"—which was too liberal, "too un-Jewish" for their liking. There were just too many *proste yidn*—uncouth ordinary Jews—who chiefly populated their fathers' congregations. They would be happier to see their sons become successful Conservative Rabbis, serving acculturated, but more worldly and educated Jews, even if it meant that the sons had to deviate somewhat from the strict religious tradition they brought over from the old country. Conservatism, they felt, was the new wave of old east European Judaism: the comfortable middle between the extremes of Orthodoxy on the right, and Reform on the left.

At least half of the class, including these sons of Orthodox Rabbis, came to the Seminary for only one reason—the same reason I had: to study and be with Mordecai Kaplan. While we were attached sentimentally to the old religious rituals and practices, we felt that traditional ideology was not being adequately expressed in terms Jews could now find meaningful and relevant. Nor, for that matter, were too many religious Jews—Orthodox, Conservative, or Reform—taking into account the two major revolutions that had become part of the spiritual baggage of many of our contemporaries: both modern Zionism and the modern moods generated by scientific thought and discovery.

We had also come to the Seminary in the full expectation of

discovering other teachers on that world-renowned faculty of the same stripe as Kaplan, even if they could not accept his specific reformulations of Judaism. We had hoped to encounter there other great men who had some reasoned and thoughtful system of Jewish belief and behavior which would renovate Judaism without the excesses of Reform—and make it more livable for us. What we found was almost shocking to our nervous and mental systems: There was virtually no other faculty person who even bothered himself with these problems. Worse still—with the glaring exception of Kaplan none seemed to care. As detached scholars—they were Rabbis, of course, but saw themselves as school-men first—they were principally preoccupied with their own esoteric research. What little they shared of themselves with the students always revolved around their own areas of specialized inquiry. Mostly, words: either ancient Biblical exegesis or legalistic Talmudic hermeneutics.

It was only toward the end of my student tenure, shortly before graduation from the Seminary in 1945, that Professor Abraham J. Heschel, a Polish Jew who had been teaching at the Reform seminary in Cincinnati, the Hebrew Union College, came over to New York and joined our faculty. Soon, he, too, became a charismatic magnet of the students—although, of course, he emphasized Jewish mysticism and rejected Kaplan's essentially rationalist, religious humanism. For the most part, however, Mordecai Kaplan was virtually all that there was about the Seminary that appeared relevant. As one of my colleagues put it: "Other faculty were teaching texts; 'Kappie' [Kaplan] was thinking thoughts." They were giving the "important" core courses, while he was really teaching "Kaplan," as Professor of Homiletics—officially considered among the lesser subjects, and almost sneered at by the rest of the faculty.

It was important, of course, to understand the Biblical text, to fathom the Talmudical argument, or to know (by heart?) the reams of dates and Rabbinic author-and-title lists that went by the name of "Jewish History" as it was then taught at the

Seminary. But if truth be told, I was often bored by this overemphasis on mere technical "Jewish skills." To me, they added up to words, words, and more words—but no rational system, no logical process, no comparative analysis. They seemed to shield, rather than to reveal, the real Judaism from coming into view. I knew that I needed additional perspective, and I petitioned successfully for permission—along with several other classmates—to enroll simultaneously with my Seminary classes, for graduate degrees in sociology and history, at nearby Columbia University.

Professor Kaplan kept insisting that Judaism was not a religious denomination—as the versions of Orthodoxy and Reform had made it, in America—and that Conservative Judaism should adopt his view that "Judaism was the *evolving, religious civilization* of the Jewish People." It also encompassed language and literature, music and the arts, as well as a unique polity. It was this basic definition—it was more than a definition; it was actually a way of thinking about *oneself* as a Jew—which appealed to virtually all the students, almost without exception.

Kaplan taught that Jews should recreate in America the organic community they had built in Europe, because he saw that each congregational union was going off in different, competing directions. He believed that it was the overall Jewish community, not the congregations or their partisan seminaries, to which Jews owed their largest loyalties. He invented the concept of the Synagogue-Center—owned and operated by and for all the Jews of the community, and not merely by a handful of those who could afford to pay membership dues in their "own Jewish country club"—which they euphemistically called a synagogue. He introduced the view that it was not incompatible with historical Judaism to innovate rituals— taken from the environment or from life in Jewish Palestine. One of these was the "Bat Mitzvah" ceremony for young girls, which has now become a standard feature in thousands of congregations around the world, although before him, there had never been a parallel ritual for girls, of the kind that young boys had enjoyed for many centuries.

Yet, the more I studied "social theory" at Columbia, the more I would return to Kaplan's classes, feeling that he was really not creating a new Jewish theology as much as he was dealing in the sociology of Judaism as filtered through the "pragmatism" of John Dewey. Though he himself was a warm and emotionally alive human being, his teachings about God— as "reconstructionist theology"—seemed distant and aloof, far from the existential needs of us little people. I had the feeling that he was asking us to pray to some impersonal life-force, or as he called it, "the Power that makes for salvation, or well-being."

Some of us began to affirm Kaplan the man, the Jew, the thought-provoker and innovator more and more, even while we thought less and less of his Reconstructionist theology. We felt that he was asking us to leave our mystical, poetic relationship with the historical God of Israel, and to address ourselves, instead, to a cosmic process. Instead of saying, "Dear God," it seemed to some of us that he was suggesting we pray, "To whom it may concern." Nevertheless, now that he is past one hundred years old, there can be no doubt that Mordecai Kaplan is a seminal thinker and has had great influence over thousands of Jews, not to speak of the hundreds of his students who have served as Rabbis throughout the United States and Canada. We did not all become Reconstructionists, but he made it possible for many of us—and I am one of them—to imagine ourselves as Rabbis, in the first place.

Not many months were to pass, however, before I started to harbor serious doubts about having enrolled at the Seminary. I came fact-to-face with a version of American Jewish life— "suburban Judaism"—which I had never met before. My brief encounters with suburban Judaism were more than enough to make me decide never to serve a congregation in Metropolitan New York, and almost enough to prevent me from ever thinking about occupying a pulpit of any kind, anywhere. I even began seriously questioning my desire or ability to serve my people as a Rabbi. Certainly not as a congregational leader.

Suburban Jews? Jews—by virtue of this new engrossment with green acres away from the city core—radically proclaiming themselves as a child-and-property-centered community? This was a fundamental departure even in so checkered a communal history as ours. For me, it came as something of a shock. In my Seminary classes I was learning the "secret" of our spiritual growth despite millennial dispersion: It had almost everything to do with our connection to the culture of cities—not to its remote outskirts, and surely not to our rare rural experiences. I had been especially intrigued by the fact that even some enlightened Christian rulers had understood this "law" of Jewish life. In Germany, as early as 1084, an energetic and farsighted Roman Catholic Bishop, Huotzmann Ruediger of Speyer, wished to extend his small Rhineland Community into a city, and so he did the unthinkable: He *invited Jews* to settle there. He explained why: "To amplify a thousand times its dignity and commerce. I have invited Jews" to live securely among his own people. He offered them a generous charter, a strict guarantee of their rights, and agreed to build a wall around their quarter to protect them from the insolence and possible violence of the mob. Over the next several hundred years, other church prelates followed his lead.[1]

These bishops understood well that the city and not the village—the *urbs*, not the *villa*—was the repository and generator of culture, and that a spiritual dynamic was possible only when there was a center of commerce joined to lively human exchanges between varied and differing layers of the population. Instinctively, they believed that both culture and commerce would be possible in small towns like Speyer, Cologne, and others, when there were Jews happily settled there.

---

[1] J. Aronius, *Regesten zur Geschichte der Juden im Frankischen und Deutschen Reiche bis zum Jahre 1273*, Berlin, 1902, Numbers 168 and 588. See also James Parkes, *The Jew in the Medieval Community*, London, The Soncino Press, 1938, pp. 160-161.

Jews and cities are inextricably linked by the intimate ties of a culture which has been forged in diverse cities Jews have helped to enrich all around the world. This is why twentieth-century Jews living in rural New Jersey—or in farming communities in Argentina and Canada, for that matter—were spiritually closer to a body of tradition created and shaped centuries before in Warsaw, Vilna, or Odessa, than to the lifestyles of their farmer-neighbors a half-mile down the road, or their small-townsmen across the street. This same phenomenon, my professors explained, was also at work in Palestine, where so many Jews were now living on the land and working it as *kibbutzniks*. Though the kibbutz might only be across a single field from Arab peasant-neighbors, its farmers were culturally closer to the Jews of Manhattan than to the Arab *fellaheen* in the very next village.

I was learning that Jewish history is largely a history of distinguished urban communities set within different nations and peoples and reflecting different times and places, yet related to each other by a tradition which could transcend the limitations of space and time. Jerusalem, Alexandria, Baghdad, Cordova, Speyer, Amsterdam, Vilna, Berlin, New York—all were thousands of years and miles apart. Each had produced its own culture-heroes, products of the uniqueness of their own distinctive communities—Palestinian, Ashkenazi, Sephardi, Italian, and now American. Yet all were made into a single cultural family. They studied the same texts, argued and analyzed the same commentaries, and read and wrote the same Hebrew language. Each developed its own unique character—yet they were linked to one another because of three important factors: a considerable population living together as a community; a common history over a considerable number of years; and most important—they created a considerable number of schools and teachers, something only a city community can support and attract.

What would happen to Jewish life and culture if Jews

became modern "peasants"—and reversed the laws of their unique social history? Would they think, act, and look like all the other villagers, around the corner, or across the street? These questions, I discovered, were not in the hearts or minds of North American Jews as their movement out of the city began to take shape.[2]

The first waves of suburbanization were set in motion in New York's Jewish community as the Forties opened and America was just beginning to turn an economic corner, after so many depressed years. Upward—and outward—mobility, again. Jews, and others, responded to the end of an era by beginning to move out, at first in very small dribbles, to where the grass began to grow.

The mass movement of Jews out of Brooklyn, Manhattan and The Bronx, to Queens and Long Island—and even to the nearby States of New Jersey and Connecticut—did not reach massive proportions until several years after the War's end. But even those smaller gestures, begun a few years earlier, were sufficient to require some sort of professional assistance for communities like Pleasantdale, New Jersey, which was only a ten-minute drive from the Oranges—and but a few moments longer to Newark. The late medieval Protestant principle was now to be invoked throughout Jewdom in Metropolitan America—*cuius regio eius religio*—every separate region required its own autonomous religious authority. It was to become the new pattern: every two miles or less another "Jewish community" in America!

That quiet, uncrowded area, situated in the rolling countryside of West Orange, was known only to a small number of

---

[2] For a fuller discussion of "Suburban Jews" see Herbert Gans, *The Origin and Growth of a Jewish Community in the Suburbs: A Study of the Jews of Forest Park*, in *The Jews: Social Patterns of an American Group* (ed. by Marshall Sklare), The Free Press, Glencoe, Ill., 1960, pp. 205-248; also, Seymour Leventman, *From Shtetl to Suburb*, in *The Ghetto and Beyond: Essays on Jewish Life in America* (ed. by Peter I. Rose), Random House, New York, 1969, pp. 33-56.

New York and Newark families as an even better resort area than the so-called Borscht Belt of the Catskill Mountains. It was certainly much closer; only a few miles from "the City," "the air was like Denver, Colorado." And the food in Pleasantdale's Jewish hotels and boarding houses, it was said, "was as good as, or maybe even better than the fare at similar places in Upstate New York." (New York City dwellers, the country's most provincial metropolitans, persist in regarding any point north of The Bronx—even Westchester County—as located in "Upstate New York.")

By 1942, enough former Jewish dwellers of Newark or The Bronx had bought homes in Pleasantdale—about forty or fifty families—to make it necessary to turn to the Seminary in search of professional leadership. This new community was not the immediate beginning of a tidal wave. Its two hundred souls had only constituted a kind of toe-testing and not yet the full-scale plunge into the mighty streams that would lead Jews later, in great numbers, to one suburb after the other, where their dark and dreary city apartments could be replaced by a patch of green, and their children had a place to romp.

But for me, as their "Rabbi" it was a foretaste of all that was—and would be—wrong with suburban Judaism in America. (Consider that, by the 1980s, the suburbanization of New York City Jewry had reached proportions of plurality.)

I was, in fact, what was then called their "weekend Rabbi." From Friday afternoon through Sunday, I was "Rabbi" Rosenberg, but all through the week, my Seminary professors made it very clear who I really was: They called me "Mr. Rosenberg." My deflating-inflating experience was shared by several other classmates, who were similarly "called" to other suburban areas, mostly on Long Island. "Called?" Protestants have popularized this euphemistic, spiritually charged language for pulpit employment. They really mean "hired." I was hired, not called, for something like $1,000 per annum.

The hiring took place *in situ*, as the archaeologists like to say, so I could "get the feel" of the place. We met inside the single-story white-frame house that had recently been purchased as their new synagogue, and over whose front door lintel hung a freshly painted sign: The Jewish Center of Pleasantdale. It was a Sunday morning late in August, and they were concerned about the forthcoming High Holy Days, just a few weeks down the calendar. (Synagogue officials in America always seem to panic—over one subject or another—sometime in late August, as the High Holy Days beckon.) Could I sing? Yes. Lead the services as Cantor? Sure. Read the Torah? Only if no one else could. (Oh, well, maybe Epstein will do that.) What about the Shofar—could I blow it? Why not? And so the interview went, amiably enough, for an hour or longer. Of course, if I were "engaged," I would also be expected to conduct Late Friday Evening Services every Sabbath, and morning services the next day. And teach their children twice a week—on Wednesday afternoons, and Sunday mornings. I would be the only teacher; the only "anything," as one of the men put it.

I looked at the two men who were hiring me—my friendly interviewers sitting across a makeshift table, and started interviewing them. Why were they interested in this sort of thing? When did they come to the community? Were there enough Jews in the area to count on for Sabbath services, at least a *minyan*?

"Rabbi," the younger man answered (I already knew, from this, that I had gotten the position), "there are always a bunch of Jews across the street at the Goldman Hotel whom we can rustle up and bring over if we're short." As to why they needed a "Rabbi" themselves, and what strengths they felt the community possessed, I had to wait for the real answers to those questions to come only after I had seen them in action, as their "spiritual leader," several months later.

The younger man, Eddie Goldfein, the new President of the Center, was probably in his mid-thirties. He was born and raised in The Bronx, and had moved to the area only a few years earlier. Like many other new suburbanites of the time, he had four children—each neatly spaced two years apart. While he had to commute to Manhattan every day—he was, he said, in the *"schmatte business,"* a sales representative of a ladies garment factory—he now had *lebensraum* for his family, something he could not have had even in the fanciest apartment on the "Grand Concourse." "Call me Eddie," he insisted from the very first. But when I reciprocated his friendship, he refused to call me by my first name. "Oh no, I can't do that," he said, looking very seriously at a twenty-one-year-old student. "If you're going to be my Rabbi, you are 'my Rabbi.' " My sophomoric head enlarged immediately, and I did not demur. (Over the years, however, I would muse about this obsessive need many Jews have to "possess" a Rabbi of their own. "*My* Rabbi," they would always proclaim, as if they really owned him.)

The older man was the "father of the community." Jake Traberman, already in his seventies, was a Russian-born Jew who had retired from his small retail business in Newark, about ten years earlier. He came to Pleasantdale, he said, "because I always liked mountains, and the healthy, fresh air—*frische luft*, Rabbi, if you know what I mean." He obviously had his doubts about my Yiddish.

Jake began explaining the history of the *shul*. The house we were meeting in—the *shul*—had been originally own by "Ma" Goldman, the undisputed ruler of the area, not just the Hotel but as far as your eyes could see. It was used for "extras"—as expansion space for her hotel guests on crowded weekends. In between times, a few of the oldsters in the community like Ma Goldman herself, arranged for a *minyan*, as required—for a *Yahrzeit*, or a *Kaddish*, now and then. But "when so many young families started to move in I went to Ma Goldman and asked her if she would be willing to sell the house to the 'community,' *if* we could get a community going."

"That's where I come in," Eddie interrupted, picking up the story. "I and fellows like me.

"Jake began knocking on doors, getting the younger men

together for an emergency meeting. Then, when he told us the story, how this house was available to us for purchase from Goldman's, we all chipped in, put down a deposit, took out a mortgage and bought it. Now we had a building, but we still had no organization. So the boys drafted me as President. We soon had a Board of Directors, and we were in business.

"Just think of it; me, Eddie Goldfein, President of a *shul*! If my father were alive he'd have a tremendous laugh. He couldn't get me inside a synagogue before I was Bar Mitzvah. And it's almost twenty-five years now, since my Bar Mitzvah. That's the last time I had anything to do with a *shul*."

He was speaking as an average New York Jew, a product of the place and the time. You didn't find too many American-born Jews under the age of sixty inside any synagogue in the City after the end of World War I. But "for the sake of my four kids," as Eddie put it, "I think I have an obligation to do something." Now he was speaking as a typical exurbanite Jew, whose desire for space in the suburbs "for the sake of his kids" had also created a new need: to create a "Jewish environment" out of nothing but sheer "self-interest"—his own hopes for his own children. History, culture, theology—these seemed to have nothing to do with it. The community of interest was built upon self-interest. But there was, nevertheless, a very traditional ring about all of this; Goldfein and company were still part of the greater Jewish family—historically and geographically. Although it was their own kids' future they always talked about, it was the *Jewish* past they were unconsciously searching out—roots for that future to cling to.

It never was an easy task to get Goldfein back to *shul*—President or no President. After the High Holy Days had concluded, he and his fellow officers thought that they, too, *had concluded*. After all, "their job," as they put it, was to attend meetings. "It's the Rabbi's *job* to attend services, and look after the rituals."

We spent the next three weeks of Saturdays vainly waiting for the "tenth man" to appear—sometimes, even for the fifth or sixth soul to cross the *shul's* threshhold. Without ten men, a *minyan*, it was impossible, of course, to conduct Sabbath morning services. Finally, at the end of a very "arid" Jewish month, and in sheer desperation, I asked Traberman to put out a telephone S.O.S.—Save Our *Shul*—to Eddie and a few of his colleagues. Would they please run down, for only an hour or so, with a complement of friends, so that we could conduct a Service, on the next Saturday morning. I had been having no trouble on Friday nights—the women were baking cookies, acting as hostesses, and making certain to bring the whole family—including their reticent husbands—to our Late Friday Evening Services and the Social Hour that followed.

Goldfein and his friends did come, and I soon learned why they had stayed away, so religiously, from Sabbath morning services. They knew no Hebrew, or so little as to be frightened even of muttering a few phrases, here and there, as a coverup.

I did not know this fact of suburban Jewish life in New York, in 1943, until that Saturday morning. We had only ten men, and all ten would be "honored" during the reading of the Torah, with an *aliya*, by being called up to recite the traditional benedictions they had not recited since last "called to the Torah"—on their Bar Mitzvah day.

When I handed Eddie the Torah Crown, expecting that he would place it atop the Scroll where it belonged, he was so flustered that, not knowing what to do, he proceeded to crown himself, placing it ever so gingerly on his own head. Perhaps he thought that would make him appear very presidential and that was what heads of *shuls* should look like. Everyone guffawed, even those who were not exactly sure why they were laughing.

I knew then that I could not spend the rest of my life in suburbia, teaching grown-up men materials really intended for children. I remembered that critics of American education had labeled some third-rate universities as only "super-kindergartens"—teaching grown people inconsequential things they should have already learned. True enough, I was very young then, and suburban Judaism has already grown up, too, since those salad days—and this was only Pleasantdale. But on balance, were any of the other congregations across the land— even the most vaunted—really very much different? Could they be made to serve the higher purposes men like Professor Kaplan had set for us?

I had the confusing feeling that suburban Jews were living up to Hollywood's description of "religious America." To be successful in their eyes, I began to see, we Rabbis had not only to be just like them, but also to measure up to what Protestant ministers and Catholic priests were supposed to be like. I remember advertisements for a film about a "great American minister" and how it summed it all up. Describing the late Rev. Dr. Peter Marshall, former chaplain to Congress, in announcing the movie about his life, *A Man Called Peter*, the signs read: "He's a first name kind of guy...He's everybody's kind of guy...He's a lovin' kind of guy...He's God's kind of guy...He plays baseball with kids."

Some forty years have since passed. I still ask myself, as I survey the fairly barren Jewish landscape—out there where the grass is green and the trees grow tall—whether American Jews, are ready to cast aside that Exodus-like, desert mentality, and finally settle down to a maturer and deeper Jewish life.

If they do not do this soon, they should not rely on "Hansen's Law" to redeem *their* grandchildren—fifth generation *shtetl*-descendants—from joining the growing ranks of self-obliterating Americans of Jewish parentage.[3]

---

[3] Marcus Lee Hansen is an American sociologist, author of the view that third generation immigrants in America want to remember traditions which their parents—the second generation—were anxious to forget. Hansen's "Law": "What the son wishes to forget the grandson wishes to remember." See Marcus Lee Hansen, *The Immigrant in America*, Harvard University Press, 1940, p. 76.

PART TWO

RABBIS AND CONGREGATIONS

Chapter 5

DENOMINATIONS

I had discovered, even while still a Seminary student, that suburbanization was a mixed blessing. It may have helped to attract younger couples to a synagogue for the first time; but it was also responsible for reducing the quality of spiritual life by adopting the lowest common denominators as norms. It seemed to transform the traditional synagogue into an active community center; but it did not encourage it to aspire to become a place of high Jewish culture.

However, it would take some years longer before I would realize that the twentieth-century North American synagogue itself—urban as well as suburban—could actually pose a grave threat to the fullest experience of Judaism in a free society. It could serve to divide Jew against Jew—all in the name of God.

I had enrolled at the Seminary precisely because I was attracted to one man—Mordecai M. Kaplan. He, more than any other, was teaching American Jews that religious pluralism was a special blessing conferred on them by democracy, which they should gratefully espouse. These options—Orthodox, Conservative, and Reform—were not to be regarded as rival denominations, nor should any of them be seen as possessing exclusive, absolute truth. Rather, they were to be accepted as valid and authentic religious alternatives for Jews to choose freely—even eclectically—in an open society.

So it was that once upon a time, in my own almost-recent experience, Jewish denominationalism had actually served as a symbol of free inquiry—of Jewish partners in parallel search. The denominations were surely not what they have now become: rivals split into warring, separationist camps; disputants, not partners. Today, a growing sectarianism, powered by the unexpected militancy and triumphalism of the religious right wing, threatens to split the organic Jewish community apart. Yet, despite highly advertised claims these days, that Orthodoxy is the "Torah-true" wave of the future, it is doubtful if North American Jews are likely to jettison their innate need for religious pluralism—not only outside, but also within, their own precincts. Nor is it fully clear that the resultant rush to appear more Orthodox, even by those who are not culturally or personally suited to such a lifestyle, is anything more than a temporary, *institutional* phenomenon. Indeed, I would argue that a strictly traditional, monolithic approach to Judaism—despite its present appearance of success—will never become more than what it really is now, the choice of a small minority of North American Jews.

In the short space of just two decades or so, much had changed since I graduated the Seminary. By 1967, the "new ethnicity" as it was called (or was it really the "old" that merely resurfaced?) became a highly visible factor in American life. It was popular and acceptable to affirm your Jewishness in strong and undeniable terms, now that Black Power had made all Americans into what had just emerged as a new noun—"ethnics." Even "Wasps" now considered that they were a legitimate ethnic group—since everyone else was, too. For Jews, the year 1967 was a watershed for still other reasons: the Six Day War of June, and more particularly the months of April and May which preceded it.

In those six days before mid-June—when the war was victoriously and sensationally concluded by Israel, and in lightning speed, against five Arab armies—bloodcurdling Arab threats to annihilate Israel raised the specter, for almost all of North America's Jews, of a new Holocaust in the making. Large numbers of previously indifferent Jews, and even many alienated "came out of the woodwork," as some of them later told me themselves. Since then, there has been a definite shift toward greater emphasis on Jewish tradition among Reform and Conservative congregations. But it was the Orthodox who were clearly the beneficiaries of the new wave of sentiment. Just two decades before, they had exhibited all the signs of a dying movement, and now, toward the late 1960s, they were emerging as a force to be contended with in American Jewish life. In a very real sense, the "fall and rise of Orthodoxy" in this century has been one of the most spectacular phenomena of recent Jewish history. Nevertheless, as ever before, the community still exhibited signs of contradictory and paradoxical extremes. While traditionalism was rising at an unprecedented rate among the "officially synagogued," a new kind of secular Judaism was also growing by leaps and bounds. It is best characterized as the "civil Jewish religion" of the very large number of the nonobservant. But it, too, was also the product of the new ethnicity sweeping the country.

To obtain a clear understanding of what was at work, not only in the Jewish community but elsewhere in America, I find it refreshing to listen to what an astute observer of the religious scene—a Christian sociologist—has to say. Martin E. Marty puts it this way:

> "Ethnicity is not all of one piece.... From the viewpoint of social behavior, at least two styles of affirming peoplehood became apparent [in the 1960s]. We can call them Ethnicity A and Ethnicity B, to avoid any hint of the pejorative in dealing with either. The behavior patterns of the two will not necessarily always differ markedly, but the style and tone of each has grown out of different grasps of ethnic or racial backgrounds. Ethnicity A was inescapable, automatic, and

reflexive. It issued from people who may have experienced 'pluralistic ignorance,' having been unaware that there were alternatives to their tribe and its ways. Or they may not have been free to borrow from these alternatives. Needless to say, this form of behavior seemed always to have been in the process of dying out, since new immigrant or otherwise unexposed groups were decreasing in number. Ethnicity B was at least partly escapable, intentional, and reflective. The black who once 'passed' now wore an 'Afro,' and instead of obliterating African traces in worship, now elevated them. The Jew who had his name Anglicized restored the original name and perhaps, turned orthodox and observant.

"Ethnicity A produced forms of activity that were associated with newly arrived immigrants who looked out on a hostile world or into a mirror, seeing there only fellow ghetto residents and their ways. Occupational gatekeepers might mediate a larger world before the age of media and mobility, but after it began, only with strenuous efforts such as those taken by Lubavitscher Jews in Brooklyn, Hutterites in South Dakota, Doukhobors in Western Canada—through chosen geographical remoteness or high ghetto walls—could anyone minimize outside influences.... The Lubavitscher Jews wore distinctive garbs, followed all orthodox dietary laws, shunned intermarriage, and were overtly hostile to strangers. They incarnated some of the styles of the small community or *shtetl* of Eastern Europe, and in their transplantation of the same were immediately recognizable as part of what we are calling Ethnicity A. A secularized or Reform Jewish coed on a university campus in 1967 might have thrown in her lot with the Arabs. Her choice would have been based on conscious identification with what she thought was the Third World, over against an Israel that to her looked to be part of American imperialism. As time passed, she would become unsure of herself and her loyalties. Eventually, she might reaffirm Judaism and choose to follow its orthodox forms. Quite likely, she would write a book advocating Ethnicity B.

"Or the experience of mixed marriage and conversion has

often led to affirmation of Ethnicity B. Thus a Gentile girl loves a Reform Jewish young man on a college campus. After careful exploration of alternatives she converts and they marry. She is determined that their child will grow up conscious of their Judaism. She will take pains to have a family visit to Israel; they will tend to Jewish practice. Soon they challenge the Jewish parents-in-law to do away with family's 'traditional' Christmas tree. The child receives a Jewish name as his father had not. An acquired ethnic sense demands a different kind of nurture than an inherited one."[1]

I need only add that Dr. Marty is not looming outlandish fabric out of the whole cloth of his sociological imagination. As a Rabbi, I have witnessed all of these developments at first hand. And I could adduce even more poignant examples of how "Jewish" some very "far-out" Christian *and* Jewish young people have become, in just the past few years or so.

None of this could be seen in the American Jewish community I had entered as a Rabbi, in the mid-1940s. Indeed, it was then fashionable to define all three groups—Orthodox, Conservative and Reform—rather mockingly. It was suggested then that all three were really the same, except for one measurement: They were only two blocks apart. By which was meant: Reform Jews drive up in their cars, openly and unabashedly, and park in front of their temples, on the Sabbath; Conservative Jews, more sensitive to the prohibition against riding on the Jewish Sabbath, parked a block away from the synagogue, *when* they attended services, while the Orthodox made certain to park two blocks away. I should also add that since the Forties, virtually all Conservative congregations have added parking lots to their synagogue grounds—which tend to be very active on Saturday mornings, especially

---

[1] See Martin E. Marty, *A Nation of Behavers*, University of Chicago Press, Chicago, 1976, pp. 164-166. For purposes of comparison with the early 1960s see also *What Do We Believe: The Stance of American Religion*, Meredith Press, New York, 1968, coauthored by Martin Marty, Andrew Greeley, and Stuart E. Rosenberg.

on the occasion of Bar Mitzvahs. This, too, is part of the paradox.

Each of these branches of religious life which have proliferated into what may now be called American Judaism is denominated by a label that has been appropriated from the general, Western environment. There have, of course, always been plural Judaisms. Biblical Judaism was vastly different from what Talmudic Judaism became in the hands of the Rabbis who shaped it. Sephardic Jews—those who lived in medieval Spain and Portugal, then migrated, after their expulsions, to Holland, Turkey, Greece and the Mediterranean basin—practice a Judaism that is a variant form of the tradition, developing as it did in different circumstances from Ashkenazic Jews. These latter had lived first in ancient, then medieval, Germany, before they moved eastward to Poland and Russia, beginning with the sixteenth century. Italian communities preserved different rites and customs altogether in the shadow of the Vatican. Still another variety grew up in the midst of Islam—the old Jewish settlements in Asia, North Africa, and Yemen, in the Arabian peninsula. There were black Falasha Jews, too, in Ethiopia, who dated their community back to the biblical days of King Solomon. And Jews had lived in China and India for many hundreds of years. Not one of these Jewish communities—differing as they did from one another—was called by a denominational name. Although each considered that they were traditional purists, none was called Orthodox. That happened only in America.

To refer to any form of Judaism as Orthodox—as if it were made of a single, smooth block of Herodian stone—is to be off the historical mark. To confuse matters even more, when Jews use the term Orthodox to describe those who claim to be unswervingly traditional—"living a Torah-true Judaism," as they describe themselves—what they really mean to say is "orthoprax." Pious Jews everywhere, despite their variations on the themes of tradition, do share a basic religious *practice*.

But no intelligent Orthodox Jew would want to say that even "his" Judaism represents a closed system of *uniform belief*. Historically, in Judaism, belief was always a highly personalized matter, with room for poetic and mystical flights of fancy, while religious practice tended to be standardized and more uniform, taking into account the local variations mentioned earlier. The *performance* of *mitzvot*—the 613 divine commandments—was obligatory—but the way they were interpreted and perceived differed widely.[2]

Those other two appellations, Conservative and Reform, are also of recent vintage. "Reform" was the name given to the Judaism proposed by emancipated, late eighteenth-century Jews in Germany and Bohemia. But even their innovations were geared primarily to religious practice, and not so much to their beliefs. They sought to "Westernize" the "Oriental" religious behavior which they saw in Judaism. They added German to a synagogue liturgy freighted with Hebrew, a language of the "Orient." Western-style music and instrumental accompaniment were substituted for the *a cappella* cantorial chants that seemed to them to echo the sounds of some Middle-Eastern bazaar. They incorporated sermons in the vernacular into the services to prove that they were true Europeans—not to mention their desire to explicate the tradition to their children in a language they both spoke and understood.

This religious "Reformation" was a far cry from Martin Luther's. At the outset, it was only a minor tinkering with a few bothersome externals of the religious practice. Only when they came to America did they turn these few improvisations into an institutionally based Reform Movement, centered in the Hebrew Union College, a seminary for the exclusive training of Reform Rabbis which they founded in Cincinnati in 1875. From then on, they attacked the entire *halaka*—fundamental

---

[2] Books dealing with the "Reasons for the Commandments"—*Taame Ha-Mitzvot*—have been extremely popular for centuries. Few of them agree on the intrinsic meaning of the *Mitzvot*, leaving room for personal interpretation.

Jewish religious law—as antiquated, and no longer merely changed a few annoying, "superannuated" ceremonials.

Conservative Judaism, too, had to wait about half a century before it became a visible movement in the American Jewish world. It started out life in America as a tiny protest against the reforms emanating from the Hebrew Union College in Cincinnati, with a small, new rabbinical school of its own, founded in 1886. Later, Reform Jews like Jacob Schiff, the great German-Jewish tycoon and philanthropist, and others, sought to Americanize the east European Jewish immigrants who started streaming to the eastern part of the United States, fleeing Russia in great numbers, after the Kishinev pogrom of 1903. They seized upon this small coterie of teachers in that minuscule New York school, The Jewish Theological Seminary of America, knowing that Russian and other east Europeans would not accept Cincinnati's Reform brand of Judaism as an opportunity to help the new immigrants break away from their *shtetl*-style synagogues, now that they were in America.

Ironically, in their passion to Americanize Jews quickly, it was Reform philanthropists who created the Conservative Movement, by endowing and enlarging the Seminary in New York. By the 1930s Conservatism—a name intended to reflect the fact that the Judaism being taught to prospective Rabbis at the Seminary was traditional, yet American—came into vogue. It would not call itself Orthodox—although many of its professors were strict traditionalists—because that word, *at that time* in the United States, was already identified with foreign, East-European styled synagogues. They built their Seminary on Morningside Heights because they wanted these new immigrants to create a fully American (not merely Americanized) version of Jewish tradition as soon as possible. If the "mother institution" were integrated into the American intellectual world, so, too, they believed, would be the synagogues attached to the Seminary, led by the Rabbis whom it had trained to serve.

Until the resurgence of ethnicity in the late Sixties, all three groups saw themselves, with only slight variations, as religious partners in America. But with the arrival of this new hour in Jewish religious life, it became increasingly difficult to meet with our Orthodox rabbinical colleagues—and to work together with all three groups—to plan and deal with a whole range of questions we faced together—even religious matters. Since that time, Orthodox Rabbis have displayed increasing signs of separatism—even a militancy—when it comes to community cooperation on religious issues. All of the Jewish religion is now regarded as their own special preserve. In many respects, they have been buttressed by the monopolistic rabbinical position which the Orthodox enjoy in Israel. But it is even more likely that the sense of their own power is the result of forces closer to home: the growth of a more committed Orthodox Jewish community in North America.

Earlier, they had presided over congregations which were essentially indifferent to Jewish observance as *a system of personal behavior*. Their members consisted principally of people who have been aptly described as being only "residual Orthodox"—the synagogue of their choice, which they did not attend in any case, might just as well be Orthodox, like the one they remembered their immigrant fathers and grandfathers had attended. Now, Orthodox rabbis reflect a changed constituency. Many of their congregants openly advocate the "principles" of a solid-rock, unbending and changeless Orthodoxy. And it should go without saying that when Orthodoxy moves in these more rigid directions, Conservatism and Reform also follow suit—they, too, are following the trend to the right. The single, most influential factor in the re-traditionalizing of mainstream Orthodoxy in America has been the phenomenal success of a form of Judaism that had arrived in North America in appreciable numbers only after World War II—Hasidic or pietistic Judaism.

Indeed, one of the most startling and remarkable developments in recent years is the flourishing state of contemporary Hasidic Judaism in North America. Most notable of these groups are the *Habad* Hasidim, or the Lubavitcher, as they are popularly known. *Habad* is an acronym of *Hokhma-Bina-Da'at*, the kabbalistic term referring to germinal, developmental, and conclusive knowledge. Lubavitch is a small town in the Mogilev Province of White Russia, to which Dov Ber, son of Rabbi Shneour Zalman of Lyady, the founder of the *Habad* system, had moved in 1813. His followers, thereafter, were known as Lubavitcher Hasidim.

The present head of the movement—The Lubavitcher Rebbe—octogenarian Rabbi Menahem Mendel Schneerson, had studied mathematics and science at the Sorbonne in Paris, and became the seventh successive dynastic leader of the movement after the death of his father-in-law, in 1950. The latter, Rabbi Joseph Isaac, came to the United States after the outbreak of the Second World War and set up headquarters in Brooklyn. From there, with tremendous organizing skills, he founded a worldwide network of schools and higher academies of learning. But it was under the leadership of the present Rebbe—Menahem Mendel Schneerson—that the Lubavitcher became the most influential of all Hasidic groups, with networks of young followers on almost every American campus, and in communities as far away from Brooklyn as Leningrad. (The latter Hasidim are "underground," of course, and I met several of them during my visit to that city in 1961.)

The power of the Rebbe is enormous. He holds court at his modest headquarters on Eastern Parkway, in Brooklyn, a once-elegant Jewish neighborhood now almost totally Black which he and his followers refuse to abandon. From midnight until the early hours of the morning, a steady stream of disciples comes to him, to receive answers to almost every conceivable kind of query: business decisions; marriage and divorce; infertility; vocational choices, etc. His word becomes their law: They adore, worship—almost deify him. He enjoys a form of "papal infallibility" which has been denied to most other rabbis and leaders from the time of Moses to the present. Lubavitcher "believe" in their Rebbe almost as much as they believe in their

God. And this is why non-Lubavitch Jews, while often admiring his accomplishments and spiritual vitality, tend to look upon these Hasidim as members of a "Rebbe cult"—amazing, yet in many respects frightening, too. I have seen too many young university students from responsible and traditional Jewish homes turn their backs on their own parents—all in the name of "their Rebbe's" strict teachings about Judaism. Although Lubavitcher insist that they practice *ahavat Yisrael*—respect and regard for fellow Jews of all persuasions—they are less than tolerant of any brand of Judaism other than their own. They worship only in their own congregations, attend only their own schools, marry only fellow sectarians, and in general, lead a self-ghettoized, enclavic form of Jewish life.

In point of fact, however, despite the high visibility of these Hasidim—and it should be added, their flair for publicity and promotion-minded techniques, including "mitzvah-mobiles" and billboard advertising—Orthodoxy is still not the wave of the Jewish future in North America. Most non-Hasidic members of modern Orthodox congregations are not completely immersed in the milieu of the tradition, as a full piety would warrant. I have a simple, minimal test whereby it can be easily determined whether the person who says that he is Orthodox, really is: the test of thought-modes as expressed in linguistic styles. A truly Orthodox person, even one who is an English professor, as Samuel Heilman has pointed out, will speak *Yenglish* when discussing Jewish religious subjects. Yenglish is a special linguistic brew—Yiddishized English—which reflects the character and the situation of genuine Orthodoxy. It is a manner of speech which not only intermixes English with Hebrew, Aramaic and Yiddish, but alters the English syntax as well. "Thus, a Professor of English, no less, can say: 'How *medakdek* (careful) do you have to be in learning out this *posuk* (scriptural verse)?' "[3]

---

[3] See Samuel Heilman, *Synagogue Life: A Study in Symbolic Interaction*, University of Chicago Press, Chicago, 1976, p. 232.

In 1968, when Dr. Mordecai Kaplan was eighty-seven years "young," and long since retired from the faculty of the Jewish Theological Seminary of America, he moved out of the Conservative movement and founded his own rabbinical school in Philadelphia. Reconstructionism, once the left wing of Conservative Judaism, had now become a *fourth* American Jewish denomination. Only a handful of congregations, however, in the United States and Canada, openly identified with his newly formed denominational movement—a pariochalizing tendency he had always eschewed before—by designating themselves as "Reconstructionist synagogues." His school, moreover, has been graduating relatively few rabbis—women as well as men—and few of them have been called to key congregations. But does this mean that Kaplan's ideas have failed, and that his rationalist-naturalist approach to "Judaism as an evolving civilization" has now been eclipsed by the three other groups, Reform, Conservative, and Orthodox? This is the verdict that most critics—friends as well as foes of Reconstructionism—have arrived at.

I would emphatically deny that such is the case. The spirit of "right-wing" Judaism has overtaken only the three established denominational *institutions*—the synagogues and temples of North America. Less visible to the eye, but powerful and ever-present, nevertheless, are the dominant life-motifs of the largest majority of North American Jews. They may not call themselves Reconstructionists—certainly, they rarely belong to the few Reconstructionist congregations that do exist. But they are practicing what may be called "civil Judaism"—spurred by that self-same "new ethnicity" we have already described. As I see it, civil Judaism is very much related—in its basic spirit, if not in precise ideological terms—to much of what Mordecai Kaplan had been advocating all his life.

If you asked the average North American Jew, just what civil Judaism is—or implies—he would probably tell you that he has never heard of that term. But many are living as that kind of Jew, without knowing what name to give it—even though they will tell you that they belong to one of the three major Jewish denominations. What have all these civil Judaists in common, and why is their lifestyle, at base, the truest denominator of what most American Jews believe and practice today?

To begin with, the very idea of civil Judaism has only very recently begun to attract the attention of students of Jewish life. None of them, to my knowledge, however, seems to recognize that when you finally set down all of the attributes of this form of Jewish belief and behavior—and they have only commenced to examine this belief through behavioral studies— you come very close to viewing Jewish religion in America as Dr. Kaplan had been teaching and writing about it for over sixty years now. The best statement of the core beliefs of this civil Jewish faith has only recently appeared. It lists the following fundamentals:

1. "A commitment to Jewish group survival as a 'sacred' value and a validation of Jewish existence as the fulfillment of a 'mission' or 'destiny' which calls for the exemplification by Jews of the ethical values of responsibility, justice, and compassion."

2. "Civil Judaism more specifically affirms eight major tenets:

    a. "The unity and distinctiveness of the Jewish people.

    b. "The resultant responsibility of each Jew and of the Jewish community collectively for the security and welfare of all Jews.

    c. "The centrality of the State of Israel as symbol of this unity and mutual responsibility.

    d. "The enduring value of the Jewish tradition and the importance of its perpetuation.

    e. "The persistence of threats (both internal and external) to the survival of the Jewish people and tradition.

    f. "*Tzedakah*, understood both as philanthropy and more broadly as action on behalf of social justice and welfare, as a primary mandate of the Jewish value system.

    g. "The virtue of active participation in the broader

society and the compatibility of each participation with 'good Jewishness.'

h. "Theological pluralism: the relative insignificance of classical theological concerns and the affirmation of individual conscience as the ultimate arbiter in matters of religious practice, belief, and lifestyle."

Arching above all of these concerns is "the deep feeling of Jewish community—of a unity of destiny and experience which binds Jews together at a level beyond" their personal or social differentiations. Central to the "mysticism" of Civil Judaism is the State of Israel as the positive symbol of the myth of death and rebirth; this idea lies at the heart of contemporary Jewish self-understanding in North America. "What American 'civil' Jews support so vigorously is a mythically potent Israel... which...acquires its powerful hold on the attentions of these Jews, by virtue of a myth and meaning system which transcends its own reality...though the 'real' Israel may not correspond precisely to its (mythic) image among American Jews."[4]

But when Dr. Kaplan was eighty-nine years of age, in 1970, *he had already said all of these things* about the meaning *of Judaism in America*—much more profoundly, of course—in a book with a challenging and even revolutionary title, *The Religion of Ethical Nationhood*. (He had meant to re-direct and reverse the bulk of earlier theological systems which had usually described Judaism as a "religion of ethical monotheism.") I have returned to that book many times—as I have to other of his writings. But lying quietly on its pages is a single sentence which keeps jumping off the page, powerfully reminding me why I had thought to study with him. "The Rabbi should not be a walking sarcophagus of dead ideas about religion, but an interpreter of the inner or outer life in terms of religion that are understandable and relevant."[5]

---

[4] Jonathan S. Woocher, "The 'Civil Judaism' of Communal Leaders," *American Jewish Year Book: 1981* (Vol. 81), Jewish Publication Society, Philadelphia, 1981, pp. 149-169; but especially pp. 149; 168-9.

[5] Mordecai M. Kaplan, *The Religion of Ethical Nationhood*, Macmillan, New York, 1970, pp. 193-4.

Yet most Jews I know—especially the Conservative and Reform varieties—need the comfort and reassurance that someone is keeping the tradition *for them*. They want their Rabbis to do *at least that* for them; to be their surrogates when it comes to their own religious obligations. "*It's the Rabbi's job*," they say, without having to say it, "to do what we should be doing, but won't." Considering these Jewish games, and the level of synagogue life in most North American communities, I sometimes believe that, too often, the religious teachers Dr. Kaplan was calling for are themselves misunderstood and regarded as *irrelevant* by their congregations.

All too often, Jewish leaders seem to be saying to their Rabbis: "Speak out, by all means. But keep it under your breath!"

What, on earth, then, could they possibly want to hear from the pulpit?

Chapter 6

THE PULPIT

Jews have been hearing sermons—on and off—for at least two thousand years, but they always felt free to listen but not to hearken. After all, parables and homilies were not divine laws but human stories, and they knew their Bible: Even it suggests that there are two sides to every tale. But in America they made the pulpit the crucial measure of what they thought Judaism should be telling them. And to make that point very clear, to themselves and their spiritual leaders, they proceeded to invent something altogether new to their history—the "trial sermon." Most Rabbis on this continent today were hired by audience-congregations deciding what they wanted to hear, and how they wanted it said: That oratorical test had to be passed.

My first recollections of sermons take me back to my grandfather's Orthodox *shul* and remain deeply etched in my mind for all the wrong reasons. I do not remember the sermons themselves but I can never forget what havoc they wrought among the worshippers. I have memories of stampeding Jews almost coming to blows, not over *what* the Rabbi said or should have said—that was a much later development—but because he had said anything at all. Which is to say that I discovered very early in life that Rabbis in America were controversial figures merely because they were Rabbis. Very few of their congregants could even agree on the nature, function and role of their spiritual leaders in the New World.

Those who objected to Rabbis preaching sermons were usually recently arrived immigrants from East Europe who had never before encountered in their home communities what seemed to them so foreign a custom. They held firmly to the view that preaching was really a Christian, not a Jewish practice. Of course, they were mistaken, as I later discovered, but this did not prevent them from expressing open hostility to synagogue sermons by boycotting their hapless Rabbi in blatantly aggressive style every time he mounted the pulpit to preach. We did not come here, they would vehemently exclaim, to listen to speeches. We came to *daven* (pray) and to *lehrn* (study). And down the aisle and out of the *shul* they did march.

A mere two decades or so later, after I myself became a "Rabbi, Preacher and Teacher"—the precise title our ordination diplomas from the Jewish Theological Seminary of America conferred on its graduates—I would discover that their acculturated adult children were freely admitting that if they did attend synagogue services it was not to pray but to "enjoy" the Rabbi's sermon. And what they enjoyed most was to hear him "tell somebody else off."

I was probably no more than eight or nine years old when I began to realize that a revolution of sorts—nothing short of a *kulturkampf*—began taking place every Saturday morning. A continuing parade of noisy, exiting worshippers, children and grownups alike, were running out of the prayer service at a trot, slamming the heavy, brass-plated *shul* doors behind them, and milling excitedly in heavy knots outside in the vestibule. Instant bedlam broke out where reverent, if not altogether silent, devotions had been performed, just moments before.

Month followed month and without letup these angry recessionals continued to punctuate the Sabbath morning services—always at the appointed hour and always for the same reason. They stomped out precisely on cue: at the moment our newly appointed Rabbi began clearing his throat and nervously tugged at his flowing black beard as he inched toward the pulpit.

It made no difference that Rabbi Friedman spoke in English only once a month—heavily accented sermons spiked generously with simple stories—delivering his other three weekly discourses in a "rich and scholarly Yiddish," as my grandfather approvingly explained to me. Four times a month they walked out on his sermons. It was a matter of principle: Their life was at stake.

A half hour or so later, when the sermon was finished, the disgruntled demonstrators quietly returned to their accustomed places and resumed their fervent prayers alongside of those they had left behind, as if nothing unusual had transpired. Their "strike" was over. They had not won it that Saturday morning nor on any of the Sabbaths that followed. In fact, they never did win it, which explains why there was at first only a single synagogue on that street, and then there were two.

My grandfather, of course, would never discuss those weekly synagogue altercations with me, then or later. But you might say that I easily knew where he stood, simply because he sat. He remained quietly and firmly riveted to his seat while the Rabbi preached, refusing to join the line of march, but also refusing me permission to leave the room, even when I protested that "I have to go to the bathroom." "Why always just before the Rabbi speaks?" he kept pressing me. So it was that I endured many a sermon I could not fathom, especially the Yiddish ones, through which I fidgeted the most. Still, I vividly remembered a few of the Rabbi's pet expressions, which I would continue to hear from the mouth of many another Yiddish orator across the years. Some words he kept repeating explosively until he himself could catch their bouncing echoes, and these, even now, dance around in my head: *yiddische shiksal* ("Jewish destiny"), *yiddische hofnung* ("Jewish hope"), *yiddische lage* ("Jewish situation"), and *yiddische schmerz* ("Jewish pain").

On a few occasions my grandfather did relent, probably because he was afraid of the risk and did not want to face the consequences that might have ensued in the event I was really telling the truth. Then, I would quickly catch the hand of one of my boy friends who was tagging along with a protesting father or grandfather, and join their march toward the large vestibule.

There, things were more exciting—and for a nine-year-old, infinitely more frightening—than inside, just waiting for the sermon to end.

On the face of it, of course, there was nothing out there to unsettle me. These people looked very much like the members of my own family. A few were ancient-looking and wore long beards. But most were about as old as my grandfather and were dressed in the same synagogue outfit he wore—striped trousers and those imposing Prince Albert tailcoats. There were a few younger men, probably closer to my father's age, and like him they were all clean-shaven "businessmen." Curiously, in the midst of this boiling adult cauldron a small clutch of sullen children loitered; a few of them were my "Saturday morning friends"—*shul* chums.

It was not the sights that scared me, but the sounds. Their loud, emotional exchanges made my heart pound its way clear out of my chest. They were shouting at one another, reinforcing their shared conviction that it was sacrilegious for Orthodox Jews to interrupt the Sabbath Service with sermons, like the *goyim*. Their stout explanations to the pre-convinced assembly were intended as self-justification for walking out on a Rabbi who "allowed himself to behave like a *galach*"—a Christian minister or priest. "This is not a Temple like with *Reformed* Jews; it's a *shul*. And we're not *deitscher yidn* (German Jews). If *he* wants to give *sermons* let him go by *them*, and make his Shabbos on Sunday like those *goyish* Jews do!"

I had listened in on only a few of these protest meetings, yet I never forgot what I heard. Each time, however, after their opening, rasping preambles of self-encouragement, furies would die down, as one or two of the more learned and respected among them would begin to give his own sermon, in more measured and thoughtful fashion.

What I heard from these men as a child re-echoed years later when I met up with others like them—those who were still living out their lives as Jews as if they had never left the East European lands of their origin. I would hear the same ideas and observe similar styles of behavior wherever I lived, whether in upstate New York, Canada, or Israel. The world, as they saw it, was at war with them; Judaism under siege; America and modernity a snare; and they would defend "the tradition" at any cost. In effect, they were engaged in a lifelong battle of self-preservation—a noble goal, except that I discovered that the way of life they were zealously guarding was not the only form of Judaism that ever was. It was, rather, the only Judaism they knew or cared about—what they, or others like them, had experienced in East Europe a century and more ago—and they continued to read all of the Jewish past only as their teachers had taught them to see it in their ghetto islands of the East. But they had made the abnormal normal. (Only much later did I realize that this display of heroic illogic is an integral part of the paradoxical logic of Jewish survival, and has nothing in common with the self-deceiving games played by other, less caring, Jews.)

It became clear from the way they addressed the issue of Rabbis, sermons and preachers that they were living under the shadow of the same dark cloud of guilt characteristic of so many others of their generation of immigrants. Old Country teachers had cautioned them before their departure that in America they would be tainted by the foreign ways of the Gentiles, openly or unknowingly. Their hometown Rabbis had forewarned: If you go to the United States you will not only be leaving home, but also your Jewishness. And, as if examining permitted and prohibited foods in the light of the religious dietary laws, they repeatedly judged that "Golden America" was *treif*—not kosher. It was as unfit as a place for Jews to live as it would be unfit for them to touch, raise, or—Heaven forfend—to eat, pig!

As proof of how seriously they viewed the problem, some of their noted Rabbis had ventured across the Atlantic to repeat the message to them, even after they were settled in New York and other large Eastern cities. "Return home," they pleaded, by which they meant, of course, that only there, in that closed and cloistered community of Jews did Judaism have a chance to survive. Even the recent memory of pogroms past, or the specter of those still on the horizon, did not shake their determination. The threat of the open society in the tinseled melting pot that was America troubled them much more.

The protesters in that synagogue vestibule and other vestibules like it had good reason to worry now, as they wistfully recalled their teachers' stern warnings. It was bad enough that they were living in a social environment they could no longer control—the "streets," they said, were no longer Jewish as they were back home. Bad enough, too, that their people were being attracted to and often overwhelmed by a glittering new American culture. Not only their very own children, but many of their friends were even discarding their own precious and private language, a tongue to which they had virtually attributed a sacred, saving power. In barely ten years, from 1917 to 1927, New York's three once-thriving Yiddish newspapers had lost more than 200,000 of their readers.

"If we are in trouble elsewhere, outside in the streets, at least we are masters in our own house," I heard their chief spokesman explain. "Here in our own sacred place we have a right and a duty to live undisturbed by the outside world. We must keep this place Jewish and not allow ourselves to be swallowed up by the *goyim*, by bowing down to them and imitating their way of life. Today, it's only the sermon—even if it's in Yiddish, who needs *that* Christian merchandise? Tomorrow, it's everything else Jewish—our families, our homes, our whole community. We Jews have enough of our own without imitating others. If we keep on borrowing from outsiders, we'll soon be bankrupt."

It was as much their sense of guilt and wrongdoing for having breached the warning words of their own teachers, and not only their feelings of loyalty to the ancestral tradition, which powered their fervent defense of an unadulterated Judaism in America. And in the process they became advocates in search of an adversary, heroes who needed villains. Everything old was precious and venerable; everything new, threatening and destructive. In their wounded passion, they often confused the two: what was new was sometimes much older than they thought, and what was old was often not that old at all, I later discovered.

"Jews had a Moses," I recall that pleasant old defender of the faith telling us, out there in the hallway. "What was he called? Moses our preacher? Of course not. You know that we Jews refer to him as 'Moses our teacher,' *Moshe Rabbenu*." He went on to explain that for Jews, Moses was no arrogant, self-inflated preacher of words of his own choosing and imagining. They saw him only as a humble and faithful human conduit of God's word, conveying the Law to his people—and through them to the world—stammer and all. No one knows the place of his sepulcher; no tomb or monument confers eternity on his life or sanctifies his death. He does not live on, enshrined in synagogue altars, nor does he come alive in congregational pulpits. For traditional Jews, his only memorial is the Torah, the books of the Hebrew Bible. And Rabbis, they fully expected, should stick to those books—in their classes—and not "follow Christian ways" from a pulpit. I was impressed but totally confused. If they were right, I asked myself, why was Rabbi Friedman—and my grandfather with him—leading us astray?

In East Europe, their Rabbis had no pulpits, I later discovered. They didn't have personal congregations over which they they presided, either. But there were community lecture rooms and study halls in which they taught the words of Torah. Worshippers would either come early to *shul*, or remain after services. It was always the Rabbi's study sessions in the community's study rooms at the *shul*—the *Beth Ha-Midrash*—that counted for more than all the public prayers. For all their ritual punctiliousness those Jews believed that when you pray you are really telling God what it is you want; but when you study and understand His word, you discover what God wants of you. Rabbis and most Jews, all across those lands—where, for the past five centuries they had lived so populously—prayed, of course, every morning and evening. But they could have prayed alone, at home, as sometimes they did. It was only study that made the "prayer house" a *shul*, and it was only in a setting with a table full of books, discussing ethical problems and surrounded by inquisitive adult men firing piercing questions at him, that one was recognized as a "real" Rabbi. No wonder those men walked out on Rabbi Friedman's sermons.

A fear of Jesus and his followers continued to grip the hearts of these pogrom-weary East-European Jews, even in Golden America. They had come to think of him—though they would never even mention his name—as a beguiling sermonizer whose smooth and ambitious tongue had deceived unsuspecting, even dimwitted Jewish audiences from awesome hill-top "pulpits" overlooking the Sea of Galilee. So there was something about any pulpit which intimidated them. It reminded them of the Church, and of their own bad fate which legions of Christian preachers, perched securely on their sanctified podia, had helped to bloody.

They had bad memories of sermons: bitter and baleful, recent and ancient. They could not forget the beatings and killings that usually followed or preceded the major Church festivals of Christmas or Easter in Europe. To these terrorized Jews, sermons were warcries bellowed forth by Christian clerics from their comfortable sanctuaries, to rally a hopelessly impoverished peasantry against defenseless Jews, as a sop for their own miserable lives. Nor could Jews forget that in the very shadow of the Vatican, at the foot of the Tiber River near the gates of the Roman ghetto, their compatriots were regularly coerced to attend Church services on *Saturday* mornings— of all times—to listen to sermons. Sermons filled with vituperations against "perfidious Jews" and the "scandalous Torah," and singlemindedly geared to force their conversion to the "one true faith of Christianity."

As a result, sermons—even Jewish ones—came to have an aura of conversion and emotional exhortation about them. It goes without saying that they didn't countenance conversion to Christianity. But you might say that neither were they flattered by the possible implication that they were in need of artificial stimulants from a Jewish pulpit to bolster their own Jewishness. "We Jews," they summed it all up, "don't need speeches *about* Judaism; we need to study the Torah."

Still, my grandfather remained a staunch supporter of Rabbi Friedman's sermons—even those he gave in English. He simply looked around the synagogue every Sabbath and observed that the younger fathers, and mothers too—even though the women sat upstairs, away from their men, in the Ladies' Gallery, as in every other Orthodox *shul*—were beginning to attend with greater regularity, "now that there was something to hear." But true scholar that he was, he also knew that despite its omission in East European synagogues, the rabbinical sermon was actually a Jewish invention, and not a subversive or foreign addition, as his colleagues were claiming. "The Talmud itself," I overheard him reprimand some of those antagonists, "is full of sermons, and the great Rabbis of old were the first preachers."

He was right, of course, but when one considers what has happened to the Jewish pulpit in America from his days to our time, those "strikers" were not altogether wrong, either. I am now convinced that they were not far from feeling the truth—in their visceral understanding, at least, if not from history's unfolding of the case. I should explain why—after I myself have preached a few thousand sermons—I can warmly relate to their innate sense of the fitness of things as sensitive Jews.

One of the problems facing those East European Jews in America stemmed from their culture shock—not only as a result of the novelty and strangeness of American life, but also because of the public religious policy of Jews on this continent. They discovered here that the synagogue and rabbinate were both private affairs, and oddly enough, were also institutionally united. Rabbis functioned in America as the paid spiritual leaders of what were actually private membership organizations, each autonomous and unrelated to the other, even though they were called congregations. Back home nothing like that existed; everything Jewish was under the control of

The Pulpit 115

the whole community. Rabbis and congregations operated only under the aegis of a powerful community council, the *Kehillah*.

Despite their consternation and confusion, their Jewish intuitions were somehow related to older Jewish styles. From the first days after the Temple's fall, until just a century or so ago—and then, only in the West—Rabbis had been the teachers-judges-scholars of the entire community, not just private congregational officials. In fact, their influence did not emanate or radiate from the synagogue at all, but rather from the recognition accorded them as senior scholars of the academies of higher learning. It was their prestige as renowned jurists and scholars and not as preachers that had made it possible for the very first of this new breed of Jewish leader—the Talmudic Rabbis—to gain and hold sway over Jewish hearts and minds.

Examining *The Talmud* closely we find that those Rabbis had ingeniously created a method whereby they were advancing, enlarging and developing the Mosaic Law, all the while they maintained that they were really keeping it intact. Their method of preserving a tradition—not by ossifying it, but by amplifying its meanings—is precisely what American constitutional jurists have been doing in the name of "due process of the law." You interpret the old rules. Without tossing them away, you give them new resonances and novel application, as the times unfold and the needs arise. Those Rabbis had their own name for the method they invented. They called it *midrash*, or search. You search and re-search for hidden, implicit connotations. And if you study their *midrash* method carefully you discover that it was actually applied in two different ways—and I am convinced—for two different settings, and in answer to two differing needs.

First, and most remembered, is the legal *midrash* (*midrash halaka*), the new rabbinic legislation which, of course, did not repeal but did widely extend the biblical laws of Moses. Then, there is what I call the moral and folkloric *midrash* (*midrash agada*). This extensive material deals with the ethical and theological implications of biblical teachings—how to lead the good life—which they exemplified poignantly in story, fable, parable, fantasy, and homily.

Many students of *The Talmud* see it as a sort of rabbinical mélange—you might say hodge-podge—of laws and lore, edited about 550 C.E. after centuries of accretion and accumulation in the higher academies of Palestine and Babylonia—without careful regard for logical order, chronology, or systematic classification. Not for naught has it been called neither a code nor a literature, but a veritable sea; certainly, many a student has drowned in it, ceremoniously or otherwise. But if you carefully separate out its moral parts from the purely legal sections, you have put your finger on something those East Europeans in my grandfather's *shul* failed to realize: You have found snatches of thousands of sermons those Talmudic Rabbis had first offered in ancient synagogues. They aimed carefully at their two separate targets: legal *midrash* for the academicians and jurists; moral *midrash*—or sermons—for the masses.

Later, over the centuries, across Africa, Asia and Europe, early medieval Rabbis made the synagogue pulpit into a popular forum for what we would call "adult education." While many of their sermons were later published in Hebrew, they were originally delivered—at least in countries like Spain, Portugal, Italy and Turkey—in the vernacular. Hebrew remained the language of the virtuoso-scholar—reserved for the academy—where these same Rabbis lectured on law. But to make certain that they would reach "the people," in the synagogue they preached in "their language."

In the high Middle Ages, however, like the outstanding university scientists and scholars of our day who never venture out of their laboratories or libraries to lecture before lowly students, the great Rabbis became content to let lesser ones do the preaching. They were preoccupied—as life became more complex and the times more harrowing for Jews—by their service as community judges in the rabbinical courts, or fully immersed in the writing of their learned tomes. Some even carried on a voluminous legal correspondence with inquiring Rabbis and fellow Jews all across the globe, sending long and well-researched briefs—*responsa*—to those who wrote to query them about erudite or esoteric matters of religious law. Most felt like the vaunted twelfth century Spanish Rabbi, Maimonides—Moses son of Maimon—who did not preach himself because he was busy authoring great legal and philosophical treatises. But he held the art of preaching in great esteem and ruled that every community must arrange to have a respected and wise Rabbi as a regular preacher in its synagogue. He was so interested in the success of the preacher—because of the importance he attached to the sermon—that in one of his *responsa* he stipulates that a person who ascends to the pulpit "should rehearse his speech at least four times before its delivery."[1]

---

[1] Rabbi Joel ibn Shuaib, who lived in Spain just before the expulsion of the Jews in 1492, and who practiced the art of homiletics with great effectiveness, in a little-known but important book, published in Venice, Italy a few years after his death, goes even further. He counseled the preacher "to concern himself with two essentials in his sermons: (1) the integrity of the subject matter, and (2) the perfecting of his manner of expression.... Regarding the first, he must be careful...that whatever he will say, his listeners will derive benefit. Though his sermons be very profound, he must make them clear enough for the masses of the people to gain something from them on their level. Yet no less must he have regard for the more intellectually inclined who may be present when his subject is presented to the simple folk. On the second principal concern, the form of the sermon, three considerations are paramount: (1) the length—it should not be the least bit longer than is absolutely necessary... (2) the structure—the sermon should be well organized, not lacking in proper order, 'now in the streets, now in the broad places' (Proverbs 7:12); (3) his phrases and words should possess grace and dignity, and they ought to be delivered in a pleasing way according to the following conditions: Along with an attractive style and an inherent order within the sermon, the preacher must also make proper use of his voice in addressing the people so that they should understand even from his external manner of speaking that his words have value for them."

In East Europe, however, the sermon began to lose favor. Most of the Jews who arrived there came at the beginning of the sixteenth century, moving eastward to Poland in vast numbers, from the German-speaking states in the West. Soon, these Eastern communities became the dominant intellectual and cultural centers of world Jewry and Talmudical scholarship came to occupy the highest rung of their ladder social status. Their achievements in this field, together with the critical mass of their numbers—in 1600 they totalled a few thousand; by 1800, they were one million strong; and by 1890, even that number had quadrupled—gave them unrivalled supremacy as a Jewish community.

There would always be a share of ordinary, unlettered people among them, however, and the Rabbis of these communities began to shy away from the untutored and the uncouth. They preferred to view themselves as Maimonides would see himself—as scholars, jurists and learned authors—not as preachers who had to address the common folk, Sabbath after Sabbath. But unlike him, they did not encourage sermonizing. Assiduously, they cultivated their image as detached scholars, until, in their bailiwicks, the title "Rabbi" and the label "Preacher" moved poles apart. They were busily occupied in the academies creating young scholars for the next generation. So they backed away from the older tradition and refused to deliver popular sermons. Before long, a new mode of synagogue life was institutionalized in that area of Europe: Rabbis who were not Preachers, and Preachers who were not Rabbis. Now, the Preacher was merely a *Maggid*—a storyteller. Now, too, the East European public would be entertained periodically by preachers, while the Rabbis could lecture on esoteric subjects to their elite students in the classroom.

When East European Jews began streaming to America, beginning with the 1880s, once again, their preponderant numbers, in contrast to the already settled Jewish population, helped them to place the stamp of authority only on "their Judaism," the life they had known and practiced. In 1880, almost all of New York City's Jewish population of 85,000 were of German-Jewish origin, the migration of that West European group having begun with a trickle in the late 1840's. A bare twenty years later, the metropolis already boasted of half a million Jews, only one-fifth of whom were of German background. And by 1925, when quotas were set in place sharply restricting immigration from South and East Europe, over one and a half million East European immigrant Jews had found their way to America, from 1881 to that time.

Many years have passed since those "sermon strikes" in my grandfather's Orthodox *shul*, in Brooklyn. When I myself became a "Rabbi, Preacher, and Teacher" and had studied much on the subject I came to appreciate and understand their dilemma. But their grandchildren and great-grandchildren, for the most part, do not. They have even aggravated the problem more. After half a lifetime of preaching, I have discovered that contemporary Jews of all stripes and persuasions still want entertaining preachers, just as their East European ancestors wanted to listen to the *Maggid*. There is only this crucial difference: Their forebears may have "listened" to the *Maggid*, but they hearkened to the Rabbi—because he was their teacher, scholar, and judge. *They*, alas, are only looking to be entertained by their Rabbis-Preachers—they rarely hearken, and sometimes, do not even really listen.

A critical look at what they have made of the Jewish pulpit in America in a few short years, and some of my own experiences as a preaching Rabbi, should help prove the point.

To compete with the new rabbinic roles of Reform congregations—who had introduced the weekly sermon to America via Germany—as well as to keep pace with Conservative congregations who quickly aped them and did the same, even Orthodox Rabbis, like Rabbi Friedman, found themselves preaching every week. Not long ago, two sociologists, studying the loss of authority suffered by the American Rabbi, interviewed a traditional East European spiritual leader, transplanted to a Mid-western state. His views fairly summarize their findings. You can feel the pain of his plaintive words, and almost hear the sighing. "The main thing," he said, "here the Rabbi gives speeches, he is supposed to; sometimes the speeches please the people and sometimes they don't. They go out and say, 'He's no speaker.' I have seen myself people leaving from some of the biggest Rabbis, great Talmudic scholars and they say: 'No speaker. He's no speaker. He's no Rabbi.' So what's he worth? Nothing."

And here, too, even the Orthodox Rabbi had to be careful not to say the wrong things from the pulpit. His sermons had to deal with acceptable things. "In my city in Europe," that same Rabbi continued, "if someone opened up [a store] on Friday night—that is, he was open ten minutes late—I went out and made him close up. Here all my *balabotim* (influential lay leaders), all my officers, have their stores open. I don't say anything to them because I know that they won't listen. I don't say nothing. I know the people won't listen to me...I can't say what I should. Should I say, 'Why do you keep your stores open on the *shabbos* [Sabbath]? Close the stores!' They'll laugh me out of *shul*."

Still, congregations in America say they "need" sermons. Virtually every Rabbi knows that he is re-graded weekly by his congregants after every sermon, even by those who may not have been physically present to hear him. Reports are apparently available from a voluntary telephone network that seems to go into action after every Sabbath service—Friday evening, or Saturday morning—supplying commentaries on "what the Rabbi said." So it is not about a mere "decent" sermon, but a "great" one that the Rabbi wants to hear them tell, and, as he hopes, retell down the line.

"A great sermon, Rabbi!"—their way of handing out good marks to him—is essentially one that is emphatically and even stingingly "other-directed." It is always others whom congregations enjoy hearing berated or criticized. Thus the words "a great sermon, Rabbi" are usually immediately followed by the

The Pulpit 121

standard, a glowing exclamation "You sure gave it to them!" Rabbis have instinctively learned not to tell their congregations very much—and hardly ever to "tell them off"—but only to tell them about *others*.

Who are some of those "others"?

The list of straw men who have become easy and sure-fire targets for pulpit sharpshooters, and which serves as reliable and safe cannon-fodder for the Jewish preacher, falls into several predictable categories: anti-Semites and anti-Semitism; certain kinds of Christians—especially missionary types, and often, even Christianity itself; the Arabs, or latterly, "Islamic expansionism"; anti-Jewish Blacks; assorted anti-Israel critics; the United Nations; and, of course, the Palestine Liberation Organization. But "other Jews" comprise part of the safe-and-certain subject categories, as well: those who are not attending synagogue, unlike those who have come to enjoy the sermon; those who did not contribute charity to Israel, or to the synagogue building fund; or those who gave, but not nearly as much as those present in the synagogue (this, of course, can sometimes be a rather awkward assumption); or, those, "unlike most who are in attendance," who are seen to be mismanaging their lives as Jewish parents, children, husbands, or wives. (The implication here is that coming to *shul* regularly helps one overcome such problems, in the spirit of Madison Avenue's "the family that prays together stays together.") To these "others" must also be added still another assortment of Jews, ranging from American novelists who write about them in the fashion of Philip Roth, to the Orthodox rabbinate—particularly the Israeli variety—if you are standing in a Reform pulpit; or all the "non-traditional Jews," if addressing an Orthodox congregation.

The subject of anti-Semitism—treated historically, or as a topical reality based on some recent issue or event, locally or elsewhere in the world—inevitably creeps into a clear majority of the sermons given by American Rabbis. It is the Jewish counterpart to Christian ministers haranguing their parishioners about the Devil, or its latest incarnation. These talks are sure winners; but they merely reflect the vainglorious and pointless victory that comes from preaching to the converted.

Rabbis surely owe it to themselves and their congregations to remain alert to those persons or movements which threaten the fundamental integrity and safety of their people—"Jewish Jim Crows" are dangerous men, indeed. Recent history—not excluding the fiendish chapter of Nazi Germany and its Jews—testifies that too often it has been necessary to awaken Jews themselves to the perils looming before them, but which they lacked the eyes to see. But these necessities and urgencies are a far cry from the extremes to which many Rabbis are willing to go, in search of their fair game—or better still—easy applause. Too many of our "wounded" sermons smack of "us against them." Many of them remind me of that well-worn story of The Elephant and the Jewish Problem, which became the subject of a dissertation written by a would-be Jewish sociologist who found anti-Semites hiding everywhere—even the wild animals in the jungle were most unfriendly and were discovered to have attacked Jews.

Survival anxiety—which to the detached and removed observer often appears to be nothing less than group paranoia—continues to preoccupy the Jewish pulpit in America, however. It may be traced to what has been pejoratively dubbed a "Holocaust mentality." But what Rabbi can forget that six million Jews—one third of his people—were slaughtered, while, it becomes increasingly clear, governments like the United States looked on with great diffidence, or even outright indifference? Despite their new freedom, Jews feel much more threatened than some of their large, expensive, and confident-looking "synagogue plants" would suggest. Rabbis are always faced with frightened Jews—no matter how prosperous—who continue to exhibit disturbing signs of declining morale because of the self-doubts that arise from some of these more recent problems: the rising rate of intermarriage, which creeps up with every passing year; the general unwillingness of the

Arabs to normalize their relations with Israel, or even to recognize its existence as a Jewish State; the sense of growing isolation of that state—and with it, the Jews of the world—from the rest of the global community, particularly in the wake of the energy crisis; the rise, first of the New Left, and then of the New Right, both of which tend to see the Zionist enterprise either as a stumbling block to better East-West relations, or as a burden to be jettisoned in order to curry the favor of the Arab oil-producing nations; or the wave of anti-Jewish terror that began to spread following the Israeli incursion into Lebanon, in 1982.

Despite all the benign talk in the late Sixties—in the wake of Vatican Council II—of growing "Jewish-Christian Dialogue," Christianity is still viewed as a source of constant worry. For a whole year, for example, as recently as 1972, Rabbis were bombarded with counteroffensive materials prepared by "anti-defamation"-oriented national Jewish organizations, alerting them to something that was a widely felt fear in the community, but which never did materialize. Yet, Key '73, that massive, national effort of hoopla and hallelujah, engineered principally by American fundamentalist Christians to revitalize their own churches during the course of that year, never was, or did become, the clandestine cover for a program to convert the Jews, as had been forecast by those Jewish officials who get paid to sniff out all possible enemies, even before they attack. More recently, similar anxieties over American churchmen's Moral Majority are being revealed regularly in critical sermons by Rabbis that one can hear from coast-to-coast—and even in Canada, where the movement does not even exist. Sporadically, too, even when only a stray handful of militant black Americans spews forth some anti-Semitic nonsense, in predictable, knee-jerk fashion, thousands of Jewish pulpits bound back, providing these marginal minority "leaders" with the very notoriety they are seeking.

And on and on it goes: Hardly a week passes without Rabbis speaking about "those others." But they are in a bind. "Others" have become so much a part of the expectation pattern of their listeners, that not to lash out regularly against real (or even imagined) troublers would let their congregations down. The problem here is that most Rabbis are afflicted by the same malaise—*mutatis mutandis*—as reflected in the earlier lament of that Midwestern Orthodox leader: They can not easily "say what they should," or they will be "laughed out of *shul*"— maybe even nudged out. So mostly, they are content to remain predictable, saying what they believe their people want to hear.

Even while still a rabbinical student at the Jewish Theological Seminary of America, in New York, I already had a foretaste of these things to come. "When you are invited by a congregation to give a 'trial sermon,' if you really want the job, you must be careful of two things before you step into the pulpit: Never wear brown shoes, and never preach on a very contentious subject!" This was the sage advice earnestly dispensed in a class curiously known as Practical Theology. Our professor, Dr. Max Arzt, had recently joined the Faculty of the Seminary, after a long and fruitful career as the Rabbi of a Conservative congregation in Scranton, Pennsylvania. He would always commence his academic year by referring to various types of Rabbis, categorizing them neatly, and forecasting the likelihood of their "success" in the pulpit. Invariably, that first lecture concluded with a quotation from the address given by a venerable Old-World type Orthodox Rabbi of that city, on the occasion of a Farewell Dinner, as Dr. Arzt was leaving his former congregation to join the Seminary Faculty. "There are really only two kinds of Rabbis," he quoted from that sage's laudatory remarks: "a 'sent Rabbi,' and a 'went Rabbi.' The first kind, congregations themselves send away. But the second is one who went away on his own, leaving the congregation! Rabbi Arzt is not a 'sent Rabbi;' he is a 'went Rabbi.'"

His forte was pulpit-pew relations—or "pewish problems," as I facetiously dubbed his course—and although he was both studious and scholarly, as you can already surmise, he had an enormous sense of humor. He never tired of helping us fill our waiting notepads with reams of "jokes and funny stories suitable for the pulpit," and other valuable memorabilia. (Practical theology?) He did have a great smile, and with his infectious grin he would consistently counsel: "Smile your way through your sermons. Especially your 'trial sermon'—and then if you land the job, keep smiling, at least for the first year in your new congregation." None of us, I am certain, can forget another of his oft-repeated admonitions, even if in practice, we sinned against it: "You can't go wrong with a sermon if you make it short. If you don't strike oil in twenty minutes, quit boring!" But my lovable teacher and friend Max Arzt will probably be best remembered by an entire generation of American Rabbis for standing up on the floor of a convention of hundreds of Seminary graduates in the late 1940s, and announcing—this time, in deadly serious tones, without cracking a smile: "Will all those Rabbis here assembled who are happy with their congregations now proceed outside to meet in the telephone booth."

I confess that when I first heard him say that I could not fully fathom the bitter laughter which greeted the joke. Most of those attending that convention had already been serving congregations for many years, but I was a recent graduate, and content with my congregation, Temple Beth El, in Rochester, New York. Not long after my graduation, in early 1946, I had arrived in that upstate city.

I was particularly pleased with myself for having "stuck to my guns," and landed this important congregation at the "ripe" age of twenty-four, even after refusing to give a trial sermon. Though I have always enjoyed preaching and was not considered a poor speaker, I simply could not accept the idea of auditioning; it demeaned both Rabbi and community. While still at the Seminary, I had determined never to accept any rabbinical posting if the sermon was made into the major measure of my work in the congregation. To my pleasant surprise, after explaining my position to Beth El's search committee, they readily agreed with my view, although they "never heard of this 'new' approach before." The interview had provided an opportunity for me to explain my philosophy of Jewish life and my views of the roles and relationships of Rabbi and congregation. "Besides"—I remember summarizing my definition of a "Rabbi, Preacher and Teacher"—"a Rabbi should be an even better listener than he is a speaker. And you can't 'try out' as a listener."

In Rochester, as often happens in such communities, competition between the "upward-mobiles" of the major Conservative and Reform congregations was extremely keen. Rabbis were judged by the number of people regularly attending their Late Friday Evening Sabbath Services. To my good fortune, Philip S. Bernstein, the Rabbi of our "rival"—the city's lone and venerable Reform Temple, B'rith Kodesh, founded by the first German settlers in 1848—although twenty years my senior, was extremely supportive, cooperative, and brotherly. He had already made for himself a worldwide reputation as the official Adviser on Jewish Affairs to General Dwight D. Eisenhower, representing the three branches of American Jewry—Orthodox, Conservative and Reform. He was also a much-beloved figure among the hundreds of Jewish Army Chaplains serving overseas during World War II.

Phil was not very strong in the pulpit—he had so many other gifts and talents—and despite his international fame, he still had to work hard to "fill the house" at every one of the Temple's Friday Evening Sabbath Services. He would therefore announce sermon topics dealing with his world travels; or offer subjects purporting to be "behind the scenes" revelations about General Eisenhower, or Patton, or his visits to the White House. And then, there were book reviews galore, always in the guise of sermons, always of best-sellers, and always prefaced in the "advertisement" by the words "A Rabbi Looks At..." and then the book's title.

He was doing what all Rabbis believed they had to do: publishing "magnetic" sermon titles in his weekly Temple Bulletin that might attract hefty "audiences." He also perfected another typical procedure of the times, practiced by Rabbis of all three persuasions. He would dispatch press releases every Friday morning to the newspapers and radio stations containing quotable excerpts from the still-undelivered sermon for that evening, in order to land prominently on the front pages and in the radio news reports, Saturday morning. To succeed at this, of course, the sermon had to be newsworthy; it had somehow to address itself to some topical and blazing political issue. None of these efforts, however, succeeded in creating a consistent and loyal body of Temple-goers. It was always a constant battle to figure out still another intriguing subject for the next sermon; there was no carryover, no echoes from one Sabbath to the other. All of us Rabbis faced the same challenge.

There can be no question that as a highly intelligent and sensitive man of broad culture, he had finally become bored by all of this. Phil was a native son of Rochester, born to East European parents at the turn of the century, who became a Reform Rabbi in 1926. He demonstrated his strong Zionist proclivities by refusing to enroll at the Hebrew Union College in Cincinnati—a hot-bed then of old-line, classical Reform Judaism, whose faculty were rabid anti-Zionists, in the style of that day. Instead, he became the very first of only two graduating students at Dr. Stephen S. Wise's newly formed, fledgling Jewish Institute of Religion in New York, a school Wise established to fly the flag of liberal Judaism, but also the banner of Zionism—both as an antidote to, and adversary of, Cincinnati brand.

The very year Phil graduated, he was called to serve as Assistant Rabbi at B'rith Kodesh, in the city of his birth. This came as something of a shock to the community, in view of his own strong Zionist views, and the well-known fact that B'rith Kodesh, like virtually all the other well-established Reform Temples in the country, was still ardently anti-nationalist and opposed to a "Jewish Palestine." Not to mention, of course, that Phil's parents were immigrants from Russia who came from "the other side of the tracks" in Rochester, while the Temple's leaders were already the affluent grandchildren and great-grandchildren of the ensconced German Jews, whose local men's clothing factories had long since made them into millionaires. A wide religious and social gap stood between them and the much more recently arrived East Europeans—the "cheap labor"—who worked for them in their successful lofts, as cutters, operators, and tailors.

He was a man of great courage who taught me wise and unforgettable lessons close to the outset of my rabbinical career. More than all else he devoted himself—good "bridge Jew" that he was—to melding together the disparate and mutually antagonistic elements of the community: the rich and poor, the haughty German Jews and the lowly East Europeans. For him, the sum of all the parts of the community was infinitely more important than any single segment or congregation, no matter how prestigious. In the pursuit of this vision, to my pleasant surprise, I discovered that he, too, was not interested in preaching, *per se*. From time to time, we spent long hours in elaborate discussions about those pulpit "war games" Rabbis were being forced to play by their fiercely competitive "audience-style congregations."

Early in 1951, he invited me to his study for dinner, together with about a dozen or so leaders of our two congregations, to meet a man who was then perhaps the most powerful single official in organized American Jewish life: Henry Montor (born Goldberg and in Montreal). Montor had arranged to come up from his office in New York City and was in Rochester on a very special, delicate assignment. For many years, he had headed the national United Jewish Appeal which, though officially the central fund-raising organization in America for all of Israel's immigrant resettlement and absorption needs, had actually come to represent the basic establishment-leadership of North American Jewry, through local welfare funds and federations of Jewish charities. Now, however, he had just created the "State of Israel Bond" organization, at the urgent bidding of Prime Minister David Ben Gurion of Israel himself. The U.J.A. leadership, across the country, was in an uproar. They saw this new bond organization as an upstart interference with their own established methods of raising money for Israel. What is more: They were also enraged at B.G.—the Israeli Prime Minister—for setting up "traps" in America that would unsettle their own leadership. Ben Gurion's adroit maneuver in getting Montor—their own "U.J.A. man"—to leave his position to head up this new "Bonds for Israel" group seemed to them a mere ploy—a transparent device to put them off their guard, and perhaps even dislodge them from their entrenched leadership position.

But Phil and I were in full agreement with Ben Gurion's new move, and with Montor's purposes. We argued with our friends for long and difficult hours until well past midnight, foreseeing, with B.G., the time when Jews might not be willing or able to give money to Israel, while they might still be enticed to lend it by purchasing bonds. Besides, every government in the world floated bonds, and here was a way to help Israel constructively, without it having to serve as the perennial *schlemiel*—the "poor relative" who depends only upon alms from his family. By one o'clock in the morning an agreement was finally hammered out and the first State of Israel Bond organization and campaign was launched in Rochester. This was a major breakthrough, since our community would be among the first in the State, except for New York City (which is really a "jungle" of Jews thrown together, not a community, at all), to pioneer in this new, and ultimately highly rewarding, direction.

And as Rochester went, so went the nation. Since 1951, billions of dollars have been loaned to Israel—and repaid by Israel—to help build schools, hospitals, roads, and a developed industrial structure, all this by means of State of Israel Bonds now sold throughout the world and even purchased by major North American banks and public corporations. Ironically, however, our "settlement" that night was reached only because Phil and I joined together as Rabbis of two congregations which laymen had wanted to see as rivals until the end of time, or so their behavior made it appear. We became the Rochester Co-Chairmen of the new organization and campaign for Israel Bonds. We also consented to the conditions our leaders had energetically laid down: "Don't 'raid' our ranks, get your own team. Don't ask for bond purchases from people who have not first pledged to support the U.J.A."

After everyone—including Henry Montor—had wearily left his study, Phil and I settled in to talk some more. He was nearly ecstatic. The community was being brought closer and closer together, and we had demonstrated to our startled leaders just what was most important to us as Rabbis—the largest Jewish good. Then he began to interpret what he saw as the meaning of what had just transpired, and what his own feelings were about the rabbinic patterns and roles we should increasingly emphasize together. "This is the kind of leadership our people really need," he kept repeating, "and if you ask *them*, all they want is *sermons*! Let me tell you that I couldn't care less if I was never called upon again to preach, if they would only let me build a community that can work together smoothly to achieve great things for the whole Jewish people."

"So why do you keep on playing their game?" I asked naively, joshing him about that "famous" series of sermons he had given a few years before titled "A Rabbi Looks At the Kinsey Report," which had succeeded—as he knew it would—in bringing out several thousands of people, in the wintry cold, on three successive Friday nights. He frowned, but then quickly a boyish smile broke out, lighting his eyes and crinkling his face. "Let me tell you something delicious about that," he said, as soon as the noise of our raucous laughter subsided.

"I gave those talks just before leaving for my midwinter break in Arizona. So what happens on the day I am about to leave? My assistant Rabbi comes to my house to ask permission to give a three-week series of sermons which he wanted to

The Pulpit 131

preach during the time I would be away. What do you need my permission for, I tell him. Well, he says, you might not like the idea. What idea, I ask him. So he tells me: 'Look, Phil, you packed those people in for three solid weeks with your Kinsey sermons, and now you leave me holding the bag, here in the bitter cold, to preach to empty pews. They won't come back so quickly. And what will I look like—a "nobody" standing all alone in the pulpit in a freezing Temple, with no one to talk to? So, I've come to ask if you wouldn't mind if I continued your series.' How do you expect to title your series? I ask him, without blinking an eye. And what do you think he answers? 'An Assistant Rabbi Looks At the Kinsey Report!'

"Of course," Phil went on, "I told him that I couldn't let him do *that*. And that was when I also realized that *I* couldn't let myself do that kind of thing, any more, either." And then, looking me squarely in the eye, he added: "Our real effectiveness as Rabbis is not in the pulpit, in any case; no matter how many people we bring out with our sermons. Our strength is here, in the Rabbi's Study—with ordinary people, or with our leaders—helping to change their lives, and to change the shape and face of the community."

Next Fall, on the High Holy Days, those words of Philip Bernstein forcefully came back to me, after preaching a sermon at the Rosh Hashanah service—or rather, to be more exact—two almost-identical sermons, one after the other. This is how it happened. In those days, my congregation still lacked the funds to build a new structure, although it had already outgrown its quarters—at least for the Holy Days, when we had many more in attendance than there were seats in the sanctuary. We had a beautiful old building, which was purchased from the Park Avenue Baptist Church in 1917 by upward-mobile second-generation East European Jews, who were then moving into "Christian neighborhoods," and converted into their newly-organized Conservative congregation, Temple Beth El. On those special occasions, like Rosh Hashanah and Yom Kippur, we would invite a Seminary student to lead the services in what we still called—imitating the ways and days of the Baptist Church—"the Vestry Room," located on the second floor of the Temple. These were known as the "Parallel Services," where those who had joined the congregation in more recent years were seated. But the student Rabbi—for some silly reason he came to be called "the Parallel Rabbi"—would not always preach at his service; the members expected that, as their Rabbi, I would deliver a sermon to both of the divided halves of the congregation. So it became necessary for me to give a sermon downstairs in the main sanctuary, and immediately thereafter to rush upstairs to the Vestry Room to the "Parallels" who were waiting for me, to deliver a sermon to them as well.

On that fateful morning I spoke about the need for family love and understanding, and the importance of grandfathers and fathers in helping to keep their loved ones together. I had been moved to speak on this subject because a certain B.R., a man of some seventy-five years of age, who had amassed a fortune at his iron-and-steel smelter in Rochester, was destroying his family because of petty obstinacy on his part—his money had blinded him to larger values. I had spent weeks counselling with him and other members of the family, trying to put together the broken vessels they had made of their homes. Throughout the sermon, B.R., who sat front and center, in his important pew, as a wealthy, founding member, seemed to be fidgeting and restless. In the back of my mind, as I spoke with great emotion, I was going through a possible scenario: After this sermon—and what I have now done to him publicly by my forthright condemnation of tactics similar to those he had employed against his sons and daughters-in-law—he would surely be after my scalp. He was bobbing up and down in his pew as I continued toward my peroration. The sight of him now only heightened my feeling that I probably had been inveighing too harshly against the likes of him.

When the sermon concluded, I dashed through the doors behind the pulpit and began scrambling quickly up the narrow, rickety steps that would lead me to the Vestry Room, where I was now expected. Halfway up the staircase, I was stopped in my hasty tracks by a gruff voice. I knew that voice in my sleep. It was B.R., as I had feared. Was he going to start fighting with me now, right here on the stairway, even before the morning's services had concluded? "Rabbi," he called out, "are you going to deliver the same sermon upstairs?" Nervously, and with beads of perspiration streaming down my back, I half-turned and croaked sheepishly: "Yes, Mr. R., perhaps not in the exact words, but the same ideas." "Well, in that case," he shouted, "I am following you. I want to hear it again." My heart sank. "I want to hear it again, Rabbi, because this was your greatest sermon. You really gave it to *them*! Give them hell upstairs, too; those young people need it!"

Yet, even if most Jews rarely hearken to the sermon, and even if they do listen they sometimes hear the wrong things, shall Rabbis simply write it off as an exercise in futility? And what of those men who earnestly preach week after week? Is their hard and often stirring effort worthless and without benefit? I do not believe it is. Philip Bernstein was right, but I have since realized that it was only his sincerity and wisdom in the pulpit that made it possible for him to be hearkened to in the quiet of his study—by the "ordinary people and the leadership," the very ones he ached to reach and to influence as Jews. Although I myself have had a bountiful share of "great sermons"—as my laymen extravagantly called them—the ones that were really important to me were those which went beyond the pulpit and led people to follow me to the classroom, or to come to my study, as their Jewish teacher, friend and counsellor.

By themselves, sermons are woefully insufficient and as a measure of things Jewish, terribly self-deceiving—to Rabbis and to the members of their congregations, alike. Jews will not be converted by sermons—not even to Judaism. That is the truth those "sermon strikers" in Brooklyn instinctively knew.

But "Rabbi-Preachers" who use the sermon to attract their people to them as "Teachers" are not only faithful to the Jewish past, but also mindful of the Jewish future.

To do this, a Rabbi will cast out of his mind the spell of numbers and the adulation of the crowd. It is enough if he helps to change and joyfully reroute even one single life—quietly, when nobody is there to see or to know, save the student and his teacher.

And about that achievement, he dare not even tell his congregation from his pulpit.

Chapter 7

BAR MITZVAHS, WEDDINGS AND FUNERALS

At Brooklyn's Casa del Rey, on that Saturday night in July, 1935, we did not invite Rabbi Friedman, who had officiated that morning in the synagogue, to my Bar Mitzvah dinner party. It wasn't that my parents didn't like him, were ungrateful for his friendship, or ashamed of the way they were celebrating my coming of age in New York. "You don't embarrass Rabbis," I can still hear my mother saying, "by inviting them. They have more important things to do than to run around from party to party, saying nice things and making speeches to little Bar Mitzvah boys right in the middle of the dance floor. I'm sure Rabbi Friedman won't be offended."

But only a decade or so later, the suburbanization of American Judaism had not only changed the traditional rabbinical role, it also reversed the social expectations of many synagogue Jews. "*I* would be offended," was the more usual plaintive comment of the celebrant's mother or father, "if our Rabbi didn't come to our Bar Mitzvah (or wedding) party. It would be a slap in my face. After all, I've been a good dues-paying member of the *shul* all these years. If he didn't attend, it would be as if I never even belonged."

The invitation was not usually extended to the Rabbi

because he was a personal friend. More often than not, he had rarely been invited to their home on a private basis, and would not be, even after his public appearance at "their party." Would the Rabbi's presence confer social status on the hosts? Yes and no. It depended on the self-importance of the member in question. But there was another need, at an hour like this, even more important than that—*Jewish honor*, or *Kavod*. In that member's eyes, the presence of the Rabbi helped make the one statement he felt he needed on the occasion of a Bar Mitzvah or a wedding: "We may not attend the synagogue frequently, except for the occasional family *simcha*, but we are good Jews, nevertheless. See—our Rabbi is here to prove it!"

When, in the 1950s, with the agreement of their unsuspecting spiritual leaders, synagogues virtually surrendered to professional caterers and were transformed into "homes away from homes," Rabbis became increasingly hostage to their member-hosts. They were now virtually regarded as a part of the synagogue plant. If they were not exactly the *pater familias* of the extended congregational family, they were surely seen as the masters of all ceremonies—especially those that now took place in the synagogue's catering halls. It became a mark of honor to most members if the Rabbi was the "first to come and almost the last to leave" their Bar Mitzvah or wedding party.

Nobody could forewarn us about such a possible turn of events while we were students at the Seminary. Homiletics courses could never prepare us for the new realities of the pulpit; and even Practical Theology could not be very practical. We were taught about Bar Mitzvah and weddings and funerals academically—as they were "supposed" to be—not as if American Jews hadn't turned these into something they had not been before. Our Seminary professors did not tell us that we would rarely be called upon to serve as scholar-judges—or learned expositors of ancient textual wisdom—as were our earlier counterparts. We were to enter a different world: the world of make-believe Judaism. Not only would our sermons have to be far removed from the scholarly discourses of our rabbinical forerunners, but, it turned out, we would be spending most of our public hours—especially if we ministered in the larger cities—waiting and making small talk in between courses, at the catered affairs we were expected to attend—and attend, and attend.

It is sometime in the 1960s. You are a stranger visiting New York City and have ventured into the dank subterranean world of the metropolis's public transit system. From a maze of glossy billboards huckstering a variety of food products and other wares, a smiling Chinese face floats toward you, straight off the once-white tile walls of the entrance way. He is happy, satisfied—and munching on a sandwich. And in the words of his Madison Avenue creator, he's telling you: "You don't have to be Jewish to enjoy Levy's Rye Bread."

It was, it seemed at the time, a small attempt to help some enterprising Mr. Levy unload a slice or two of his extra dough—a sporting chance to gain entry into the ethnic market. After all, American Jews had already been in love with chop suey for several decades. Why not reverse the roles?

But advertisements like this one heralded an American Jewish revolution in the making. Clear across the continent, in the years that have since followed, dozens of "Kosher-style" Jewish foods have become staples of supermarket sales; not to speak of the fast-food deli(catessen) shops, bagel emporia, the wagonloads of "hot pretzels, and in the larger cities, shops specializing in Israeli street foods—shish kebab (skewered lamb) and pitta and fallafel (flatbread and deep-fried chick-peas).

Considering that by the 1970s the old ethnicity had reemerged with a vengeance, this Jewish revolution in America's culinary habits would appear to be wholly unremarkable. But there was a strange irony to all of this. Kosher restaurants in the big cities—they were always virtually non-existent in smaller communities—now became scarcer than hens' teeth. While other Americans were now quickly gobbling up "Jewish foods," Jews themselves were rapidly abandoning older lifestyles. At home they were still "eating Jewish"—though with diminishing concern for the dietary laws—but when it came to dinners out "on the town," they were in the vanguard of the pan-ethnics. The fanciest Indian, Japanese, Polynesian and other exotic restaurants could always count on Jewish customers to help fill their dining rooms.

Still another Jewish revolution had already come upon the scene, by the side of this one. The former has probably helped to salve the conscience of some Jews in regard to the incongruities of the latter. It would help make up for some of their lost Judaism by appealing to their Jewish appetites. I am referring, of course, to the little-documented, though universally experienced, domination of American synagogue life which had been won by the professional Jewish caterers by the mid-1950s. Never mind that these enterprising, market-wise purveyors and chandlers of Jewish victuals eagerly provide synagogue diners (some even offer a "take-out" service) with "Kosher shrimp cocktails," made of halibut, of course; won-ton soup, instead of *matza* balls, or *kreplach*; or egg rolls in place of gefilte fish. (It should be noted however, that few, indeed, have done away with chopped liver.) What really matters is that they have helped to change the entire nature and shape of the traditional *rites de passage*—from birth to burial—by re-locating the center of Jewish gravity from the altar-tables of the home to the kitchens and banquet halls of synagogues and temples. "Ask and you shall receive"—Jews got what they asked for.

I confess that I find it impossible to swallow the suggestion of an otherwise distinguished American rabbi-theologian who has written unsmilingly that "God lurks behind the chopped liver. The caterer, for all the vulgarity he may have fostered, must be seen as a low-level, latter-day Levite, serving the ritual assemblies of the Jewish masses, the commonality that is the Jewish people."[1]

---

[1] Eugene Borowitz, *The Mask Jews Wear*, Simon and Schuster, New York, 1973, page 117.

Much closer to the mark—and to my own spirit—is Philip Roth's reply to rabbinical critics who had attacked his stories in which he devilishly depicted the *embourgeoisement* of his fellow American Jews. Whether describing the catered affair in *Goodbye, Columbus*, or suburban Jewish reaction to overt displays of the tradition in *Eli, the Fanatic*, Roth revealed that he had "been attacked from certain (Jewish) pulpits and in certain (Jewish) periodicals as dangerous, dishonest, and irresponsible...and for creating a distorted image of the basic values" of Judaism. To which he responded that he wished that his critics would have told him instead, "You have hurt a lot of people's feelings because you have revealed something they are ashamed of." Far from becoming the darling of Jew-baiters for his critical stories about American Jews—as his Rabbi-critics had charged—Roth informed his antagonists that he was not "invited to address any anti-Semitic organizations. When I did begin to receive speaking invitations, they were from Jewish ladies' groups, Jewish community centers, and from all sorts of Jewish organizations, large and small.... If there are Jews who have begun to find the stories the novelists tell more provocative and pertinent than the sermons of some of the rabbis, perhaps it is because there are regions of feeling and consciousness in them which cannot be reached by the oratory of self-congratulation and self-pity."[2]

It is not, as we have seen, that Jews were never exposed to sermons in the years when the tradition was still abuilding; it is only that they now "enjoy" them for all the wrong reasons. Nor were Jews ascetics; they knew how to celebrate life—and death, too. But they did so in a manner far removed from the materialistic and conspicuous ways in which their contemporary descendants magnify and sanctify their God at these crucial, "spiritual" moments. Jews broke bread together—as spiritual companions—on almost every occasion of religious significance. Indeed, their Muslim neighbors long ago minted the

---

[2] Philip Roth, "Writing about Jews," *Commentary*, April, 1963.

proverb that "Arabs celebrate their rituals in the cemeteries, while Jews do so with their pots."

Some wrongly believe that the current excesses are excusable because most American Jews are "descended from families who had been deprived materially over the centuries," and that "when the Depression gave way to the post-World War II economic boom in which Jews shared, all the hopes created by years of underprivilege poured forth in a flood of acquisition and consumption.... [In any case] most Jewish materialism is lavished on enhancing the marriage, home and the family."[3] But this is sheer, unadulterated filiopietism.

It is surely not the way I learned about home, the family—and the older uses of Jewish poverty—from my grandfather. He frequently shared with me antique Yiddish proverbs that cut to the heart of the matter: *Az m'est Shabbos kugel, iz men di ganzeh voch zat.* "If you eat pudding on Sabbath, you can be full all week." And: *Fun iberessen cholyet men mer vi fun nit deressen.* "From overeating one suffers more than from not eating enough." One of his favorites, too, was the Talmudic saying, in Aramaic: "Only the near-empty box, with few coins inside, makes a lot of noise." "If there is something valuable within you," he would say, "you need not rattle your worth; it will speak for itself."

It seems to me that *culturally* deprived Jews—not those who know their own spiritual worth as descendants of a tradition that de-emphasized material acquisition—have transformed religious rituals into something new and absurd. In their hands, and assisted ably by their caterers, Bar Mitzvahs, weddings, and funerals now serve as the equivalent of modern Jewish theater.

Whereas those ancient, humble rites were designed to set Jews apart from their pagan neighbors, by enshrining symbols and *sancta* meant to reflect the teachings of ethical monotheism, they have now become almost indistinguishable from the notorious bacchanalia of Rome. All primitive religions erected

---

[3] Borowitz, *ibid.*, p. 117.

their own defense systems intended to appease the wrath of their gods at crucial and delicate junctures of life—birth, puberty, marriage, and death. On such occasions, they offered sacrifices of their most precious possessions: a child, an animal, or bounties of the crop. Alone among the ancients, the Jews approached those moments sacramentally—they behaved in a manner that suggested that human life was a sacred adventure in purifying one's thoughts in order to perfect one's deeds. The rituals were given them to perform, the Talmud taught, "in order to refine their human nature"—by subduing their animality. These rites were not seen as opportunities to propitiate the blind spirits and forces which control men, as the pagans believed. For Jews, this was a rational, orderly universe, governed by a God of justice and moral law, and to speak to Him, on these great occasions of life, you behaved as "refined creatures," made in His image, should: reasonably, morally, humbly and discreetly. There was no need to prove your prowess in controlling Him. Look what happened to the builders of the Tower of Babel, my teachers always reminded me.

Solomon Schechter, the great Rabbi-scholar who came to America from Cambridge, England to build the Jewish Theological Seminary early in this century, had said that in an age when all Jews prayed, a single, standard and unrevised Prayer Book was sufficient and satisfactory; but when Jews stopped praying—altered, re-worked, and new prayer books were published almost every day. I think that the same process is at work in the rites of passage publicly practiced by most North American Jews, today. The less they know of their meaning, the more they theatricalize their performance; the less they believe in them, the more they act as if they did. But what these *arrivistes* have made of this "theater of the absurd"—their almost-pagan celebrations of Jewish *sancta* and religious rites—is not Jewish, even though it "looks Jewish." Everything about them may appear to match—the tablecloths, the décor, the suits and gowns, and of course, the color of the *yarmulkes*, or skull-caps, that caterers distribute at the door. But there is one missing link, basic to all these marvelous matches. Judaism—and the unique spiritual meanings these rituals are intended to convey.

What are some of those religious messages that have not yet reached these ambiguous, decultured Jews? And what are the hidden costs to their sensitivity, not only as Jews, but also as God's creatures "refined by the tradition"?

Birth

For Jews, the synagogue is a sacred place, but it never was what it has now become—the *only* sacred place. Above the synagogue itself is the Torah-law-and-teaching, and its preeminence transcends and exceeds its physical place. So it is that when a male child is born, the rituals that accompany the first days of life need not take place within the synagogue. Scriptural law prescribes: "And on the eighth day the flesh of his foreskin shall be circumcised." Whatever the origin of this rite, it has come to play a principal role in setting Jews apart from the world of paganism and idolatry. The ritual itself is known as the *b'rit*, the covenant or agreement. Its very name suggests its deep meaning. It reminds Jews that they are the "children of Abraham," the people of the covenant who, together with the Patriarch, made and still keep the pact with God, to live in accordance with laws and beliefs that clearly distinguish them as a separate community—"a kingdom of priests and a holy nation."

But these initiatory rites, performed by a religious functionary called a *Mohel*, or circumciser, are not only occasions for remembering an old covenant, as the seed of Abraham, but also the time for reconnecting with the recent past. They also center on people for whom there is still a living memory among family members, for as part of the ritual, the baby is also given a Hebrew name, which among Ashkenazi Jews is almost always that of a recently deceased near relative. So it has developed that at the time of birth they linked themselves spiritually not only to their ancient concept-models, but more

Bar Mitzvahs, Weddings, and Funerals 143

especially to the real-life ancestors they themselves knew and loved as Jews. It had become a time for proclaiming that the spiritual past—both the distant and the near—still lived, and will continue to thrive in the life of this newly born Jew. A female child is similarly named at a synagogue service, when the father attends shortly after her birth and is called to the Torah reading, and prayers for the mother's health are also offered.

Since the *b'rit* usually takes place in a hospital—many Jewish hospitals provide small "circumcision rooms"—only a handful of guests can be accommodated at the ceremony. Sometimes, there is barely room for a *minyan*, the quorum of ten males required for the conduct of public Jewish ritual. As a result, the festivities on such occasions are usually restricted, even these days, to the modest repasts of earlier times: some wine and sweet cakes. But when I arrived in Canada, I discovered that Jews there had seized upon a folk-ceremony that grew up in Europe—the *ben zakhar*—which American Jews have all but forgotten, and which gave them the wider field needed for conspicuous displays of food and drink, *sans* ritual adornments or meanings.

The Talmud mentions *shalom zakhar*—a visit to the child's parents on the occasion of the birth of the male ("if a boy is born, peace comes to the world") to express happiness and offer congratulations. In later medieval times, *shalom zakhar* became known merely as *ben zakhar*—"the male child"—and it took place on the Friday night following the boy's birth, when relatives and friends visited the parents, and were served with fruit and wine. It was a modest celebration—which may explain why most American Jews have no remembrance of it, and have virtually eliminated the *ben zakhar* from their list of required Jewish festivities. But Canadians? I attended my first—and last—*ben zakhar* in Toronto, in the spring of 1956. Although it was held, of course, on a Friday night—and I had made it a practice never to attend social events outside of my home or synagogue on that night—I was curious to see just

144 THE REAL JEWISH WORLD

what a *ben zakhar* really was like. As an American-reared Jew, I had never seen one, and had only read about the Old Country style, in history books. I don't believe, however, that what I encountered that Friday night in the gilded ghetto of Forest Hill Village, in Toronto, could have been anything like the *ben zakhar* the living grandparents of this newborn infant male—or any others—had celebrated in their home Polish communities of Apt, Drildz, Zaglembia, Stashow, Shidlow, or Slipia.

It was more like a wedding party—or should I say, a rehearsal for a "Bar Mitzvah bash"—American-style. Catered. Banqueted. And with a three-piece combo in the recreation room, for the dancing set. Yet, there *was* one unintended consolation. Nobody there even pretended that this was a religious occasion. There were no speeches, no rituals, no rabbi's benedictions—only lots of noise, food, drink, and smoke. (And the "kid" was only two days old and mother and child had not yet returned from the hospital!) "We do this," the bejewelled, proud and beaming grandmother from Slipia confided to me, "because, after all, how many people can fit into the *b'rit* at Mount Sinai Hospital next Wednesday? And at that hour? Seven-thirty in the morning! I'm going to find it hard to be there myself."

(Some twenty-five years later not much had changed in Jewish Toronto. Chances are that that Canadian-born grandson of this Slipian *bubeh*, was himself calling Max—or any number of other caterers like him—when his own son was born in 1982. At least this is what one can deduce from a telltale advertisement placed in a Canadian-Jewish newspaper that year, advising this generation to do exactly what their own parents had long been doing: "Have An Affair With Max." But this seemingly titillating invitation was meant to be taken seriously and to blossom into full commitment—in the next line, the caterer was boasting that "some people would love to spend a whole lifetime with" him. Why? "Because Max caters every kind of affair (for over fifty years) you could hope to celebrate. Everything from ben zuchers [sic!] for the newborn, to golden wedding anniversaries...and all the simchas in between.... You won't have to lift a finger. And that's a nice way to go through life."

(What a letdown, you say, after such a tantalizing opener. Not at all. In many of these circles, "not having to lift a finger through life" is a very romantic prospect—surely more alluring than the bleak possibility of having to celebrate Jewish life by the sweat of your own brow.)[4]

But this is not the end of the matter if the child is also the first-born son of his mother. (This preoccupation with males in ancient Judaism is something of an embarrassment to many of us moderns. Still, *Yiddishe Mamehs*—"Jewish Mothers"— despite external appearances to the contrary, usually were in control of the family.)[5] In earlier Jewish history, the law required that first-born males be dedicated to the service of God. They were Israel's first priests. But a religious rite developed that required that first-born males, as a reminder of the role of their ancestors, undergo a "ritual of release" from their service to God on the thirty-first day of their life.

This ceremony is still conducted in observant Jewish families— the *Pidyon Ha-ben*, "the release of the son." A person known as a *Kohen*, because he traces his lineage to the priestly family of Aaron, serves as the officiant. The father brings the baby boy before him—at a ceremony just before nightfall, at home—and gains the child's "release" by making a symbolic gift offering to God, consisting of five "shekels." Generally, five newly minted silver dollar pieces are used. The *Kohen* then invokes the priestly blessing of Aaron upon the child and returns the five "shekels" to the parents, who are expected to contribute the money to charity. Today, this ceremony has lost the force of its original perceptions because there is no longer the institution of the priesthood in Judaism. Even those who are called "Mr. Cohen" are not always "working" at being

---

[4] See *Canadian Jewish News*, May 27, 1982.

[5] For an unusually incisive account of the role of the *Yiddishe Mameh*, see Zena Smith Blau, "In Defense of the Jewish Mother," *Midstream*, February, 1967.

priestly; some can barely read the ritual for this occasion. Which explains why, in most communities, it is that surrogate Jew again—the Rabbi—who has virtually taken over this duty, and if he himself is not a Kohen, he will find someone who is and bring him along. But it is the Rabbi who is expected to conduct the ritual, even though tradition has made no room for him on such occasions, unless he himself coincidentally happens to be a *Kohen*.

So barely a month after the *ben zakhar*, here's another pre-Bar Mitzvah rehearsal most Rabbis wearily attend. The ritual is quaint, and in many ways completely irrelevant to modern Judaism. Still, Rabbis have tried to make the most of it from a spiritual point of view, considering that the *Pidyon Ha-ben*, like the *ben zakhar*, has really become the exclusive province of the Jewish caterers. Rabbis will often re-interpret the older priestly ritual to suggest that even though Jews no longer practice that form of Judaism, it is a bond that ties us to the historic ways of the Jewish people. Implied in the ceremony, they will suggest, is the spiritual idea that human life comes from God, and all children—not only first-born males—have only been "loaned" to their parents.

Bar and Bat Mitzvah

For the young Jewish male there were three great moments that stood out, as festive occasions. There was, as we have seen, his initiation into the "Covenant of Abraham" on the eighth day of his life. Then, usually at four or five years of age, came the day when he was formally introduced to Jewish study, taken to the synagogue, blessed by the Rabbi or teacher, and offered honey to lick from a slate on which were written the letters of the Hebrew alphabet. "May the letters of the Torah be sweet to your mouth all the days of your life," he was told, as he commenced upon a career of unending study of Jewish teachings. Then the day arrived when he reached the status of adulthood—from the point of view of religious law—and was considered to be a member of the congregation, responsibility for his religious duties having passed from his father's shoulders to his. He became a Bar Mitzvah.

But thirteen is not the right age for Bar Mitzvah, any longer, I have been contending for some time.[6]

Studies reveal that a substantially higher percentage of American Jews have graduated college than either Protestants or Catholics. Ironically, in our secularized society, where the frontiers of knowledge are continually being advanced, and where a university education has become the accepted order of the day for most Jews, we still presume to "graduate" the "students" of our religion at the ripe and knowledgeable age of thirteen!

In the Hebrew Bible the age of responsibility was considered to be twenty. Only when a man reached that age was he thought to be an adult. We might very well be guided by this more ancient wisdom to meet the challenge which general education poses to those who have been only indoctrinated, never really educated, religiously. Religious teaching that is limited only to the pre-teens can rarely deal with the deeper issues of the spiritual life. As long as Bar Mitzvah remains a child's achievement, Judaism will become increasingly irrelevant to those whose higher general education may prepare them for life—but not for Jewish life.

What, indeed, is the meaning of Bar Mitzvah? And what has the answer to this question to do with the "right age" for Jewish religious commitment?

From the Bible itself we have no clues regarding Bar Mitzvah. Yet it seems credible that between a child's birth and his fuller maturity, some special ceremonies must have been celebrated. But beginning at least six hundred years ago, in Germany, a religious event was observed immediately as a boy reached his thirteenth birthday. This has since come to be known as the Bar Mitzvah, when a boy becomes a "child of the commandments." This event is related to the blessings recited

---

[6] See my essay "The Right Age for Bar Mitzvah," *Religious Education*, July-August, 1965, p. 298.

during the first days of life, at the time of circumcision, when family and friends prayed: "May he live to study and observe the Torah."

The religious rites at birth confer Jewish status inasmuch as they symbolize the covenant-relationship of the people of Israel with their God. The Bar Mitzvah ceremony, however, is not an initiatory rite, as such. As a ceremonial ritual it is essentially a "graduation ceremony"—graduation into personal responsibility for the fulfilling of the commandments of the Torah, based upon a presumed understanding of its obligations and significances.

As the Jewish national state began to decay during the Roman occupation of Palestine, the Rabbis placed less emphasis upon the biblical age of maturity and civic responsibility—twenty, when the individual could bear arms—and concentrated their attention on the products of the religious schools as the principal means of keeping the Jewish people culturally prosperous. Education in the spiritual life became the major preoccupation of Jewish leadership.

These leaders, the Talmudic Rabbis, prescribed a ladder of education—a ladder which, later, ironically was responsible for the development of Bar Mitzvah as a symbolic educational ceremony signifying readiness on the part of the adolescent. They taught: "At five years, the age is reached for the study of Scripture; at ten, for the study of Mishnah; at thirteen for the fulfillment of the commandments; at fifteen, for the study of the Talmud...." Since, in those days, a young man of thirteen had already engaged in an intensive study of the Hebrew Bible as well as the rabbinical interpretations codified in the Mishnah, he was rightly deemed ready to undertake the obligations of the Torah, as a responsible member of the Jewish community in his own right. Responsibility was related to religious literacy and literacy was achieved only as a result of diligent and comprehensive study of the meaning of that responsibility.

Like other Jewish rituals and observances, Bar Mitzvah is not a counterpart to a Christian sacrament—say, confirmation—in which an inward, invisible change takes place, by means of

God's grace, in and through the Church. It is, rather, a sign, remembrance, and a symbol—but most of all, it is a *status* in Jewish life, which does not even depend upon the ceremonial itself. Bar Mitzvah does not mark a change in the individual's nature, since it is not a sacrament. It only marks the age when a change should occur in his obligations to the commandments of the Torah—*because his religious education has prepared him for this change.*

(In recent decades, North American Rabbis have democratized this view, extending it by application to young women as well. As a result, in many non-Orthodox communities, Bat Mitzvah for girls in their thirteenth year, now parallels Bar Mitzvah for boys, in almost all respects.)

But we find ourselves living in a time and in a situation when the change in obligation to the Torah and its teachings is less and less perceptible, partly because the role-model of middle-class North American Jewish parents rarely encourages religious commitment. But equally to blame is the plain fact that the over 340,000 students presently enrolled in afternoon, supplementary religious schools (sometimes called "Hebrew," or "Congregational" schools) cannot achieve the kind of Jewish literacy by the age of thirteen which was commonly experienced until just a few generations ago in Europe, where both the home and the school were saturated with Jewish knowledge. Moreover, the general environment in the Old World was not regarded as worthy of assimilating, and Jewish education was usually the only schooling available to the "alien Jews" of nonemancipated communities in countries like Poland and Russia. Yet, the same Talmudic Rabbis who regarded thirteen as the age of religious discernment because they—and the generations following them—had produced the educational system to match their spiritual goals, also taught: "The study of the Torah outweighs in importance all of the other commandments...for the illiterate man cannot be a pious man."

But despite our most pious hopes, religious literacy of the older Jewish order is not achievable today for most Jewish children in North America. (Not even the over 110,000 students attending elementary Jewish day schools, where Jewish subjects are taught for an average of three hours every day, can match the religious knowledge, say, of many of their great-grandparents, just three generations ago, in East Europe.) In earlier times, the principal subjects studied by Jewish children were Bible and Talmud but these were taught in ways that encompassed a world-view. Nor did they have to be *taught* a Jewish language—Yiddish in Europe, or Judeo-Arabic in Sephardic countries; they simply *caught* it, at home, or in the "Jewish streets" of their towns. They learned to pray simply by praying—in synagogue or at home—with their families. In North America, they have to be *told about* prayer by their teachers, and then *taught* the skills. They have to learn a language—Hebrew—they will probably never speak or read.

Then, of course, there is the whole problem of "justifying" the need for Jewish education, in the first place. "My son isn't going to be a Rabbi" was the constant refrain parents used to repeat to me every time I would urge them to encourage a better attitude toward Jewish studies on the part of the child. To counter those negative views about the need for and the worth of Jewish learning altogether, educators and Rabbis scurried about devising new techniques that would make it easier to "sell" the educational product they were having difficulty "marketing." The result was many new courses introduced: subjects like comparative religion, the role of Judaism in a democracy, etc. Ironically, however, the multiplication of more sophisticated subject-areas increased as the demand for a reduction in the hours of instruction grew. A vicious circle developed. The more acculturated children and parents became, the more conscious they were of their "Americanism," and the more modern they were in their own eyes—the less time were they willing to make available for the Jewish afternoon school.

There were always higher priorities: piano or violin instruction, clubs and athletics in their public schools, or family weekends away from the city at their ski-chalets or country homes. As a result, despite occasional successes, the Jewish educational enterprise in North America, by and large, can be accurately described as being "a mile wide and an inch deep." As far as I could tell, many of those who "graduated themselves" by dropping out of Hebrew School the day after their Bar Mitzvah, must have thought that the Children of Israel never left Egypt. They had barely covered Genesis, and never finished Exodus.

In the European past, many Jews had the benefit of higher Jewish learning but were denied the possibilities of a general university education because of anti-Semitic regulations. In such circumstances, their cultural and religious loyalties to Judaism were firmly grounded in the soil of Jewish knowledge. Even when they rejected the Judaism they had been taught, they did so thoughtfully and critically, like those *Litvak tzelem kepp*! But the situation in America has been reversed. While there has been a new and growing emphasis upon more intensive elementary education—with the phenomenal rise in day schools across the continent—very few Jewish college graduates can also boast of having received a *higher* Jewish education.

Mahr Braverman was right, and I have rediscovered his truth over and over again. It is clear that those who attend even the most intensive Jewish day schools but do not continue beyond the elementary school years (as most do not) have achieved very little for themselves. Not only do they forget what they have learned in their day schools by the time they reach college, but even their intensive elementary education cannot stand up to their new sophistication as college graduates with two or more academic degrees under their belts. They rarely unlearn the Jewish materials they had been taught as children, in childish ways. In fact, the more general education they acquire, the more critical and secularized their thinking process grows. And if they have not complemented their new knowledge with an approach to Judaism which is equally mature and adult, it is likely that they will forever identify its teachings only with the naive and primitive meanings they were taught as children. The Bible, I have always contended, is not a book for kids!

Jews today really require a new ladder of religious education. Rabbis and intelligent laymen should revise the Talmudic scale in the light of the deflationary spiral spawned by the secular, open, and free society of North America. The Talmudic structure should be changed in the light of the Rabbinic dictum: "...the illiterate man cannot be a pious man." "Bar Mitzvah should take place no earlier than at eighteen," I used to tell the parents I would meet, months before they were planning their "big" Bar Mitzvah for their sons, or the almost-as-lavish parties for their daughters' Bat Mitzvah. "Good idea," they would always respond, courteously. "But don't do a thing about it until my kid's big day is over, or else instead of quitting Hebrew School the day after, *he'll walk out on you right now!*"

And so it went; and so it still goes. The big Jewish debuts of my Flatbush, which were really Jewish finales, still go on and on, all across the country. We laugh and joke and poke fun at each other, telling stories about the "Superbar Bar Mitzvah"; or the "Safari Bar Mitzvah" catered by headhunters in mid-Africa; or the weekend Bar Mitzvah splash for two or three hundred guests, sponsored at Jewish hotels in the Catskills of New York State, the Laurentians of Quebec, or the deserts of California, by loving Jewish parents. Games Jews play. And parents defend these inanities by telling themselves that they have to "keep up with the Cohens." "How will my little boy feel if we don't do for him, what 'they' did for their son? After all, he's his friend." Or by the lowest, most devastating blow of all: "Rabbi, how can you expect my son to love being Jewish if he won't have a big, *beautiful* Bar Mitzvah to remember?"

Weddings

The Jews, called Semites, Orientals, and Non-Aryans, were actually among the very first Europeans. They reached Germany sometime in the first or second century of the Christian era, and by the early fourth century—almost one hundred and fifty years before the Germans themselves finally crossed the Rhine—there was already a flourishing Jewish community in Cologne. The Greek historian and geographer Strabo, a contemporary of Julius Caesar, and who died fifty years before the Jews were dispersed and exiled from Jerusalem by the Romans in 70 C.E., had already written of Jews in his *Geography* that "it is hard to find a spot in the inhabited world where this race [sic] does not dwell or traffic." And by the ninth century, a well-known Arab travel writer, Ibn Khordadbeh, in his *A Book of Roads*, was describing the amazing ubiquitousness of the Jews as follows: "They take ships in the land of the Franks, on the Western Sea [Marseilles, on the Mediterranean]...and make for Antioch.... They embark in the Red Sea and sail to Eltar [the port of Medina] and Jeddah [the port of Mecca].... They sail down the Tigris...for Oman, Sind, Hind and China.... They also make different journeys by land...starting from Spain or from France to Morocco, then to Tangiers, whence they march to Kairowan and the capital of Egypt.... Sometimes they take a route from Constantinople, passing through the country of the Slavs...or they embark on the Black Sea and arrive at Balkh [Afghanistan] betaking themselves from there across the Oxus, to continue their journey toward Yourt, Toghozghor, and from there to China."

I often pondered these historical facts as I traveled through Europe. Except for the Jewish Catacombs in Rome—saved for history, undoubtedly, by the Roman Catholic Church for its own theological reasons—there are virtually no visible signs of the antiquity of Europe's Jews. The oldest standing synagogue in all of Europe is the *Altneuschul* in Prague, built in 1270—though under the rule of Stalinist Czechs it looks more like an empty, haunted house than a synagogue. Apart from Prague, virtually all of Europe's oldest synagogues go back little more than three centuries. Why are all the others—the truly ancient ones—no longer to be seen? They were, of course, razed during the intolerant Middle Ages. Yet, you ask yourself, as you travel these lands, if the synagogues were all destroyed, how is it that

European Jews survived? And the clear and simple answer sheds immediate light on the very nature of Judaism itself. Synagogues were leveled and covered over, but not Judaism. For Jews, the stage for most of their sacred acts and beliefs was their home, not their synagogue. This explains why marriage was considered by Jews to be a person's highest station in life. Through it, the home came into being, and because of it, Jews survived.

Judaism begins with the conviction that since man is a creation of God, no element of his nature is inherently evil or sinful. This is why it frowns upon celibacy and has never regarded marriage as a concession to the weakness of human flesh. On the contrary, marriage is considered to be a sacred duty, a fundamental *mitzvah*. The Rabbis taught, with characteristic psychological insight: "He who reaches the age of twenty and does not marry, spends all his days in sin—or, at least, in the thought of sin."

Because it never recognized Greek dualism—the antagonism between body and soul—as a true picture of human nature, Judaism continued to insist upon the essential unity of man's nature. The body was not evil in itself, nor was it a source of evil. Man worships God with his body, as well as with his soul, the Rabbis taught. The first *mitzvah* in the Mosaic Law, they pointed out, was the commandment "to be fruitful and multiply." (Genesis 1:28.)

The home is so central to Judaism that it is actually symbolized at the Jewish wedding service itself—in the form of the bridal chamber, or canopy—the *huppah*. Until very recently, weddings did not take place inside the synagogue itself because the community could not accept the idea of placing the *huppah*—which, after all, represents the bridal chamber—directly in front of the Torah Ark. Yet, a bridal canopy was always kept on its grounds, because the favorite place for marriage ceremonies—apart from the home—was in the courtyard of the synagogue, under the open sky. There, under the stars, the ceremony served as a reminder to the couple that

Bar Mitzvahs, Weddings, and Funerals 155

they were the children of Abraham, and like him, they would multiply "like the stars of the heavens."

Before the ceremony begins, in a secluded and private place, the parents of the couple join them, as the groom places the veil over the bride's face and repeats the blessing given to Rebekah, the Matriarch, by her mother and brother before she left home to marry Isaac: "Oh sister! May you grow into thousands of myriads." (Genesis 24:60.) Among ancient Semitic peoples (and in Muslim countries, still) the veil was a sign of her unavailability to other men, as well as a symbol of the bride's modesty. And the blessing spoken by her groom highlights again the purpose of marriage, according to Jewish tradition: to establish a home and to raise a family. This soft and charming prelude to the nuptial ceremony is known as *Bedeken*— "the covering of the bride." When it is concluded, the wedding march begins, and the families take their places under the canopy. They do not sit as spectators from afar, and the father does not "give the bride away." The two sets of parents accompany and lead their children to the *huppah*, and remain part of the ceremony. Jews are reminded at the wedding ceremony itself that there are no "bartered brides" and the new couple will always remain linked to *both* their families—as one large, extended family.

As part of the ceremony, the officiant offers the bride and groom two cups of wine, the symbol of life's bounty. Wine will later be used in their home at virtually all religious occasions. It represents the gifts of God's goodness and their joy in sharing them. The ring is symbolic of the consummation of the marriage and of its sanctity, or *kiddushin*, as the marriage ceremony itself has come to be called in Hebrew. As the groom places it upon the bride's finger he announces the meaning of the entire ceremony with these words: "Behold, you are *consecrated* unto me, with this ring, according to the laws of Moses and the people of Israel." He places the ring upon the forefinger of her right hand probably because of its prominence. (Rembrandt's luminous and touching painting of the "The Jewish

Bride," which hangs in Amsterdam's Rijksmuseum, clearly shows her wearing the wedding band on this finger.)

The various provisions for the man's maintenance of his wife and the mutual obligations both have to each other are detailed in the marriage contract, called the *ketubah*. These include both the physical and spiritual needs of the man and the woman. The text of the *ketubah* was composed during the period when the vernacular of the Jews in Palestine was Aramaic—during the time of Jesus—a language most scholars believe was his mother tongue since, like most other Galileans of the day, he spoke little Hebrew. To this day, as a link to those oldest of *ketubot*, the marriage contract is still printed—or sometimes written by a calligrapher—in that ancient Semitic language.

After the *ketubah* is read aloud, "Seven Benedictions" are recited. These are devoted to an expression of thanks to God for the institution of marriage and the family, for having implanted his image on the human race, and for the joy of the wedding and the happiness of bride and groom. One of these benedictions, in addition, offers a prayer for the restoration of Jerusalem. Ancient Jewish sentiment, based on Psalm 137, reminds the Jew to recall Jerusalem "above your chiefest joy." And that is why this prayer is included at such a supremely happy moment as the wedding service. For the same reason, the traditional ceremony concludes with the groom breaking a glass under his heel, to memorialize the destruction of Jerusalem, even while he celebrates his own fulfillment as a man.

When I would meet with prospective brides and grooms to describe some of these lovely and uplifting rituals and value-symbols, I could almost always sense a hidden feeling of embarrassment on their part. So this was what a Jewish wedding was all about! And they had come with different questions on their mind. Quite different. But they quickly recovered from their uneasiness and invariably would launch into the matters *they* thought were important about the wedding ceremony.

Many were bright and eager, thoughtful and intelligent

Bar Mitzvahs, Weddings, and Funerals   157

young people. But they were often so intent on reviewing their own detailed check list that they had little patience with the "Jewish content" of the wedding. Their questions were almost always addressed to the mechanics of the ceremony—the music, or the number of ushers and bridesmaids, and the like. Like Bar Mitzvahs, Jewish weddings are often approached as events, or at best, as ceremonies, and the idea that they represent values that should last a lifetime seems to elude the otherwise preoccupied celebrants. Their overattention to the demonstrative displays of the occasion diverts them, and they often miss the private spiritual purposes of their very public enterprise.

But one must be grateful for even small mercies. Since caterers have taken over these religious celebrations, it has become acceptable—even among most Orthodox—to conduct weddings inside the sanctuaries or chapels of the synagogue, followed, of course, by a catered meal or reception on the premises. At synagogue weddings, Rabbis were not about to be completely ruled by the show business mentality of many of these catering impresarios—with their outlandishly colored, garish tuxedo jackets, and their matching skull-caps. In their own congregations, at least, Rabbis could usually set ground rules that would keep weddings within the bounds of the traditional spirit.

In Israel, however, only Orthodox Rabbis are licensed by the Ministry of Religions to perform wedding ceremonies; they are agents of the state. Yet, synagogue weddings are not allowed following the traditional practice before religious centers also became catering establishments, in America. Still, ironically, the crassest imitations of so-called American-style weddings now flourish in Israel. There, enterprising beauty salons join forces with catering establishments or wedding parlors, and together they offer a complete package, including "Cinderella" outfits for the entire wedding party, available for the night. An American Orthodox Rabbi attests that "the extravagances of a wedding [can] bankrupt families...and this is presently occurring at an alarming rate in the State of Israel among traditional families."[7]

The excesses which take place in North America can be understood as a reflection of a free and voluntary society where no ultimate religious sanctions can be applied. Jewish life, thus, becomes "consumer-directed," and Jewish law can only be maintained *inside* the synagogue. Yet, in a rabbinically dominated community like Israel, where the government itself regulates marriage and stringently applies the standards of *halaka*—religious law—to the performance of weddings, one would have hoped that traditional sumptuary laws would also be applied to the way in which marriages are celebrated.[8] With

---

[7] Maurice Lamm, *The Jewish Way in Love and Marriage*, Harper and Row, New York, 1980, p. 176. Further, on page 179, Rabbi Lamm, while correctly stating that "the rabbi has no part in effecting the marriage itself," adamantly but *incorrectly* insists that only an Orthodox rabbi ("a rabbi who is a scholar of the law"—his code language for Orthodox rabbi) may conduct a wedding: "The presence of the rabbi gives the wedding the character of an official act.... His primary value is not as a public speaker or a master of ceremonies, but as a scholar, able to assure that all the actions meet the centuries-old standards of the Jewish people. Cantors who are not ordained as Rabbis should not perform marriages (though they perform at marriages). The fact that the [secular] state [in the diaspora] may authorize them is irrelevant; the Jewish religion does not. A wedding should be postponed if there is no ordained rabbi available on the date selected."

Actually, Jewish history attests to the fact that it was not until sometime in the fourteenth century—when the rabbinate becomes, for the first time, a paid, professional calling—that the Rabbi regularly attended the wedding ceremonies as a religious official of the community and received a fee for his services. Before this time, the marriage ceremony was performed either by a member of the bride's or groom's family, close friends, or a distinguished lay member of the community. To this day, Jewish law, *per se*, does not require that an "ordained rabbi" serve as the marriage performer.

[8] See discussion of traditional "sumptuary laws" in Salo W. Baron, *The Jewish Community, Its History and Structure to the American Revolution*, The Jewish Publication Society of America, Philadelphia, 1942, Vol. II, pp. 301-307:

Bar Mitzvahs, Weddings, and Funerals   159

the Orthodox rabbinate in full control, why don't its members simply refuse their services in cases where they clearly know that they are participating in a religious ceremony which "can bankrupt families"?

Inside their North American synagogues, to their credit, many Rabbis have withstood the powerful pressures of their "member-consumers" to emulate the ways of caterers on the outside. It was mostly in those "casas," "manors," "gardens," or "chateaux"—the euphemisms chosen by Jewish caterers for their own plastic-slick, tinseled wedding halls and banqueting establishments—where made-in-America ceremonies began to root themselves, in mindless ways. These were especially appealing to those who had no *shul* or Rabbi of their own, or

---

"Of special significance were the numerous ordinances restricting the use and display of articles of luxury.... Beginning with the fifteenth century more and more communal organs, regional as well as local, felt the need of issuing a *pragmatica*, or some other ordinance 'regarding these extravagant and conspicuous displays.' Various reasons were advanced in justification of such sumptuary ordinances: the envy of ever-suspicious Gentile neighbors usually aroused by a display of costly garments or jewelry and by revelry in feasting; the attempt to keep up with the neighbors which led to the impoverishment of numerous families and converted many a celebration into a sorrowful occasion; the frequent indebtedness of extravagant celebrants to Gentiles and the ensuing enmity in the case of bankruptcy; the obliteration of what were considered legitimate distinctions between rich and poor or, on the contrary, the underscoring of such distinctions...."

"When unchecked by the community, lavishness in dress and festivities were quite natural to groups of pawnbrokers and merchants who owned much jewelry and precious materials as their stock in trade, and whom boisterous family festivals in part compensated for the general lack of amusements and the drabness of life created by both outside hostility and the stringent requirements of Jewish law."

The Chief Rabbinate of Israel, which would have the necessary power to issue such *pragmatica* to its Orthodox constituents at least, has remained painfully silent and quietly aloof from any of these problems. Yet they are hardly different today from what they apparently were five hundred years ago in Europe.

those Jews who had already fallen into cultural limbo. The caterers' *ersatz* chapels pretended religiosity; they seemed just right for most Jews in the larger metropolitan centers, who were themselves unsynagogued and, at times like these, found themselves in dire need of a sacred place. So they rented these halls for their weddings, as well as so-called Rabbis—usually they were Cantors who invented for themselves the Jewish title of "Reverend." They, too, were leased in the very same contract. Caterers happily provide their own "house Reverends" for these occasions, just as they offer "their own" florists, bands, photographers, videotapers, and chauffeured livery.

New York is not America, but it is the capital city of these commercial ritual-emporia, whose showy "new-style" weddings, for the past several decades, have been winning the favor of more and more satisfied customers. As the Jewish "fashion center," its modes are eventually borrowed by other large metropolitan areas—especially the dozen or so North American Jewish communities with a population of over 100,000. (The latter often use hotels in place of catering halls, since their more limited numbers, unlike metropolitan New York's three million Jews, can not easily support "private" catering establishments.) Still, initiated observers claim that once you have seen one or two of these weddings, you have seen them all—permuted or combined—that is to say, at least until an even more bizarre ceremonial idea has been hatched out by an enterprising caterer. Essentially, however, the bigger weddings fall into two categories: the Saturday night ceremony, usually held at a late hour in deference to the Sabbath day, and the Sunday evening wedding party.

Even as early as the 1940s, if you were attending a Saturday night wedding, say, at the Aperion Manor on Brooklyn's King's Highway, you would have been well advised to have dinner before leaving home for the affair. My invitation announced that the marriage ceremony would take place at "nine o'clock in the evening," but only the untried and inexpe-

Bar Mitzvahs, Weddings, and Funerals 161

rienced would regard this statement as a truth to be taken literally. Those who were old hands at such things knew that "Jewish time" is usually counted in leisurely, Mediterranean beats, and that when "they say nine o'clock, they really mean ten or ten-thirty." Most public Jewish events—save those arranged by the more acculturated—are still calculated in advance, to start at a much later hour than the time officially announced.

True to this form, the wedding guests first began to filter into the hall around ten o'clock, to be greeted by the "receiving line"—prior to the ceremony—with very little, except tidbits of finger food, to eat. (The "punch bar," of course, was open.) The bride was cloistered "somewhere upstairs," out of view, but the groom was busy flitting about from couple to couple, and knot to knot, weaving into and around the family's reception line. By eleven-thirty he was totally exhausted and "disappeared."

It was about this time that the master of ceremonies (was it the caterer himself or only one of his assistants?) began hushing all and sundry, urging them to take their places at the other end of the hall. Accordion-pleated room-dividers were removed by two neatly attired attendants, revealing a "wedding chapel," which looked as if it had been designed and gilded in Hollywood—complete with a winding, spiral staircase a good two stories high. It was close to the stroke of twelve before everyone had been almost silenced and had finally made his way to the "chapel" side of the hall. So now you knew. This was designed as a midnight ceremony, called for nine o'clock in the evening.

"Will she make it?" That question was on everyone's lips as the amply proportioned bride suddenly appeared at the golden door atop the staircase, which had opened magically, at the sound of an Oriental gong. Obviously, she had been carefully rehearsed—probably by the caterer's assistant. Slowly down the steps, clutching tightly at the balustrade, she came—step by deliberate step—accompanied musically by a boy soprano singing "Here Comes the Bride," the wedding march composed by Richard Wagner, the notorious anti-Semite.[9]

The religious ceremony thereafter, under the bridal canopy, was decidedly anti-climactic. Other more immediate and physical matters were of primary interest to the Jewish congregation in attendance at these "sanctification ceremonies"—the *kiddushin*—of bride and groom. The caterer knew about these. Throughout the midnight supper that followed, he continued to beam. He had, his face said, brought great pleasure to so many: first, by his magical bridal march; and now, by his "delicious food."

Nothing nearly so "dramatic" takes place in the smaller Jewish communities, where only about one quarter of the continent's six million Jews reside. For one thing, the ratio of synagogue members in these places is much higher than in centers where Jews number more than 100,000. The proportion of the synagogued increases significantly in inverse ratio to the size of the local Jewish population.[10] Smaller Jewish communities also tend to look askance at "New York Jews"; they

---

[9] German composer (1813-1883) whose anti-Semitic writings were well-known and highly regarded, especially by those who looked for reasons for making their hatred of Jews culturally respectable. He had branded the Jews as "the demon causing mankind's downfall."

[10] Several studies estimate that only from 47 to 50 per cent of American Jews belong to any synagogue. This would indicate that of the approximate total Jewish population in the United States of 6,000,000, only about 2,800,000 to 3,000,000 are synagogue members. Of this number (five per cent of the total population estimated as being *fully observant*) only about 300,000 are *committed* Orthodox Jews. While there are relatively fewer Orthodox in cities of under 100,000 Jewish population, synagogue affiliation in many of these cities often runs as high as 75 per cent. In cities with over 100,000 Jews (especially New York and Los Angeles) synagogue affiliation is appreciably lower than the national average of 47 to 50 per cent. See Daniel J. Elazar, *Community and Polity: The Organizational Dynamics of American Jewry*, Philadelphia, Jewish Publication Society of America, pp. 71-73; p. 403.

live out their Jewish lives in more conservative fashion, and retain greater loyalty to their own local, timeworn community habits. I had served as Rabbi of Temple Beth El in Rochester, New York from 1946 to 1956, and during that period of time there still were no fulltime, professional caterers serving that Jewish community of some 22,000 souls. But in the 1950s, I would be reminded that the New York style I had last seen a decade earlier was far from dead—if anything, it was becoming more and more entrenched. I was to return to the Casa del Rey—scene of my own Bar Mitzvah dinner party—surprised to find it refurbished and expanded, and full of celebrating Jews.

By then, Rochester's Jews were no longer using "Jewish time" as the gauge for their public events, services, or celebrations—only Eastern Standard (or Daylight) Time—and naively, I had completely forgotten that millions of other Jews were still abiding by that older, Semitic clock. One of my favorite cousins had invited me—or so we both thought—to officiate at his Sunday evening wedding, announced for "five-thirty P.M." His bride's family—like another two million or so of the Jews living in Greater New York—were not members of any congregation. They did what most all those others did on such occasions. They rented a catering hall, and the "new" and "improved" Casa del Rey was their choice. Because of my own congregational commitments at home, I was forced to arrive late and breathless—some thirty minutes after the scheduled starting time even after urging my cab driver to break the speed limits, on our wild and reckless ride from Idlewild Airport to the door of the Casa.

I ran nervously into the lobby, fully expecting that some members of my family would be there to greet me, to rush me headlong under the canopy in order to start a ceremony I was responsible for delaying. But there was not a soul in sight. Was it all over? Was I in the right place? I stood in that empty foyer staring incredulously at the shimmering walls and ceilings, covered over completely with antiqued, smokey-looking mirrors, and could find no way to gain further entry. Where were the people—and where were the doors to the chapel?

I soon discovered, to my amazement, that there was not one door, but three—each opening up to three separate halls. The "new" Casa was new indeed. It was hosting three different sets of merrymakers, all at once—two weddings and a Bar Mitzvah party. And at the very same time I also discovered that my family's wedding was far from over; it had not nearly begun, and would not for at least another hour and a half. Not until that other wedding ceremony had finished with the three-hundred-seat theater-styled chapel connected to these partying and dining rooms. Until then, I was invited to join in the "dansant" and cocktail party that everyone there knew—except me, it seemed—*had* to precede the ritual ceremony.

Ceremony? It was not exactly the kind of ritual arrangement I would have recognized as a Jewish wedding service. In the first place, there was a theatrically inspired caricature of the bridal canopy, the rectangular cloth that is usually placed over four posts, and which serves as a symbol of the Jewish home—the *huppah*. The set-designers of the Casa had concocted something that floated overhead, held in place by the thinnest of wire-strings: no doubt, somebody's idea of a protective "cloud of glory" to cover the bride and groom at the "altar." It was made of some kind of luminescent material, and when the guests first entered the chapel, they were expected to be overwhelmed by its sight. Colored lights coming from the ceiling played all about it, giving the illusion that a rainbow cloud was hovering over the sacred proceedings.[11]

The singing "Reverend" and his female partner were also more than I expected. Obviously, no one may officiate at a

---

[11] Jewish caterers in America have apparently had a long history of "working out" new, gadget-like arrangements for wedding canopies. Irving Howe tells us that "the Victoria Hall at 80 Clinton Street (east-side New York) advertised an 'electric bridal canopy' in 1900, and the Grand American Hall ('strictly union') featured 'thousands of electric lights' three years later." See his *World of Our Fathers*, Harcourt Brace Jovanovich, Hard-bound edition, New York, 1976, p. 221.

wedding at this place without them. They virtually told me that I was really superfluous—"wouldn't you rather sit down with your family, and enjoy our performance along with the other invited guests?" In the end, I remained standing under the so-called *huppah*, letting them "perform"—merely adding a few personal comments to the couple at the end, in the form of a family greeting and blessing. Until then, it was this duo "all the way"—she, in a decolleté evening gown at the back of the room, when she wasn't moving toward him, at the front, with his technicolored "rabbinical robes." Together, they were a kind of Nelson Eddy-Jeanette MacDonald religious team, keeping all eyes and ears attentively glued to their sounds and movements. "We are why people choose the Casa for their weddings," "the Reverend-Rabbi" soberly explained to me after it was all over. As if, by then, I didn't know.

At my own Bar Mitzvah party in this very place—a hovel then compared to its new glitter—I could at least escape outside by "playing tennis" with my friends. Now, I was a sedate Rabbi. I remembered Margolis. I sat throughout the proceedings—in deference to my family—and smiled at every one. It finally dawned on me, however, that I was distinctly in the minority. Most of the rest were smiling because they really enjoyed this kind of wedding. Very few of them believed that any other style—certainly not the "old fashioned ones"—could be as beautiful.

Death and Funerary Customs

To the religious person death comes as part of the natural plan of life. But to the truly devout—as most Jews were until only a relatively short time ago—death is something to prepare for throughout life. For them, death was not the end of life.

In the Jewish tradition, the only time a person was called upon to "make confession" privately (he does so openly and publicly as part of the congregation on each Day of Atonement) was when he realized that he was about to die. Observant

Jews always recited *vidui*, confession, at such moments. It is a rite connected with the belief in life after death. In their last conscious moments they addressed these words to God: "May it be your will to heal me completely. Yet, if it is determined that I die, I will accept it at your hand with love. Father of the fatherless, and Judge of the widow, protect my beloved ones...."

And their final words are those which stand at the center of all Jewish belief: "Hear, O Israel, the Lord our God, the Lord is One"—the unshakable affirmation of the unity of God and the world He created.

There is also a democracy of death built into the Jewish tradition for the past nineteen hundred years. This is symbolized not only by the garments with which the deceased are clothed but also by the kind of coffin that is permissible within the bounds of the *halaka*. At one time in older Jewish history, the wealthy were buried in costly garments. But Rabbi Gamaliel II, a distinguished scholar and leader who lived at the beginning of the second Christian century, asked that he be interred in a cloth shroud similar to those used by the poor, to stress the equality of all persons before God. Since that time, utter simplicity has been the governing principle underlying all aspects of burial.

The traditional Jew in East Europe—and in Israel, today—was buried on a bed of intertwined reeds—in no coffin at all. This "Jewish way" was chosen to underscore the biblical description of man: "For dust thou art, and unto dust shalt thou return." (Genesis 3:19.) In this fashion, the living returned the dead rapidly to the womb of earth, confident that man's spirit, not his body, was the essence of his being. In Western Europe and America it became acceptable for Jews to use coffins, but care was always taken to choose what has now become known as an "Orthodox casket"—a simple wooden coffin, unadorned with metal of any kind, and usually made of inexpensive pine. No adornments or worldly goods were to be interred with the deceased, save the shroud, a prayer shawl wrapped over the shoulders (in the case of a male) and, where possible, a small bag containing earth from the Land of Israel. The Jew returned to his Creator in prayerful garb, united to the land of his fathers in death as in life.

Returning the body to the earth as soon as possible after death was regarded by Jews as the highest tribute they could pay to the spiritual image of the deceased. It was as an act of neglect and discourtesy to allow the physical remains of a person to remain unburied; after all, he was no longer a spiritual being, now that his soul had departed his body. As a result, it became the practice—copied later by Muslims, as well—to bury the Jewish dead within twenty-four hours of their demise (except on the Sabbath and Festivals) if at all possible. There was also a great deal of good psychological insight here. The longer a beloved remains unburied the heavier the strain on the bereaved. It is better for the mourners to begin their mourning in a spiritual way, as soon as possible, rather than subject them to a stressful time in the "valley of the shadow of death"— confronted with the physical presence of their spiritless deceased. The laws surrounding death and mourning were as concerned with the vitality of the living as they were with the honor due the departed.

From earliest times, it was customary to take leave of the dead at a brief religious service which took place at the home of the family, or at graveside. As with weddings and other significant occasions, Rabbis usually played no part in the ritual aspects; their role centered on explaining the laws of burial and mourning, as teachers or judges. Together with all other members of the community, they were expected to console the grieving, and to pay their respects to the mourning family by visiting their home, where they were gathered together for a week of mourning—by visiting the *shiva*. There, on one or two occasions, they would conduct a study session dealing with the appropriate Talmudic laws of mourning. Characteristically, in traditional Judaism, it was the layman who played the central ritual role, if he were pious and learned enough to be chosen as a member of the *hevra kadisha*—literally, the "holy society," but actually, this was the community's "burial society."

Until only recently, membership in the *hevra kadisha* was regarded as a communal honor of the highest significance, bestowed only upon the truly pious. It has slowly been replaced, in America, by the Jewish mortician, who has become, even as he is now known, the "Jewish funeral director." Concomitant with the rise of this new Jewish profession—an entrepreneurial business, as is Jewish catering—the role of the Rabbi was also dramatically altered. He became the officiant at all funeral services, which, by now, take place from the usually sumptuous chapels established by the directors. He was also regarded as the eulogizer and "official comforter" of the congregation. Though his members did not often request him to offer learned discourses at the *shiva* in their homes, they surely expected him to make as many "house calls" during their week at home as possible.

The frequency and the timeliness of such "condolence visits" were soon to become a mark of social status among middle-class Jewish congregants. In many communities, it also could make or break a Rabbi—if he were not *seen* to be a good pastor, merely by "dropping in" to the *shiva* (even if he sat and said almost nothing), he might not be rehired. But then, again, fair is fair. It was the Rabbi who should have known by now what his Seminary professors neglected to teach him. Jews were no longer seeking rabbinical leaders whose erudition as scholars enabled them to expound Jewish law and communicate its life-values. In death and as in life, he was to serve as their essential public show-piece—either as their surrogate Jew, or their Protestant-styled pastor and ceremonial shepherd.

When it came to essential Jewish practice, however, American Jews did what Jews had been accustomed to doing. They consistently ignored traditional rabbinical advice and created their own death-style, as they had their own life-style. Ostentation replaced modesty, and instead of simplicity, extravagance ruled the day. Now, sleek funeral parlors, "directed" by commercially oriented Jewish morticians, easily convinced them that the nicest way to honor their dead was by means of conspicuous displays. There were expensive metal or mahogany caskets; several "visitation nights" at the parlors to "pay respects to the deceased" by viewing the open bier and admiring "the way he looks"; and green, grass-like mats placed by funeral directors over open graves, to shield mourners from the reality of "dust unto dust." All of these—and other—ritual novelties were, of course, manufactured in middle-class America. It goes without saying that they were at extreme odds with what the tradition had been saying about life and death, for the past twenty centuries—and the way Jews had responded to what they heard.

One of the most masterful and unique creations of that tradition was the spiritual atmosphere with which it had endowed the Jewish house of mourning. It carefully prescribes several graduated stages of grieving—from almost complete withdrawal to a slow and escalating return to normal life. It does not try to sweep death away but encourages the free expression of grief by the mourners in the privacy of their own homes. It is aware of the need to vent one's inner feelings in order to avoid irrational guilt, which often accompanies moments of grief. It knows of the mourner's need for solitude in the early hours following burial of a beloved; but it is also aware of the benefits of community, and so it builds into the *shiva*—the week of intense mourning—opportunities for linking one's own sorrow to the sorrow of others, in appropriate ways.

When mourners arrive home after interring their beloved dead, neighbors have already prepared the traditional "meal of condolence"—a simple, symbolic repast usually consisting of hard-boiled eggs and rolls. (The egg represents the continuation of life; the rolls, the full circle of infinity and eternity.) Their friends are encouraged by Jewish custom to depart early, to leave the mourners to themselves during these first hours of intense grief. The Talmudic Rabbis taught: "Do not try to console a mourner too early—when his deceased lies before him." This is why eulogies were delayed until thirty days after death; and why the tradition discouraged visits to the house of mourning by friends or neighbors, during the first three days of the *shiva* week. After this period of time, it was believed that the mourner should be prepared to accept comfort; to talk about life and death; and to speak openly to others about the teachings and virtues of the departed. The isolation and pain of the earlier days slowly recede as the achievements and dreams of the deceased are rehearsed aloud, by both the mourners themselves and their friends.

The most highly regarded condolence visit was not one in which the caller spoke small talk, or about worldly affairs—but only by calling the deceased back into life by quoting some of his high-minded sayings. S.J. Agnon, Israel's Nobel laureate for literature, would reach even higher on the scale of Jewish values when he would visit a house of mourning in Jerusalem. It was his custom to enter such places without speaking to anyone, but silently to seek out a rabbinical book from the shelves. He would seat himself at a table in another room, away from the others, and begin to study aloud appropriate spiritual texts from the Talmud. Soon, other visitors to the house would move closer, sit beside him, and join in. All this, without cues, comment, or commotion. Then, at the close of this brief learning session—an exercise all silently understood as a spiritual act to memorialize the deceased—the mourners would rise instinctively to recite *Kaddish*—the doxology in praise of God, which children recite for one year, three times a day at public services, after the passing of parents. Agnon had linked the memory of the departed to the words of the Law, and the bereaved had sealed this spontaneous, pious exercise with words of praise for the gift of life and of memory. In this way, they had made study of the Torah into an act of prayer, which is precisely the way the tradition had always seen it. In this way, too, the tradition had been used as a psychological and spiritual tool of consolation. There were no petty, embarrassing attempts urging the bereaved to take heart, or to be courageous in the face of their pain. By simply behaving as Jews, comfort was silently offered through this heartfelt and shared expression of piety and devotion.

On the thirtieth day after the burial it was customary to gather together with friends and relatives to listen to a public lesson—much like the kind Agnon had offered in private—dedicated to the memory of the deceased, and also to hear praises of his life—or what we call a eulogy. This "ceremonial" usually followed a brief visit to the cemetery earlier in the day, where a tombstone was unveiled and the mourners recited the *Kaddish*, in the presence of a *minyan* of ten or more males. And all of these memorials and devotions were usually self-actuated, without benefit of clergy, or of their oversight.

It has been correctly observed that the "American Way of Death" is a reflection of the "American Way of Life." So, too, North American Jews mourn today in ways alien to their history. The "meal of condolence" has been contracted out to caterers who have added heavily to its lean menu; it is sometimes served not once, but every night of the seven days at home. In our society, bereaved persons hardly know what to do with their aloneness, so most *shiva* houses have become noisy affairs, with so many visitors jammed into them that they mostly can speak only to each other, and barely to the mourners. The *hevra kadisha* has been almost completely displaced by funeral directors. The Rabbi's eulogy, like his pulpit sermons, has become the center-piece of public discussion: it dominates the committal prayers and displaces pious study. He is expected to come often to the mourners' house; especially meritorious in their eyes are early visits so they can boast to their friends that "the Rabbi was here the very first day!" Jewish neighborliness still abounds, and kindness is ever-present and cherished, but with so many professionals paid to take care of things, there is little room left for Jews to do "*Jewish* things" by themselves, any more.

But we always knew how to do Jewish spiritual things by ourselves: perhaps our inability to do that now is our greatest single problem. By ourselves, we worked our way out of our grief across the centuries—our personal sorrows as well as the collective pain we experienced at the hands of dozens of varieties of Crusaders and pogromists, in all our generations. It was our Jewish behavior, as much as our Jewish belief, which kept us from dying as a people. Indeed, the uniqueness of our faith, in the midst of the culture of others, was always bolstered and deepened by the distinctiveness of our ways.

Throughout a lifetime—from the day of birth to the day of death—Jewish rituals possessed a poetry all of their own. They helped to promote inwardness, gratitude for life, and the capacity to persevere in the teeth of tragedy. They brought peace, not the sword, to Jewish hands and minds, and helped teach that spirit was stronger than matter. The special flavors of their commemoration and celebration made moral and sensitive men out of people who could easily have become savage and cruel, considering their lot in the world. They learned well the Talmudic lesson: "The rituals were given them to perform, to refine their human nature." Above all, there was a naturalness and simplicity about the ways with which Jews confronted those crucial moments of life.

Can the vigor of that naturalness and simplicity take hold of Jewish life again—in North America? Can a way of life that energized them even as ancient empires and medieval structures were crumbling, and kept them immune from the darkest ages of others, reconquer these sons and scions of spiritual giants? Now, they excel in education, science, music, art and literature—not to mention their inventive business ingenuity. They are unbelievably caring—and loyal to the idea of a Jewish People, especially when under attack. They have serious lessons to teach the Christian and Muslim worlds in philanthropic achievement and community responsibility. They are sensitive and sensible. They believe passionately in the democratic ideal. They have taught themselves to share, with their own and with others.

But will the spirit of the ritual tradition—the way they themselves live as Jews—survive in their hands? Can it prosper in the midst of freedom, as it did for ancestors in their adversity?

I believe that it can. There is already a glimmer of hope that it will. As the 1970s came to a close there were definite signs—if only among a small minority of younger families—that some were seeking a more authentic personal Jewish experience than their parents had ever bothered to think about. As children of *arrivistes* who had to prove to themselves that they had indeed succeeded, their generation had no need for, nor did it find fulfillment in, the exaggerated, suburbanized, Jewish lifestyle of its parents. Indeed, they were rebelling against all of this, and unexpectedly willing to experiment with the very old, while rejecting the tinseled, middle-class novelties that had repelled them. They wanted to do Jewish things by themselves, they were wary of surrogates.

But they were the counter-culturalists, in search of their own, more genuine Jewish selves. Some remained on the sidelines of the organized community, still shy of the large or established congregations, or bored by their old labels; others were founding or joining smaller, more intimate and less-denominated, cultural and spiritual fellowships. Yet, before their spirit can become more rampant among greater numbers of North American Jews, they will need allies from the top. For something really dramatic to take place, a new community-structure and a different kind of synagogue are required.

The crucial problem in the days ahead, as always before in such seminal and transitional moments of Jewish history, is not only with the choices of the followers. The character, strength, and quality of the leaders will truly determine the Jewish future.

Chapter 8

THE CORPORATE SYNAGOGUE

PART ONE: HOW IT HAPPENED

Eddie Goldfein had first joined, then became President of his then-infant synagogue in Pleasantdale, New Jersey, in the 1940s—"for the sake of my kids." As these younger families began to contribute their share to the mounting baby boom following World War II, they were faced with the need to educate their growing children in some Jewish school—even if only to prepare them for Bar or Bat Mitzvah. It would be impossible to send them—two or three afternoons a week—to schools located too far from their new Jewish neighborhoods or suburban communities. In a way, they began practicing "castor-oil Judaism"—they didn't very much require it for themselves, they thought, but it was good for the children. Many congregations, therefore, first built religious school buildings and youth centers, even before tackling the task of erecting their sanctuaries and social halls.

But if this new and powerful drive to build congregational schools—which virtually displaced the older, downtown private or community schools known as Talmud Torahs—had originally been the "first cause" of most suburban congregations, it would soon lose its primacy. Once they erected their other imposing facilities, the school would become only one of many other interests and responsibilities. There were those

The Corporate Synagogue 175

large building funds that had to be amassed, the social halls and catering facilities that had to be built and managed, not to mention the support staff required to supervise and maintain them. In the process, many congregational schools would reduce their hours of instruction, and otherwise compromise the quality of Jewish schooling as religious education receded in importance, and became less than primary in the hierarchy of values and concerns—and the financial support—of synagogue leaders.

This problem, too would become the bane of some "history-minded" Rabbis—especially those, like myself, who had been trained as educators, and who regarded Jewish education as the central, historical purpose of synagogue life. Large congregations—the unplanned result of growing affluence and social mobility—could not easily coalesce into a single community of interest. As a result, the dominant desires of most of their indifferent members—for less, and not more Jewish education—would become a challenge for Rabbis to overcome. Some threw up their hands and "diplomatically" sought to "make the best of it." For others, it could remain a constant, vexing bone of contention. Sometimes, as we will see, rabbinical efforts to spur ever-larger congregational commitments—of energies and funds—to serious Jewish educational accomplishment, would be deeply resented, even by lay leaders who liked to be regarded as thoughtful Jews.

If, by the 1980s, some North American Jews had begun to seek newer, more intimate, and smaller-scaled religious fellowships, this mood was a far cry from the dominant spirit of their parents in the 1950s. In that earlier decade, Jews were busily "moving up" in every way possible. Part of that movement included a radical change in their religious geography. As they made their way from the crowded city cores to the open spaces of exurbia, they also began building new and larger synagogue buildings.

Powered by the prosperity following World War II, and ably

assisted by a crop of successful and creative Jewish architects—congregations were emboldened to purchase large tracts of land. Enough of those tiny, competitive, scrubby synagogues downtown, they were told. The time had now come to do what Americans do: to "think big." And so, they changed the physical map of Judaism, as monumentally scaled, imposing synagogue "plants" became the rage, with the aid of outstanding designers like Eric Mendelson, Percival Goodman, Louis Kahn, and other notables. In suburban Philadelphia, Jews had even invited the celebrated architect Frank Lloyd Wright to create a daring building for them, which he did, conceiving it as a "traveling Mount Sinai."

The new, spacious, often rambling buildings, were very costly to erect. Thus, large-scale membership drives were undertaken—usually appealing to their sense of "Jewish pride" in their "Jewish citizenship," and not to inherently religious motivations. These were necessary in order to broaden the base of those now required to shoulder the burdens of heavy mortgage and maintenance charges. Clearly, more members require more staff: Rabbis, Cantors and professional choirs, where perhaps none of these were required before; teachers, secretaries, youth and janitorial workers. In addition, a new profession virtually sprang into being overnight, borrowed from the corporate world: the Executive Director of the congregation. That title alone reflects the importance that necessarily came to be given to the business and managerial aspects of these institutions.

They were powerful expressions, but how did they fit the mold of the past?

Historically, synagogues were never uniform in design, exterior shape or style, and they ranged from tiny, single-roomed huts and hovels to massive and ornamental cathedral-like structures. The Rabbis of the Talmud had called them "small sanctuaries"—in their bid to urge Jews never to build synagogues that could rival or outshine the splendor of the fallen Temple of Jerusalem. Archaeologists have unearthed a number of ancient synagogues which were ornately built and deco-

The Corporate Synagogue 177

rated, but all of these seemed to have been small neighborhood houses of worship, not large central synagogues.

Not many medieval communities in Europe could comply with the Talmudic law that the synagogue should be built on the highest spot in town, and should itself be the highest building. One Rabbi had even gone so far as to maintain that "any city whose roofs are higher than the synagogue will be ultimately destroyed."[1] (Roofs, of course, were flat, and used very often for living quarters, and he wanted to make sure that people would not "look down" on the synagogue.) The law was probably honored more in the breach than in the observance, simply because kings and rulers forbade Jews to enlarge, elevate or beautify their synagogues.

Much closer to the experience and memory of most American Jews—who hailed from East European backgrounds—were the simple, barely adorned one-or-two-room *shuls* that sprouted all over their Pale of Settlement in Russia or Poland. While living in Jerusalem in 1968, I tried to recapture the feeling Jews must have had in these prayer-and-study rooms of their recent past, which they transplanted to the Holy City, after their arrival from Europe. I tried, but could not visit them all. Every time I thought I had completed the circuit, there were still scores of others to discover—over stores, on second or third-story landings of apartment buildings, or in garage-like huts at the end of blind alleys and winding lanes. People shuffled in and out, at all hours of the day and night. They sat at old wooden tables on hard, backless benches. Some huddled to themselves in corners, meditating; others were joined in small knots, reading aloud from faded and yellowed folio pages of the Talmud, and arguing fine points of law.

I recalled how my friend and teacher Professor Abraham Joshua Heschel had described these *shul-yidn*—synagogue Jews—of East Europe, and what I saw in Jerusalem then mirrored his own depictions of earlier days: "An old book

---

[1] See *Mishnah: Megillah* 4:23; also *Babylonian Talmud: Shabbat*, 11a.

saved from the countless libraries recently burned in Europe, now at the Yiddish Scientific Institute Library in New York, bears the stamp, 'The Society of Wood-Choppers for the Study of Mishnah in [the town of] Berditschev.' "[2]

The synagogues North American Jews were erecting beginning with the 1950s were all designed to fit in well with the landscape—usually, several acres of it. But did these houses of prayer also spring out of the soil of history and tradition? Or was this development still another American Jewish mutation? There are those who earnestly believe that scale affects and changes quality, and that form, especially in synagogues—when it does not follow function—can lead to dysfunction. "Bigness is badness," they say, taking a page from Louis Dembitz Brandeis. "More is less," they insist, repeating the words of Mies van der Rohe. Even Abraham Isaac Weissman of Jassy—my grandfather—used to say: "*Tzu shein is amol a chissoren*"—"Too pretty is sometimes undesirable." One thing is clear: These buildings—many were elegant and magnificent—were surely the outspoken statements of the Jewish loyalties of those who labored hard to plan and erect them. There is much less certainty, however, concerning another question, which I would contend is the core issue—and it has nothing to do with the size, shape, or physical appearance of their synagogues. What did these Jewish leaders really want their congregations *to say, to do, and to be*—when they pointed these religious pinnacles skyward? Were they monuments to and testimonies of their spiritual strength and understanding? Or was this only their way of cementing into concrete the hallmarks of their own worldly successes?

In the emancipated climate of the New World, where the question of "being Jewish" seemed to have been transformed into a personal, individual option, synagogues would be regarded as "private organizations." Because Jews now lived in the midst of fellow citizens—not estranged but interconnected—

---

[2] Abraham Joshua Heschel, *The Earth is the Lord's: The Inner World of the Jews in East Europe*, Henry Schuman, New York, 1950, pp. 46-47.

who comprised a "nation of belongers," some of them joined as members of synagogues, sometimes even whimsically and thoughtlessly. And because America was also dedicated to the principles of *laissez-faire* and the entrepreneurial spirit, Jewish congregations, too, came under the same spell of privatism. They were the personal affairs of their own members.

It would follow, then, that the private proprietary rights of most Jewish congregations in America could almost never be called into question—certainly not by non-members. They came to regard their own rules and regulations as transcending Jewish history and custom, as if they were "divine rights of property"—their new Torah, which others, outside of their walls, could not tamper with. Like so many other American clubs and associations, they considered that their real purpose was principally for the enjoyment and benefit of their own members. They did not feel called upon to justify or to rationalize their actions, style, or programs—except to their tight membership islands. And even these shifted with the moving sands of the joiners; as neighborhoods changed, members came and went, and with their coming and going, earlier stances and postures were rapidly altered. Thus, almost overnight, Orthodox synagogues became Conservative; Conservatives were made over into Reform—and on and on the "conversions" went. Like America itself, one could hardly look for philosophical consistency among those whose lives were ruled by pragmatics.

But the Great March of the 1950s—that continent-wide exodus from downtown to uptown, or, as in most cases, from areas of older settlement to the newer territories of the suburbs—offered the American synagogue an opportunity of historic proportions for self-conversion. Young families were flocking to them, even if only for the sake of their children, so that they could learn what the parents were not taught at all, or had allowed to decay through disuse.

Together with their enlarged membership and increased support, the new synagogue-school buildings and public halls provided these congregations with dramatic challenges never before available to their predecessors. They could become a vital and influential cultural force in their communities, and no longer center their concerns in themselves, by merely serving as the private and privileged clubs of their financial supporters. If they would link their newfound strength to a larger spiritual vision, they could remove the synagogue from its splendid isolation, and cause it to emerge as an innovative and valued teaching center—truly a *shul*—for all who would come to it: young and old, poor and rich, Jew and Gentile. They had the chance of making the synagogue into a higher academy of Jewish life and thought.

On the other hand, if they remained narcissistic, turned in on themselves, became pre-occupied with expansion for its own sake, and continued to amass more and more members merely to buttress their own organizational strength, they would fall victim to a prevalent American habit: the idolatrous worship of sheer size, mere numbers, and big buildings.

I had been taught by my grandfather that Jews don't always start out full-grown but need nurture and guidance. Then, he said, quoting ancient wisdom, "*Mi-tokh she-lo li-shma ba li-shma*"—"Even those who commence for all the wrong reasons can end up doing things for the right reasons." When I came to Toronto from Rochester in 1956, to serve as Rabbi of Beth Tzedec Congregation, I kept repeating his dictum to myself over and again. Two years later some people were already calling it "Beth Tzedec University." It was relatively simple: I "shamed" its leaders. If they could spend over $15,000 annually for floor-waxing their beautiful building, they should be able to spend even more on serious adult education for the entire community.

Let there be no mistake about it. These large congregations all over America represent a mixed blessing. By their very nature, they pose a serious dilemma; one for which there is no satisfactory or fulfilling solution in sight. Both Rabbis and their congregations—if they will be honest with themselves—must realize that they are destined for unhappy unions if they do not learn to solve it. Simply put, it is a new Jewish problem, spawned in America: the problem of "the lonely crowd"—congregations without a sense of their own community, not even a "community of interest."

I regard any synagogue group whose membership reaches or exceeds 1,000 families as a giant-sized congregation. Adding the families together, we have a community of about 3,500 souls—larger than the population of most towns and some small cities anywhere in the world. It would surely take any Rabbi more than one lifetime to know all these people intimately, let alone to serve them effectively, as pastor and counselor—"to be there when I needed him," as the phrase goes.

Let us examine some crucial and tell-tale data. Based on admittedly incomplete statistics—the best we have, unfortunately—I conservatively estimate that there are at least 300 such Jewish congregations in North America, out of a total number of some 4,500 synagogues. Yet, the combined population of these "giants" adds up to about 1.1 million men, women, and children. This means, in effect, that almost one out of every two of the affiliated—who total about 2.6 million—has consciously chosen to join large congregations, some of which border on, or surpass, 2,000 families.[2]

It was argued that one large congregation would be better than two smaller ones, because of the efficiency and economy of scale. Yet, this did not prevent budgets from soaring and soaring, and since synagogues are customarily supported by the dues charged, so did the cost of belonging—even with

---

[2] Based upon conservative estimates, Daniel Elazar provides raw data for the year 1970-71 of synagogue population and finances. The numbers I have employed are based upon extrapolations from Elazar, in addition to observations of the scene—economically and demographically—in 1983. None of these numbers can be exact, but they are offered to provide the reader with a basis for empirical judgment. See Elazar, *op. cit.*, pp. 72-73; 272; 305-06; 403 (notes).

ever-increasing numbers of higher-taxed members. It may now be safely assumed that few of these 1000-and-more-member congregations can support their undertakings without an annual budget in excess of half a million dollars—some indeed approach and exceed the one million dollar mark. For many of these congregations, concern for meeting budgets has become an all-consuming passion. As a result, there seems to be no limit to the number of new members they continuously seek.

Even as things are, membership in a large congregation is probably much more expensive than in many smaller ones. It costs each of their members $1,000 or more a year to belong, if you include—as one must—the annual installments paid on their longer-term building-fund pledges. These pledges often serve as an "initiation" or "entrance" fee, and they usually range upwards from $2,500, payable over several years. These are surely not congregations for the wood-choppers of Berditschev—the likes of whom were undoubtedly the great-grandfathers of many of their members. Indeed, they may not even be the right congregations for many who do belong—merely to keep up the appearance of suburban success.

Inevitably, in the American scheme of things, people who pay these amounts of money tend to regard themselves as "investors"—or at least, as shareholders. The corporate mentality creeps into the synagogue life-style, and members want their money's worth—according to their own lights, of course. But there is always that older, Jewish ambivalence at work, as well—they know that a synagogue should be more than a business arrangement, and they want to believe that as members of this religious community, they are still part of an intimate fellowship of Jews. This is why, despite the myriads of committees and sub-committees, or the proliferation of budget-oriented activities, they resist accepting some of the rational benefits of bigness. They know in their hearts that Jews are a minority among minorities, and somehow, despite the trappings of corporate living which these excessively large congregations reflect, they seek an intimacy that continues to elude them.

The Corporate Synagogue 183

One would have thought, for example, that the problem of Rabbi-congregant distance—which flows from their condition as a lonely and anonymous crowd—could have been partly overcome by borrowing models from the corporate world: division of labor, chains of authority, and the use of specialists, wherever possible. Or that they might even examine the way in which some cathedral churches—Protestant and Catholic—manage such problems. But no matter how many rabbinical associates or assistants they engage, the Senior Rabbi is always "their Rabbi"—and they often regard any seeming inattention from him as a serious personal affront. If the Assistant Rabbi visits a hospitalized person, and not the Senior, the member often feels slighted. Even if both visit, it can elicit negative comment from the member. "Your assistant was here three days ago," I would sometimes be told by Beth Tzedec members who said that they were accustomed to "dealing with the boss." "I suppose," some would even say, "you have little time for people like me. I may not be active but I'm still important to myself. Next time, don't send your assistant—come to see me yourself." I venture that there is not a Senior Rabbi of a large congregation who has not been "complimented" in similar ways.

The Senior Rabbi of these large institutions is always regarded as the generalist—the "jack," if not the "master" of all trades—and attempts of division of labor have rarely succeeded among the adult members of the congregation. A young Assistant can deal with junior or youth members—the school, or the clubs. But even then, if the rabbinical head of the congregation does not take an active interest in these matters, too, it will be said that he has no real contact or concern with the young. As long as attitudes such as these persist toward the Rabbi and his functions, despite all outward appearances of calm, most of these cathedral-communities will often comprise significant numbers of confused or unhappy members whose major criteria for their synagogue's purposes are far removed from the way many Rabbis see them. Which may account for

184 THE REAL JEWISH WORLD

the fact that scores of Rabbis—some who have outgrown congregations such as these; others who never wished to "tangle" with them at all—have either left the pulpit altogether for university teaching, or had set their sights on Academe, to begin with. It may also explain why so many members of these congregations—especially after their son's Bar Mitzvah—have said: "I really don't see why I should belong anymore. There's very little there, *for me.*"

It is ironical that once the Bar Mitzvah is over many suburbanites should feel little need for the synagogue, when so many of the now-large congregations, it would seem, had only come into being because of the children.

PART TWO: A CASE STUDY

Toronto's Beth Tzedec Congregation was already equipped with its six-million-dollar plant and supported an annual budget of well over $500,000 as early as the late 1950s. It was born of the merger of two smaller downtown congregations that had been established as Orthodox synagogues in the 1880s—*Beth* Ha-Midrash Ha-Gadol and Goel *Tzedec*—and which found themselves competing for members and building fund pledges. Both had set their hearts—at about the same time—on erecting their own places of worship closer to their new residences in Forest Hill Village. Instead, a marriage of convenience was arranged. They joined forces, took a new name, and began a full-scale drive for additional supporters. Soon, Beth Tzedec boasted of almost two thousand family-members. It was an instant giant.

Late in 1955, it opened its massive new bronze doors to a sixty-foot-high sanctuary that could seat 3,600 people when expanded by removable walls. The synagogue also had a large Chapel; shiny new kitchens; two lavish banqueting halls; a professional caterer, offering "French-styled cuisine"; a sumptuous bride's "boudoir"; paneled committee and board rooms; and a congregational school building which housed over one thousand pupils. Your eyes were also greeted by spotlessly polished marble floors, draped wall-hangings, and a huge foyer dominated by a spiral staircase that seemed to float down from the high ceilings. As its Rabbi-elect, I came from Rochester that December—on the Festival of *Hanukka*—to dedicate Beth Tzedec's new structures, in the presence of the Queen's vice-regent, the Honorable Vincent Massey, Governor-General of Canada. Early the following spring, I moved to Toronto to serve as Senior Rabbi of the congregation.

While still a graduate student at Columbia University in Manhattan, I chanced upon a weird but tell-tale "Map of the United States: A New Yorker's Conception"—in the campus book-store. It was designed to remind native New Yorkers, like myself, of their not-so-splendid isolation and insularity. It was, in fact, not so much a map as a pictorial rendition of a state of mind. New York was pictured extending westward to the outskirts of Chicago; its southern boundaries were placed close to the edge of the Gulf of Mexico; Philadelphia, Boston, and Pittsburgh were not noted; and Chicago was a tiny blip, hard by the West Coast.

New York, New York. Half of America's Jews lived there, and even to those of us who studied at Columbia University, our city was the alpha and omega of the coutry, the navel of the universe; virtually the only place the sun rose and set. And as for non-New York Jews, they may have been good Americans, but who had heard from them, as Jews?

Consider then the oblivion ordained for Canada, in our own unconsidered view. Living in Rochester, on a clear day you could see forty miles clear across Lake Ontario into that foreign, unknown country. But even in that neighboring upstate city, who bothered to look and who ventured to see? I had not—for almost ten years, not for Canadians, and certainly not for Canadian Jews.

In fact, it was only in 1955, when I began to receive numerous telephone calls from a Toronto congregation then searching for a new Rabbi, that my interest in looking into the background of that country and its Jewish communities was first aroused. To my surprise, I soon discovered that there, on my doorstep in Rochester, was a vast subcontinent—a "ribbon" of a country, though—about which neither my teachers in university or in the various Jewish schools I had attended ever even bothered to mention. But the more I began to study about Canada, the more intrigued I became. This *was* a country; it did have *its* Jews; it *was*, and *was not*, America.

From coast to coast, fewer than twenty million Canadians then inhabited, for the most part a narrow, hundred-mile band of land north of the United States. There were over five-and-a-half million Jews in the United States—one quarter the total population of Canada. Six out of ten of America's Jews resided in the metropolitan areas of four cities—New York, Philadelphia, Chicago, and Los Angeles. Each of those cities had a greater number of Jews than the fewer than 250,000 then living in all of Canada.

There was also the problem of territory and distance. In all, the Canadian Jewish story in 1956 was little more than a "tale of two cities"—Montreal with about 120,000, and Toronto with approximately 85,000 Jews. One had to travel one thousand miles westward to encounter Winnipeg's 18,000 Jews, and beyond the Rockies to the water's edge in Vancouver to come upon another 5,000, those days.[3]

Canadian Jewry, I discovered, was characterized by problems of time and space, too. To the obstacles emerging from its geography there also had to be added the problems arising from its history. It was one of the youngest Jewish communi-

---

[3] When the 1981 Canadian Census finally appears in print it is likely to show a total Jewish population of over 300,000, but there will be notable Jewish demographic changes in several key cities, in contrast to what had existed in 1956. These are some of the changes expected to be reported: Montreal down to 100,000; Toronto up to 120,000; Winnipeg down to 15,000; Vancouver up to 15,000; Edmonton up to 5,000 from about 3,000; and Calgary up to 7,500 from 3,500.

ties in the world, and immaturity and inexperience are characteristic of the young. But this communal youthfulness, I thought, could also be a very welcome blessing—it could allow for openness, experimentation, and non-dogmatic flexibility in adapting to social change. Despite the ever-present temptation for most Canadians to do things "the American way"—Jews included—and despite the colossal influence of their neighbors to the south (especially on Jews) something of the Old World charm still hovered over Canadians. Europe was still part of their personal experience.

The idea of Europe still alive in North America intrigued and attracted me. I soon learned that "the Jewish neighborhoods"— *der yiddishe gegend*—of Toronto and Montreal were still very much like those I had loved on New York's Lower East Side. Living then, as I did, in an Upstate New York community, where most Jews were already fully Americanized—anxious to be just like everyone else and to walk the earth as full-blooded Yankees—I began to realize that another kind of "American way" was still flourishing, nearby.

Immigrants arriving in Canada—and in those days, more than half the country's Jews were recent arrivals from overseas— discovered two major cultures, French and English, and could not easily come upon a well-defined conception of Canadianism. Moreover, they were not exhorted to adopt a specific Canadian way of life; and from what I could tell, then, none existed, as such, in any case. But neither were they greeted with the frightening spectre of flag-waving, nativist, superpatriots, who denounce foreigners as potentially disloyal. True, from the earliest days, Canada was regarded in law—not only in fact—as a Christian country, and Jews numbered so small a minority that there could hardly be any appeal from the fact of a Christian Canada. Nevertheless, Canada did offer all ethnic communities that so desired, in law and in life, opportunities to foster their own lifestyles in flourishing sub-cultures within the diverse mosaic of the country.

All of this provided those facets of Jewish communal life

which were anchored in the folk-spirit and the national psyche an easy and acceptable accommodation in their newly adopted domicile. Zionism was integral to the Canadian Jewish experience from the very outset, not as a philanthropic enterprise as in the United States, but as a clear extension of the East European way of life Jews arriving in the country had brought with them after the Great War. Similarly, the Yiddish language, theater and press, and a host of other folk vehicles of the Jewish national spirit could never be regarded by these Jews of Canada as alien to their Canadianism. They did not have an identity crisis. The ethnicity of Canadian Jews—their Jewishness—had helped to preserve their faith—their Judaism—and not vice-versa, as had been attempted in the United States. This attracted me, because I had always believed that this was precisely the way normative Jews had always behaved until they were westernized—in Germany, then America—in the nineteenth century. Had Jews not behaved the way they did throughout Christendom, they might long ago have converted to the Church. Once they lost their sense of nationhood and had become only a religious faith-group, they would surely have gone over to Christianity in great numbers. A minority faith that is not linked to a folk and a culture of its own tends to be gobbled up by the majority.

The first Jews I met in Canada appealed to me, because of all these discoveries I had learned and had come to understand about the nature of the country and its "Jewish minority." Ironically—*at that time*—it was this "foreignness" of these Canadian Jews that began to magnetize me in their direction. After almost a year of repeated refusals to offer myself as a candidate for that congregation in Toronto—Beth Tzedec—by means of a "trial sermon," I finally agreed to visit Toronto and to meet the Search Committee as well. We met several times over a period of two days and nights, downtown, near the hotel. I had still not seen their "dream synagogue," then only nearing its completion, but I liked the way they responded to my "Jewish challenges," as some of them called them. I did not yet know what it might mean to be a Canadian—more than two decades later I still don't exactly know—but they gave me the feeling that they were Jews above all else. They looked and dressed like all the other American Jews I had known, yet I immediately identified them as European Jews, still fresh from the Polish *shtetl*, though most of them were either born in Toronto or had come from overseas as very young children. These were *folksmenschen*: They had a Jewish mother-tongue; a few quoted Hebrew texts intelligently; they had always been fully committed to Zionism and its Jewish world-view. Some of their children fought for Israel in 1948, and they were proud of them. They had even agreed that we could establish an intensive Day School if a sufficient number of children would enroll. Nor did they back away from my proposal that they make their new synagogue into a veritable *beth ha-midrash*—a vital academy of adult learning.

For me—and for other colleagues—the principal malaise with life as a congregational Rabbi had always been related to that same problem encountered during my student days, at Pleasantdale. American Rabbis, it seemed, were eternally cast in the same ambiguous and frustrating role: university professors condemned to teaching kindergarten. We were consigned to serving "pinch Judaism." The recipe was always the same: an occasional pinch of tradition; small doses of nostalgia; dabs of the "old-time religion." Bits and pieces of ancestral ways and smatterings of Jewish memories—but never enough to come out whole, or to put down deep roots into the soil of our own history. Nor enough to become a creative diaspora community, by the side of Babylonia, Spain, or East Europe. It was that patch-quilt of sentimentality-without-culture that made me fear for the future of American Judaism. If only these people would worry about their own "Jewish culturation" and would give up their relentless race to acculturate as Americans, there might be some hope. In the 1950s, that hope was not yet in sight.

But those Toronto Jews I had met seemed to be different.

They may have been heading inexorably toward the same goal and fate as most American Jews—in ways still hidden from my view—but they were more recent arrivals, and they still remembered the fundamental skills of their heritage from the Old World. As they spoke, reminisced, or prophesied, I kept repeating to myself: They may not be too clear about where they are going, but they still remember who they are and where they came from. I found myself comparing them favorably—even identifying them—with many Jews I recalled from days growing up in New York. I liked what I remembered about those immigrant New York Jews—not yet completely spoiled by the vain pursuit of becoming 110% Yankee. They had built schools like the Yeshivah of Flatbush and Herzliah, and sought the fullness of Jewish life and culture—for their children, at least. They had not altogether turned their backs on the Jewish experiences they brought to America from their East European homes. The hyphen in their hyphenated Americanism was not seen as a minus sign, but as a proud, self-connecting link. They had dared to be themselves.

There was, I would discover, something about the political climate in Canada that also helped. Jews in America, perhaps even more than most other immigrant groups who landed in that country, had developed an exaggerated and tenacious patriotism: America is God-blessed, the promised land, the best and most favored of nations. To my pleasant surprise, I found that Canadian Jews—like other ethnic groups in the country, but unlike their American cousins at the time—did not regard citizenship, as such, as a prerequisite for happiness, or monocultural espousals as the ultimate mark of loyalty to the state. There was another way in Canada: multiculturalism, or the "Canadian mosaic," as it was then called. Unlike America, this was still a land of immigrants, and it was appropriate for the non-French and the non-English to foster their own native language, literature and community life, as proudly as those two founding "nations" of Canada. To be a devoted Jew, living within your own strong ethnic community, was no threat to yourself or to the country. No one was worried that such ties could be interpreted as a diminution or weakening of one's "Canadianism"—a word that still has no fixed, focused, or final definition.

Canada's Jews did not have to hide their ethnic minority status—they proudly displayed it—as Jews felt called upon to do in Will Herberg's America. There, until the so-called "new ethnicity" emerged in the 1970s, Jews had invented all kinds of subterfuges to shield their minority status. They said that if Jews were only a very small part of America, Judaism, at least, represented "one-third of the country's three major faith-groups"—at the side of Protestantism and Catholicism.[4]

Without ever using the name, in my America—growing up as a Jew in New York—I had always been an "ethnic." This was my way of realizing the Jewishness and the Zionism I had melded into my way of life and thought. Relocating in Canada in 1956 was not like moving to a foreign country. For me, as a Jew, it was more like "going home"—spiritually. I regarded Jewish Toronto as a rare frontier in the midst of a cultivated city. It was still pliant and malleable. Perhaps, I told myself, it was ready to rebuild, in its own ethnic image, some of the Jewish institutions I felt were already foundering in the United States. The synagogue, for example, especially the "giant synagogue."

Which is not to say that all would be milk and honey. Beth Tzedec members, for many years, would still war with each other, in the name of their pre-merged older synagogues. "I'm from the McCaul Street *shul*—'Beth Ha-Midrash Ha-Gadol,'" they would proclaim; or "I'm from the still-older *shul*, 'Goel Tzedec'—the University Avenue Synagogue!" They stubbornly retained this internecine tribal posture for some time to come, causing me to walk a tight rope between two spiteful, non-

---

[4] See Will Herberg, *Protestant, Catholic and Jew: An Essay in American Religious Sociology*, New York, Anchor Books, 1960. According to this theory, ethnic and nationality groups are Americanized—in the third and fourth generation—within the three major religious communities, Protestant, Catholic and Jewish.

integrated groups. It reminded me of the biblical civil war between the ten northern tribes of Israel, and the Judah-ites in the south.

Nor were all of the members as well oriented as the leaders I had first met, and who had impressed me so favorably, during our initial talks. Imposing the synagogue was, but few fully understood what they had built, nor how to put it to its best use. If my grandfather were alive to see their building and to meet many of the members, he would probably have said: "*Zei veissen nit mit vos m'est es*"—"They don't yet know with what you eat it." Some, especially those who wintered in Florida or California, were already talking and thinking like their American Jewish counterparts. They saw this new synagogue as their own "big toy"—a private and luxurious club for those who could afford the joys of belonging.

There were even those—the more competitive business types—who were full of gloating. "At last," they beamed, "we are on a par with Holy Blossom Temple." That uniquely named Reform congregation had made the leap to this same posh area of Forest Hill Village more than fifteen years earlier, and now, these recent émigrés to the Village had built their own new synagogue just one block away from the "mighty one." It wasn't, of course, that these members of Conservative Beth Tzedec were anxious to assert a more traditional Judaism than the one espoused by Holy Blossom. It was, even they would occasionally admit, a matter of "class"—now *they* had "it," too.

It was because of some of these people that more-cultured Jews in Toronto—unaffiliated with either congregation—coined a sardonic description of the new building Beth Tzedec had built only a hundred yards away from Holy Blossom Temple, down the slope of Bathurst Street. "Once," they said, "there was only the 'church-on-the-hill,' but now there is also this new 'night-club-in-the-valley.' "[5]

---

[5] A sociological study of Forest Hill Village, published in 1956, gave other reasons for the overstated needs of some of these types: "The Jews, who began to move into the area during the Thirties [Holy Blossom members]

The Corporate Synagogue   193

Even after the building's dedication in December 1955, there were angry meetings, in which both "former-*shul*" partisans threatened immediate disunion. When "amalgamation" had been legally effected the year before, a Board consisting of some thirty members was not elected, but put in place corporately, by the lawyers of each group, based upon a "deal" that had been struck. Seeing itself as the more prestigious of the two (it boasted of greater wealth) the University Avenue group had pushed successfully for two Board seats for every one granted to McCaul. It was agreed that this arrangement was to last for about a year, at which time "free elections" would be held. It was this, their first election of Board members, which caused havoc. The McCaul people, their antagonists alleged, must have been plotting at secret meetings to overthrow that "nice balance." How else explain the fact, University leaders bitterly complained, that *they* elected more than twenty of "theirs," to less than ten of "ours." They were crying "foul," while their now-successful adversaries hotly replied that "all was fair in love and war"—they had never forgiven the "deal" which had put them to disadvantage and made them look like "second-class citizens in their own home."

I began receiving frantic long-distance calls from Toronto urging me to "hurry up and sign a contract." I never had a contract during all the years of my rabbinate, and had not asked for one now. "Please sign," they exhorted. "When you do, it will help put an end to the terrible squabbling. That way,

---

were business and professional people, with higher-than-average incomes, who had come to [Forest Hill Village] in the hope of escaping from a more purely Jewish community.... Many Jews have moved into the community during and after World War II. The liberal core of original inhabitants [Holy Blossom members, in the main], many of whom have severed almost completely their ties with orthodox Judaism, and who prize their half-acceptance by the Gentiles...felt threatened, like the Gentiles, by the later Jewish influx, regarded by both liberal Jew and Gentile as vulgar, ostentatious, ignorant, and detrimental to the community." See John Seeley, et al., *Crestwood Heights: A North American Suburb*, University of Toronto Press, Toronto, 1956, p. 287. (As explained later in this book, "Crestwood Heights" is a pseudonym for "Forest Hill Village.")

we'll know that you're still coming—no matter what you may be hearing about us now." They wanted me to sign on for five years. "If you sign now, then we'll know you'll really stay and put out this fire."

I was hearing about their continuing inner warfare, not only from Toronto, but from friends who had heard about it and who were calling to dissuade me from "burning myself." But a word is a bond. I went to Toronto to assure those nervous and tense leaders that I would indeed come there as previously discussed, and would be happy to remain—as long as they put their abundant resources to work in ways that would make their synagogue a dynamic and vital influence in the life of the whole community, and not just serve as a private membership club—surely not as the "night-club-in-the-valley."

In my heart, I could only justify so large a congregation if it would properly exploit its greatest strength—perhaps its only and singular raison d'être: While it could not ever be an intimate fellowship in the older European style, it could become an imaginative and magnetic force, a cultural center of unusual attraction for the community at large. They agreed then, but many years later, long after those early fires were put out, a new crop of would-be leaders swept themselves into office. They had become tired of seeing "their synagogue" serve others and not only themselves. They longed, they said, for the "good old days" of close fellowship—something that never was or could be at Beth Tzedec, or the likes of it. Actually, they were reverting to an earlier type. They sought to re-privatize the congregation and to jettison its newly cherished and hard-won Jewish doctrine of community responsibility.

The Board

"...I never go to synagogue unless I have to...but I'm on the Board of Directors...I don't know why."[6] Of course he knew why. He just didn't want to reveal personally what social scientists can tell about him.

---

[6] John Seeley (and others), *Crestwood Heights: A North American Suburb*, University of Toronto Press, Toronto, 1956, p. 215.

The Corporate Synagogue   195

Though he called it *Crestwood Heights: A North American Suburb*, almost everybody in Toronto recognized that sociologist John Seeley's widely heralded study, which appeared in 1956, really dealt with Forest Hill Village—once the rockbound, tree-lined, enclavic stronghold of upper-class Protestant super-achievers. By then, it was becoming a shared preserve. Members of Holy Blossom Temple, followed a few years later by Beth Tzedec families, were moving in rapidly, until they were almost equal in number with the other mansion-owners, the Wasps who came first.

Listening carefully to what that synagogue Board member—and many other Forest Hillers like him—told or didn't tell his researchers, Seeley ultimately concludes that "...churches and synagogues [serving Crestwood Heights] are administered by men who occupy the position of greatest power and responsibility.... Attendance is frequently associated with the maintenance of status and the wish to make good business contacts."[7] Yet, if you did not know that he was describing a religious congregation you would be certain that he was discussing the reasons why many such men join—and seek leadership of—town or country clubs. Status? Business contacts? What had these to do with serving on a synagogue Board? Almost everything, it turns out. In this respect, even the most Jewishly oriented member of Beth Tzedec's Board—then or now—could not easily free himself of this widely accepted "Village style." The mores of this "North American suburb"—epidemic in similar communities throughout the continent   represent an exasperating challenge to most Rabbis. These are the "reasons" for the choice of Board members in most large congregations. In my case, at Beth Tzedec, for a long time, there was a core group—people like those who had first invited me to come, on the Search Committee—who were on the Board because of their positive and loving Jewish concerns. Still, it was always a taxing, balancing act, involving all of my moral

---

[7] John Seeley (and others), *Crestwood Heights: A North American Suburb*, University of Toronto Press, Toronto, 1956, p. 215.

strength and passion, to neutralize those who sat on the Board guilty of the "last temptation"—"to do the right thing for the wrong reason."

In the end, of course, few Rabbis—no matter how highly regarded or respected by the community at large—are a match for the overwhelming power of self-anointed Boards comprised of people who maintain "business contacts" and who rely on one another to defend and maintain their shared status. A Rabbi may appear to be the "Chief Operating Officer" of the synagogue corporation. Everyone knows, however, that he really serves at the pleasure of the Board—not even the "shareholders" have much to say. I surmise that "Seeley's Board member" surely knew about all these matters of power and status, but for obvious reasons, he was not about to admit it. None of us likes to talk about that "last temptation."

Nor was the talk of disunion I had heard about before I came to Toronto a creative or helpful force. It died very hard. Small-town *shtetl* Jews—in the Old Country and here—used to sit at wedding banquets in two separate "camps"—those "from the bride's side" and those "from the groom's side." For many years, that's the way it was at Beth Tzedec. The families of the two marriage partners—the old downtown congregations—multiplied contending cliques and cabals. They did not always trust each other. That was still another price they paid for almost overnight becoming a corporate giant. Often, unknown even to themselves, instant congregations will pay dearly for other things, as well. It takes a generation or more to build mutual confidence, and years of joint effort to learn how to evaluate and find, dispassionate, talented, and dedicated lay leaders who can work together smoothly. This is how a "community" is built. But congregations that are quickly taped together—especially if like this one, they are large, and consist principally of mobile people, highly conscious of their newly won status—tend to squander their energies on political infighting among the recently arrived. Built rapidly by businessmen achievers, they attract a highly competitive group of rivals, in search of high profiles and public prominence. Invariably, there are enough of these among ambitious lawyers, doctors, accountants, and other professionals who are seeking quick entrée into a larger world of clients or patients. Before long, the struggle for power and status dominates elections to the Board and adds unsavory flavors to the taste of congregational life.

These are some of the unpleasant side-effects of quickly assembled, huge synagogue associations. Older, established groups have long since outgrown most of these petulant, enervating petty rivalries. They have their own organizational traditions to fall back on; they have well-tried patterns of behavior that can be called upon to help smooth over the hurdles of new challenges and decisions. There is no need to swallow whole, without knowing how to assimilate them, all of the problems that face them. Instant synagogues are young upstarts who can't wait for mature wisdom to accumulate, and they don't; they have been assembled and put together—and they are ready to go. And go, they do—in many conflicting directions at once, without the calm confidence and self-assurance that seasoned leadership knows how to muster. There were, of course, a number of such mature people on Beth Tzedec's Board—holdovers from the downtown days. But after the grand new building went up, a lot of new ladder-climbers rushed to join "the Club." They sprinted their way toward the top by "running for the Board."

As soon as the High Holy Days had concluded, in the Fall of each year, the Board would appoint a nominating committee, which would invariably consist of a handful of their own business or professional associates, whose main function was to fill the places of the few Board members who had deceased or retired. By and large, the lion's share of the Board was renominated, year after year. And with similar regularity, small groups would manage to get themselves nominated by written petition from among five or more friends. Numerous pre-election political strategy meetings were held in private homes. Then, suddenly we would see the aspiring new candidates at synagogue services—most, for the first time—and they electioneered more than they prayed. Sometimes, personal letters were sent to key members of the congregation by friends of nominees, urging their election. Then came the elections, usually held on a Sunday morning at the synagogue, following the corporation's annual meeting. Despite attempts to "get out the vote" by a variety of ruses—including car pools—usually less then ten per cent of the members participated in any of these annual exercises in "Jewish franchise." The scene was always the same: a lot of noise, tension, and fierce fighting among a few contestants and their bands, which succeeded in souring the feelings of two thousand other members who never came to vote in any case. And the results were equally similar, year after year: two or three new faces—usually those who had not been nominated by the committee—and the rest returned to the Board, given a vote of confidence—by one another, their families, and their immediate business associates, the only ones sure to vote. In such a political environment, it is easy to see how non-issues were made into issues, issues into non-issues. The whole synagogue election process became an annual reminder of my high school days at James Madison, where personal popularity and "good looks" were the real vote-getters, not the imagined and irrelevant "political platforms" of the candidates for school office. But this is what happens when synagogues become corporation-like social clubs. They confer power on immature status-seekers who are searching for little more than self-gratification.

Sometimes, however, when a new group is hungry enough for power, and anxious to show that it, too, has arrived, it can sweep away an entire Board. It can do this if it acts as a party-bloc, and spends enough money on public relations advisers to help create "issues," even though it is really only concerned with a single issue: to get elected fast, and not have to wait on line for other Board members to retire or die. A notorious example of this took place at Beth Tzedec, in 1972.

Advertisements in the public press were paid for at great expense; weird sit-ins were staged, with heavy, pre-arranged media coverage; and similar "guerilla" tactics were copied and applied, under the supervision of a criminal lawyer, hired by a small group to orchestrate its efforts. A sophisticated network of propaganda machinery was also established. All of these things, and more, were undertaken by a mere handful of people intent on wresting power in a hurry. Even then, in what became one of the most hotly contested and widely publicized synagogue elections in North American history, less than twenty per cent of the bewildered membership bothered to vote. But the "prize" these brash and brazen "democrats" had sought was won: control of the corporate power of the giant, with all the marks of their own social success that they thought this implied.

In spite of these side-shows, many less sensational, but more enduring Jewish achievements took place at Beth Tzedec. They serve as a reminder that the giant synagogue does have unique possibilities. But only when it learns how to exploit its power in the service of Jewish life and culture.

Jewish-Christian Dialogue

When Arnold J. Toynbee's monumental ten-volume study of history was finally completed in 1954, it dawned on the Jews that they were an unknown quantity, not only in the popular imagination, but even among the so-called savants of the Western world. Together with most other ancient cultures and groups, he summarily dismissed Judaism—even ancient Judaism—as merely a "fossil of the Syriac civilization." If even the "fathers" were a dead branch of a grafted tree, what could he say of Jews and Judaism in the twentieth century? Toynbee was a strong-minded Christian, not only a historian, and in his view, only "Western Latin Christianity" was alive and well; contemporary Jews and Judaism were nullified as surpassed and transcended, long years before. You might say he believed that Jews were living in darkness and didn't know it.

American Jews were especially offended. In sermons, lectures, even in books—especially Maurice Samuel's, *The Professor and the Fossil*—they lashed back at the English scholar with all their passion, taken by surprise at his lack of knowledge and understanding of the Jewish heritage. They shouldn't have been so shocked—or wounded. At the time, and to this day, precious few Jews paid any attention to the need to educate even "well-educated" Christians. Then and now, most North American Jewish institutions and organizations were far removed from this concern. Instead, they engaged in activities that were geared to putting out "anti-Semitic fires"—real or imagined ones alike. Their principal interest in Christians was—and is—geared to the negative enterprise of "anti-defamation." They would set the record straight, as a matter of good community relations, whenever non-Jews caused them hurt or offended their Jewish sensibilities. Their purpose was—and is—to prove that "Jews are just like everyone else."

This reticence to teach Christians about Judaism is, of course, well grounded in their earlier tragic experience, a holdover from Jewish history. After the fifth century, when Christianity became the state religion of the Roman Empire, the older classical Rabbinic desire to teach the world and to reach out for sincere proselytes, had to be cast aside.[8] And in the ghettos of Europe, or the *mellahs* of North Africa, it would be unnatural—not to say impossible—for them to establish spiritual or intellectual contacts of a serious nature with either the Christian or Muslim world. If there were any of these, they were always pre-rigged polemical debates—not democratic

---

[8] See Matthew 23:15. The author claims that Pharisees will "traverse sea and land to make a single proselyte." This suggestion of an active and vigorous proselytization among the Talmudic Rabbis may be an exaggeration. Yet, the prideful references of the Talmud to such luminaries as Rabbi Meir, Rabbi Akiba, Shemaya, and Avtalyon—tracing their origin to proselytes to Judaism—leave no doubt that the authors of the Talmud were not averse to "recruiting" still others like them. See also the excellent chapter "Conversion of Gentiles" in George F. Moore, *Judaism* (Vol. 1), Harvard University Press, 1932, pp. 323-353.

dialogues—set up by a triumphalist Church to prove Judaism's inferiority to Christianity. (Shades of Toynbee?) These usually culminated either in the burning of Jewish books, repressive ordinances, or even outright expulsion of Jews. True, the royal family of Adiabene, a province of Parthia, had converted to Judaism in the first century of the Christian era, and its Queen, Helena, spent many years in Jerusalem. (Her body was later brought there, to be buried in a tomb that is still standing.) Later, in the fifth century, the kings of Himyar in southern Arabia adopted Judaism, and in the first half of the eighth century the upper classes of the Khazars—a kingdom in the Volga-Caucasus region of Turkic stock—were converted as well. Still, as the eminent poet-philosopher Rabbi Yehuda Ha-Levi of Spain had written in the twelfth century, when Christians and Muslim fight, Jews—who are in the middle—are made to suffer, too. Would they not also be hurt if irenic discussions between *un-equals* replaced disputation and warfare? Jews thus came to fear dialogue as much as debate.

But what if Jews would see themselves as equals, and regard Judaism—not as an imprisoned, ghettoized force intended only for themselves—but as a partner with other religions in the world? There were very few Jewish leaders, even in the middle of the twentieth century, who were willing to face that question courageously and unapologetically. One of them was my teacher, Professor Louis Finkelstein, who had become President of the Jewish Theological Seminary of America just two years before I entered this school. Unfortunately, most of the students and faculty downgraded his efforts. They mistakenly regarded them as "fund-raising devices" intended to lure Jewish tycoons to endow funds at the Seminary—not for rabbinical studies, which they would hardly then endorse—but for what were pejoratively labelled "inter-faith good-will" activities. I felt that he was right and that they were wrong. Under his leadership, and with his inspiration, every Tuesday, during most of the academic year, the Seminary was run on two tracks. In addition to the usual classes at its Rabbinical School or Teachers' Institute, lectures and seminars on Judaism were given to scores of America's Christian leaders, scholars, and clergymen. Known as "Institutes," they covered Jewish ethics, Jewish religion, and Jewish philosophy. While still a student at the Seminary I vowed to myself that if ever given the opportunity, I would establish institutes such as these in my future congregation. If Jews were equals—and not frightened half-persons—they had an obligation to speak to the world. And if a synagogue were to become a place of higher learning—a *beth ha-midrash*—it had to teach the whole community—non-Jews, as well. Unlike those public-relations-oriented Jewish agencies—which I would discover also included the vaunted Canadian Jewish Congress—the point of departure would not be "how Jews are similar to Christians," but to teach about Judaism and Jews just as they are.

In Rochester, these thoughts led to the establishment in the mid-1940s of an annual "Institute of Judaism" held at Temple Beth El and to which I invited the leading faculty members of the Seminary. All-day sessions were held at the synagogue, in which several hundred Protestant and Catholic clergy participated, studying at the feet of my own teachers. It was good to see Dr. Mordecai Kaplan, Professor Louis Finkelstein, Dr. Simon Greenberg, Professor Abraham Heschel, Dr. Shalom Spiegal, Dr. Max Arzt, Dr. Robert Gordis, Dr. Moshe Davis, Professor Harry Louis Ginsberg, and others, year after year, in the midst of my own congregation—not only expounding to its members and the larger Jewish community, but to the leaders of local cultural and religious life generally. But one day a year was all that Temple Beth El's meagre budget could support in those years, and it could only be a symbolic gesture—not the kind of continuing educational program I had really wished for.

Those encounters, however, led to others. Before long, I found that I was also teaching a course on Jewish Thought at the local Colgate-Rochester Divinity School, a leading interdenominational American Protestant seminary. What happened to me—and to Judaism—there made me realize how far away the synagogue had drifted from its real agenda: to become a house of learning and prayer, as the tradition had put it—for all people.

The first few minutes of that "urgent and important meeting" called by Dr. Justin Wroe Nixon seemed an eternity to me and had all the hallmarks of an international crisis about to erupt. Nixon, Professor of Christian Ethics at Colgate-Rochester, was the man who had arranged for that course in Jewish Thought to be offered—the first time even this liberal Protestant theological school had opened its doors to a specifically Jewish subject or to a Jewish teacher. Now, he was sitting across from me at his desk, his twinkling eyes narrowed down to angry slits, forehead creased with emotion, furry white eyebrows moving down, until they seemed to cover his eyelids. As he spoke with slow and deliberate passion, I kept thinking of the title of the path-breaking book written by our fellow faculty member, the distinguished Church historian Conrad Moehlmann. Called *The Christian-Jewish Tragedy*, it had attacked Christians for their insensitivity to Jews. Now I was certain Nixon was turning the tables—not his other cheek—toward me. "I feel betrayed, especially after all I personally did to arrange for your course in Jewish Thought," he began, as I sank deep into discomfort. "Our students are confused and upset. Some are calling for radical changes in our curriculum. They are saying that they know very little about the 'Jewish Jesus'; almost nothing about the way the Old Testament is understood by Jews who know it in the original, not in English translation, as they do; and they're clamoring for courses in Talmud and Jewish religious philosophy. They say that taking your course makes them feel like religious illiterates. But even more disturbing to me is that they are now accusing us—their Christian teachers—with covering over the vitality and reality of the Jewish people and culture. They claim that all they ever get from us on the subject are old theological saws to the effect that Judaism just withered and died once Christianity came on the scene. What have you been doing to them? Don't tell me that you're a secret Jewish evangelist intent on converting us! Come now, is that the way to build bridges?"

I wasn't about to reply to that last question. After all, what had zealous, missionizing Christians been doing about those "bridges" during the last 1,900 years? They weren't exactly busy making love to Jews. Fortunately, there wasn't any need to answer. My nonplused silence allowed for a small break in the tension he had stimulated—and then, suddenly, his ruse was up. He broke into uncontrollable spasms of laughter, and before I knew it, he was protesting loudly: "Boy, I bet you thought I was serious about all this; you must have figured I was about to launch a pogrom." When I finally regained cooler composure, which also took some time, he began to explain what he really wanted to discuss: the strange reticence of Jews to tell the world about Judaism and Jewish culture.

"Why are your people so tight-lipped, almost mum on the subject? Isn't it important to them? Or is it perhaps that they know so little about Judaism themselves that they fear to venture beyond their own world? Still, look at so many of us. Christians are probably more ignorant of Christianity than Jews are—and by that, I mean *Christianity*, not Judaism! Yet, that does not stop them from behaving as if no other religious group amounted to much—or existed, for that matter. For heaven's sake—and I literally mean that—you are a teaching people. Don't Jews understand what that means?"

I could not get myself to tell him what I only surmised then, but have since come to know very well. No, Jews do not always understand what it means to be a teaching people. Especially not those Jews who were busy building those huge synagogues in the mid-1950s, nor many of those who still belong to them today.

It was this kind of challenge which I placed before the Board of Beth Tzedec in Toronto, within weeks of my arrival. At the very least, I felt that this particular congregation—in its special circumstances—needed imaginative projects that would, once

The Corporate Synagogue   205

and for all, lift it beyond self-preoccupation, and help to divert attention from its daily, continuing performance—those petty skirmishes, otherwise known as "*shul* politics." More to the point: I quickly discovered that the Toronto I had come to, was still pre-modern in its all-consuming Christian passions. Sunday "Blue-Laws" were still in operation, prohibiting public activities of all sorts on "the Lord's Day"; the Orange Lodge, consisting of Protestant zealots, was still very persuasive and pervasive—especially its anti-Catholic and anti-Jewish dislikes; and while people spoke of "ethnic values" they kept themselves at a comfortable distance from any "others" but their "own kind"—especially the Anglicans and the United Church people (mostly a merger of Methodists and Presbyterians) who dominated English Canada. In the most elementary matters of community relations, Toronto in 1956 was at least fifty years behind the metropolitan centers of the United States, where the "melting pot" had been the theoretical base for rapid "Americanization."

In a curious way, there was also the question of all those marbled, shiny floors and pulpits—the plush drapes and broadloomed banquet halls. What were they for? Was this powerfully built institution to be mothballed even before it went on active duty? Was it to become a museum, a mausoleum of Jewish life, even before it became a living center of Judaism? In this connection, as I have hinted, comparison with maintenance costs alone—to keep the building spotless and shining—became my ally in launching the Beth Tzedec Institutes in the mold of Professor Finkelstein's models at the Seminary. While I had hoped to build them almost exactly alike—with all-day sessions once a week—the idea itself was so shocking to my Board that I was content to conduct them once a month. Soon, they became a fixed focus of Toronto's intellectual and spiritual community, and prominent poets, scholars, and lecturers from all over the continent would contact us themselves, in the hope of receiving our invitation to lead and participate in various sessions.

The increasing value and centrality of these learning programs for the larger community produced an unusual but tell-tale anomaly: It made ambitious members of the Board vie with one another to chair the Adult Education Committee which assumed the lay responsibility for these Institutes. That had never happened before in this congregation or many like it. Always, the "political" thing to do had been to chair the Banquet Hall Committee, the Finance Committee, the Budget Committee—and other power-sensitive-and-related congregational arms. But, in my time at Beth Tzedec, the Adult Education Chairman became the person who "counted": several men, eager for the Presidency of the congregation, began to use that high-profile position as their royal road to the synagogue's highest office. Few of these committee chairmen, however, regarded these inter-religious educational programs with religious seriousness or personal relevance. Yet, I saw them as an integral part of learning about ourselves as Jews, and thus had put them under the aegis of the Adult Education Committee.

In 1966, at the opening session of the tenth consecutive year of these Institutes, I tried to make clear why I felt that these Jewish programs—sponsored and supervised by a Jewish congregation—were not only properly concerned with Jewish-Christian dialogue, but were also deeply related to the need of Jewish adults for higher Jewish education. The trouble, however, is that most members of large congregations still point their sights elsewhere, mostly inward, as if they still lived in the *shtetl*. Or worse still, many still see their synagogue merely as an "emergency service station"—useful to them only when *they* need its benefits, personally, for Bar Mitzvahs, weddings, and such like. They have yet to make their congregations into academies of higher learning for the whole community.

What I said then, I would contend, applies with even greater force today:

> "Catholic-Protestant ecumenism is designed to help Christian partners to the dialogue to live in charity until the

day that all Christians regard as their ultimate fulfillment—when 'all may be one,' and the scandal of Christian disunity is eradicated. But how should the Jew react to Christian ecumenism and its possible consequences? Does 'Christian unity' resolve old questions or does it, rather, pose new problems for him? What religious responses can he possibly make to those ecumenists whose search for Christian unity is now extended to him and to his brethren?...

"While proselytizing between Protestants and Catholics has now been set aside by the spirit of Christian ecumenism, can the same be said of the continuing Christian need for Jews to 'enter into the fullness'? Father Gregory Baum, a leading Catholic ecumenist in Canada, has been quick to admit that 'Jews have suffered so much from an aggressive Christian missionary approach.' This, he goes on to explain, is why 'they are extremely sensitive and easily suspect the Christian partner in conversation of being inspired by a will to convert. Jews are afraid that the friendliness of the Christian and his eagerness to engage in dialogue are simply the ways of a new missionary technique: while the old missionary came with threats, the new one comes with a smile....'

"*I would call for vigorous training of our lay people in the techniques and methods of religious dialogue as part of intensive adult education courses in Jewish religious thought.* Jews who can engage in such open discussion will know how to meet Christianity, how to evaluate, criticize, and appreciate it, and unhappily, if necessary, how to defend themselves against possible deviations from the spirit of ecumenism and dialogue. Those laymen who are simply warned to avoid the dialogue will not really avoid it—in an open Christian society it is a cultural inevitability....

"Those who exercise Jewish scholarly or rabbinic authority and who claim to serve as leaders abdicate their religious role and forfeit their leadership function by not using this new moment *as a major spur to higher Jewish learning and religious culture.*

"We have very special Jewish messages to bring to our Christian partners-in-dialogue. Those messages, to be sure, emerge from our special history within the context of the traditional Christian world, but we also have Biblical and Rabbinic messages which transcend that history's place. The latter will serve as a long-stifled but now eagerly sought Jewish contribution to the enlargement of religious life and thought. It will emerge out of the dialogue. The first set of messages, however, must serve as a preamble to serious conversation, and they may, indeed, form the ground rules for our dialogue with Christians. Indeed, without prior acceptance of these as fundamental postulates, there can be no true dialogue:

> "(1) Judaism is a living religion; it never died; it does not exist as a propaedeutic to Christianity. The Jewish people is a living people with its own religious, cultural and historical destiny. We cannot begin to speak as Jews facing Christians unless the spiritual integrity of a living Judaism and of a vital people of Israel is accepted as 'a massive fact.'
>
> "(2) Anti-Semitism and anti-Judaism, history teaches, feed upon each other, and they are twin phenomena. We cannot begin dialogue with Christians whose insensitivity to these facts prevents them from recognizing the past role of the church in preserving Christian hostility to Judaism, and therefore, to Jews.
>
> "(3) We cannot speak as Jews facing Christians unless they can say to us what we can say to them: We do not seek to convert you; we are willing to leave to God's doing what is surely God's planning."[9]

---

[9] This appeared in *Journal of Ecumenical Studies*, Philadelphia, Temple University, Volume 4, No. 4, 1967. In an expanded version, it was also given as an address to the national convention of the Rabbinical Assembly in Washington D.C. See *Proceedings of the Rabbinical Assembly*, 1967, pp. 70-83; in still larger form it has also appeared in *Encounter Today: A Quarterly on Judaism and Christianity in the Contemporary World*, Autumn, 1968, Paris, France, pp. 153-165.

Jewish Education: "Continuing Studies"

North Americans, it seems, have finally decided that education is indeed a lifelong process—if not a career. Even professional schools—medical, dental, engineering—have determined that they will not look upon their graduates as free opters of "refresher courses" after receiving the degree, but are urging them to sign on for expanding programs of professional continuing education which their faculties offer. Perhaps all of these and others like them have finally caught on to the wisdom of Robert Maynard Hutchins, the innovative and humanistic educator and former President of the University of Chicago. He is reported to have urged that colleges grant degrees to those who have taken their course—only twenty-five years *after* graduation; and then, only on condition that these "students" prove that they have remained students. They must demonstrate that they have continued to grow in learning.

This view that there are no former students—only students—is, of course, an old and characteristic Jewish attitude. If, as many believe, the idea of elementary schools for children is Chinese, then the idea of education as an ongoing and uniquely adult preoccupation is the invention of the Rabbis of the Talmud. Mature people need mature study, they insisted, and they socialized their insight by creating the necessary institutions to transmit it in tangible form. One was the "Renewal School" for adults, which emerged in Babylonia sometime in the third century of the current era. The other, of course, was the synagogue itself.

The Renewal School, as it may be called, was conducted at the great Talmudical academies in Babylonia for two whole months—during one month in the early Spring; then again, for a month, six months later. It was considered important for mature men to attend, to renew, or "complete" their studies on these two occasions, every year. Known as the *Kallah*—which probably means "completion"—this was far from a "finishing school," but one that continued the adult male's education, year by year, throughout a lifetime. But not everyone could travel such great distances from their home to these academies, and so, in the hands of the Rabbis, every local synagogue was considered the proper venue and vehicle for regular, daily, adult study.

The Rabbis were very strong in their views about the need for a life of unbroken dedication to study. To make the point crystal-clear they enacted religious legislation which suggested that a *Beth Midrash* (house of study) could also be used as a *Beth Tefilla* (house of prayer), but that it was not proper to have a house of prayer that was not also a place of study. The law was specific: They allowed a house of prayer to be converted into a house of study, but not the reverse. In this way, they succeeded in building continuing education into the daily habit of Jews. As we have had occasion to note—the synagogue became a school, or *shul*, the name by which it is known in Yiddish.

By the 1950s, however, the synagogue in North America had become, like so many other institutions there, a child-centered place. Parents not only joined congregations for the sake of their children's Bar or Bat Mitzvah—and the preliminary schooling which these juvenile-oriented rituals required—but also to provide them with a Jewish social environment during their formative years. They themselves were largely absent from the synagogue. From then until now, almost every Rabbi has had to tell parents, "Please don't send your children to services. Bring them with you." Not only did they stay away in droves from religious services, they were also not keen on "going back to school" themselves. They were too shy, too reticent, or possibly too ashamed to reveal their own lack of Jewish culture, to enroll in any of the sparsely attended adult classes offered by most congregations.

Of course, the Institutes of Religion and Ethics blazed a path that helped melt away some of this indifference at Beth Tzedec. As more and more people in the general community started to flock to these interesting and often dramatic sessions, even members of the congregation usually removed from such activities sat up and took notice—and they, too, began to attend, if only out of curiosity. But still another scheme was employed to rouse them out of their accustomed lethargy. It was related to something I had already learned while still a student-Rabbi in Pleasantdale.

I had discovered then, in the 1940s, that if upward-mobile Jews can not often be serious *avant-gardistes*, they do enjoy the idea of being "with it," as they say—doing "in things." They are not only among the earliest purchasers of the newest household equipment and trappings—television and other electronic wizardry—but they also rate high as *afficionados* of the stage and screen. Similarly, they buy the best-sellers—especially those that reach the market with *éclat*—and help those books stay "on the lists" for weeks and months. For related reasons, Jews of this variety—and they comprise the bulk of the membership of large, suburban-style congregations—may not easily accept the idea of "studying in class," but they will be eager to hear a lecture, when it is given by a well-known public personality, even a very serious lecture. Knowing all this, during the two years I spent in that suburban New Jersey congregation—only on weekends—it was possible to fill every one of their two hundred seats for the monthly "adult education evenings" I had arranged. The membership itself consisted of only fifty families, but they and their friends thronged the hall to sit in the presence of the great Jewish teachers and leaders whom I had enticed to come and address them: from my favorites—Dr. Mordecai Kaplan and Dr. Stephen S. Wise—to fine Jewish writers and lecturers like Maurice Samuel, Marvin Lowenthal and Horace Kallen.

At Beth Tzedec, I took an old and obvious garment—a lecture series—and stretched it into a new piece of cloth, with far-reaching benefits. The plan was to transform the learning experience into engaging and exciting events and happenings, centered in charismatic personalities whose inner spark would help ignite the public passion for Jewish life. I wanted something of the greatness of "great Jews" to rub off on my people. This would happen only if education became what Jacques Barzun has wisely called "the grand entertainment." The congregation had to enjoy itself, not in fleeting, passing pleasures, but in the sure knowledge that it had shared personally in memorable moments that could neither be exchanged for others or duplicated. I had known such long-lived joys; they came from some of the mighty Jews I had encountered over the years. Now, I wanted to introduce some of these same grand spirits who had reached me to the members of my community. I had hoped that they, too, would be touched by their strength and power as thinkers and leaders, and to remember as I did—not just another public occasion—but how good it was to feel the presence of greatness and to savor it long afterwards.

This is why we instituted our Great Week-Ends With Great Jews a few months after I came to Toronto. The program was carefully designed to spin off into many other thoughtful areas of community life. We did not ask these imposing men of Jewish life and letters to come and leave—after a single night; they were to spend three or four days with us, as "house guests." Nor was theirs to be just another series of talks, although, of course, there were a number of public sessions which they led, and which, in the aggregate, several thousand people had attended. They were given numerous opportunities to meet various leadership groups in the congregation—the youth, as well as the men and womens' organizations—in intimate "think sessions." These were not mere encounters with subject matter, but with real people, all around the same table.

In these ways, over the years, large numbers of otherwise marginal Jews were made to feel the prolonged and lingering presence of some contemporary Jewish heroes of the spirit. People still remind me of their own favorite recollections. Some recall vividly the warm and loving presence of Moshe Sharett, the poetical former Prime Minister of Israel, and his interior spiritual sparkle and broad humanism. Others bring to mind the long weekend with Erich Fromm, renowned social

The Corporate Synagogue 213

thinker and psychoanalyst, to whose lectures and discussions busloads had streamed from all over Ontario, and from faraway Quebec as well. They remember the intimate glimpses he offered of his early manhood (until he was in his mid-twenties) as an observant rabbinical student in Germany. There are those who cannot forget a Saturday evening lecture given in a sanctuary jammed with over two thousand people, when Professor Yigael Yadin of Israel offered the very first graphic presentation in North America of his startling archaeological finds at Tel-Hazor. University professors who came and sat with the rest of us still remember the excitement of those hours. I think back upon them with special attachment, too. During that same week-end, friends invited to my home to meet Yadin were suddenly struck with the idea of building a museum at Kibbutz Ayelet Ha-Shahar, opposite Tel-Hazor, which now houses artifacts he had discovered there, and which he had so dramatically portrayed at Beth Tzedec.

There were many other great moments at these "week-ends." Elie Wiesel, speaking to us long before he became well-known as the mystical writer-witness to the Holocaust, rousing huge groups to new heights of spiritual insight; Gideon Hausner, prosecutor of Adolph Eichmann, taking us to all the death camps of Hitler—and then back to the new Jerusalem—with acute detail he described the enormity of the Holocaust; Yaacov Herzog, wise and noble student of Jewish life, whose sweeping knowledge of Israel and its place in history gave his listeners a new pride in their Jewishness. The names and the occasions can be multiplied many times over. Those who were there could not forget the scores of "great Jews"—the wise and inspired men and women of our generation's authors, teachers, scholars, artists, and persons of affairs. Their imagination and gifts of spirit quickly settled in on many in the congregation, and this led to what I had hoped might become the new Jewish involvement of the synagogue: the personal commitment of some of its members to serious, continuing Jewish education—in smaller, homogeneous groups, or even one individual on his own.

There was thus born a variety of new-styled teaching enterprises. They ranged from a group of six or seven different home-study circles, consisting of ten or fifteen couples each, to college-youth Sunday Morning Seminars with the Rabbi, where my subject areas ranged yearly from Martin Buber, Paul Tillich, and other religious existentialists to the Jewish motivations of Sigmund Freud and Erich Fromm. Weekly study of Bible texts with an intimate and searching group was inaugurated; it took place every Sabbath morning, prior to the service. Three evenings a week, a College of Jewish Studies was convened for advanced adult students; in the Bible course, given in Hebrew, several young Christian scholars had enrolled alongside Jewish students from across the city.

A new position was also created, the Scholar-in-Residence. The incumbent was expected to offer assistance to individual adults who needed bibliographical or other personal guidance for their own self-study, or who wished to discuss personally serious ideas in depth. Along with the Rabbi, he also served as an ambassador for Jewish learning within the congregation, and in the community.

These new and different undertakings were, of course, in addition to the usual adult education classes run by most Jewish congregations of any size; or the weekly Sunday Breakfasts with the Rabbi, sponsored by the Men's Club, and the study programs conducted by the women through their Sisterhood. There were also annual "retreats" in a country resort, weekends of spiritual refreshment and Torah study, which were conducted as part of our adult educational program. I called them our "Kallah," although one weekend in America could not exactly be said to equal two months in ancient Babylonia. And several of our young men were given personal instruction in Talmud. They went on to enter the Jewish Theological Seminary.

All of these cost money—too much money, Board members used to say—some would actually howl about it and remain forever hurt and unforgiving when I reminded them that I was serious about this "idea of a synagogue" I had insisted on even before accepting the invitation to serve as their Rabbi. Some sought to block my efforts by complaining that I was lobbying; they were not happy with my close connection to the budget-making process in various committees. "A Rabbi should not get involved in the finances of the congregation," they would insist repeatedly. My answer was simple: A synagogue's budget is a philosophical and religious statement; if it spends more money on polishing the building than on Torah and education, it might as well say what it really wants to be. A Rabbi must preserve the character of a synagogue. I never went so far as to remind them of that other description I had heard—the "night-club-in-the-valley." I assumed they might get the point themselves.

It is confidently predicted that within a few years there will be over 125,000 children studying in Jewish day schools in North America; there are already over 110,000. While most of these are schools conducted by community groups banded together in support of Orthodox, or Orthodox-styled, educational goals, something altogether new has come upon the scene in the wake of American laws requiring busing in the public school sector. Even Reform congregations—which always regarded such schools as "parochial" and even anti-democratic—have joined in the recent trend toward separate elementary schools for Jewish children, which a few even sponsor themselves, now that private schools have become popular and acceptable among middle-class American non-Blacks.

In the 1950s, most Canadian Jews were much less concerned than their American cousins about the problem of self-ghettoization which Jewish day schools might cause and perpetuate. But the Forest Hill life-style of many Beth Tzedec members, at the time, did not always match that of most other Canadian Jews—and so it was not easy to convince them that their congregation should establish and maintain an intensive school for Jewish and general studies which appeared to separate their children from all the rest. My own happy experiences as a child at the Yeshivah of Flatbush had proved to me how wrong this view was. But by then, there were even more compelling "Jewish reasons" that made me place the establishment of a day school at Beth Tzedec very high on my agenda. And those Board members who had invited me to come surely knew all about them. Some remembered very well, and they helped; others conveniently forgot, and fought the plan all the way. But one year after I had arrived, a day school was established by the congregation with only eleven beginning students. It has now grown to a school of over 1,000 children housed in two separate locations, and run by its own Board, under the name of United Synagogue Day School of Toronto.

Those compelling reasons can be summed up in a single sentence: Monolingual Jews—without some Jewish language of their own—are shut out of Jewish life because they do not possess the keys to Jewish culture. They are destined to twist Jewish life and experience out of shape and meaning, or even to dry up as Jews and completely depart from the community. In pre-modern religious ages of the past, it was enough for Jews not to be Christian or Muslim, to keep them within their own boundaries. Even then, the support provided them by their own spiritual life needed comprehensive underpinning: the reinforcement that comes when you have your own language, literature and cultural folkways.

In the first three centuries following Jesus, when religious lines were still fluid, and before they were locked out of the Holy Roman Empire, the earliest Jews to embrace Christianity in significant numbers were those who had lost touch with their own language—and thus their culture as well. These were the Greek-speaking Hellenistic Jews of the early diaspora. Then, more recently, after the rise of the modern nation-state, when the Church was no longer the sole denominator of social identity, those Jews in Central and Western Europe who had no Jewish language of their own were the first to seek "emancipation" by leaving the Jewish community completely in order to become "good Germans" and the like. It is estimated that by

The Corporate Synagogue 217

the 1920s, fully half of the Jews living in major Western capitals like Berlin or Prague had intermarried and left the historic fold.

Throughout the centuries, Jews remained fully at home with one another because they shared some Jewish tongue. They created their own versions of languages spoken in the regions in which they lived: Judaeo-Aramaic, Judaeo-Persian, Ladino, Judaeo-Arabic—and in fifteenth century Germany, Yiddish. All of these became "Jewish languages" because they were Hebraized. Not only were they written in the Hebrew alphabet, they were also loaded down with Hebrew words and expressions taken from the Bible. It is not fatuous to claim that all of these diaspora tongues were employed as strategies to keep alive the older Hebrew language and culture. If Hebrew had been allowed to remain only a liturgical language for synagogue use—as it is with a plurality of North American Jews—it would have died long ago, and many Jews would have passed out of the community with it.

In Europe, monolinguists are a rarity; in North America they are the rule. In Europe, Jews often spoke many languages but, except for those few urban centers, retained Yiddish as their own *lingua franca.* For some years now, almost all that remains of Yiddish on this continent—and elsewhere—are a few bastardized and garbled quotations of favorite sayings of departed grandparents; or scrambled and stray words and expressions that have come into American English via New York Jewish comics, writers—and cab drivers. The Yiddish schools of only forty years ago have all but disappeared, especially after the rise of the State of Israel, with its strong emphasis on modern Hebrew as the authentic language of the people.

The Hebrew day school appears to be the only available answer if we are to stem the tide towards monolingualism. It appears to me that only if children are immersed in a total environment—their school, for example—can they imbibe a language, and through it a culture. It is no longer only a matter of developing an elitist group of Jews who have been exposed

218   THE REAL JEWISH WORLD

to intensive Jewish training from childhood on, as Joel Braverman believed. It has now become a matter of life or death for Jewish culture in the diaspora. Perhaps, in part, the "new ethnicity" has re-vitalized North American Jews to an awareness of this need—one that was very difficult to demonstrate to them as recently as the 1960s. Young mothers and fathers today, whose parents had all but rejected the idea of a day school when they were children, have begun to see for themselves what the older generation often refused to understand. It would have been easier to have this generation around—not some of their parents—when the "battle for the day school" was still raging at Beth Tzedec Congregation in the late 1950s. It may have saved a lot of personal wear and tear.

A Jewish Museum

"Judaism is a civilization," Mordecai Kaplan taught us, and when it is fully reconstituted, after centuries of erosion and attack, it will not only speak again in its own Hebrew language, but sing its new music, frolic with its new dances, and create its new art. In keeping with these themes, when the Warburg mansion on Fifth Avenue and Ninety-second Street in New York was donated to the Jewish Theological Seminary, the "Jewish Museum" was opened there in 1947, hard by the Metropolitan Museum of Art. By now, it has become a major American cultural center.

In Rochester, we had begun to collect a few pieces of religious silver and other Jewish antiques, and set up a few display cases, and we called that a "Jewish Museum," too. But with the constant help we received from the New York original, and more particularly from its talented Curator, Dr. Stephen S. Kayser, we were able to borrow traveling exhibits and loans to help our small beginnings appear to be what we were calling it.

The foyer-entrance to Beth Tzedec's new building, when I arrived in 1956, looked more like a hotel lobby; it was bare of Jewish connotations and silent on the meaning or purpose of the grand edifice that stretched out beyond. It seemed to cry out for the "beauty of holiness," as the Psalmist might have put it, or for some matching eloquence from the symbolism of the Jewish past, to confront the luxury of the circular royal-blue rug imbedded into its marble floors. To me, that lobby said: Warm me up; convert me to Judaism; the least you can do is to make me into a living Jewish Museum. In a few years, with the assistance of Dr. Kayser in New York, we became the Canadian Branch of the Jewish Museum of the Jewish Theological Seminary of America. A big title, but we had only a few pieces of our own; the rest were on loan to us from New York, on condition that we build our own collections as soon as possible. Some time later, I tracked down Perli Pelzig, the Israeli artist and mosaicist, and he created a major mural some thirty feet high, to cover a large bare brick wall—floor to ceiling: "The Joys of the Torah." It was already getting warmer.

Today, the Cecil Roth Collection is a permanent part of the Beth Tzedec Museum, which now has large quarters of its own, in a section that was added to the building in 1965. The story of how this important collection came to Toronto is as unusual as the man who once owned these beautiful objects of Jewish religious art. It all began very innocently with a trip to Cleveland, and it would lead to Oxford, England and Jerusalem, Israel, before the Roth Collection would find its home at Beth Tzedec's museum in Toronto.

It is, of course, a cruel irony that one of the greatest collections of Jewish religious objects and other memorabilia should now be found in Prague, Czechoslovakia. The old synagogues of the Jewish quarter are without congregations. All have been turned into beautiful but lifeless "Jewish museums" by the governing Stalinist-Communist authorities. Thousands of Jewish artifacts sit silently in their cases or hang from the walls, looking out on a country that had become Hitler's "warehouse" of Jewish memories. The Nazis had gathered them together from various regions and shipped them to this part of the world either to destroy them along with Judaism, or to establish a world center commemorating and symbolizing the passage of Jews—and their culture—out of history and onto the dungheaps of time. Whatever their purpose, Hitler's henchmen have helped to highlight a tragic fact: Not only is Middle Europe now almost *Juden-rein*, but the once-proud possessions of its synagogues have either been destroyed or removed far from the reach of the redeeming hands of living Jews elsewhere. Only a few private persons have been able to "keep alive" some of the quaint and charming religious *objets d'art* that adorned Jewish life in recent centuries, and their very personal collections are the product of a lifetime devoted to a loving and arduous search.

Knowing all this made me jump to attention at the "The Temple," the Reform congregation in Cleveland. I was there as guest preacher for its Rabbi, Dr. Abba Hillel Silver, to address the Sunday morning lecture-services he was still conducting. Following these exercises, he took me on a tour of the building and showed me the congregational museum as well. "We've been collecting the objects," he said, "for many years, now. We have no more room for any others. Otherwise, we would try to acquire Cecil Roth's items. You know, he's leaving Oxford to live permanently in Israel, He's just finalized plans for his library and manuscripts to go to the University of Leeds, and I hear via the grapevine that he may now be ready to make similar arrangements for his Jewish art objects. But for all I know, he may have sold the collection by now."

There was no time to waste. After our lunch, I rushed back to the hotel and placed a call to Cecil Roth in Oxford, where he was Reader in Jewish Studies. It would be futile and frustrating to wait until I returned to Toronto to ask for a Board meeting to consider the possibility of purchasing the collection; that could take weeks, if not months. Cecil Roth was a distinguished writer on Jewish art, renowned historian, and an old friend; he had also been our guest at "Great Week-Ends" and had relatives in Totonto whom I also knew. "Yes," he finally admitted in his high-pitched nasal voice, "the collection is still available. But only on certain conditions." "Would you be willing to have Stephen Kayser come to inspect it on our behalf?" I asked, without a clue as to whether Stephen would be available or willing to run this errand for me. He agreed, but it would have to be in the next few days, as he was going abroad shortly thereafter. I phoned Stephen immediately at his retirement spot in Santa Monica, California, and put that detail into place. Now, all that remained was to get my people to agree to the whole idea.

The next afternoon, back in my study in Toronto, I was telling two trusted friends—key leaders of the Board—that whatever we did would have to be fast, decisive, and elegant, to use the language of General Bar Lev, spoken two years later, in describing the Israel Army's success in the Six-Day War. They agreed to have Dr. Kayser leave the next day for Oxford. "If the Board objects later, we'll pay for his trip ourselves," they said. To which I added: "And if the synagogue won't pay for the collection, I'm sure I can get one or two individuals to donate it." They smiled, then winced, hoping I didn't mean them.

The following week, Stephen Kayser returned to Toronto full of glowing reports about the "wonderful and beautiful objects" he had just itemized, and handed me an inventory of each piece, together with his estimate—both artistic and commercial. "Roth is willing to sell the whole collection to you for the price indicated. But he wants to keep the cream in his hands for removal to his new apartment in Jerusalem. You can have about one half of it now, but the remainder stays in his safe keeping in Israel until his demise. That's the only way he'll agree. He has other offers, but he likes you and this congregation, and I surmise that as a good Englishman he has a warm spot in his heart for Canada." And then he winked at me, with this: "But you'll have to make up your minds quickly." He knew, of course, that *my* mind had already been made up in Cleveland.

I had already been in Toronto almost ten years by then, and I knew my Board. If this were a matter dealing with stocks or bonds they might be quick to "make a deal." But what if it were only what it actually was—only a collection of old Jewish religious objects? They might be interested if they thought they were getting a bargain, or that these items would skyrocket in value, over the years. Still, I chose not to present the case for its acquisition on these crass terms. There was, I thought, a better way: to have someone present this to the congregation. How could they refuse a gift? What I didn't count on, of course, was the problem of housing the collection adequately. And that's precisely what became a point of contention for the next two Board meetings. Finally, with the collection now assured them from patrons I had contacted, and with the help of those two key leaders, we got the Board to agree to build an appropriate home for the collection: a large Museum room, all for itself. Considering that they were in the middle of a building-expansion program at the very time, it was better to erect this lovely addition than, say, extend the banqueting facilities even more. In the end, the Roth Collection beat our Bar Mitzvah parties; but not without a contest or those endless, contentious hours at the Board.

Cecil Roth, historian and art connoisseur, Jewish teacher and writer, died five years later. I was surprised by his morbid forebodings, even his superstitions. He kept telling me that he would never live beyond seventy. Strangely, he was seventy-one when they laid him to rest in his beloved Jerusalem. Scores of illuminated *ketubot*—Jewish marriage contracts—most from Renaissance times in Italy, had been hanging on the walls of his penthouse apartment in the Talbieh section of the city. One of them narrowly missed being hit by a bullet that ripped into the outside door leading to the roof-terrace. The incident had occured early in the week of the Six-Day War in June, 1967. Jordanian Legionnaires had been pumping bullets into this neighborhood, from the top of Mar Elias, a Greek Orthodox monastery on the road to Bethlehem which they had transformed into an advance-attack post. When I returned to his apartment after his death, I could still "see" Cecil pointing to the bullethole, as he did throughout 1968, when I used to visit him frequently. "You see," I could still hear him saying, "*your* collection is charmed. It survived the Arab attack. It won't be long before it gets to you. But if—Heaven forfend—there's another war here soon, I'll see to it that it remains unharmed, even if I have to go outside myself and tell the Arabs to stop shooting at Canadian property." And here it was, barely two years later, and I was called upon to eulogize him at a large memorial meeting held at the Van Leer Institute in Jerusalem, thirty days after his passing. Together with me, the other memorialists included Abba Eban, his fellow "Anglo-Saxon" immigrant to Israel; Geoffrey Wigoder, a ranking member of the editorial board of the *Encyclopedia Judaica*, the monumental work Roth edited; and the ambassador of Italy to Israel. In 1969, just a year before he died, Cecil Roth was appointed a *commendatore* of the Order of Merit of the Italian Republic for services rendered to Italian culture.

I had heard ominous rumblings and rumors coming from the direction of some Israeli government officials that we might have trouble shipping these objects out of the country. They would have to consider very carefully, it was said, whether these pieces, now housed in Jerusalem, should be regarded as "national treasures of the Jewish people"; if so, they said, "Israel, not Canada, would be the appropriate place for them to be kept permanently." This was most unsettling news, and I quickly arranged for the legal services of my old friend, Gideon Hausner, once the State Prosecutor of Adolph Eichmann and then a Member of the Parliament with close ties to government circles. He was swift, efficient, and effective. Within ten days after taking the matter in his hands on our behalf, several large containers loaded with the remaining "Jerusalem section" of the Roth Collection arrived in Toronto. A short time thereafter, in the presence of his widow, Irene, Dr. Stephen S. Kayser, and many of his friends, all of Cecil Roth's prized pieces were finally reunited at stirring dedication ceremonies held at Beth Tzedec. Altogether, the collection was a gem. One of its rarest items is the only known "Chinese Megillah"—a Scroll of Esther with colored sino-styled illustrations, hand-painted by Chinese Jews living in Kaifeng, the capital of Honan Province, whose ancestors settled there in the days of the Sung Dynasty, probably as early as the ninth century. Soon, it became necessary to appoint a part-time curator, as guided tours were required for the many visitors from all over the world who made it a point to come to the Museum. It also became what it had to be—a teaching arm of the synagogue. Special lectures relating to Jewish art, with leading experts on hand to explain this little-explored area of Jewish culture, became a permanent feature of the expanding adult education program. Still, only a tiny portion of the congregation allowed itself to take these things seriously, despite the growing awareness in the larger community that Beth Tzedec had become a major teaching institution, with a mighty impact far beyond its own clubby membership.

I was coming to the unhappy conclusion that almost nothing serious could bestir most of those who had joined this congregation. Few were there for love of Judaism. Fewer still understood that bigness could beget grandness, and that a sense of nobility comes with personal commitment and obligation. It was not in the hearts and minds of people such as these to reach out for exciting Jewish achievements. But for a handful of people, the collection would never have reached Toronto.

Yet, it is clear that a small, intimate and sharing congregation, unlike this or other mammoths, could never hope to achieve these or any other large benefits for the greater community. This is the one saving grace to their bigness. And the pity: Pining after what they are not, these synagogues have severe difficulty becoming what they could be. Too often, they remain "private locals" when they have the power to be "public cosmopolitans." That earlier, bedeviling middle-class need of conspicuously displaying Jews in North America—to make their giant synagogues serve principally as a showcase of their

The Corporate Synagogue 225

dominant material desires, and not as centers of Jewish spiritual culture—dies exceedingly hard. It lingers on as the overwhelming *leitmotif* of their congregational leaders—ever-ready to give their constituents what they want, not what they need—who still see themselves as corporate executives, even when they are no longer businessmen, lawyers, or accountants, but housewives and mothers.

In the spring of 1982—almost ten years after I had departed from Beth Tzedec—and in the midst of an agonizing war between Israel and the P.L.O. in Lebanon—it was still business as usual. A Toronto newspaper was headlining the fact that "Beth Tzedec, the largest synagogue in Canada and one of the three largest in North America, has elected its first woman President...mother to six children...she now has become 'parent' to 8,000 members of Beth Tzedec." And what was the sensitive, spiritual word that would now be spoken to the paper's religion editor on this momentous Jewish occasion, during those trying, heart-wrenching days? My grandfather would have read it and said that one would not know whether to laugh or to cry.

"Already, she says," the editor duly reported, "she's finding it's a full-time, though wholly volunteer job [sic]. She chairs the executive, is an ex-officio member of the synagogue's 22 committees, carries out policy, oversees staff problems, confers almost daily with the senior rabbi (discussing) 'everything *from getting the landscaping done to hearing complaints about parking.*' "[10] (Emphasis added.)

Alas, a whole generation had already passed—almost thirty years since they had first built the instant giant—and the congregation was still awed and preoccupied by all the wrong things. They still do not fully know who they are, why they are there—or what to do with what they have.

---

[10] *Toronto Star*, June 19, 1982.

PART THREE

JEWISH LEADERSHIP IN NORTH AMERICA

Chapter 9

THE NEW ESTABLISHMENT

There are, an old folk saying has it, only two kinds of Jewish leaders: the "Jews of the Kings" and the "Kings of the Jews." But when I first heard my grandfather repeat that aphorism at one of his Sabbath afternooon "Tea-and-Torah parties," he demurred. "The best of our leaders," I overheard him say, "are neither. They are not like those Jews of the Kings—aping the medieval court Jews who fawned on their imperial masters, seeking first—and for themselves—the special favors of their office. Nor are they like most of the monarchs of Israel whom even the Prophet Samuel had warned against: 'Kings of Jews' today, like the ancient ones they imitate, only lord it over us for the love of their power and in pursuit of their vanity."

A long and stirring discussion ensued among his learned friends. "What in the world are you saying, Reb Avraham? What leader doesn't sometimes use his power for the wrong reasons?" "Not the ones I have in mind," my grandfather answered calmly. "No, we don't need kings of Jews or Jews of kings. We need Jewish Kings; and I emphasize *Jewish*. Who are they and what are they like? Have you forgotten your Talmud? Does it not itself record the question 'Who are our real kings?' And do you not remember its answer? 'The Rabbis are our Jewish kings,' which the commentators explain by saying that they are not kings, or lords, at all; only learned men faithfully serving their people, and not seeking to be served by them. Yes, more than ever, we need learned, committed Jews as our leaders, today. We need Jewish Kings."

The fact is, romantic that he was, my grandfather was again idealizing the past, although as usual he was on the right Jewish track. Even the leadership styles of the ancient teachers he revered were uneven and varied. There was, for example, the taciturn Shammai who ruled his constituents archly and with stern authority, while his contemporary, the gentle Hillel, was all humility. Yet, both lived in the same Talmudical age, and were equally respected. Later, in the medieval period there were still other changes that reflected a different social and political reality. Jews were virtually the vassals of the local Bishops and feudal lords, and their leaders had little means to help or save them in the face of the great exterior powers of church and aristocracy. But always the disciplinary power of Jewish community leaders over their people was enormous, because a strong, shared ethos was at work: Jews work together and stand together in the face of the external threat. Their leaders could be relied upon because, in the end, all Jews—the lowly and the mighty—shared a single Jewish fate. Theirs was a *communitas*—with a unified view of life. But in the new world, "voluntarism," freedom, and materialism changed much of that.

Still, something of the Old World did make itself felt in crucial ways, at a critical juncture in Jewish history. A handful of unusually sensitive men had come to America from Germany in the mid-nineteenth century without whom the lives of many East European Jews could not have been the same. One of them, Jacob Schiff, became a byword for years, and I remember my grandfather lauding his name. He and a few others who surrounded him, my grandfather repeatedly said, represented the very best of the "Kings of the Jews," although as a rich "German"—a *deitsche*—Schiff was still somewhat suspect, and far from the ideal he himself had in mind. Courageously acting out the principles of their *noblesse oblige*, the Schiffs, the Warburgs and others of their "crowd" had insisted on the right of East European Jews to find refuge in the United States. Without them, many immigrants might never have arrived there at all. They built institutions and agencies which assisted hundreds of thousands to immigrate, and then to adjust to the new life. Never mind that, once-arrived, assisted, and successfully settled, the newcomers often regarded their benefactors as adversaries, and they soon embarked on their own blueprint for a new Jewish community structure in America—much of which still stands today. But few of them would be able to match what Schiff and his friends had achieved. Oscar Handlin, eminent American historian, explains it this way:

"Of this historic obligation of the rich toward the poor Jews such a man as Jacob Schiff was eminently conscious. Raised in the Frankurt ghetto and later familiar to the banking circles of Europe, he was a maker of railroad and industrial empires. Riches and power were for him not ends in themselves, but means to assist the Jews in performance of a universal mission. He saw himself, the *nogid*, or man of wealth, as a *shtadlan*, or intermediary between Jews and the rest of the world; and what bound him to Jews everywhere was the conviction 'that as Jews we have something precious and of high value to mankind in our keeping, that our mission in the world continues, and with it our responsibilities of one for the other.' In those words he expressed the sentiments of the successful and powerful men of his generation."

Power, leadership qualities, authority, and matters of social status are no longer the same in the Jewish America the East European immigrants and their offspring have fashioned. Decisions made for Jews by those who speak in their name are often unrelated to truly profound Jewish needs. A new breed has come into authority for whom Jewish leadership is essentially the pursuit of but two pragmatic goals—good public relations and successful fund-raising campaigns. There are not many "Jewish Kings," although in the almost-fifty years since I first heard that expression that Sabbath afternoon, I have met a motley lot of "pretenders to the throne." Some were woefully miscast, serving by default—amiable enough, just incompetent. Others, roguish wolves in sheep's clothing, were only thirsting for more and more dominion. They were not only "conspicuous consumers," in the language of Veblen—but also conspicuous promoters of their own self-advertisements. Fortunately, there were always a few great and glorious ones, too, whose reach exceeded their grasp, and who sought little for themselves and much for their people.

What was it like for leaders in times past, and what are the new dynamics of their calling today? What follows here is a short story of Kings: Kings of the Jews; Jews of the Kings; as well as that rare, but important species—Jewish Kings. It may help provide clues to the deceptive and self-defeating games many Jewish "leaders" are now playing before the eyes of their mostly mute and consenting followers. But leadership is a direct function of followership, and perforce, this tale also reveals as much about both modern and contemporary Jews themselves—and the radical changes in social values they have willingly accepted, in order to alter their old, and bolster their new, self-image.

If one can pin down moments in time which become major turning-points in history, then it can be said that in Paris, in March 1807, Jews officially said goodbye to the Middle Ages and entered the modern era. Nine months earlier, Napoleon Bonaparte had set the stage for this remarkable change in Jewish direction by calling for the establishment of what amounted to a Jewish "World Parliament"—it was actually known as "The Assembly of Jewish Notables"—to meet in the French capital in order to find answers to twelve crucial questions he put before it. He wanted to know whether Jews could still retain their ancestral religion if they would be granted civil rights. Could they become citizens, like the Christians, while still practicing Judaism?

One hundred and eleven relatively undistinguished delegates to this "Jewish Parliament" were elected by their local leaders from most of the communities in Central, Western, and Southern Europe. German-speaking Jews came from Alsace-Lorraine; Sephardic Jews, banished from Portugal, but now living in the south of France, were also there; and French-speaking Jews from Paris, Bordeaux and Marseilles were joined by representatives from the Kingdom of Italy. The "Assembly," having answered all of Napoleon's questions in the affirmative—yes, Jews could remain "religious" while accepting national citizenship in their respective countries—gleefully acceded to the Emperor's request that their own conclusions now be given "ecclesiastical" imprimatur. Impervious to all obstacles of history and in typical Napoleonic style, he demanded nothing less than that they proceed immediately to reconvene the Great Sanhedrin—the Supreme Tribunal of seventy-one judges in Jerusalem which had not met for the more than seventeen centuries since the Temple fell. On October 6, 1806, they sent this proclamation, written in four languages—Hebrew, French, German and Italian—to the "whole Jewish world":

"A great event is about to take place, one which through a long series of centuries our fathers, and even we in our own times, did not expect to see, and which has now appeared before the eyes of the astonished world. The twentieth of October has been fixed as the date of the opening of a Great Sanhedrin in the capital of one of the most powerful Christian nations and under the protection of the immortal Prince who rules over it. Paris will show the world a remarkable scene, and this ever memorable event will open to the dispersed remnants of the descendants of Abraham a period of deliverance and prosperity."

When the "almost-messianic" event actually did take place—not in October as planned, but in the spring of the following year—it was, in a sense, anti-climactic: All the answers already provided by the "Assembly" were quickly approved. What ensued, however, has often happened since—when weak-kneed, modern, "emancipated" Jews feel called upon to prove their loyalty to the state, to the world, or even to mankind! They were more than 100 percent "loyal"; they were "110 percent loyal"—and then some.

After strangely pleading that Rabbis no longer exercised power over Jewish communal life, they stressed the view that, in any case, the authority of the Jewish community over its members had broken down by lack of organization and lack of funds, ever since communal dues had become voluntary after the French Revolution. They were really telling Napoleon, themselves, and the rest of the world that the "Jewish people" as a corporate entity had ceased to exist. And to prove the point, in case it had been missed, they proceeded to adopt a rarely-quoted but very tell-tale declaration. Thus did they decree: "A French Jew considers himself in England as among strangers, although he may be among Jews.... To such a pitch is this sentiment carried among them that, during the last war, French Jews have been fighting desperately against other Jews, the subjects of countries then at war with France." Little wonder that East European Jews, who never forgot this sentiment of their "emancipated" brothers in the West, scornfully regarded the "freedom" they had sought as nothing less than a new form of slavery. That is, until some later came to America themselves and unwittingly made it possible for their children and grandchildren to behave no differently, in their own lust for recognition as loyal Americans—even if they themselves did not.

Strangely, all their fawning on him, and their protestations of utter loyalty, did not prevent Napoleon, just one year later, from issuing a decree against "his" Jews for "lack of patriotism," accusing them of shirking war service and of espionage on behalf of his enemies. But this was only a temporary measure which was soon modified. The trend had already been set toward more and more public Jewish displays of their desire to live as fully respected citizens of the state. With the establishment of the "bourgeois monarchy" under Louis Philippe, the last vestiges of public discrimination against them seemed to have been eliminated. In 1846, Louis Philippe himself shrewdly and ironically observed that he, too, had recognized "the capability of the Jews to become civilized. Regardless of the religious tie which unites them in the various lands, they have succeeded in becoming Frenchmen in France, Englishmen in England and so on.... They were almost wedded to the good qualities, sometimes even to the faults of the nations in whose midst they lived."

I have great pity for those harried and confused men of Napoleon's "Great Sanhedrin" who, like Jonah's gourd, "came up in a night, and perished in a night." Despite their relative recency as modern Jews, even their names have been all but forgotten by subsequent generations, unlike the well-remembered and frequently quoted ancient Rabbis of the real Sanhedrins of Talmudic times. Yet to examine the fruit of their efforts is to discover the seed of much of modern—and contemporary—Jewish behavior. Their answers to the Emperor reveal the way emancipated Jews, from their days forward, have tried to interpret and define themselves in terms of the expectations of the dominant culture of the nations among whom they lived. They fashioned all of Jewishness into simply another religion, and in the service of this prevailing view they actually invented the modern word "Judaism." It helped them achieve a neat orderliness and definition: A Jew is one who practices Judaism, just as a Christian follows Christianity. Each is the same, despite external appearances; one has a synagogue, the other a church. In relentless pursuit of the blessings of their new citizen-neighbors—whose differences they saw as enshrined in a church—they re-defined themselves by twisting out of their own historical path. While Jews had always believed that they constituted a nation, or a people, who "lived a Jewish way of life," these *nouveaux-moderns* could only see themselves as private persons, citizens who "practiced Judaism"—or, if you will, as members of the "Jewish church."

The very term Jew harks all the way back to the fifth pre-Christian century, when King Ataxerxes of Persia called his overseas province centered in Jerusalem by the new name "Yehud." The Romans followed suit, four hundred years later, and latinized that name into "Judaea." Thus, Jews—the *Yehudim*—or those who lived in Yehud, or Judaea—were nationals of that province, not members of a religious sect like the Christians. They were "Judaeans"—"Jews," not Mosaists, or Sinaists. Still earlier, in the Hebrew Bible, the Jews were called *am*, or *goy*—a people, or a nation—they constituted a corporate civilization, not a church to which they were converted. Until their sometimes mindless, often ill-starred, love affair with what they thought was modernity, Jews had never built dichotomies between what we now separate out as "culture," "religion," "the state," or "the nation." In short, they were a closely-knit family, whether at home in Judaea or later, dispersed across the globe.

But something new and strange occurred when they came in their vast numbers to the open society of America. Here, modern, emancipated Jews of the West were faced head-on with the still-medieval Jews of the East. The "family" began to splinter into pieces. What had been a community would now become little more than a cluster of private, voluntary organizations, vigorously competing for prestige and the role of "Jewish spokesman," no less than for dues-paying members. To complicate matters even more, they were caught in the trap of the dominant illusion of the day: America was a "melting pot," and to be a "good Jew" was to be a "good American," just "like the Gentiles." Their leaders, of course, were the first to prostrate themselves before this new American deity. The richer, the more "American" they became, the more power they would wield over their Jewish neighbors.

To be regarded as a successful Jewish leader was to be seen as one who could "curry favor"—or possess clout—with "Gentile

America." In a classic novel of American Jewish experience at the turn of the century, the hero of Abraham Cahan's *Rise of David Levinsky* reflects on his participation in this process, a mere twenty-five years after his arrival as an immigrant from Russia:

"I was born and reared in the lowest depths of poverty and I arrived in America—in 1885—with four cents in my pocket. I am now worth two million dollars and recognized as one of the two or three leading men in the cloak-and-suit trade in the United States....

"Most of the people at my (resort) hotel are German-American Jews. I know other Jews of this class. I contribute to their charity institutions.... Though an atheist, I belong to one of their synagogues.... I am a member of that synagogue chiefly because it is a fashionable synagogue. I often convict myself of currying favor with the German Jews. But then German-American Jews curry favor with Portuguese-American Jews (who arrived here before them) just as we all curry favor with Gentiles and as American Gentiles curry favor with the aristocracy of Europe."

Yes, Kings of the Jews they were; but not Jewish kings.

And even many years later, when East Europeans in America were no longer immigrants, or impecunious, but settled and economically secure, they were no different. They were mobile and on the move, as one scholar has neatly summarized: "Just as the middle-class Baptist or Methodist is likely to join a suburban Presbyterian church in the course of his rise to a position of elite affluence, and then move on to an Episcopal church in order to assimilate into the upper class, so the Orthodox East European Jew rises out of the ghetto and joins a Conservative synagogue uptown or out in a largely Jewish suburb, and perhaps eventually finds a Reform congregation even more congenial to his tastes as he moves into a predominantly German-Jewish upper-class community."

Nonetheless, these Jews are not exactly carbon copies of those Baptists and Methodists, despite the old saw that Jews are "like everyone else, only more so." Their "smooth" upward movement is often burdened by feelings of guilt and confusion, and dumps its load of pain and inner tension. These feelings of guilt over their worldly success are not shared by too many other achievement-oriented Americans. Unlike Jews, they have no need to linger over haunting memories of Hitler's Holocaust, nor do they live in constant fear of still another to come, considering the recent and chilling Arab threats to "drive the Israelis into the Sea." Nor do they have to keep in mind the earlier fulminations of the German-American Bund, or the machinations of old Henry Ford and his ilk; the crackpots of the right, lusting for the Jewish scalps "because all Jews are lousy Communists"; or the radical terrorists on the left, who foment anti-Semitic acts "because all Jews are capitalist whores."

Unexpected forces such as these help to account for their ambivalence as Jews, and the paradox of their "off-again-on-again" will to survive as a community. They did not expect to remain a family—they wanted to join America on what they thought were America's terms—yet, in spite of themselves, they remain a family. They sought to escape the Old World and to destroy its memories in the New. Yet, even if they do not wish to remember, the changing, threatening parade of events does not permit them to forget. American Jews still read their morning newspapers in fear and trembling. They ask, "Will the news, today, be good or bad for Jews?"

Jews have lived through turbulent years in the past three decades or so. For reasons often beyond their control, the establishment of the State of Israel in 1948, in many ways, created more problems for them than it has yet been able to solve: the absorption of hundreds of thousands of depressed, "displaced persons"—some "graduates" of the concentration camps of the Nazis, and others refugees from Arab lands or Communist-bloc countries—all of these jobless, homeless, speaking a potpourri of languages and reflecting a mixed-salad of cultures; the Six Day War of 1967 and the Yom Kippur War of 1973; the menacing terrorism of the Palestine Liberation Organization and their assorted colleagues-in-arms around the world. Not to mention the persistent problems at home: rampant intermarriage and widespread Jewish illiteracy. There was room for hope that in such supremely testing circumstances, creative, and even revolutionary, leadership styles would have emerged.

Yet, this recent chapter of our story of Kings is the saddest of all. The "monarchs" of today often speak as though they were responding as fully and totally committed Jews who are forever linked personally to the long-term survival interests of their people as a cultural and spiritual force in the world. There are very few Jacob Schiffs among them. Alas, so many of them are fleeting and ephemeral, cresting as "leaders," and then disappearing from organized Jewish life after the most recent emergency appears to have subsided. They measure up neither to the importance of the times, nor to the honors that have been gratuitously bestowed upon them by a myopic community. (Only the "sectarian" Orthodox community—led by the Lubavitcher Hasidim—have responded with profound new vigor, even with originality and inventiveness. But, they do so, unfortunately, as we shall see, by going back to their medieval East European lifestyle, shutting the door, and bolting the lock, on the gates of their airtight, home-made ghettos.)

There was even additional help from the environment itself. The acceptance by most Americans—in the wake of the Black Revolution of the Sixties and Seventies—of the new ethnicity as a valid expression of Americanism—also provided the newly sensitized Jewish community with uncommon opportunities for finding and raising up brave and bold, new-style Jewish Kings. A few did arise, but they are a minuscule, relatively unheeded, minority. From coast to coast there currently exists a leadership lag that is as vast as it is pitiful. Men like Jacob Schiff and his kind—those vaunted, German-style "Kings of the Jews"—retained, at the very least, a life-long commitment to "helping" Jews and "supporting Judaism"—

even if they lacked intellectual strength and a fully developed philosophy or understanding of Jewish life.

Today, we are still stuck with the fundraisers and the public relations types who pass themselves off as Jewish leaders. By and large, they only flit from one "campaign" to the other, and then flicker out, without ever having paused to think about the final object of the games they are only temporarily playing.

Many sensitive Jews have been deterred from offering themselves as candidates for Jewish leadership, as a result. A goodly number whom I have met feel as does Daniel Bell, but few have put it down so pithily and perceptively as he:

"In the *embourgeoisement* of Jewish life in America, the community has become institutionalized around fundraising, and the index of an individual's importance too often is the amount of money he donates to hospitals, defense agencies, philanthropic groups, and the like. The manifest ends are the community functions being served, but frequently the latent end is the personal prestige—*yichus*. This kind of institutional life may even lend itself to historic forms of corruption: of simony, when those who have risen high in Jewish organizations receive their awards in appointive office in Jewish life; and of indulgences, when leadership is the simple reward of wealth. And in performance of charity as a way of Jewish life, self-satisfaction may take on the face of righteousness. The most sensitive of the Jewish agency professionals, lawyers, and business men have often deplored this situation, yet are trapped by the system."

How does the "system" actually operate? What are these "simonists" really like? What makes them tick—and then run? Why, in Heaven's name, are they there, at the top, at all, considering that their people need "Jewish Kings," not just temporary "office holders," to lead them? And perhaps most important of all is the question Jews customarily ask concerning things others are doing to them, not about what they do to themselves: "Is this good or bad for the Jews?"—this new establishment of fundraisers.

The New Establishment 241

I have to make something clear. If I said that Jewish life suffers from a system which exalts mere fundraisers as leaders, I should stress that I really do not dislike the fundraisers themselves. After all, I, too, am one of them, and have been, it seems to me, almost from the beginning of time my memory can recall. As a social democrat, I find it very agreeable. It is a painless, non-revolutionary way of re-distributing wealth for the public good.

I was four years old when I had made my first contact with Palestine—or *Eretz Israel*, as we called it. It was at my grandparents' home in Brighton Beach, which our family used to visit every Sabbath, from Friday night through Sunday, after all of us had moved to Brooklyn. Just prior to lighting the white candles in her large silver Sabbath candelabrum, every Friday evening, my grandmother made certain to drop some small coins into the two or three *pushkas*, the tin charity boxes that were quietly waiting for her personal attention, atop the china closet. As a pre-school child I could not make out the writing on the *pushkas*, but she patiently explained that this money would be sent, when the boxes filled up, to Rabbis and scholars in Eretz Israel; I remember her mentioning *yeshivot* in Jerusalem, Hebron, and Tiberias. Both the names of these "holy cities" as well as the importance of remembering poor Talmudical scholars when ushering in the Sabbath stayed with me for a long time. Palestine was indeed a Holy Land, and bringing it into our homes every Sabbath helped to make the Sabbath day holy.

Then, too, the Land of Israel had become an integral part of our daily *religious* life at the Yeshivah. From our first days there, as part of every morning's brief prayer service, we had dutifully dropped our pennies into the "blue-box" of the J.N.F.—and on Fridays, in honor of the impending Sabbath, we often donated whole nickels. The Jewish National Fund— we knew it by its Hebrew name, the *Keren Kayemet*—was, of course, the land-acquisition arm of the World Zionist Organization. But it also is a crucial, if often overlooked, example of how most American Jews, who had been so remote from serious involvement in worldwide political Jewish nationalism, came to be overwhelmingly "Zionized." The process was not immediate nor even perceptible to the naked eye. But by the time Hitler's "handiwork" became universal knowledge near the close of World War II, most American Jews began to see no other honorable way out of the horrible disgrace of the Holocaust than to choose the "Zionist option." They had moved full circle in their attitudes to Palestine, and in their understanding of the role of Zionism as well.

For decades, some Jews were ritualistically and romantically collecting "charity pennies" (not even dollars) to reclaim distant deserts for those few, "crazy" Zionist *halutzim*, "pioneering settlers" in the God-forsaken promised land. Others, like my grandmother, had integrated their "love of Zion" into their religious pieties, by helping to support impecunious rabbis studying Torah in the Holy Land and its holy cities. But then, in the middle of the Great War, in November 1917, came the dramatic announcement of something new and exciting—the "Balfour Declaration"—the letter written by the then British Foreign Secretary, Arthur James Balfour, to Lord Rothschild which declared that "His Majesty's Government view with favor the establishment in Palestine of a national home for the Jewish people, and will use their best endeavours to facilitate the achievement of this object...." Theodor Herzl, who was the founder of the World Zionist Organization in 1897, had died in 1904. A man who had invented an important method for making acetone from corn grain became his major successor. Professor Chaim Weizmann of Manchester, a renowned British chemist of Russian-Jewish birth—from the tiny village of Motol, near Pinsk—would soon be the head of the world Zionist movement. In 1948, with the establishment of the State of Israel, he was acclaimed Israel's founding President.

As early as 1906, when the British Prime Minister of that day, the same Arthur J. Balfour, visited with Weizmann in Manchester, he had already impressed Balfour with his brazen but sincere statement that "Jerusalem was the capital of our country when London was a marsh." (Weizmann had just turned thirty-two!)

In the flush of excitement that followed in the wake of the Balfour Declaration—and in the face of the tremendous relocation problems caused by the vast Jewish population movements set in train as the war in Europe ended—Weizmann and his colleagues had established the Keren Yayesod, the Palestine Foundation Fund. They had optimistically anticipated that the Fund would quickly succeed in reaching its goal. The sum of 25 million pounds which they had set, would enable the Jews to acquire all the lands absentee-Arab *effendis* were then eager to sell to the Jews; enough, indeed, to establish a "Jewish Commonwealth" on what would be Jewish-owned soil. In April 1921, accompanied by Albert Einstein, the acclaimed physicist and "Jewish genius," Dr. Weizmann came to New York to launch the historic campaign to "buy back" Palestine by putting forth his hands for gifts from Jews, from city to city, and town to town.

His encounters—for the first time on their home base in America—reflect that great Jew's agonies with the "Kings of the Jews" then reigning in America. The old-line German-Jewish community, as enshrined in classical Reform Judaism, was violently opposed to Weizmann, to Zionism, or to any form of national Jewish selfhood. They were, after all, by their own lights, "Americans of Mosaic Persuasion," not members of a people or a nation called the Jews.

At a crucial political juncture in the United States, in 1919, Zionist leaders had petitioned President Woodrow Wilson to support the Balfour Declaration.

The German-Jewish leaders, headed by Adolph S. Ochs, publisher of *The New York Times*, immediately after this petition was reported, had taken out a large advertisement in that newspaper, addressed to Wilson, "warning and protesting against the demand of the Zionists for...a national unit to whom...territorial sovereignty in Palestine shall be committed."

Weizmann was outraged and adamant. I can still hear the loud laughter of my late, lamented friend Meyer Weisgal, the Chancellor of the Weizmann Institute in Rehovot, Israel, and one of Weizmann's trusted American aides. There, at the beautiful scientific memorial to Israel's first President, sitting on the lawn of his campus home, in 1974, Meyer loved to repeat one of his "favorite Weizmann-Ochs revenge stories." "For years afterward," chuckled Weisgal, "Weizmann loved to walk into a room full of blue-blooded American Jews—assimilated to the hilt—and inquire in the Yiddish language they never understood, about the health of Adolph Ochs. *'Wass macht der Ochs*—How is Ochs?' " Of course, the reason for our laughter was simple. Both Weisgal and I knew that Weizmann was *really* saying: "How is that dumb brute of an ox?"

Ochs and his crowd were bad enough. But what hurt Weizmann and his European colleagues even more was the lack of "true Jewish leadership" on the part of what they regarded as the "so-called Zionist" leaders of America at the time. Their mentor was Louis Dembitz Brandeis, a native of Louisville, Kentucky, whose parents had arrived in America from Prague shortly after the aborted liberal Revolution of 1848. President Wilson had elevated him, in 1916, when he was sixty years old, to the bench of the Supreme Court of the United States—the first Jew to have reached that eminence in the country's history. This appointment came after a long and illustrious career as a Boston lawyer who had made a name for himself fighting for the rights of the oppressed and downtrodden. Weizmann had pinned his hopes on Brandeis and his "Zionist" followers, but soon after arriving for that "sacred mission to America," on behalf of the *Keren Yayesod*, he came to see Brandeis and his American Zionists as little different from the assimilationist-bound, Reform German "protesters" and their servile Rabbi followers. In his eyes, they, too, were "110% Yankees" and nothing less than "Jewish cowards."

I saw Palestine as a Jewish cultural center and "homeland," but not necessarily a Jewish state. But as a very young Rabbi of twenty-three years of age, it was the magnetic charm and visionary outreach of Weizmann which would capture me. I became his follower and avid disciple after a private meeting with him, arranged for me while attending a Zionist convention in Atlantic City, New Jersey, a mere two months after World War II had ended in Japan. I was stirred to my deepest parts by the dogged determination of this tireless old man of seventy-one sitting next to me on a couch. Nothing and nobody would shake his faith in the future fulfillment of his Zionist dreams. From that day forward, Weizmann occupied a special place in my Jewish pantheon. Although I, of course, had known about him from afar, that electric meeting led me to seek to emulate his style of Jewish leadership—come what may—and since that day I began studying everything he ever wrote or said in the pursuit of Jewish goals. Who could have prophesied that night in Atlantic City, in the midst of the darkest hours of modern Jewry, that in less than three years the British would renounce their mandatory powers over Palestine, would leave the area, the Jewish State of Israel would be proclaimed, and Dr. Chaim Weizmann would be applauded by the entire Western World as its first President?

In the mid-1970s, about twenty years after his death, a series of volumes began appearing, one by one, titled *The Letters and Papers of Chaim Weizmann*. In the tenth volume, which saw the light only in 1977, Weizmann's "strictly confidential" letter to a British Zionist colleague appears for the first time. I have read and reread that letter many times because it offers a remarkably candid picture, by a sophisticated Jewish leader, of what American Jews and their spokesmen were then like—even the "Zionists." They remained in the same condition for decades, virtually unmoved and unchanged, until Hitler's monstrosities jolted them into the real world.

This is what, in the strictist confidence, he wrote in 1921 from Boston, to his friend in England, a short month after landing in America, for what he had mistakenly believed would be a "successful and triumphal tour."

"I am so tired out and worried that you must forgive me if I am not very coherent.

"On arrival here I found a very difficult situation. Brandeis and his group (they are about fifty in all) have captured the machine of the Z.O. (Zionist Organization) in America and have with an iron hand and, by political methods and stratagems absolutely unknown and inconceivable in Europe, kept down everything and everybody who dared to have an opinion of his own. I have never thought such a political terror possible. Anybody who expresses an opinion different from the officially recognized one is simply steamrolled out of existence and branded as a rebel, and that is the mildest term applied to an opponent. It was so amazing and overwhelming that it took me weeks to grasp it all...the attitude of Brandeis and his colleagues to the international Z.O. is similar to the attitude of America to the League of Nations and to Europe. The Americans have done it all, and have won the War (have made the Zionist movement and Palestine), have done it all altruistically as they have no interest (American Jews won't go to Palestine in masses).... The parallelism is very striking. *Wie es sich christelt, so jüdelt es sich*! ["As the Christians do, so do the Jews"]....

"The masses of the American Zionists and Jews have nothing in common with B. and his group, which is only a small oligarchy of men with a certain social position in this country but without influence on Jewry, with the exception of a few assimilated, non-Zionist or anti-Zionist Jews. Ninety-five percent of American Jewry are those who understand a one-hundred-percent Zionism full-blooded.... I am writing this note from Boston, which is Brandeis's town, the citadel of assimilated Jewry.... At one dinner yesterday 20,000 [dollars] were raised, and so it goes on in every city. We don't get big contributions, but the masses are giving in smaller sums, but in large quantities. It is a terrible exertion, but we can get from New York alone all the money we require on one condition— that we send here a good man who will work hard and build up a Zionist Organization leaning on Jewish democracy. The present (American) Z.O. is a bluff, non-existent for all practical purposes. Their membership has dropped from 150 thousand to 17 [thousand]....

"B. [Brandeis] is an American first and a Zionist only a few minutes in the day, and therefore has lost touch with Jewry and with the actualities of Palestine.... The Jewish masses will remain faithful to Zionism...whatever American politics may be. This is not the case with B. and his group...they...make an impression on a few Jewish cowards who pose as 110% Yankees, but not on the Jewish people....

"The American Zionist leaders are also frightened of [Henry] Ford and his [anti-Semitic] propaganda and would therefore like to hide their Jewish lights behind a bushel. In short, all those people are at the best pro-Palestinians, philo-Zionists, 'Zionists for others' but not for themselves, and here is the whole difference....

"You will give me a day [when I return to England] and I shall tell you all about it, the awful times here—but we shall get the dollars! I have about 4½ promised millions now, and did not even begin to scratch the surface"....

But Weizmann's Jewish optimism did not win the day. The success of Zionism had to wait for the post-Hitler, post-Holocaust years. Even his beloved "Jewish masses" did not fully follow his lead. Some were Socialists, who despised Zionism no less than the Reform German Jews. They regarded it as a bourgeois delusion, one that would only distract the common folk from what should have been its principal, all-consuming goal—full and final liberation through *international economic programs, not by means of a paltry Jewish national* state. Moreover, there can be no doubt that they also saw political Zionism as a bothersome competitor within the small American Jewish community of the day, an annoying obstacle in their difficult struggle to capture the attention and loyalty of their middle-class-oriented fellow factory-and-sweatshop workers.

Others, the Orthodox religious, felt that Zionism was a brash, secular intrusion on God's own design and promise for his people; Zion could only be rebuilt by divine means, and it was arrogant and wrongheaded to try to force His hand. Still others, known as "territorialists," believed that Palestine was an impossible dream; it was better to seek national autonomy for Jews someplace in Africa, or even Siberia, with cooperating governments, and not vainly wait for the Arabs to vacate their land, or even to sell it, acre by acre. Still less were they willing to fight Arabs over "rights" to the land.

Then, of course, there were the Yiddishists—the secular diaspora-culturalists—who were deeply offended by the Zionist downgrading of the value of the whole diaspora experience. Unlike the Zionists who regarded the diaspora as a degrading and deforming exile experience, Yiddishists saw it as an enriching historical epoch, which had produced important literary and cultural values.

The majority, however, were content to be or to become "better Americans." They had few, if any, political thoughts as Jews. And in unideological America, what political thoughts they did possess were not usually even remotely related to their Jewish condition, but reserved principally for the next municipal or federal elections. "Do we vote Democrat? Or do we vote Republican?"

Perhaps the most crucial reason for Zionism's slow and difficult start in America had even more to do with America itself than any of the intramural rivalries which still divided the Jewish community. Clearly, by its very nature, Zionism, alone among all other Jewish movements, was antipathetic (or so it seemed) to the very "dream" of Jewish immigration to America itself. Here were these myriads of Jewish refugees from Eastern Europe, who had uprooted themselves at great personal sacrifice from their long-established ways in their "old home," who were still struggling—before the Great War, at least—to accommodate their lives to the New World environment; and not finding it very easy, at that, to establish themselves in

America. And now these "ideologists"—these Zionist *luftmenschen*—come along, and tell them, in effect, that they had traveled to the wrong country, and should be turning their sights eastward again—this time to Palestine, that barren, arid land they had avoided going to from Russia in the first place! Not that Zionist leaders in America those days were urging immediate *aliya* to Palestine, but their Zion-centered rhetoric was enough to fill any average, struggling immigrant Jew in the United States with guilt for having chosen the "golden land" over the "promised land."

Louis Brandeis, the acculturated Zionist leader, *had* to speak differently even to the American Jewish *masses* than Weizmann did. And it was Brandeis's "Zionism" which became the American norm, not Weizmann's. The soon-to-be-appointed Justice of the Supreme Court laid down the "rule" in a 1915 address that would be followed by American Zionists for many years to come: "Practical experience and observation convince me that to be good Americans, we must be better Jews, and to be better Jews we must be Zionists." Even then, most American Jews preferred to be seen as good Americans, without having to rely upon either Judaism or Zionism as indirect props or supports for their patriotism, as Brandeis had urged.

Which is not to say that American Jews were not philanthropic, and magnificently so, in the period between the two world wars. They poured out scores of millions in their largesse to sponsor rescue efforts and immigration resettlement schemes. But these projects were non-political in nature, mostly monies donated to the American Jewish Joint Distribution Committee. The "Joint," as it came to be known, was the central hub for almost all fund-raising efforts to rescue and rehabilitate overseas Jewries—and to resettle them in South America, Mexico, Canada, and even some in the United States—despite strict immigration quotas there, which went into effect beginning with 1925. But none of these efforts were directed to Palestine; that would be too political. *That* was for those few, "wild" Zionists to worry about; not for the general American

Jewish community. And there were not many Zionists in America, those days.

World War II changed all of this. Efforts on behalf of beleaguered Jews en route to Palestine increased, as "humanitarian" projects to resettle unwanted "displaced persons"; not yet in a Jewish state, but at least in a "Jewish Homeland." But it was only after the war that the Jewish community was finally converted to political action, otherwise known as Zionist activity, including hush-hush funding for the purchase of arms and "illegal" ships to help empty out the remnants of the D.P. camps in Europe.

There were even secret "luncheon meetings," some of which I attended. These were convened by Rudolph Sonneborn, multimillionaire scion of a wealthy German-Jewish family of Baltimore. He had been a naval aviator in World War I, played football at Johns Hopkins University—an easy and sure candidate for total assimilation into the "Wasp-dom" of America. Like some others of his tribe, he was, however, converted to "Zionism" by the recent events of Jewish history in Europe and the Middle East. At the urging of David Ben Gurion, who came to visit him as head of the *Hagana*—after V.E. Day, in July 1945—Sonneborn agreed to help raise large funds, secretly, in order to finance the purchase of old ships which would run the British blockade against Jewish immigrants to Palestine, and try to land them safely there, under cover of the guns of the men of the *Hagana*. Scores of thousands of them were turned back and detained by the British in D.P. camps they had set up on the island of Cyprus.

Within a few months, Sonneborn's surreptitious money-raising for ships, became an even more clandestine operation—now it was also geared to the purchase of arms and ammunition for the *Hagana's* anti-British underground efforts. "The Sonneborn Institute," as his group was euphemistically called by a small group of knowing insiders, began meeting weekly, every Thursday noon for "lunch," in the El Patio Room of the Hotel McAlpin. Each week, different individuals were drawn to these "lunches," people came to drop their checks, and those of their friends back home—which ultimately ran into the millions of dollars—from Jews all across the United States and Canada. The donors knew nothing about these meetings; they were merely asked to help "beat the British and save Jewish lives." But at the Hotel McAlpin, key *Hagana* leaders were discreetly telling those insiders who were present of their successes against the British. Their message, without attribution or further elaboration as to details, was relayed like a "human chain letter," by those of us in attendance at the "Institute," to hundreds upon hundreds all over the continent, who were meeting in their recreation rooms, at home—probably on otherwise lazy Sunday mornings—at intimate meetings, where they had gathered to write out their checks.

Irving S. Norry, a close personal friend and a member of my Beth El congregation in Rochester, was one of those who had been drawn to Sonneborn early on. Like Sonneborn, he was no Zionist, but as a successful young entrepreneur—he owned a prospering electric equipment company in town—he had come into contact with some of Sonneborn's friends. As a result of the excitement generated by Sonneborn's group, in 1946, Norry took over the dormant, almost-defunct local district of the Zionist Organization of America, and as president, revived it and made it into a vital force in the German-dominated Rochester Jewish community. When he completed his two-year term, he asked me to take over his presidency—which I did—and he went on to larger and more important international Jewish political work. While he still remained active in his local business, his "Jewish interests" now dominated his time and life so much, and required so much travel, that he reorganized his firm, and put its day-to-day operations into the hands of an executive vice-president. He became a "full-time" Zionist leader. I could see the same process taking place among many of his "Institute" colleagues, whom I met while attending these "luncheons" in 1947 and early 1948. Like him, they were now fully politicized and "Zionized."

252 THE REAL JEWISH WORLD

As a clear sign of how far Zionism had now begun to pervade the ranks of even third- and fourth-generation American Jews—many of whom had long since forgotten their Jewish connections—one had only to glance around the room at these furtive sessions. They were all leading business executives, most of whom had probably never been to a "Jewish meeting" in their lives. The money they raised, from all over the United States, was astronomical. But they had a new sense of self-esteem and national pride: They were building an underground army to defend Jews in what would soon become a free State of Israel—not just donating money to "Jewish charity."[1]

Some of them became so zealous in their new-found preoccupations as Jews, that they even took exceptional risks—possible arrest—for helping to export arms without licenses to their beleaguered comrades in the Jewish army-in-the-making, the *Hagana*. But there seemed to be no other way to stop the British forces from rounding up and detaining thousands upon thousands of Jewish refugees who were trying to make the shores of Palestine in those leaky "illegal" boats. Irving was one of these risk-takers. He was unlucky enough to have been apprehended and arrested in March 1948, charged with buying and storing six thousand dynamite caps without a license. He pleaded guilty to the charge, and was given a suspended sentence, without ever saying, at the time, why he had acquired the detonators. Many, by this time, could have guessed why—even the Irish judge before whom Norry was to appear and with whom I personally interceded, as his Rabbi. (Irish-American judges readily understood why Jews had to fight the rigid British, who were helping to complete Hitler's unfinished work, by preventing Jewish displaced persons from entering Palestine—or any other haven, for that matter.)

But even many young Jewish professionals who, at that time of their lives, would not go as far as Irving Norry, or other

---

[1] For a fuller description of Sonneborn's Institute and this unexpected development in American Jewish life, see Leonard Slater, *The Pledge*, Simon and Schuster, 1970, New York.

successful, independent entrepreneurs like him at the Sonneborn Institute—for fear of losing their hard-won ground in the non-Jewish world—were suddenly and profoundly jolted back into "the Jewish camp." I think now of young Sol M. Linowitz, who like myself had recently come to Rochester. We became very close friends, as did our wives, Toni and Hadassa—they with their four young daughters, we with our three baby girls. He was then barely thirty-five years old, and had just been mustered out of the United States Navy, as a Lieutenant (j.g.). Coming as we both did, and almost at the same time, into a rock-bound conservative Republican city like the Rochester of that day (dominated by the Eastman-Kodak establishment on the one hand; and in the Jewish community, by co-religionists of early German settlement who were now tycoons in the men's clothing industry) helped to draw us two "New York Jews"—liberal Democrats by earlier nurture—very close together. I was also enchanted and regularly convulsed by his delicious renditions of humorous folk stories, which he delighted to recount in a rich and flavorful Yiddish.

Still, in 1946, Sol—who would later cap a distinguished ambassadorial career when appointed as President Carter's personal representative to the Egyptian-Israeli negotiations following the bilateral Camp David peace treaties—was a prototypical reflection and example of the "American ambitions" then prevailing among many bright sons of impecunious East European Jewish immigrants. Although born into a Yiddish-speaking family in Trenton, New Jersey (not New York City!), once landed in Rochester he perceived himself principally as a future successful *American* lawyer—especially since he had graduated from Cornell Law School with top honors, after completing his undergraduate course at Hamilton College, a small "Wasp"-dominated school, in upstate New York. He had been at the head of his class in both schools, and one of only a handful of Jews in a sea of career-oriented, Protestant, Anglo-Saxon classmates. It could be expected that when he chose to live and practice in a city like Rochester, he would quickly set himself to the task of staking out a successful professional future in the broader community. Instead of joining a Jewish law firm, or hanging out his own shingle, he sought and found a prestigious "Wasp" legal office, and even from the ranks of a lowly junior, he was determined to make it to the top in *their* world.

One day, Sol came to see me, troubled by a decision he was hard-pressed to make. He had landed a new client, Joseph Wilson, a well-respected local Catholic layman and the owner of a small printing plant then called the Rochester-Haloid Company, probably named after Haloid Street where it was located. Joe had recently taken over this family business from his father, and had succeeded in acquiring the patent to a new dry photocopying process quaintly known as "xerography." The Wilson firm was anxious to protect its patents worldwide, and had engaged Sol to help them do this. There was a problem, however, Sol explained. This relatively small family operation, which had recently gone to the public to sell shares which then barely traded on the local "exchange," was unable to pay him for his extensive legal services. Instead they had offered him stock in "Rochester-Haloid." "Should I or shouldn't I?" Sol was now asking me. There was no great risk, I suggested, particularly, since he wasn't exactly overwhelmed with too much other law work, at the time. "Why not take a chance?" I said, naively hoping for the best.[2]

The rest of the story, of course, has unfolded into a thrilling saga of American economic and business history. It also totally changed Sol's life and career, as a person and as a Jew. In a few years, Wilson's company would add a new word to our language when it changed its name to The Xerox Corporation; Sol would be named its General Counsel, and soon became the

---

[2] I was not nearly as courageous as the advice I had given Sol. When he suggested that I buy some of his shares from him—the price was then about $1.00 each—I excused myself; my salary was then a mere $3,000 per annum. He, of course, kept his shares, and needless to say was profoundly enriched soon thereafter, and much more over the years.

The New Establishment 255

Chairman of the Board. And not only did Rochester itself become a different city—the new home of thousands of workers and scientists in the burgeoning, infant high-technology industry—but in a crucial sense, a new era had begun in the annals of international social and cultural history.

All of this was heady stuff indeed, but for me it serves as a stirring example of the new strengths that would also accrue to American Jewish life and leadership in the persons of people like Sol M. Linowitz. For Sol could now afford to transform his personal *angst* for success and survival into creative anxiety for the survival of his people. *Because*, not *despite* the fact that he—and other professionals like him—had indeed made it to the top, Sol would not only never forget his Yiddish, but would also seek out ways in which to contribute to the strengthening of Jewish life everywhere. Like the businessmen, the Irving Norrys of Jewish America, those like Sol Linowitz, whose professional careers would no longer be in doubt, and who became firmly entrenched on the American scene, would see it as a matter of *noblesse oblige* to rally to their beleaguered people. The Holocaust now became a searing personal reminder to them of what Jewish powerlessness had helped to engender. Their private success fired their desire to see their own people normalized again, and made ready to take its rightful place among the nations of the world.

Now that the Holocaust was becoming part of the collective conscience of American Jews, they began to become more sensitive to the intrigues of international politics—including the deceptions of their own government in Washington, led by the double-dealing of their "friend," F.D.R. Their ties to their fellow Jews took on an immediacy and an urgency. They no longer seemed to have any other option but political action on an ongoing basis. This was war—a war against themselves, as Jews, and not just against the homeless and displaced survivors of Hitler's death camps. By June, 1948, even Adolph Ochs's *New York Times* was ready to accept the newly proclaimed State of Israel—at least, after both the governments of Harry

Truman and the Union of Soviet Socialist Republics had already recognized it.

It was about ten years earlier, during the Arab riots of 1936, that my Yeshivah-mate, Morty, and I had gone a long way towards this jolting route—and within the short space of only four or five weks. From then on, my life was radically altered. And not by Zionists, Arabs, the British, or Roosevelt—but by Jewish Communists—they called themselves "anti-Fascists"—and their fellow-travelers. Later the "sophisticated" Jews at Madison also helped: their apathy and self-indulgence, their complete lack of social and political consciousness were strong prods to my own Jewish awareness. I would do everything I could not to become one of them.

My response to the wanton bloodshed in Hebron, and the taking of Jewish life by Arab attackers, was, at first, purely emotional and humanitarian. "Let's answer those Arabs with the J.N.F.," I kept urging Morty. After careful consideration over several days, he finally agreed to a plan I had worked out: We'd ride the subway trains and collect money for the Jews of Palestine. Nobody had told us to do this sort of thing—no teacher, friend, or "organized" Jewish body. In fact, we had learned of this style of campaigning from other youths we had watched on the trains—those who were busy collecting funds from fellow passengers to fight against Fascists who were then killing innocent people with aerial bombardments in Spain. If our parents, or even our teachers at the Yeshivah High School, had heard about our proposed venture, we were sure they would have considered us at least partly *meshugah*; almost, if not completely, mad. So we mentioned the plan to no one, not even to our closest Yeshivah schoolmates, for fear of being called "nuts," or called down for behaving like "those Commies."

As we first saw it, our venture did not have political meaning at all. We looked upon our personal "J.N.F. project" as our peaceful and moral response to continuing British intransigence and Arab violence. It was, we were convinced, the only just and righteous way the Jewish people could acquire unwanted Palestinian lands from those rich *effendi* landlords who had already more than they needed, or had given up on much of arid Palestine. Moreover, we believed it to be the best way to defend the small number of Jews who were struggling there against big odds; our help would make it possible for new settlers to augment the tiny numbers of the struggling Jewish "Yishuv."

That first Saturday night we stealthily left our homes and made our rendezvous at the Brighton Line express station platform at King's Highway. We took with us our "blue boxes" and our homemade blue and white armbands we had emblazoned with the Star of David, and quickly tied them around our coatsleeves before getting ready to board an oncoming train. I remember letting three or four trains pass before we finally gathered the courage to enter, to begin with our pleas.

On Saturday nights, a different crowd traveled the subway. It was unlike the sardine-packed, weekday mobs of burdened people who lived in Brooklyn and made the long and boring trip into Manhattan where they plied their trades or wares. Saturday nights were special: Nobody was strained; nobody in a hurry; nobody unwilling to listen to a stranger. It was a night for celebrations and for easy hours "on the town."

After finally boarding, we moved to different corners of the car, where each of us made our prepared pitch. My voice was highly strained. I quavered, but managed to pull through. Then, we quickly moved around, passing our boxes, as we went. We did not have to wait long, however, to hear the ring of our success: pennies from heaven. We had just reached Newkirk Avenue—the first express stop—and we had already collected about a quarter in pennies. Very few adults refused us. There were, of course, many Jews among the riders, who seemed eager to "shell out" for Palestine.

We happily continued with our collecting for several hours, and returned home after two full round-trips to Forty-second

Street, Manhattan, with loaded boxes—probably about five dollars between us. We were overjoyed and vowed to keep up our "program" for as long as we could. All week long we could think of only one thing: Saturday night and our part in helping to buy still another strip of earth to settle more Jews on the land. That would surely help our brothers in Palestine against future defenselessness. We did not begin to think of arms, military support, or any kind of political activity. It was really a combination of the sentimental moods instilled in me on the Friday nights at my grandparents' home, together with the daily joys at the Yeshivah—the magic blue box that would buy back our ancestral homeland and help to rebuild its glorious cities. We thought only of helping to recreate the land, mound by arid mound, *dunam* by *dunam*. We were romantics, nothing more, helping to make the desert bloom with roses and Jews.

But it did not take more than a few Saturday nights on the train until we suddenly knew that we were most certainly involved in a political, if not a military project. We were catapulted into the real world.

This shaking realization was the direct result of an encounter about our fourth time out, with an earnest but obstreperous "team" of Spanish Civil War "collectors." They had apparently spied us out the first night we rode the trains, but waited to see if we'd ever return before moving against us. Then, when we did return, week after week—and successfully, to boot—they made their bold "strike." I never forgot them, or what they said, in their mocking derision. Instantly and instinctively, they succeeded in "politicizing" me as a Jew for the rest of my life.

They were mostly Jewish, with a couple of Italians thrown in. There must have been at least eight of them. They were husky, upper-school seventeen- and eighteen-year-old students, from Abraham Lincoln High. At the DeKalb Avenue station they ordered the two of us off the train and onto the platform. They surrounded us, shoving us to a far corner of the platform where no other passengers stood. We had no idea what they wanted, or what all the fuss was about—after all, not

The New Establishment 259

even the train conductor had objected to our collections. We were not exactly sure of what was coming next: a fight, a lecture, or a raid of our boxes.

It turned out that we almost got all three.

One of them started for our boxes, but the ringleader, the oldest among them—I was certain that he was Jewish—waved him off with mock disdain. "I suppose we *should* take that money, and give it to the *more* deserving—to *our* people," he slowly announced, feigning bravado. "But *we* don't operate that way. We anti-Fascists have conscience. We'll let *you* Zionists keep your filthy lucre.... But only this time.... We'll see to it that you never come back again.... You only get in our way...*you* and all your other *rich Flatbush slobs*."

We were, to put it mildly, frightened out of our wits. Somehow, we managed to conceal our fears, and in the most gentle way we knew, tried to put forward our "liberal" solution. Why not room enough for both of our groups; the trains were surely big enough for more than one. But instead of placating them, our simple and obvious "solution" only succeeded in infuriating them even more. A shouting match followed. We were completely on the receiving end as every one of them stood up to take "batting practice" against us. All hell had broken loose. It was a harangue never to be forgotten:

"You're only confusing people with your crummy boxes and stupid *Jewish stars*."

"You should take their money and give to us. Jews don't need money!"

"Jews don't know how to fight, anyway. The real fight is against the warlords in Italy and Germany, those Fascist bastards!"

"It's the *workers* and *peasants* that count, not those religious Jews in Palestine, sitting on Arab land."

"The only battle worth fighting is the struggle of the little guys—the *workers* and *peasants*—and all the little guys of the world. Not for *you* Zionists."

And then, as their anger turned to more rational efforts at

giving us "fatherly advice"—but in not so gentle tones—the chief spokesman tried to summarize:

"Don't you see—you dumb little clucks—that you've been had. Completely taken in by your phony Zionist masters.... The trick is not to win a wrong battle over the Arabs, for the sake of a few Jews who don't belong there in the first place.... What you've got to do is win the 'big one'...you've got to beat the imperialist bastards who are out to get all the Jews, too.... But what are you guys doing? You're fighting for the Jews only, when you should be joining the international struggle of all the little people of the world—the workers and the peasants—Jews can't win it alone.... And damn it, you kids better learn that lesson now.... If you don't join us, and all the anti-Fascists, *you Zionists* will get it from us, too.... *Because if you're not with us, you're against us....*"

As their hot words and accusations kept pouring forth with increasing force and frenzy, my frights and fears were rapidly turning into black feelings of loathing and shocked anger. Several times, when I was about to cut into their vindictive chorus, Morty tugged strongly at my coat-tails. He was wiser than me. There was no point in trying to "win" against them. They were very sure of themselves, convinced converts to their blazing ideological cause. And who were we? We were two little kids, not quite fourteen, out by ourselves in the world for the first time in our lives, only trying to "do some good."

At the first opportunity, when it appeared that they had exhausted themselves, Morty cleverly maneuvered us away from the tight circle, and before I knew it we were aboard the next train headed for home. I remember not being able to talk; we remained standing silently, all the way to our station, King's Highway.

I was too proud and too angry to do what I had really wanted to do—to sit down, somewhere out of sight, and cry my eyes out. Instead, we quickly ran down the stairs from the elevated train platform and made our way to the dark streets below. We began our long walk home, very slowly, and for the first time since the "attack" a half hour earlier, began to talk to each other. But what we said was only the prelude to a new beginning, a new world-view that had been opened up to us that night—and not by our teachers, our parents, or by any of the sermons of our rabbis.

"*You Jews... You Zionists*"—for the next few days, my head was reeling from these words, spoken with such scorn by the Jewish headman of those tough Lincoln kids. It had finally happened. I had come face-to-face for the first time, I told myself, with anti-Semitism. But not at the hands of any Irish kids at St. Brendan's Parochial School, near my house. My maiden encounter with anti-Jewish hate was a shocker, mercilessly dealt me by Jews themselves. My idyllic, sheltered world was suddenly and devastatingly crushed; I had lost my virginity as a starry-eyed young Jew, raised in a world of "liberal do-gooders."

I had become a Zionist only after I was a Jew; and a "fundraiser" with heightened political consciousness—only after I was a Zionist. But I regarded the raising of these funds from Jews only as an instrumental necessity, not as a substitute religion. Money offered for the redemption of Jewish lives, my grandmother's *pushka* first taught me, was a *mitzvah*, or a religious duty, of the highest order. It was *tzedakah*, charity in the sense of righteousness. As a Zionist, I now realized that these monies also represented political clout. We could actually plant Jews firmly on the land—and this was not only a religious act but also a matter of social and historical Jewish fulfillment. But most North American Jewish leaders have transformed *tzedakah* into a gigantic fundraising machine and apparatus, and made it into their central Jewish preoccupation—their magnificent Jewish obsession. They have been phenomenally successful during the past thirty-five years, as we shall see. I would argue, however, that some of the means have not been worthy of the ends. The hidden costs of their financial success may yet bankrupt us spiritually.

It was early in the summer of 1966. Three men—Orthodox,

Conservative and Reform—top leaders of Toronto's Jewish community, had come to my study. They were asking me to do something no other big-city Rabbi had yet done in Canada, although several had in the United States. Would I accept the invitation of the selection committee to serve as the Chairman of the United Jewish Appeal of Metro Toronto in the year-long Campaign that was soon to commence? "I need a few days to consider your gracious invitation. I would like to obtain the consent, too, of my congregational Board of Governors. But if I should accept, gentlemen, I will insist that we get rid of the 'fan dancers,' the 'neon lights,' those terrible 'Honor Rolls' and other assorted abominations of our fund-raising 'machine.' " For years, I had been forcefully speaking out against these things from my pulpit, but without success. What is more: I was regarded by many of these leaders as disloyal because of it. They realized that I was now "playing my card," which *they* would have to accept if they wanted *me* to accept. Looking at each other sheepishly, they smiled thinly, and one by one, reluctantly nodded agreement.

By this time, and for some time before, large urban Jewish congregations in the United States were usually headed by leaders who, in the jargon of sociologists, outgrew their status as "locals," and had matured into "cosmopolitans." The interest of locals is principally confined to a fragmented segment of the larger community—their own neighborhood, social group, or—as in the case of the organized Jewish community—to their own synagogue. Cosmopolitans, on the other hand, view the community globally, and inevitably, Jewish leaders who fall into this category regard themselves as players on the world Jewish stage, and their interest is geared to the totality of the Jewish universe. And as for the spiritual leaders, it was usually only those Reform Rabbis who served the "distinguished" old-time congregations established by the first Jewish settlers—like Philip Bernstein in Rochester—whose lay leaders sometimes encouraged their participation in the wider spheres of Jewish activity. But in Canada, even as late as 1966, despite the pressing Jewish needs all around the world, the Boards of

Conservative congregations were still peopled mainly by locals whose "parish mentality" extended almost exclusively to their own membership roster and not much farther.

I knew these facts of Canadian Jewish life, of course, and ever since I arrived in Canada, had struggled constantly to transform the parochial, *shtetl*-induced attitudes of my Board into a more responsible view of Jewish leadership—to enlarge our outreach as a congregation not only to the whole Jewish world, but to Canada as a nation as well. On the surface, and in the minds of most people on the outside—who thought that they knew—my efforts in this connection were seen to be "victorious." Yet, as subsequent events have proved conclusively, that congregation to this day remains, by and large, what it always wished to be: deeply narcissistic, committed almost entirely to its own private needs. Like many other congregations—especially the largest and the wealthiest, who see themselves as totally autonomous—it still resents and resists "pressures" from the "outside," and regards the intrusion of the cosmopolitans into its own local territory as annoying, or even threatening.

Realizing all this, the search committee had diligently done its homework in advance. Prior to its meeting with me, the committee of three leading Jews had apparently spent a good deal of time with individuals and small groups, persuading recalcitrant board members. They told me much later that they had "won" on the basis of their argument that my serving as Chairman of the community's most prestigious and important U.J.A. Drive was not only "good for the Jews," but would reflect "honor on the congregation" itself. Soon, a special synagogue board meeting was called to consider the matter. In return for my promise not to neglect my duties as their Rabbi, I was given permission to accept the invitation to serve for the next twelve months as the head of the campaign. Still, I instinctively knew that in their hearts, and in the provincial minds of some other members lurking behind them, they would never either forgive or forget this "needless loss" of their Rabbi—

"our employee, after all"—to the community. Nevertheless, I gladly accepted both my challenging new assignment and my possible future fate.

There were now those bothersome "abominations" to look after, immediately: the fan-dancers, the neon lights, and the Honor Roll.

Chaim Weizmann never did raise those 25 million pounds sterling which, if produced at the time, could have averted many of the crucial, long-range problems still plaguing Jews. More Jews from East Europe, and more land in Palestine, would have been in place at the neediest of times—both before and immediately after the Holocaust. He was rebuffed by the wealthy leadership and could only turn to his treasured masses as his one great hope; but even with the greatest of desires, they were too poor to make much of a difference, financially. Once, in 1927, reminiscing about this, he told an audience in Czernowitz—in the very heartland of those who would later go to their death in Hitler's infernos—that the real strength of the Zionist program came from the masses: "Before Herzl came to us poor, he knocked at the doors of the rich. Only when he found their doors closed he came to us and he found us ready." "Ready," yet one must sadly add, "but not able."

But beginning with 1946, with the first post-war year, the American Jewish community mobilized the rich in dramatic, exotic, and often bizarre ways that had never been employed in the two thousand years during which Jews have engaged in voluntary self-taxation, while in exile. From that time until 1983, communities across the United States and Canada, through their central U.J.A. campaigns, have raised the staggering sum of over ten billion dollars. Added to these charitable gifts for central Jewish causes was the successful State of Israel Bond effort, in place since 1951. In thirty years, well over six billion dollars of Bonds were also sold, at very low rates of interest. Moreover, if one were to add up all the funds contributed directly by the six million Jews of North America to all Jewish charities—at home, abroad, and for Israeli institu-

The New Establishment 265

tions—the sum has been reliably estimated as exceeding an amount of over two billion dollars, annually. *That* is *big business*! Unfortunately, this "Jewish G.N.P."—which I have sometimes jocularly dubbed as the "*very gross* national product of the Jews"—has been achieved by the vulgarization of the traditionally high standards of *tzedakah*.

It is particularly saddening to observe some of the bad side-effects this "Israel-charity industry" has produced, especially among educational institutions there. There are about 65,000 students enrolled in seven universities and centers of higher learning and research. Each of them conducts vigorous annual fund-raising campaigns in North America, and the share of monies they raise is not related to their actual needs, but rather to which "personalities," in every local community, head the effort. Social status is everything; educational purpose and program account for very little. As a result, these universities are constantly vying for the favor of the most desirable establishment figures to lend their names and their support to *their* organization of "Friends" in these North American communities. They reward many of them, by "electing" them members—in special cases, even Chairmen—of their own university Board of Governors. Or by naming buildings after them, if the "price" of their donation "is right." If they cannot match these biggest of the donors, they are at least certain to receive plaques of all kinds.

As a further indication of the centrality of fundraising even to *universities* in Israel, until recently, three of the seven schools were headed by Presidents who were the country's ambassadors to either the United States or Canada, or the United Nations. In their former positions, they had ample opportunity to make the rounds of hundreds upon hundreds of dinners, cocktail parties, and "parlor meetings," using their influence as well-known and well-positioned diplomats to raise funds for the United Jewish Appeal—the central Jewish fund-raising apparatus for Israel in local Jewish communities—clear across the continent. After they retired from the diplomatic service, they were almost immediately seized by these universities to become the heads of their institutions. Though they knew little about higher education, they had become experts as fundraisers. As a result of their efforts, and of similarly aggressive money-raisers who head other Israeli universities, massive sums have been collected in the United States and Canada—and elsewhere, notably in Britain, France, and Mexico—most often, to erect, almost obsessively, a brace of superfluous buildings in the form of "Institutes," "Centers," and the like. It is widely known as Israel's "edifice complex."

Yet even more costly a price is being executed in regard to the nature and quality of higher education itself, as a result of this ready source of gift dollars from North America to Israeli universities. These campaigners called University Presidents have paid too little attention to the academic needs of their students and faculties, despite the fact that they boast—to uncritical, undiscriminating Jewish businessmen-donors in America—of the academic excellence of their schools. They willingly tailor their programs to accommodate their donors' wishes, not so much to satisfy the university's true needs. There is also duplication and overlapping of programs. In a small country, with only seven such institutions, it seems hardly necessary to have so many of them maintain competing "Institutes on the Holocaust," or "Centers for Peace," or other programs—many of them fitted out with special buildings—which are chiefly the result of the whims and fancies of the wealthy contributors, rather than based on a set of national priorities in the various fields of scientific research or intellectual inquiry.

Sadat's peace initiative culminating in the Camp David treaty of 1979, is a recent case in point. It was transformed into the vehicle of a string of university promotion campaigns in North America. Almost every Israeli school was competing for dollars in the philanthropic marketplace: All at once, each proposed similar "peace-based programs." There were going to be a half-dozen "Institutes for Israel-Arab Co-operation" in

The New Establishment 267

the country, under different names or rubrics, of course, but with each university running its own. It did not matter that there was no serious response from Cairo to join these widely publicized Egypt-Israel academic "exchanges." What mattered to these market-minded Presidents, and to their Boards—mostly big donors from America—was that Sadat had "offered" them a gift they could not afford to refuse: the opportunity to raise additional funds for their schools, for programs they only talked about but could not put into effect.

It goes without saying that serious-minded members of these faculties, not to mention the students themselves, are profoundly disturbed by many of these "charades," and upset, in general, by the rampant cynicism which these activities have inculcated in the academic leadership of Israel. What is even more disturbing: The stature of North American Jews is diminished—not increased—in the eyes of thoughtful Israelis when they see that even their most successful businessmen are merely mindless puppets, on a string pulled by even cleverer Israelis.

My own experience is that the "big donors" have more say than they should simply because eighty per cent of all of the funds Jews raise are contributed by less than fifteen per cent of the total number of givers. This is a far cry from the troubled days and relatively meager pickings of men like Chaim Weizmann. Jews have since grown into a new awareness that their affluence must be shared with their people; that they rise and fall together—rich and poor alike. Still, these successful third- and fourth-generation scions of poor East European immigrants do not always respond to these needs on the basis of the needs themselves. They have established a system of "bread and circuses": They give their "bread" only if properly cajoled, enticed, or even coerced, by a series of sideshows that have nothing to do with charity, or even with self-taxation—which may be a more accurate way of describing an annual enterprise of these proportions.

They liked "fan dancers," a generic name professional fund-raising executives have given to the whole tribe of comics, vaudevillians and assorted entertainers who have "headlined" thousands of U.J.A. luncheons and dinners, from coast to coast, over the past thirty-five years. By itself, there is, obviously, nothing intrinsically sinister in these proceedings. All of these entertainers were upright and decent men and women. Still, hundreds of thousands of charity-dollars have been paid out to them, in order to lure resistant Jewish contributors to "come out and give." It is also true of course, that a goodly number of these contributors would not have appeared at the meeting, nor could they have been solicited for their donations so efficiently or effectively—all in one place, with competitive peer-pressure causing beads of perspiration to run down their softened-up spines. So their names were called, and they gave, amid shouts like, "If you give 50 grand, Max, I'll match you." But they were taught, unfortunately, by a whole generation of fundraising-leaders, to do the right thing for the wrong reason. This has consistently contributed to a steady erosion of Jewish self-esteem, particularly in the eyes of their own children. I would cringe sitting at some of those meetings whose usual theme was "Give So They Can Live": referring to whichever community of Jews was the featured "victim of the year"—Iraqis, Romanians, Yemenites, or even more recently, the inadequately sheltered poor in Israel, principally among the North African immigrants to the country. We sat there, with these signs of "Give-Live" all around us, feasting on stuffed chicken and *ersatz* ice-"cream" (to comply with the laws of Kashruth, forbidding the mixing of milk and meat) and listened to the guffaws in response to the off-color stories these comics were spinning out in the belief that they were hilariously funny. My grandfather, if he were alive and told what was going on, certainly would not have believed. "Jews don't do such things," he would have said, and so would all of the Jewish grandfathers of the world a mere fifty years ago.

So there were to be no more "fan dancers." But no "neon lights," either; this was a more complicated matter, however, with some political and philosophical overtones.

Conventional wisdom of the fundraising fraternity in Amer-

The New Establishment 269

ica had it that Jews would be "embarrassed into giving" charity if important non-Jewish public figures or political officials came to tell them that they should. I had always felt distressed over the essential hypocrisy of this game. Why did American Jews in the tragic and difficult 1940s and 1950s need people like Senator Alben Barkley (later Vice-President of the United States), newspaper columnist Dorothy Thompson, or Senator Wayne Morse to lecture them about their Jewish duties and responsibilities? The stock answers were always ready. Jews like to hear themselves flattered by non-Jews; what's more, by putting these people on a retainer to give a stated number of fundraising talks a year, we are also insuring that "when the chips are down politically for us, they will be on our side." The answer, it seemed to me, was as bad as the question and the moral problem it had raised. There were some notable exceptions, of course, men like Pierre Van Paasen, John Hayes Holmes and their likes, who were Christian Zionists and lifelong, committed friends of the Jewish people. I saw people of this stripe in a different light; they were not careerist, self-seeking hacks, who were exploiting a Jewish inferiority-complex, to pay the rent—and then some.

I could never forget that in the early years of the War, Dorothy Thompson, one of America's most respected journalists, had been on the payroll of the leading Jewish fundraising organizations and made hundreds of "pro-Palestine" Zionist speeches. Then, in 1944, she turned herself around a full 180 degrees and began pouring forth anti-Zionist tirades, decrying what she then called Jewish terrorism in Palestine. I remember arguing, some years later, with Meyer Weisgal, who had been one of her closest Jewish friends and supporters. Meyer, too, could not defend her any longer, certainly not after she went to Cairo, became a close friend of Nasser, and even wrote the introduction to his book against Israel. Miss Thompson had taught me a lesson, but apparently her actions had little effect in changing the ways of the fundraising élite. To this day, they maintain their old styles, which, in my opinion, makes it clear that they still treat themselves and their followers as permanent alien-immigrants, outsiders to America and Canada. Apparently, they need the applause and reinforcement of condescending politicians, or of public people who are old-stock Christians, in order to bolster their Jewish morale. They will rush to mount huge fundraising affairs for Jewish causes—at $1,000 and more a plate—in honor of a Governor, a Mayor, or a Senator. But they rarely will honor their own Rabbis, teachers, professors, writers, or artists, at events such as these. "Who would come out?" they ask. "Who will give *for them?*" they almost laugh.

The "Honor Roll of Contributors" was really a "Dishonor Roll." Many communities had introduced this annual publication ostensibly to list the benefactors to the campaign held the year before. Nor were they in the least bit shy about listing the dollar amounts donated by each of the contributors. The day the Honor Roll was received in Jewish households also served as a starter's whistle signaling the opening of a bitter slugfest between bruising, competing athletes. If your name was listed and you gave less than what others thought you should have given—you were pounced upon. If your name was not included in the Roll at all, you would surely pay dearly for it. Those who did business with you would probably boycott you, your store or factory, even your wife and kids. And if some printer's devil had accidentally omitted to print your name, although you did actually contribute—and this was a frequent mishap—you suffered, silently or otherwise, because even your friends might not believe your protestations. All in all, this Roll produced an annual mess, and who knows how many arguments and spiteful acts of revenge. It was introduced to coerce and shame renegade "non-givers." In the end, it served the cause of communal disunity, breeding suspicion and disharmony. Worse still: It distorted human values as well as the meaning of leadership.

This was what the materialistic, voluntary, and democratic society of North America had done to them. But they said that they were caught in a bind, and had to "produce" both leadership and the vast amounts of charity dollars required, yet without any real authority or ultimate power. They lacked the tools of community enforcement that had been available to the traditional corporate community of the Old World. Consider, however, what has been lost to them in America, not only because it is a different society, but principally as a result of the dilution and dimunition of the religious elements of Jewish life. In the past, Rabbinical power could be harnessed to "keep Jews in line" in all of their behavior patterns, both personal and social. The laws of *Kashruth*—the ritual slaughter of animals and fowl, and the foods fit for religious Jews to eat—were often the basis for many of these sanctions. Special meat and wine taxes and various imposts on weddings, circumcisions, and burials were established to secure the necessary revenues to support community institutions. There were even "sumptuary laws" which went so far as to deal with the articles of clothing which might be worn by various individuals on certain public Jewish occasions, the number of guests and musicians who might be invited to certain functions, and the amount and type of food which might be served.

American Jewish fundraisers have often excused their own tactics by complaining that in a voluntary society they lack the religious authority of the older Jewish communities to impose any decrees. Yet, instead of inventing rational and ethical substitutes for what Jews of an earlier time and place had done in support of their institutions, on this continent they created not moral, but often immoral, equivalents. There certainly are some things Rabbis and their religious followers could be doing—at the least, *they of all people. I have never heard or seen, for example, any American Rabbi, whose congregations claim to accept Jewish law (halaka) as the basis for Jewish life,* say what Chaim Weizmann, the so-called secularist Jew, did have the courage to pronounce. In a proclamation addressed to American Zionists, in 1921, on the eve of that all-important launching of the first *Keren Yayesod* campaign, he declared:

"All Zionists must become contributors on the high standard of the *Ma'aser*, or the tithe." Tithing is a biblical commandment, yet even the most Orthodox Jew in America is not expected to contribute his support on *that* biblical basis, or in *that* proportion to his means.

I do not wish to cavil. I mention this only to point to a direction that has been totally avoided by the charity machines of American Jews, despite all of their remarkable material successes. Fundraising must be seen not as the ways *and* means of Jewish life; it is only a means, not a substitute for the way. What would happen to the leadership if, by some miracle, Israel no longer needed their funds? What would happen to the new establishment if their campaign toys were taken away from them, and their game of "Jewish golf"—their U.J.A. drives—were no longer necessary?

I would contend that one truly great "campaign" still awaits North American Jews—I say "campaign" since that seems to be the one important codeword necessary for their conditioned response. It would be a campaign, in a sense, to end campaigns: to change and correct the fundraising leadership style we have transformed into our Jewish Establishment, by seeking and finding Jewish leaders more sensitive to the older, truly established ways. We need leaders, in Weizmann's words, who do not live as Jews only "for a few minutes every day," and do not regard their commitment to Judaism as still another fundraising campaign. Without such leadership, nothing can save the fiber of our Jewish life from decay. Not even Israel, which is in deep trouble itself, not alone because of Arab hate, but also because of our own uncritical Jewish "love."

Chapter 10

THE HOLOCAUST AND SOVIET JEWRY

Like so many other young people—excluding most of my apathetic Madison classmates—I was also caught up in the imaginative remedies of Franklin D. Roosevelt's New Deal, and the panaceas he seemed to be offering to a sick American society. But I could never adore him, as did most middle-class Jews, because I faulted him for not going far enough—all the way to democratic socialism. His critics on the right, however, like Westbrook Pegler, helped me sympathize with F.D.R. and come to his defense in my many arguments with myself.

Still, unlike most older Jews, I never regarded Roosevelt as much more than a successful politician, using his own bag of tricks in order to prolong his hold on the Presidency. Much later, in graduate school, in the early Fifties, some of my earlier, unlearned and wild suspicions were confirmed. By then I regarded F.D.R. as essentially a conservative patrician. He had served as the savior of capitalism in a rocky, almost-revolutionary time in America, by means of a variety of gimmicky, sometimes overhyped, "social programs." And most, if not all of these, had one principal point of departure: to ward off any takeover of America by outright Communists, socialists, or their "fellow-travelers." Still later we saw through his double deals with Ibn Saud on Zionism, and with England on Jewish refugees. He was the ultimate politician, not someone Jews, of all people, should have so fully trusted.

It is not difficult, however, to understand why people like my grandfather and father, together with hundreds of thousands of Jewish workers and trade unionists across New York admired Roosevelt, like some might worship an unfailing, miracle-working Hasidic Rebbe. He had the magical ability to make believers out of them: to make all of these strugglers sit comfortably, side by side, as passengers in the same boat. What I had tried to explain to my father in Jewish terms had barely touched him; he could never see himself as a willing partner with his own workers; they were on "another team," the trade union's, not his. But Roosevelt had the necessary emotional persuasiveness to tie these contending groups—the small businessman and the labor unionists—into a common, single fold.

All over the neighborhood it would happen at once, and all across Jewish New York. Whenever one of F.D.R.'s "fireside chats" would be broadcast, an awesome silence would fall upon these communities, a silence perhaps greater than any ever "heard" in any synagogue, even at the holiest moments of Yom Kippur. For the President himself was addressing them personally: the *Rebbe* of Washington speaking personally and warmly, in fatherly yet regal tones to his pained subjects—or disciples. All the Jewish world fell silent before him. The American Messiah-King—as I was annoyed to see some Jews imagine him—had once again succeeded in comforting and binding up his sorely tried people: the workers as well as the little bosses—like my father—on the verge of ruin. All Roosevelt had to do was to cuddle them together close to his bosom, with his familiar and anticipated opening salutation, so warmly and roundly spoken in his unmatched, velvet voice and sonorous cadences: "M-y F-r-i-e-n-d-s."

The Holocaust and Soviet Jewry   275

There are many publics in America, and those which do not catch the ear and reach the mind of the President and the Congress will likely be overlooked and ignored, no matter how significant their wants or needs.

Political establishments do not respond to ideas-in-general, only to specific pressures, mounted by those who feel strongly about "their" issues and programs. Government policy is thus the result of many different private interests willing to work hard to fashion the "public interest" after their own image. And what is true of the American political scene is also reflected in the decision-making process of the North American Jewish community, with only a few variations on that theme.

The four terms of the Franklin Roosevelt Presidency provide a classic example of how, despite his legendary "liberalism," F.D.R. did very little—except to posture—to advance the cause of America's two major minorities—the Blacks and the Jews. The "colored" people, as they were then called, never benefited from a single piece of federal legislation to improve their disabled social and economic position in Roosevelt's America. They fought the war—first as the Army and Navy's cooks and bottle-washers, and only later, as the battles required them overseas, as warriors—in strictly segregated units. It was only in the Sixties, when they organized under the banner of Black Power, that they began to break through the long silence of American liberals in office, and to win, step by painstaking step, a modicum of civil rights in their own native land.

It was little different with Jews, except that they were further encumbered by the fact that they had "fallen in love" with the President and could not believe that he was not on "their side." But Roosevelt knew that American Jews—and their leaders—were his political captives, and as Ben Hecht has trenchantly written, "The Germans who hated him called him Rosenfeld, not because they believed he was Jewish but because he was beloved by the Jews." Jewish leadership of the day had not yet learned the real workings of the political process. They were tied to a single political party and did not realize that they had to create a public opinion in their favor, in order to make Jewish goals part of the policy of the government in Washington. They were too busy talking *for* the Jews—behind closed doors in the political offices of men in high places.

Establishment-style leaders continue to make the same mistake because they are often plagued by the age-old Exile mentality—an inferiority-complex that is linked to their perception of Jews as a perennial minority, doomed to be weaker than their masters. They fail to understand that, in North America, majorities need minorities, and that in the game of power politics a majority is only the sum of many different minorities.

They are further entrapped by the false belief that if they can only remain in the good graces of the authorities whose favor they curry, they will succeed in snatching an exta favor from them for Jews, now and then. They are, however, so intent on waiting for the next major benefit—by not "cashing in all their coupons" now—that they usually continue to stand by waiting helplessly—and waiting, and waiting.

In those black Holocaust years, establishment leaders lost the Jewish war; not only to Roosevelt and the British, but at home, too, inside their own community. Impatient and upstart grassroots outsiders took matters into their own hands and went over their heads to the masses of Jews themselves. They succeeded in creating new Jewish publics, with new opinions and new voices. After so many years of helplessness, Jews would no longer accept the *status quo*, neither from the world, nor even from their own leaders.

Jewish activism—the outsider-as-insider in command—suddenly erupted across the country as the beleaguered Jewish establishment looked on in shock and amazement. These newcomers, the oldliners protested—people like Hollywood's Ben Hecht and the many new talents his provocative Emergency Committee to Save the Jewish People of Europe had brought to the fore—were destroying "Jewish unity," acting without authorization. Activists, of course, usually do just that. They exceed the bounds of mannered nicety by not falling into a neat, single file behind commmunity leaders whose silence or impotence seemed to betray them. "Jewish unity," I would contend, is never desirable when it is used as a weapon to destroy the inner freedom of the community to express itself on vital matters affecting the life or safety of Jews. (Are Reform and Conservative congregations to close shop because they refuse to be Orthodox?) When unity is invoked by Jewish leaders as a self-protecting *shibboleth*, it is used precisely in the same way, and for equivalent reasons, as when government officials cover themselves with patriotism, in seeking shelter from criticism, by invoking the sacred words "national security." And this truth applies with equal force to Israel, no less than to North America.

It took me a long time to discover these truths, although even during the Roosevelt years I already had my doubts about the way Jewish lives were then being managed. Years later, when a new oblivion faced the Jews of the Soviet Union, I learned these lessons again, at great pain. But by that time, I, too, was living within the Jewish establishment.

Once hostilities broke out in Europe, and especially after the United States had itself entered the war in 1941, it became even more difficult for Jews to find any fault with F.D.R., even when they had every reason to do so. The S.S. St. Louis of the Hamburg-America line left Germany in mid-1939 for Havana carrying 930 Jewish refugees who had paid a small fortune to acquire Cuban landing permits, and yet they were refused entry by the immigration authorities. They sailed away, reaching a point only a few miles from Miami, Florida, while the distraught Jews aboard waited for word from Washington that they might be granted asylum and allowed to land. Permission was refused, and from the shoreline of the United States, with the harbor lights of Miami still before them, they were forced to sail back to Europe, where a goodly number were later to perish in Hitler's death camps. Of course, there were some protests from American Jewish leaders, but obviously not strong enough to prevent the recurrence of similar tragic events, both in American harbors and European ports, a few short years later.

Throughout the war, even after news of the Holocaust had reached the United States in 1942, Roosevelt remained a formidable opponent for Jewish leaders to take on, especially since they still regarded him as their beloved "chief," and never could see him in the role of opponent. They refused to ascribe to his hand the misdeeds of his State Department officials who continued to avert their eyes from the steadily deteriorating Jewish refugee problem. But Roosevelt remained steadfastly loyal to these advisers and relied upon them uncritically. Jewish leadership in America was in a sorry state: disarrayed, confused, even fearful. They did not want the President to think—even when they pressed him—that by forcefully urging a change in his policy or his continued refusal to rescue Jewish refugees and finding havens for them in America or elsewhere, they were weakening or even subverting the war effort, or causing division between the United States and England—its principal ally.[1]

Some writers naively believe—even today—that no Jewish organization could confront Roosevelt because it was felt that he and his Administration stood between American Jews and American anti-Semitism, then beginning to make large inroads in parts of the country. These covert, then later widely visible, efforts were linked principally to the isolationist, "stay-out-of-the-Jewish-War" slogans making the rounds throughout the

---

[1] In neighboring Canada matters were even worse. "Only a handful [of Jews] were given permission to enter the country. During the twelve years of Nazi terror, from 1933 to 1945 while the United States accepted more than 200,000 Jewish refugees; Palestine, 125,000; embattled Britain, 70,000; Argentina, 50,000; penurious Brazil, 27,000; distant China, 25,000; tiny Bolivia and Chile, 14,000 each, Canada found room for fewer than 5,000." See Irving Abella and Harold Troper, *None Is Too Many*, Lester & Orpen Dennys, Toronto, 1982, p. x.

Midwestern states, aided and abetted by Charles Lindbergh, the folk hero, and "Bertie" McCormick's powerful *Chicago Tribune*, and their "America First" Committee. The truth is that some Jewish demonstrations *did* take place—though not sponsored, and sometimes boycotted, by the establishment groups—against Roosevelt-inspired governmental inaction on behalf of Europe's Jews.

The irony and tragedy of this false adoration of F.D.R. can be sadly seen merely by looking at what the Nazis themselves were thinking at just that time. In Berlin, America's official non-response to the plight of European Jewry was being viewed very differently than by official Jewish leaders in New York. Josef Goebbels must have been smacking his lips when he made this shrewd but pithy entry in his diary on December 13, 1942: "The question of Jewish persecution in Europe is being given top news priority by the English and the Americans. At bottom, however, I believe that both the English and the Americans are happy that we are exterminating the Jewish riff-raff."[2]

In addition to the problems caused by "their man" in the White House, American Jews were treated, in those years, to the unhappy specter of bickering leaders and competing organizations—all of whom were engaged in posturing and in fighting either to advance the prestige of their own organization, or to defend their own particular Jewish ideology. None of the major groups can be exempted from this blame, including the Zionists in America—*and* Palestine. The major players in this fiasco were all entrenched, established groups: beginning with the German-Jewish, Reform-oriented Joint Distribution Committee, which had performed so well, under different conditions, of course, during and immediately after the First World War; to the American Jewish Congress, led by Rabbi Stephen S. Wise; and the World Jewish Congress, based then in Switzerland; and even including the Zionist officials

---

[2] See *The Goebbels Diaries*, 1942-3, ed. and trans. by Louis P. Lochner, Doubleday, New York, 1948, p. 291 (December 12, 1942).

280 THE REAL JEWISH WORLD

who dominated the Jewish Agency (for Palestine). One scholar-apologist for the nonperformance of this bloc of establishment organizations has suggested that "Zionists, including World Jewish Congress leaders, were so absorbed in planning for after the war's end that they were paying little attention to what was happening in Europe."[3]

Today, there are annual world-wide remembrances in April, on Holocaust Day—even an American Presidential commission recently set up to devise ways and means to ensure that we do not forget the Six Million. I have the gnawing notion that this "American gesture" is, in reality, an inexpensive—I almost said cheap—way of helping us forget that the U.S. War Department repeatedly refused requests either to bomb the gas chambers at Auschwitz, or at least to slow down the Nazi annihiliation program by bombing the railroad lines and junctions leading to them—carrying those horrific cattlecars overloaded with Jews en route to their death in the crematoria. On August 20, 1944, we now have learned, 127 Flying Fortresses, escorted by 100 Mustang fighters, dropped 1,336 500-pound high-explosive bombs on the factory areas of Auschwitz *less than five miles* to the east of the gas chambers. What is more: By this time, the Americans—Roosevelt included—had already known for several months that 1,750,000 Jews had been deported to die in Auschwitz during the two years preceding. Recent American historical writing objectively describes the immoral behavior of the Roosevelt-led war machine of the United States in that crucial hour of Jewish—and human—history. The generals were allowed to turn their minds away from the Jewish situation. They were permitted by Roosevelt to justify their inattention to the "Holocaust" (that inept and inappropriate usage had not yet been "invented" to describe what was happening to Europe's Jews) by claiming that bombing the gas chambers, or even the railroad tracks leading to

---

[3] See Yehuda Bauer, *American Jewry and the Holocaust: The American Jewish Joint Distribution Committee, 1939-45*, Detroit, Wayne State University Press, 1981.

The Holocaust and Soviet Jewry 281

them, was counter-productive to the war effort.[4] They glibly palmed off and filed these suggestions, asserting platitudinously—in the midst of that mind-boggling Jewish decimation—that *"after due consideration of the problem, it is considered that the most effective relief to victims of enemy persecution is the early defeat of the Axis."*[5] (Emphasis added.) I can just picture them, in their private dining rooms, served by their Black soldier-waiters, puffing stogies and quaffing beer with great comfort—"duly considering" the Holocaust.

In Israel, too, the "Holocaust" is solemnly remembered. It is drilled into students' hearts and minds in schools, youth movements, and Army training programs. There is, perhaps, even an overabundance of museums and "institutes" dedicated to the Holocaust "ghetto-fighters"—Israelis always deemphasize those whom they regard as having been "slain as sheep," without fighting back, in self-defense. From a humane angle of vision, this popular Israeli view is as warped as the extreme

---

[4] The word "holocaust" is derived originally from the Hebrew Bible and denoted a religiously inspired sacrificial act in which a "wholly burnt offering" was given up to the Lord. The Nazi extermination plan cannot, by any stretch of the imagination, be regarded as a "sacrificial" act in the sense the Bible intended. The Hebrew word used in Israel, *shoah*, meaning "catastrophe," is much closer to the mark.

[5] Each year, new access is achieved to secret unopened files dealing with these aspects of the American "war policy." They do not shed favorable light on Roosevelt, his generals, the State Department, or members of the "War Refugee Board," which was publicly viewed as Roosevelt's instrument of "concern for the Jews." The records show that for a long time, until it was too late, these people dragged their feet—perhaps hoping that the problem would soon go away: Hitler's "Final Solution" would, in fact, be achieved. The references here are taken from David S. Wyman, "Why Auschwitz Was Never Bombed," in *Commentary*, May, 1978, pp. 37-46.

In his autobiographical references to Roosevelt, published in 1949, Stephen Wise remained as loyal as ever to him, despite his personal "heartbreak" over the "shocking delays and sabotage by the State Department bureaucrats, abetted by the British Foreign Office." See *Challenging Years*, G.P. Putnam's and Sons, New York, 1949, pp. 274-279. Also see Arthur D. Morse, *While 6 Million Died*, Ace Publishing, 1968, New York.

position taken by others—many Christians and, painfully, even some Jews. For their part, these trumpet the notion that the Jews were really not singled out as special victims, for even if they were the hardest hit, they were only one group among many others killed by Nazis. Wittingly or not, both of these positions are ideologically and psychologically tainted. Both are part of what has been called an "escape mechanism"—a way of avoiding or denying the awful uniqueness and particularity of Hitler's "final solution," by refusing to confront the moral significance for Christians as well as Jews of the *helpless martyrdom* of the Six Million. Those Jews could not have saved themselves; but powerful outsiders could have intervened to stop their slaughter. I have nothing but contempt for any Christians who attempt to trivialize the Holocaust by de-Judaizing it—thus covering over their sins of omission. But worthy of criticism, too, are those Israelis who imagine that they can score points on behalf of their own contemporary warrior lifestyle by blaming those earlier defenseless Jewish victims for "allowing" themselves to be victimized.

The naked and painful truth remains, and won't go away: The Jews of America—and the free world—are also not without guilt. They did not fully do what they had in their power to do, *before* all the innocents were slaughtered. They could surely have saved hundreds of thousands of the millions. Try though I may, I can not shake off the uneasy feeling that *some* of the Holocaust "remembrancing" which has become part of the ritual-round of Jewish organizational life, here and abroad, is linked to our own lingering remorse. What we forgot to do then, we are "remembering" now. And even so, we do not always remember in appropriate ways.[6]

---

[6] For a dispassionate account of the way in which American, British, and even Zionist Jewish leaders in Palestine reacted to the incontrovertible news of the mass murders of Jews at the hands of Hitler, even by the end of 1942, see Walter Laqueur, *The Terrible Secret: Suppression of Truth About Hitler's "Final Solution,"* Little, Brown, Boston, 1980. The author's bone-chilling yet objective account avoids recriminations against these Jewish

It was in the midst of this Jewish political mismanagement and misjudgment in America that *suddenly*, in 1943, demonstrations against the administration in Washington did begin to take place—over the objection of the organizations mentioned earlier. Major mass-circulation American dailies began carrying full-page, paid advertisements in which Franklin D. Roosevelt's policies were openly attacked by some unknown hastily formed, *ad hoc* Jewish "rescue committee," sporting famous American names—Jewish and non-Jewish—never linked before to Jewish causes. This was essentially the handiwork of one young man, a follower of Vladimir Jabotinsky's hard-line and militant "Revisionist Zionism." He had come to New York from Palestine, where he was the political chief of the "Irgun Zvai Leumi"—the underground, terrorist, fighting arm of Jabotinsky's "Revisionists," which Menachem Begin would later lead, beginning with 1943. His name was Hillel Kook, but not wishing to compromise the members of his rabbinical family—he was the nephew of the late Chief Rabbi of Palestine, Rabbi Abraham Isaac Kook—for this special American mission he assumed the name Peter Bergson. Soon, he was calling upon the well-known journalist and dramatist Ben Hecht to assist in fighting the Jewish cause in dramatically different styles than had been the American fashion by funding the Emergency Committee to Save the Jewish People of Europe, and a host of other spinoff groups. They displayed creative and exciting skills in mobilizing opinion—among Jews and the widest of publics—using newspaper advertisements effectively, staging protest rallies as a continuing ritual,

---

leaders and officials for their passivity. Yet, he leaves no room for doubt that they, too, must bear part of the burden. Perhaps hundreds of thousands of Jews who perished might have been saved if those Jewish leaders had not been cowed into believing that nothing could be done to save the remnants of their European brothers *until after* an Allied victory in the War.

Henryk Grynberg's "Appropriating the Holocaust" (*Commentary*, November, 1982) is a useful reminder of what it is Jews and Christians alike should be remembering about the Holocaust—and why.

and by mounting extravaganza-pageants like "We Will Never Die," which played to hundreds of thousands in Madison Square Garden, New York, and other major American cities. They "captured" much of Jewish Hollywood, and other writers, artists, and performers were soon on their new and rolling bandwagon. Overnight, it seemed, they were gaining the support of unaffiliated Jews who were, by now, growing more impatient with the inability of the established Jewish organizations to reach the heart of America.

Bergson's Committee became a new force on the tired American Jewish scene, despite the fact that many Jews knew of its connections with the disestablished and often condemned *Irgun*, which was repeatedly "excommunicated" by the Jewish leadership in America. No "regular organizational Zionist," like myself, would openly admit it, yet many of us were deeply moved and motivated by what this new group was doing to the America we knew—electrifying it and taking it by storm.

In 1954, Ben Hecht described his feelings about the death of Jewish leadership, how Bergson's Committee had come upon the scene, and what it had accomplished. I have returned many times to his autobiography, *A Child of the Century*, a good part of which is devoted to the work of that Committee. I would do so especially on days when I was disheartened with a leadership that often disappointed my hopes for displays of a greater Jewish courage. Hecht tells how it began:

"I looked with confusion at the three men and a woman who were calling on me in my Algonquin Hotel room that day in the spring of 1941. Peter Bergson, their spokesman, had just stated that he wished me to be the American leader of the great cause in which they were engaged. I had not quite understood what this cause was, beyond that it had to do with Jews and raising millions of dollars to improve their status in Palestine, but I felt sorry for my visitors and their cause, both. They could have selected no more unqualified and uninformed and un-Palestine-minded man in the entire land. Their choice of me made them seem naive and a little overdesperate....

The Holocaust and Soviet Jewry 285

"...I was to work intimately for seven years with these three young men. [The young woman married and vanished.] Although hundreds of active cohorts were to come to this group, the three men who sat in my room that day remained for me always 'the Committee.' Through all its guises my response was always to these three. I ignored their ramifications—and no committee ever ramified itself more. It took a dozen different forms and titles and busied itself in all corners of the earth. It howled down an empire, saved myriads of Jews and armed a revolution. Eventually four hundred thousand Americans contributed millions and their moral backing to it; and such stalwarts as Senator Guy Gillette, Senator Ed Johnson, Harry Seldon, Alex Wilf, Harold Ickes, Secretary Frank Knox, Alfred Strelsin, Will Rogers, Jr., Louis Bromfield and scores of congressmen and officials carried its banners."[7]

What a difference just four people—the three men from Palestine and Hecht—had made. I never forgot that.

A government census for the Jews in the Soviet Union is not what it is for other Jews in the free countries of the world; in Russia, it takes great courage to tell an official that you are a Jew. Yet, in 1959, there were 2,267,814 Jews who told official enumerators that they were of "Jewish nationality"—in Russia, they are not officially regarded as Jews "by religion." As it was, they formed the eleventh largest national minority of the Union. Imagine how many more Jews there must have been who kept their identity a secret from the census-taker. Nor can one fault them, considering the years of manic oppression they had suffered at the hands of the tyrant Stalin. Not the least of these nightmares were the campaigns against "cosmopolitans" which began in 1948, and the trumped-up charges of the Jewish "Doctors' Plot" in 1953, which were openly directed against all Jews by the Great Leader himself. Most astute observers of the Soviet scene have no hesitation in suggesting that there were

---

[7] Ben Hecht, *A Child of the Century*, Simon and Schuster, New York, pp. 521-2.

not barely two and a half million, but closer to three and a half million Jews in the U.S.S.R., when that census was taken, in 1959.

My 1961 trip to Russia really began five years earlier, after a delegation of some twenty men representing the New York Board of Rabbis was granted official permission to visit several Jewish communities in Russia. Permission for such an official visit of American rabbis made it appear that at long last, Khrushchev was trying to wipe away the years of Stalinist oppression of the Jews. On their return, these Rabbis reported to *The New York Times* that things were indeed easing up for their brothers, under the new Chairman. My friend Rabbi Morris Kertzer, then Director of Inter-Religious Affairs of the conservative American Jewish Committee, wrote a three-part series of articles for that newspaper in which he described some of the improvement that had taken place for Jews under Khrushchev; but he pointed out that under the Soviet system, they were gradually losing all possibility of maintaining their ancient heritage. His reportage prompted a *Times* editorial writer to state on August 2, 1956, that "Judaism appears to be well on the way to extinction as the result of Government measures which have deprived Jewish parents there [in Russia] to raise their children as Jews...Communism extirpates religion...."

Both the Kertzer articles and the editorial led to a single, perhaps unintended, conclusion: Russian Jews were not much different from other religious groups in the country. They could not practice Judaism very easily—but neither could other religious groups—for when it came to religious freedom, neither they, nor most other Russians, had encouragement from their avowedly and militantly atheist government. The point, however, that seemed to be overlooked was the fact that Jews in Russia constituted, as already mentioned, the eleventh largest national minority in the country, and that even according to the 1959 census almost 400,000 of them had listed Yiddish as their mother tongue. But there were no Jewish schools, no Yiddish theater, no press or cultural organizations, in a Communist country that prided itself constitutionally on the cultural rights available to members of its national minorities. Other minorities did have these things, at least.

I knew in my heart that the Soviets never gave up on Lenin's old "Jewish verdict," and that even now, after Stalin's death, there was still a profound desire on the part of the Soviets to grind down Jewish group life and identity. After all, from the start, international Communism had been deeply antagonistic to Jewish nationalism. As early as 1903, Lenin had laid down the line that a Jewish nationality was "manifestly reactionary" and "in conflict with the best interests of the Jewish proletariat." Then, along came Stalin, ten years later, and he published a pamphlet titled *Marxism and the National Question*—and he, too "ruled" the same way. By 1925, thousands of Jewish nationalists—Zionists—were already in prison or languishing in Siberia where they had simply been "forgotten." That same year, a Moscow Zionist leader, Engineer Itzhak Rabinovich, courageously submitted a memorandum asking for the release of all Zionist prisoners, the cessation of further arrests, and authorizationn for open immigration to Palestine. But the VTsIK—the All-Russian Central Executive Committee of Soviets—rejected it out of hand, and saw to it that for his troubles Rabinovich himself was jailed for propagandizing on behalf of the hated Zionism. A few months later, in 1926, he was sentenced to three years' exile in Kazakhstan.

One of my clear windows on the Russian Jewish situation was provided by my Israeli brother-in-law, Colonel Meir Rabinovitch—or "Batz"—and his father, that self-same Moscow engineer. The elder Rabinovich had escaped from exile, snatched up his two sons, and his wife, and found his way to Jerusalem in 1929. Later, more out of spite to the departing British mandatory power than affinity for the liberated Jews of Palestine, the Soviets recognized the new State of Israel, mere days after it was proclaimed in 1948. When this unusual turnabout occurred, Itzhak Rabinovich was able to found—

mirabile dictu—the "Israel-Soviet Friendship League," over which he presided for many years, in Jerusalem. From this vantage point, he was in an extraordinary position to keep in close contact with every new wrinkle in Soviet policy which touched on its Jewish population. For years, during every one of my frequent visits to Israel, father and son would brief me on the newest trends—and the newest problems—of Soviet Jewish life. Over and again, Itzhak would repeat: "There are thousands upon thousands of Russian Jews who have remained 'secret Zionists.' If given half a chance, it will be their suppressed Jewish nationalism, not only their squelched Jewish religion, which, one bright day, will propel them to Israel. And we have to help make that known to the world, and assist them to come here."

I had desperately wanted to see the situation at first hand. Not many months after the New York Board of Rabbis had returned from Russia, now that I was living in Toronto, I applied for a visa from the Soviet Embassy in Ottawa. I never did receive a reply. The Russians never say *nyet* to would-be tourists; they simply don't answer at all. The Rabinovitches then suggested that since I was refused in Canada—where it was known that I was a Rabbi—I should try walking in cold— "off the street," as it were—to several overseas Russian embassies, and apply there for a visa. In 1958, I spent a total of three weeks waiting for such a reply—first in Copenhagen, then Stockholm, and finally in Istanbul. I did the same, a year later in Paris and London. But none came. Then, to my great joy and amazement, after I had applied once more, in 1961, to the Ottawa Embassy, a visa for a twenty-three day stay in the Soviet Union arrived: a week or so each in Moscow, Leningrad and Kiev.

Shortly after I returned I wrote an eight-part series for the *Toronto Star* syndicate which appeared in many cities in Canada, the U.S. and abroad and was also translated into Hebrew for publication in Israel's leading mass circulation daily, *Maariv*.

Even before I arrived there, I knew in my heart that a visit to Russia would profoundly affect my whole life and I did not want to miss or forget a single moment of the excitement that awaited me. I opened a new file for my own private use, stored it out of sight—and placed a label on the tab which read, "Soviet Jewry: Memos to Myself." No other eyes were to see these, because of the many confidences they contained.

Over the years, these private files grew and grew, as I began to recognize that the Russian-Jewish Problem was not only a Soviet political issue with international ramifications, but was fast becoming a hard bone of internal Jewish contention. For Jews in North America it had turned into a two-sided coin. Facing down—the polite silence and inactivity of the organized leadership, which, for so long a time, remained unwilling to "rock the Russian boat." Facing up—the "little people"—*die kleine menschelech*—so beloved of Tevye's Sholom Aleichem, who slowly but steadily readied themselves to take on the whole world, if need be, to rescue Soviet Jews.

Many of these memos were scribbled on scraps of paper—sometimes even on the inside covers of matchbooks, in tiny, cryptic Hebrew characters. This is what I wrote, as the events were unfolding, adding other items to the file that were directly related:

February 1961

Montreal: Met here today with Saul Hayes, Executive Vice-President of the Canadian Jewish Congress, whom I admire very much. He personally encouraged my trip to Russia but seriously cautioned me that the CJC resident, Michael Garber, stood squarely behind Nahum Goldmann in his opposition to "rattling the Russians." "They want to deal quietly, behind-the-scenes, with Moscow and not pull the bear's tail. So when you return and speak or write about your trip, my advice, for your own sake, is to soft-pedal your criticism of Societ policy on the Jews."

He urged me to meet privately with Dr. Nahum Goldmann, President of the World Jewish Congress, who would be in Montreal the day before I leave New York for Moscow. Promised him that I would try.

Toronto: Dr. Abba Hillel Silver, the great Zionist leader and Rabbi of The Temple in Cleveland, spent the weekend as my guest at Beth Tzedec. He delivered three masterful lectures on "Where Judaism Differed"—which is the title of one of his books. Thousands of people came, and loved him. Spent a lot of time with him, at my home, in between his public appearances. He reminisced about his great fights with Dr. Stephen S. Wise, back in 1942 and 1943, when he wrested the leadership of the Zionist movement in America from Wise. By then, that grand old man was already on his way out of Jewish leadership, and somewhat discredited for sticking by Roosevelt so closely, during those hectic "refugee tussles." "Wise was too old for the job," says Silver, "and besides, we needed a more activist kind of leadership to fight the British double-dealing in Palestine, and inside the White House as well."

Told him of my impending trip to the Soviet Union, coming up in a week or so. He suggested that I take good care of myself, and play it cool. I asked, "What does that mean, in a political sense?" He said: "We hear all sorts of conflicting stories these days about the real needs of the Russian Jews. I think that those who believe that Russian Jews even dream of leaving for Israel are telling wild stories. My view is that it's counterproductive to beat that drum. We ought to press the Russian authorities to grant Jews equal rights with these other national minorities, and fight that good fight. By mixing Zionism into the political pot, we'll only spoil the brew. We'll neither get them out of Russia, nor will we be able to influence the Russians to improve their lot at home. In fact, we will only be infuriating the Russians. If we talk about the 'Israel option' for their Jews, they'll only make things worse for our people, there."

Montreal: En route to New York, where I leave tomorrow

The Holocaust and Soviet Jewry 291

night for Russia via London, paid a courtesy call on Dr. Nahum Goldmann who was here for an overnight visit. He was charming but formidable. Only, I can't accept his position on Soviet Jews. He actually laid down the law to me, like Moses at Sinai: "Don't you get into any trouble over there, and don't get *us* into trouble when you come back. Before you say or do anything, report back to me, through my New York assistants, so we can check out what it is you should be saying about Russia." I know where *he* stands. How many times have I read his views on the question? I can't forget his statement at the World Zionist Congress, in Geneva, back in 1956, when he was in the chair, that he believed the Soviets were then in the process of scrapping their anti-Zionist policy, and that he should be allowed to "handle" them, diplomatically, and not be hindered by public outcries against them. Great man, great leader. But he reminds me of the 1940s. He too is waiting. For what? The Messiah?

Before leaving, I told him that I had recently heard that Chancellor Konrad Adenauer had referred to him publicly and admiringly as "King of the Jews." He smiled at that, approvingly. Then I told him my grandfather's story about "Jewish Kings." He wasn't impressed.

New York: Saw Dr. Meir Rosenne this afternoon at the Israel Consulate here in New York. He's a Consul of Israel, in charge of what is called the "Office Without a Name." Came at his invitation before departing tonight for Moscow, since he's the official representative of the Israel Foreign Ministry quietly "working" North America to press the Israel government's views on what should be done about the Soviet situation. When I told him that I had just seen Goldmann last night in Montreal, he gave a sour laugh. "He's not our favorite Man of the Year when it comes to Russian Jews; he's not on *our* side. We are here, in this office in America, trying to undo his wrongheaded, counterproductive approach to the problem."

I liked Meir immediately. He's a *landsmann*, born in Jassy, Romania. I judged him to be around thirty years old. Studied in Paris, and has a Doctor of Laws Degree. He'll go places, some day.[8] He gave me an El-Al flight bag to carry around in the streets, parks, or restaurants of Russia—a sure way to attract Jews to me, and then perhaps to be invited to walk and talk. Also loaded me down with a *Luah* (Jewish religious calendar)—not one but maybe a hundred of them. They're printed in Israel by the Foreign Ministry, in Hebrew and Russian, more especially for hand-to-hand distribution in Russia by Jewish tourists. Most Jews there don't even know when the Jewish holy days are celebrated, because no Jewish religious calendars may be printed.

Told him I was carrying about fifteen prayer-books, four or five phylactery-sets, three prayer shawls, and several dozen *mezuzot* (religious objects containing selected biblical verses which Jews attach to their doorposts). He said that the best way to distribute these discreetly was simply to leave them, one at a time, as unobtrusively as possible, on synagogue pews, before leaving the services. He's just back from a recent private "incognito" trip to Russia himself (I think he was in Moscow dancing in the streets on *Simhat Torah*, last fall). His experience suggests that I should have no problems clearing these items through Customs at Moscow airport—if I keep them in my valise, as part of my personal effects.

Urged me to try to put my hands on and bring out a copy of the only recent Russian prayer-book, put out in 1956 under the late Chief Rabbi Solomon Schlieffer (a Communist tool). Rosenne believes that they're virtually extinct, and it's important to check this matter out. I should also contact Yaacov (Kobi) Sharett, Moshe Sharett's son, First Secretary at the

---

[8] Meir Rosenne later became one of the chief legal architects of the Camp David Peace Agreements between Egypt and Israel, in his capacity as Solicitor-General of Israel. Before that, he was "Legal Adviser" to the Foreign Minister, Moshe Dayan. At this writing, he is serving as Ambassador of Israel to the United States in Washington, D.C. (See also a "Letter from Jerusalem," where he is obliquely referred to merely as "M.," necessary at the time, for discreet reasons.)

Israeli Embassy in Moscow, who will help me get around; he knows I'm coming. Urgent, too, to try to arrange a private interview with Chief Rabbi Yehudah Leib Levin of Moscow Great synagogue. He rarely talks to foreign Jews in private discussions. Find out what makes Levin tick. Mordechai Chanzin, the one trusted Jew in the Moscow synagogue, may be helpful in arranging a meeting with Levin. But trust no one else in the synagogues—all the other officials of these few congregations are paid informers, or even agents of K.G.B.

Rosenne will come to Israel to meet with me, in about three weeks' time—as soon as I arrive there from Kiev via Vienna. Above all, must try to keep a sharp eye in my head and be prepared, he says, to stay with the "problems" I'll soon discover for myself, for a long, long time—and to work hard, to try to overcome them. He will be helpful, throughout....

Moscow: Checked into Hotel Metropole, which seems to be reserved only for foreigners. It looks like something you see in the movies—from another time and place. The ceiling is very high, with long, cut-glass chandeliers; free-standing wardrobe cupboards—of mahogany—are all across one wall; and there are over-stuffed plush armchairs. The beds are ancient. I search for hidden "bugs." Can't detect any. At every landing sits an old woman; you have to give your huge room-keys to her, before taking the creaky, old elevator, to leave the hotel. She must report immediately to the K.G.B., I'm certain. Still, I laugh as I unpack my valises. They never opened a single bag at the airport, just as Meir Rosenne predicted. Now, to work....

Moscow: Went to Main Synagogue on Arkhispova Street. Nadya, my Intourist guide, agreed not to accompany me. But I'm sure her K.G.B. assistants in the synagogue were alerted to my coming there. That's what Chanzin said, when I met him in *shul* after morning services. Somehow, it almost seemed to me that, he, too, was expecting me—but through other sources, of course. He will try to arrange a private meeting for me with Chief Rabbi Levin. We traded words obliquely in Hebrew, passing each other information, by using appropriate biblical quotations as "code language." He works there full time and knows a lot. He was in prison camp in Siberia for a long time, as an *Asir Tziyon*—a "Prisoner of Zion." He looks it. He appears much older than the forty-five or fifty I figure his age to be. Still, because he was put away for so long, he has only one small child—a very young daughter.

Moscow: The Scene: The Main Synagogue. It was about nine o'clock in the morning. Blowing snow was falling on icy streets and the synagogue was freezing. Morning services had just concluded. About twenty ancient-looking men—they all seemed to be nonagenarians—maintained their distance from the "American" visitor. They moved quickly towards an alcove located on the south side of the sanctuary and under the balcony of the "women's prayer gallery." There, a crude, wooden table was set, covered with a greying white cloth. There were twenty chairs. They found their seats. One of them shouted *Le-Chaim*, and the others responded in kind, as they raised the water-tumblers set before them, brimming with cheap vodka. They barely spoke to each other. There was no other food or drink at the table. They finished off several bottles, then slowly made their way to the bitter winds outside. They did not have to put on their shabby coats because they did not take them off. Seeing that they were gone, a tall, regal figure appeared. He locked the door of the office which he had just shut, even though he will re-enter and unlock it again, in just a few moments—and although he knew that the office door was only three or four steps away from the alcove. He was shod in tall Russian boots and was wearing a hat made of Persian lamb and a very long black overcoat trimmed with brown fur. He smiled politely, extended his hand, welcomed the "American visitor," and invited him to his office—three or four steps back. It was the "office of the Rabbi." Although there are no other rabbis in the city, he was the "Chief Rabbi" of Moscow. His name was Yehudah Leib Levin.

"The Meeting": Rabbi Levin removed a large brass ring from his pocket, packed tight with a bunch of keys, and led me

The Holocaust and Soviet Jewry 295

to the entrance of his office. First, one door was unlocked, and we entered. Then he locked and bolted it. Then a second door—and again, the same procedure. The room was tiny, but lined with old editions of Jewish religious texts. I thumbed through a few, complimenting him on the fine rabbinical library. "It used to be bigger," he said without emotion, while motioning me to sit down. We began bantering in Yiddish, exchanging small pleasantries. He made a "speech": repeated several times that Jewish life was better now, under Khrushchev—whom he called our "Great Leader for world peace"—than it was under "the Terrible One," by which he meant Stalin. He went on and on, singing the virtues of the Kremlin as "world-protector" of the peace. He sprinkled his conversation "liberally" with phrases like "capitalist imperialism," "scientific socialism," and the need to "ban the bomb."

I did not interrupt or debate these things, but when my "turn" came I plied him with questions—Jewish rights in the Soviet Union, and such like—questions that seemed to embarrass him. He shifted in his chair, and shifted again, without really answering. Then, suddenly, without warning, switching from Yiddish to Hebrew, *he* dropped this *bomb*: "If you want to talk about 'things in the world,' we'll talk in Yiddish, but if you want to talk about the weather—'*our* Russian weather'—we must speak only in Hebrew, which nobody here but Chanzin understands. The walls have..." In my heart, I silently celebrated, and nodding approval, completed his Hebrew proverb to myself: "...ears."

I waited for him to make the first move. In faltering, medieval Hebrew, *he* asked *me* a series of run-on questions: "Are there many Jewish schools in Canada? Do most children still celebrate Bar Mitzvah? How many *shuls* in Toronto? Do rabbis meet in country-wide association? Is Kosher food easily available? Are many Jews from Canada settling in Israel? How many of them speak Yiddish or know Hebrew? Are there Jewish newspapers and magazines?"

At first, his questions puzzled me. Was this merely his way of showing courtesy by now giving me a turn at making my "speech"? Or was this a debating tactic, a maneuver to help prove, in his next "speech" to me, that Jews in Russia were not the victims of governmental interference or suppression, but suffered only from the same worldwide assimilation patterns as did North American Jews? Was he going to challenge any suggestion that Judaism was prospering in my country, and debate with me "my" statistics or "my" interpretation of trends? I did not have to wait long for an answer—but it was the one I least expected. It came from his eyes and from the arms he would throw around me, in brotherly embrace.

I began describing the variety and richness of Jewish life in North America in some detail—the Jewish day schools, the institutes of higher Jewish learning, the growing number of native-born scholars of Judaica, the gifted Jewish writers, and some of the outspoken political leaders of the Jewish community. I spoke, looking directly into his large, sad, blue eyes. As I continued, he was becoming a strange mixture of emotions: Those sad eyes were misting and filling up with tears, while a small, hesitant smile was settling on his face. And then, the moment of truth. He stood up and moved toward me. I rose and we embraced tearfully. And the only words he said, as he patted my back warmly, were these: "So you have a great and strong community of Jews in America. You must continue to be strong. We have no voice and your Jews do. *You must never forget us. We will be finished, if you do.*" I left his room and walked slowly into the stark, wintry bleakness of Moscow.

Moscow: Visited briefly—very briefly—with "Kobi" Sharett at the Israel Embassy, which is located on a quiet, winding, crescent-like street. He is a journalist by profession, presently on leave to the Israel Foreign Ministry, from *Maariv*, the big Tel Aviv paper. He is First Secretary here. The Ambassador is away on home leave—they said his wife was ill—so could not meet with him. For the moment, Kobi is in charge. He spoke very little, pointing, like Rabbi Levin, to the walls. We made a date to meet tomorrow, outside the synagogue—after the morning services. "We'll talk in the streets as we walk around," he said.

Moscow: Have not yet thawed out! Met Kobi as prearranged, and like two *meshugaim*—crazy people—we spent the whole day, today, from morning until evening, walking the pavements of this frozen city. (It's the only way to communicate with him, and vice-versa.) Our walks put the Russians to work, too; there were really three of us. As we were entering a bookstore, Kobi told me to turn around and observe a short, stocky man in a knee-length leather coat who was about seven or eight yards behind us, down the street. "That's my tail," he said, "and the poor fool knows that I know he's assigned to follow my movements. Watch for him, again, after we get out of the shop." "Maybe we should invite him to join us for lunch," I said.

Inside the bookstore Kobi told me to ask for a recently published Russian book, *The Reactionary Essence of Judaism*—a piece of anti-Semitic garbage in the guise of authentic historical "research." The store was mobbed with bookbuyers. Books are very inexpensive here in Russia and the reading public is very large. But the state stores trust no one. Before you can even get near a book you must queue up at a cashier's wicket and pay for the volume you're asking for. This book, Kobi says, has not yet reached the West, and it's important to have it translated and publicized after I return to Canada. The "tail" came wagging right behind us, as predicted, no sooner than we left the shop. We stopped at an outdoor kiosk which sold even cheaper books. I bought an anti-Semitic pamphlet which is in great vogue just now, titled *Conversation on the (Jewish) New Year*. It's loaded with the same dangerous anti-Jewish tripe. I must not forget, Kobi reminded me, that here the state publishes everything, and no printed word sees the light of day without its knowledge and encouragement. These books, he said, were actually commissioned by the government.

March

Vienna: Todah la'el—thank the Lord—after three weeks in that hellhole, landed here after a very short flight from Kiev in the Soviet Union. Vienna looked like the promised land. Even the weather is almost tropical compared to freezing Moscow and Leningrad. It's 70 degrees (Fahrenheit) here today. After what happened at the Kiev airport I felt like kissing the ground of Vienna. Before I could finally board the plane in Kiev I was detained for almost two hours—frisked, undressed and harassed—by airport police. They accused me of trading in the black market with American dollars. They knew that they were lying. But I finally realized that they were giving me a rough time only to show that they were not happy with the many contacts I had made with Jews. In the end, they claimed there was some discrepancy between the amount of foreign currency I had declared on arrival three weeks ago and the bank's receipts showing my currency exchanges in the country. Protested and demanded to call both American and Canadian embassies in Moscow from their office. They backtracked and relented. But not without filching a "fine" of $113 (U.S.). I'd wager the two policemen personally pocketed the money. They refused to give me a receipt for it. Said that if I wanted to wait for it, I would miss my plane.

Tel Aviv: Have spent two full and exhilarating days with Meir Rosenne at the Foreign Ministry here. His word is his bond. He promised to fly in from New York, to meet me here on my return from Russia, and he's here. Read him all of my notes plus personal commentaries and impressions. Yesterday afternoon, he took me to meet some of the members of the Israeli basketball team who had just recently returned from their trip to Riga. I compared notes with them. We confirmed to each other our resolve to "get them out," and bring them "home to Israel."

All day today, Meir and I have been discussinng this very issue. It is time to raise this central question—in public and among our own people, of course. The question is not, as

The Holocaust and Soviet Jewry 299

Nahum Goldmann keeps repeating, an internal Russian matter which Jewish diplomacy can cure. It is much more than a matter of civil rights for Jews under the Russian Constitution. Of course, it's that, too, but it's much, much more. This is a new and golden moment in recent Russian Jewish history. After more than forty years of anti-Zionist Communist rule and brainwashing, Russian Jews in their hundreds of thousands were not only still Jewish to their core, they were also still Zionists, hanging on to every word about Israel's fate and future. If given a chance, these people could be saved as Jews. They'd walk all the way to Israel, today. What happens to those who won't or can't get out of Russia? Does our effort to redeem, say, even only twenty per cent of them cause any harm to the other Russian Jews who stay? We think not. Their Jewish future in Russia can only be improved—*even if they never leave*—once they know that there are Jews outside who care enough about them. Care enough, in fact, to risk their own lives in bringing out those who want and can get out. So activism for Soviet Jewry must become the order of the day.

Meir cautioned me that there are many big hurdles to overcome among North American Jewish leaders who are paralyzed into inaction by the Goldmann position. We will also be told that our activism contributes to warming up the "Cold War"—creating tensions between the United States and Russia that the American government can live without. "I heard about that once," I told him. "That's what Jews and other liberals in the Roosevelt Administration told us back in the forties. They said that the Jewish Question in Germany, and the resettlement of Jewish refugees from Europe, could drive a wedge between the United States and England. Remember their horrible slogan: The Jewish difficulties will all be resolved when we win the war; wait until the war's over. So we waited—to discover that there were six million Jews dead. How many of them did we Jews in America send to their graves by not forcing Roosevelt's hand—by not moving fast enough ourselves? And most of all, by Jewish organizations fighting among themselves."

Meir urged me not to omit the desire of many Russian Jews

to emigrate to Israel from the articles the *Toronto Star* asked me to write on this trip. "Most of the published reports have kept this central question out of their descriptions. It's a political hot-potato, I know. But somehow, you've got to get that message across." He knows that I feel that way, too. "Tell it," he repeated, "but of course, without mentioning Jewish names and Jewish officials." Told him not to take me for a fool and then, leaving him, added: "It's a story *I must tell*. If you, as an Israeli tell it, cynics among our people—and the world—will say that you wouldn't expect anything different from Israelis. They are always ready even to liquidate a diaspora Jewish community in order to swell their own population with *olim* (new Israeli immigrants). But if I, and others like me, tell the story, we are not speaking as Israelis—whom many wrongly distrust on this issue—but as concerned and realistic Jewish citizens of North America, with access to the power centers of Washington and Ottawa."

April

Toronto: No luck again, today, with Canadian Jewish Congress leaders. Attended their Executive Meeting at 150 Beverley Street—of which I am not a member. This was my first appearance before an "official meeting," but I have been saying the same things publicly and to private individuals who are active in the C.J.C. Canadian Jewish Congress still prefers hush-hush diplomacy. Stalling me.

The real reason did finally come out. Sam Bronfman and Michael Garber of Montreal (Michael is President, but "Mr. Sam" still runs the show) are strongly opposed to countering Nahum Goldmann's World Jewish Congress line. The word is: Canadian Jewish Congress is a constituent and active member of the World Jewish Congress. It will not undertake a political program of the kind I proposed regarding Russian Jewry that does not have the stamp of approval from Goldmann. And that's not going to be given. Not soon, anyway. Maybe never.

Toronto: Saul Hayes called from CJC headquarters in Montreal. Heard about my attempt to persuade Central Region of CJC in Toronto to adopt a strong "Soviet Jewry position." Reiterated his own personal support, but papered over the situation and stroked me by saying that he would be able to do one thing—and that was about all—to get my position across. If the *Toronto Star* would put my eight articles on Soviet Jews into a single brochure and print up a few thousand copies, he would see to it that Canadian Jewish Congress, from Montreal, would distribute them, as a public service—to V.I.P.'s, libraries etc.—and mail them out to a selected list of their member organizations across Canada. I thanked him for his personal support and, of course, for at least undertaking to have those articles sent around the country, courtesy *Toronto Star*. It should be printed early in May, and it will carry the title "A Rabbi Reports on Russia."

May

Toronto: The Rev. Al Forrest, Editor of the *United Church Observer*, an important biweekly in Canada, called to ask that I write an article for their July issue on "religious plight of Jews in the Soviet Union." He had read my series in the *Toronto Star*, was impressed, and would like a special article based on my trip to Russia. Forrest is not supposed to be too friendly to Jewish people. Still I will write that article—not for him—but in order to get the message across in his important church journal.

June

Toronto: Another try today for Soviet Jews with C.J.C. Struck out again. They won't budge an inch. "Speak softly," one of their big-shots told me, "that's our policy." Didn't Teddy Roosevelt coin that phrase? But he said it differently. "Speak softly—and *carry a big stick!*"

September

Toronto: During the week of *Sukkot* (Feast of Tabernacles) phoned Dr. Abba H. Silver in Cleveland. Wished him a Happy New Year, and he said that he had read about my Russian articles. That has something to do with the purpose of this call, I told him. I read him a report of words ascribed to him in the current (September, 1961) issue of the local *Jewish Standard*: "Silver says that there.is hope that Soviet Jewry may, in the not too distant future, secure religious and cultural freedom." I asked him for the source of this optimism. He said that he has been talking with Nahum Goldmann about this matter and he was reflecting Goldmann's hopes. Told him that he, Silver, had not swallowed "establishment" views on Palestine and the refugees in 1943. Why should he follow them now? Received no answer to my question. And I didn't ask it rhetorically.

April 1962

My mail is filled with "hate-letters" from the Jewish-Communist-types. But also some strange sounds in the community are coming from a few of the so-called "leaders," who accuse me of "stirring up trouble." One of them even said publicly that "Rosenberg must be in the employ of the American State Department, paid to heat up the Cold War." I am sick at heart. But the Jewish battle must go on. This is 1962, *not* 1942.

August 1963

Toronto: Meir Rosenne called and suggested I arrange to meet with him in New York, early next month, when I will be visiting the Jewish Theological Seminary, attending the Conference on the Moral Implications of the Rabbinate, sponsored by the Rabbinical Assembly. Professor Abraham Heschel is going to deliver a bombshell there, with a paper on the Soviet Jews, Meir told me. He also said that Heschel would put himself "on the line" with Soviet Jewry, and planned to make this issue a continuing commitment, giving it the same kind of effort he did with Martin Luther King, beginning with his marching at Selma, Alabama. Meir would try to get me an advance copy of the Heschel speech, through Wolfe Kelman (executive head of the Rabbinical Assembly).

New York: Met with Meir Rosenne, and after dinner left Hotel Commodore for the Heschel speech. It was a great, moving, and—I am certain—historic speech. It will be a turning point in American Jewish life. Heschel is just the man this problem needs. He's got charisma, credibility—with Blacks, other minority groups, and Christian churchmen—and most of all, with the Rabbinate and many synagogue leaders. He's not a political Jew, but a moral statesman, and that's just what this idea needs. His views on Soviet Jewry will go a long way to shake up the sleeping establishment of American Jews—and, who knows, maybe even spin off into Canada too.

Attached to this note is the text of Professor Heschel's speech, "The Jews in the Soviet Union." Here are some of the paragraphs I had underlined:

> "When I was a young boy I asked myself again and again: Was there no moral indignation, in Europe, when a whole people was driven out of Spain? (The Jews, in 1492.) Was there no outcry, no outburst of anger when human beings were burned alive at the auto-da-fé?
>
> "There was no outcry, there was no public protest....
>
> "To be sure, there is a risk to be taken whenever we undertake to challenge the policy or the acts of a mighty power. At this juncture in history when the Test Ban Treaty between U.S.A. and U.S.S.R. has been signed and may, as we wholeheartedly hope and pray, initiate an era of peace

and reconciliation between the world's great powers, our plea on behalf of the Jews in Russia may be attacked as inopportune. Political experts may rebuke us for calling attention to a minor issue when major issues are at stake. Yet the process of liquidating a great Jewish community is not a minor issue....

"If we are ready to go to jail in order to destroy the blight of the racial bigotry, if we are ready to march to Washington in order to demonstrate our identification with those who are deprived of equal rights, should we not be ready to go to jail in order to end the martyrdom of our Russian brethren? To arrange sit-ins, protests, days of fasting and prayer, public demonstrations to which even Russian leaders will not remain indifferent? The voice of our brother's agony is crying to us! How can we be silent? How can we remain passive? How can we have peace of mind or live with our conscience?...

"It is the duty of the American rabbinate, with its tradition of leadership in many social issues, to assume moral and spiritual leadership in this great emergency; to proclaim, to teach, to preach that the plight of the Jews in Russia is a matter of utmost priority.

"Inform your congregants, preach, write, urge, stir....

"If I forget thee, O Russian Jewry..."

October

Toronto: After some preliminary discussion with Saul Hayes about this, decided to try "breaking into" Canadian Jewish Congress via the "back door"—by arranging for their National Religious Welfare Committee, headed by Rabbi S. Zambrowsky of Montreal, to set up a countrywide conference of Rabbis dealing with Soviet Jewish issue, from religious-freedom angle. Have spoken with Zambrowsky, reminding him of Professor Heschel's cry. Surely, this approach can raise none of Goldmann's hackles, and CJC should be able, through this route of rabbinical protest here, to help sponsor such a meeting. Zambrowsky called today to confirm agreement.

Toronto: Date now set for Ottawa All Canadian Rabbinic Conference for early in the new year.

February 1964

Toronto: Clipping of article in *Congress Bulletin*, issue of January-February, 1964 (Headline and opening paragraph): "ALL-CANADIAN RABBINIC CONFERENCE MEETS IN OTTAWA. The Rabbinic Conference, the first of its kind to be held in Canada, was attended by sixty Jewish religious leaders from every major community across Canada, sponsored by the National Religious Welfare Committee of Canadian Jewish Congress...." This article neglected to mention that three rabbis, including myself, took a copy of the Conference resolution calling for equal religious rights for Jews in the Soviet Union to the Russian Embassy in Ottawa, after the close of our meetings. But the Russians refused to receive us, and merely took the note at the front gate.

April

Ottawa: Today, Rabbi Zambrowsky, Samuel Lewin, the Congress executive in charge of its Religious Welfare Committee, and I, met with Mr. A. Popov at the Soviet Embassy, to hand him a statement of our Committee. It was first cleared with the Executive of CJC, and it made certain to say, among other things, that we were *not* requesting Russians "to grant Jews any privileges not accorded to other Soviet religious groups." I would have wished that Congress would have permitted a more forceful statement about national minority rights, Jewish schools, and of course that "no-no"—the right to emigrate for purposes of "family re-unification in Israel." Satisfied for small mercies, nevertheless. Popov wasn't exactly "popping off"—he kept quiet, listened to our presentation, gave a "Mona-Lisa smile," and that was it. But at least somebody in Moscow will know that Canadian Jews are upset with their government. I also gave him back his Mona-Lisa smile in return, when he said, as we left: "We know all about your visit and your articles on the Soviet Union, Rabbi Rosenberg." I should have demanded that he return that $113 they took away from me at the Kiev Airport.

October

New York: In New York to meet with Meir Rosenne. Dr. Heschel did it again! Attended a large meeting at Hunter College Auditorium called by the New York Conference on Soviet Jewry—one of the few public groups operating in this field on behalf of the organized Jewish community. Heschel will find out soon enough that the cry he made last night for outright Jewish emigration from Russia will cause him pain with everybody in the Jewish establishment groups—except Israel, of course. Meir confirmed my view, when I called him this morning to say goodbye.

Attached: my quickly scribbled notes of key paragraphs from Heschel's speech:

> "Russian Jews are in distress; are even deprived of the right to speak about their being in distress. This is the meaning of this gathering tonight. We must speak, because Jews of Russia have no voice. We must cry in public because they can only cry in secret.

> "We plead, we implore the leaders of Russia: Let our people live in dignity or let our people go. Let them live or let them leave!" (Thunderous applause. People stand and shout their agreement!)

February 1966

New York: Met here today with Rabbi Wolfe Kelman, executive head of the Rabbinical Assembly of America. Have been appointed Chairman of the Rabbinical Assembly convention (International Association of Conservative Rabbis) which will be holding its annual meeting, in Toronto, this May—for the first time ever in Canada. Insisted, as Chairman, that we devote "a day to Soviet Jewry." It was agreed that we would invite Elie Wiesel and Professor Heschel to address the convention—afternoon and evening—on this subject. The idea is to get the Convention to make a breakthrough officially, by calling for *emigration of Jews out of Russia*—a political step—and no longer merely contenting ourselves with polite calls for ameliorating their internal religious disabilities.

May

Toronto: Rabbinical Assembly convention moving along fine. Best session so far was yesterday's meeting—virtually the whole day—devoted to Soviet Jews. Wiesel and Heschel were breathtaking and moving. Wiesel is a spellbinder—with his hushed, understated dramatic speech. We got the resolution we wanted—passed unanimously. Here it is:

"Jews in the Soviet Union

"The status of our brethren in the Soviet Union is one of deep concern to us. We urge, in the spirit of Professor Abraham J. Heschel's message, the creation of a committee to direct itself to the manner of advising an on-going program, and the implementation thereof, which shall focus attention on this most crucial matter to the end that:

"1. Soviet Jews know that we identify with them, that we feel their pain and their spiritual slavery, that .we shall not rest or remain silent until we see the amelioration of their plight.

"2. We take concrete steps to bring to the attention of Jews and the general population everywhere, that though Soviet Jews must be silent, we speak on behalf of their suffering.

"3. The Government of the Soviet Union must permit Russia's Jews to live their culture and religion, *or else permit them to emigrate.*"

As Chairman of the Convention was able to arrange for a number of my lay friends in Toronto to hear both Wiesel and Heschel. We all agreed that Wiesel is so tremendously effective a spokesman for the "cause" that we must bring him to Beth Tzedec, to introduce him for first time to Toronto's larger community. Maybe they will pay heed to *his* cry.

June

Toronto: Received an urgent call from Meir Rosenne today. "The Central Conference of American Rabbis"—international body of Reform Rabbis—was holding its annual convention in Toronto, in a day or so, and it was imperative that they pass a strong resolution on Soviet Jewry. This was not a Canadian body, but an international group of influential rabbis, and there were some rumblings Meir had caught. Rabbi Morris Kertzer (a good friend and a former Canadian), as Chairman of the Resolutions Committee, was being persuaded by some of his colleagues to "soft-pedal" the issue. Kertzer, of course, had been to the Soviet Union in 1956 and was personally supportive and knowledgeable. He just needs some extra leverage from the outside, Meir said. Would I meet Kertzer and the members of his Resolutions Committee, and see if they can get a "good" resolution passed, in convention assembled?

Toronto: Went down to Royal York Hotel to meet with Rabbi Levi Olan of Dallas (a former Rochesterian, whose family there were also members of Beth El), now Vice-President of the C.C.A.R.—and with Morris Kertzer. Two friends. Before an hour was over, we hammered out a resolution which was passed.

This is what the Convention voted:

"Be it resolved that C.C.A.R. encourage the formation of special subcommittees on Soviet Jewry in each [Reform] congregation to implement the program of the American Jewish Conference on Soviet Jewry....

"Be it further resolved that in order to effectuate our determination to bring the plight of Soviet Jewry to all our congregations, a special *ad hoc* committee be established which shall be charged with sensitizing the Jewish and general community to the desperate plight of our brethren."

Key words, of course: *special committees in all of their congregations*, and the need to *sensitize the Jewish community*.

September

Toronto: Have made arrangements with Elie Wiesel in New York. By the side of Abraham Heschel, he is fast becoming the conscience of the community of North American Jews on the subject of Soviet Jews. Elie will come up to Beth Tzedec on Sunday, December 18th, to spend the day with us: a morning dialogue with Colonel Mordechai Bar-On of Israel; and a big, citywide meeting at four o'clock in the main sanctuary. I think we can fill that big room. He will electrify this community. Particularly, after the recent appearance of his newest book, *The Jews of Silence*. Of course, Elie also meant North American Jews when he wrote his title—not just the Russian Jews. Maybe our people here, after hearing him, will get his *double-entendre*.

December

Toronto: Yesterday was a great day in my life. Elie Wiesel did everything I expected he would. After that superb talk, he and Meir Rosenne came over to my house. All three of our daughters were home and they, too, said they will never forget the mood and aura that Elie brought to the table—as we ate, sang, and dreamed out loud. All the way to the airport, with Meir, Elie and Hadassa in my car, we sang Israeli songs of hope. It was one of my Jewish highlights—that great, big, wonderful day of yesterday—spilling over into the week—and I hope—the weeks to come in the new year.

January 1967

Toronto: Clipping from my column in the *Beth Tzedec Bulletin*:

ELIE WIESEL

I write these lines just after Elie Wiesel's call from New York City. I had asked his permission to make a record of the tape of his speech here, to our Israel-Diaspora Institute. At first he demurred, his modesty disallowing. But I explained that many of those who had heard him, and many, many who could not be present had beseeched me to let them hear the speech.

Now we're to have a record of one of the greatest talks I have ever heard—a living remembrance of an unforgettable Jewish event, a veritable religious experience, not often felt so deeply, by so many, at one time.

The record will be sold and if there are any profits the money will go to a special fund established by Elie Wiesel to help in the work to alleviate Russian Jewry's burden.

This will be a limited edition record—available on a first come first served basis.

January

Toronto: The important and reliable sourcebook, the American Jewish Year Book for 1967 has appeared. In it—and in a review of 1966 for Jews around the world—as part of its report on Soviet Jewish life in 1966, photocopied this tell-tale—and for me—personally noteworthy paragraph (Page 381):

> An interfaith delegation visiting Moscow in January 1966 reported that Chief Rabbi Yehudah Leib Levin was always closely watched when foreign visitors came to see him, and therefore in no position to speak freely. In their opinion, the plight of religious Jewry stemmed largely from "fear on the part of the Jewish leadership...of reprisals."

February 1967

Vienna: It is now three o'clock in the morning. I can't sleep—not after spending this whole evening with Chief Rabbi Elijah Katz and Mrs. Katz in Bratislava—just twenty miles across the border into Czechoslovakia. What has happened to a once-great community.[9] "How have the mighty fallen!" In the quiet of his apartment told Rabbi Katz of my harrowing experiences all of last week in Budapest, then Prague—trying to make contact with Jews who want to get to Israel.

After dinner, about eleven o'clock, Rabbi Katz arranged for us—two of my U.J.A. mission friends were along—to go by special, licensed taxi across the border from Bratislava into Vienna. Thought back once again to my Kiev-Vienna trip six years ago. Only this time, it was pitch-black out, somber in the streets of Czechoslavakia; and we were stopped four or five times down the highway leading to the Austrian border by Czech military men at these checkpoints. Vienna was bright, alive, and the night life just beginning as we checked into this beautiful Hotel Imperial two hours ago. My friends have gone

---

[9] Bratislava is the capital of Slovakia. Under the Austro-Hungarian Empire, until 1918, it was known as Pressburg. It had been the home of Jewish *yeshivot*, and was one of the oldest Jewish communities in the Danube area, having received its charter in 1291. Rabbi Katz emigrated soon thereafter to Israel, where he became Chief Rabbi of Beersheba.

312 THE REAL JEWISH WORLD

out for a night on the town. *I* write—articles for the *Toronto Star* to cable before dawn—material about those two Iron Curtain countries, and their Jews, which I couldn't—and wouldn't—file from there.

Tomorrow, I meet Russian Jews, who are beginning to get out in respectable numbers, bound for Israel—with Vienna as their first, and exciting moment, outside of the curtain, en route to the Promise.

Vienna-Israel: In Flight aboard El-Al Airliner

At the airport all afternoon. There were two plane-loads of Georgians—"Oriental Jews," from deep inside Russia; we met them on their arrival. Some of them with very large families. One patriarchal type, wearing ceremonial robes typical of Georgian Jews—with his embroidered Jewish headgear, and all. They say that in their west-Transcaucasian Soviet republic, they remain "fiercely" Jewish, and the Moscow authorities—so far away to the west—can't stop them from practicing their religious life openly and loyally. The old gentleman spoke to me in Hebrew. I was nonplused that they still preserved this language and could even speak it. He said that I shouldn't be so surprised. "After all," he boasted, "we Georgian Jews are descended from the Ten Tribes of Israel, exiled by Shalmaneser. In your countries they speak of the Ten Lost Tribes of Israel. Well, that's who we are, except that we never got lost. We've preserved our holy Jewish language and way of life—even inside the Communist world—untarnished, for over 2,500 years! And now, at last, we are going back home!"

Tel Aviv: Spoke to my brother-in-law, Colonel Meir Batz. He's set up a meeting for me with David Ben Gurion at his kibbutz in the Negev, "S'de Boker." I will taxi down from here first to pick "Batz" up at his home in Beersheba, and then we'll go on together to meet Ben Gurion at the Kibbutz, about twenty miles further south into the desert.

Tel Aviv: Ben Gurion was as rambunctious as ever this

afternoon at the Kibbutz. Batz and I spent almost two hours with him. They are old friends from the days of the *Hagana*. First, the two spoke about Batz's well-known (in Israel) "grandiose" dream of building a canal in the Negev—from Sea to Sea, the Mediterranean to the Dead Sea—to do away with dependence on the Suez, and to electrify the Negev, at the same time. Then, B.G. got onto his favorite subject, *aliya* (immigration of diaspora Jews to Israel)—but a new and—for me—surprising twist. He told Batz: "Your canal will make the Negev an industrial center, with hundreds of scientific and manufacturing enterprises. That will become the base for the huge Russian-Jewish immigration that is sure to come, in the next few years. As you know, I am past eighty, and may not live to see it—but hundreds of thousands of Russians are going to get out of the Soviet Union and come here. And we have got to be able to give them what *they* need: good *scientific* centers; *sophisticated manufacturing* plants; and lots of good, open space for beautiful houses. The best of the city and the best of the countryside—that's what we will have here for them in the Negev desert."

Glad I taped our discussion. It will be a useful historical document: maybe even a prophecy. B.G.—after a lot of coaxing—finally agreed to come to Toronto on March 20th, to address our community in behalf of the United Jewish Appeal. I've also made arrangements for Batz to spend a month in Toronto for the U.J.A. to spread the word about "his canal" and the future. "Russian Jews and the Canal," I told him, "that's a good title for your lectures in Canada."

March

Toronto: The Toronto "U.J.A. Cabinet" decided to charter an Air Canada airliner filled with top-givers "paying heavily to get on board," to fly to Montreal in order to bring Ben Gurion and his wife Paula from there to Toronto. "Guard of Honor," they called it. On arrival, at the airport in Toronto, there were about 400 children from various Jewish schools, waving Canadian and Israel flags. Limousines took us to the Royal York Hotel, where the Vice-Regal suite was waiting for the Ben Gurions.

At four o'clock in the afternoon, after a very short rest in the Hotel, the Ben Gurions arrived at Beth Tzedec. The sanctuary and other halls were over-flowing with about 4,000 children. Ben Gurion insisted at "S'de Boker" that his first speech in Toronto—he hadn't been here since the days of the First World War, recruiting for the "Jewish Legion"—must be to children, *and it must be given in Hebrew.* All the day schools cooperated, madly. Their Hebrew-speaking kids were given passes. Suddenly, "all" the Jews in town passed themselves off as Hebrew-speakers—they wanted tickets of admission. But they couldn't pass as school-children, though some of them did sneak in.

At night, Paul Martin, as acting Prime Minister, came from Ottawa, spent time visiting with the Ben Gurions in their suite, and then we marched into the great "fundraising banquet" in the Canadian Room of the Royal York Hotel.

The next morning, the newspapers were filled with stories and pictures. A great day had come and passed. One of the articles in the *Toronto Star* is attached:

> "Rabbi Stuart E. Rosenberg praised the former government leader. 'Ben Gurion made history by being history.... But even now many Jews are not ready, in the way that Ben Gurion is, to carry on the great tasks'....
>
> "Rosenberg said there are hundreds of thousands of Jews behind the Iron Curtain who would be anxious to go to Israel if they were allowed to do so"....

May

Toronto: Meir Rosenne is now rounding out six years at his "Office Without a Name," at the Israeli Consulate in New

York. He visited me in Toronto today, and he brought with him Dr. Yoram Dinstein, who is about to replace Meir. Rosenne will be returned to the Foreign Ministry in Tel Aviv in the next few months.

They said that Professor Heschel had told Meir that he had been invited to lecture to the forthcoming international conference, sponsored by Roman Catholic Church in Canada, in honor of the Canadian Centennial, to be held in Toronto, in August. Heschel mentioned that I was also invited—the only two Jews—to participate in that Conference. Leading Catholic figures from around the world would be present at this conference on "The Theology of the Renewal of the Church," together with many observers. "And there will be big press coverage," added Meir.

"Yes, I've been invited," I replied. "But what's the point? Do you have something in mind?"

"Of course, I do." I should have known; Meir (and I suppose now, Yoram, too) always "had something in mind." "Can you somehow raise 'our question' in your lecture?" I was taken aback.

"At a theological conference on church renewal, you're asking me to talk about Soviet Jewry?" It wasn't the place, I thought, for this kind of discussion. "However, let me think about it, and I'll get back to you."

July

Ivry, Quebec: Holing up here in the Laurentians—only an hour away from Montreal, and "Expo '67—in a summer cottage lent to Hadassa and me by good friends, the Cobrins of Montreal. Have been busy writing and editing *Encyclopedia Judaica* articles here, and also preparing for that major lecture—which will be published—at the Catholic Conference in Toronto, next month.

Dinstein has been phoning. He wanted to know my reactions to a problem in Montreal. Could I meet him there soon? And he added—those Israelis never forget—have I come up with a solution to the decision *we* made in Toronto, a few months ago (when he first met me) to raise "the question" at the Catholic conference? I have—but it was not my decision, and it wasn't even a decision—I protested. We're meeting soon.

July

Ivry, Quebec: Spent the day in Montreal. Dinstein wanted me to get Rabbi Wilfred Shuchat, my friend and classmate— and Rabbi of the prestigious Montreal *shul* "Shaar Hashomayim"—to change his mind. About what, I ask? "As program chairman of the Pavillion of Judaism at Expo, he refuses to mix what he calls 'politics' into a display by Canadian Jews about religion. All I've asked him—for weeks now—was to allow a simple placard on a simple easel, at the entranceway to the 'Pavillion,' showing the number of synagogues and Jewish schools, on a chart, in the major countries of the world." He was smiling now, not angry, and in a moment, we both burst out laughing. "Well, that's a good religious statistic about Judaism—not *political*, at all," I said. "But of course, you will be showing that in the Soviet Union—a country of three million Jews—there are less than one hundred synagogues and *no Jewish schools at all*. Compared to the thousands upon thousands of both in the U.S., Canada, the U.K. etc. Good point. Good plan. And such pure religion!"

It had not been easy, Yoram complained. "Not only Rabbi Shuchat, but the Congress establishment know what I want to accomplish, and they refuse to allow this. You're on the Board of the 'Pavillion,' " he said, "so use *your* muscle!" I'm on vacation here in the Laurentians, I told him, and besides I'm working on that paper for the Catholics. Which brought him to that point, which I don't for one moment believe, he "almost forgot about." "The only thing I can try to do, since I am not invited there as a political person, but as a Jewish scholar, is to see if I can weave the matter into one of my *answers* in the discussion period following the lecture. I will be talking about the role of Israel in Jewish religious and spiritual thought—so there may be a spot for 'the question,' somewhere in the question-answer period." I reminded him of the story of the Rabbi who tells his students: "Boys, ask me a question, because *have I got an answer*—ready-made for you!"

August

Ivry, Quebec: Dinstein is happy. After several trips to Montreal, my friend Jack Engels—an active supporter of the "Pavillion" took me to meet several of the other Board members, and with some pressure, even got Willie Shuchat's approval for the chart. It will be labeled, "Synagogues and Jewish Schools Around the World," and considering the obvious discrepancies between the free world and the Soviet Union, hundreds of thousands of expected visitors to the "Pavillion"—Jews and non-Jews—should readily get the silent message of the "silent Jews."

Toronto: Read my paper, "Contemporary Renewal and Jewish Experience," before a very interesting and important collection of Catholics, Protestants, and academics gathered here for the Conference.[10] My plan worked even better than I could have foreseen.

After the paper, and before the discussion period, there was a coffee-break. Observed that Monsignor John Oesterreicher, who heard the paper, was at my elbow, in the corridors, outside the lecture hall. Oesterreicher is head of the Institute of Judaeo-Christian Studies at Seton Hall University in South Orange, New Jersey. He is of Jewish parentage, converted to Catholicism, and started an important career in the Church. Now that ecumenism is "the rage," he no longer talks about

---

[10] Published in *Renewal of Religious Thought*, Volume I, of *Theology of Renewal*, edited by L.K. Shook, Palm Publishers, Montreal, 1968, pp. 265-287.

"converting the Jews"—as I believe he once did—but of "loving the Jews."

He came over to congratulate "me" on the recent "stunning victory" of the Israelis during the Six-Day War. He "loved" my paper, especially the part that dealt with the importance of Israel to the Jewish people. "You're right—as you say, Israel is itself a major example of Jewish *renewal*. The Jews are coming back into history as players, not as victims."

Suggested that without additional Jews in Israel—especially those who were disallowed by their hostile governments from practicing Judaism to the full—there would be little to remember about "our renewal," after all. It didn't take very long, and he was asking about Iron Curtain countries, etc. "Ask me these questions, John, in the discussion period that's coming up. It's too long a matter to deal with, out here in the hallway."

A few minutes later, back in the lecture hall, I was talking about Soviet Jews, their internal difficulties, and the need to get them out—to Israel—if the process of "Jewish renewal" was to be continued. Called upon the audience to assist Jews in getting out of that land so they could rejoin their people, and *renew their Jewish history.*

Throughout the lecture, and thereafter during the discussion period, one good-looking and impressive Catholic cleric sat seriously, off in a corner, to himself. He was taking notes rapidly and remained fully engaged with the lecturer. The discussion wound down, and this man approached, inviting me to a faculty lounge "to take tea together." Handed me his card. It read, "Most Reverend Sergio Pignedoli, Apostolic Delegate, Ottawa, Canada." Between sips, he said that he was now completing his tour of duty as Vatican's diplomatic ambassador to Canada, and returning to Rome in a few weeks. He was active in the Congregation for Non-Christians, a secretariat which grew out of Pope John's Vatican Council II several years before, and which sought better relations with the Jewish people. He had heard me mention—during the discussion period—that I was going to spend a year in Israel, beginning this Fall, on sabbatical leave from my congregation. "When you see Yaacov Herzog in Jerusalem, tell him of our conversation. Come to see me in Rome, and bring Dr. Herzog along. We Catholics have to learn to see the whole problem of Jewish renewal—including, as you mentioned, Jews like those in the Soviet Union—from *your Jewish perspective*. Visit with me in Rome, whenever you can. You can find me in the Vatican Secretariat of State."[11]

So Dinstein's insistence wasn't wrong after all. Those Israelis! They don't miss a trick. And they know how to touch all the bases. Will surely follow up in Jerusalem, with one of my dearest, warmest, brightest friends in all Israel—Yaacov Herzog.

November

Jerusalem: Have settled in nicely at our tiny rented apartment here, where we will be staying, on sabbatical until next July (1968). Have gone over to meet with Yaacov Herzog, now Director-General of the Prime Minister's Office—running the show for Levi Eshkol. Gave him Archbishop Pignedoli's message. Yaacov had met him before, and said the new word from him was very "useful," especially the reference to Russian Jews. He would arrange to see Pignedoli, soon, on his next trip to Rome. He also asked me to go down to Lod Airport, whenever possible, and to "tee up" the times with him, to meet the planes

---

[11] Archbishop Sergio Pignedoli returned to Rome from Canada in 1967. He became President of the Congregation for Non-Christians. In 1973, he was elevated to the College of Cardinals and, according to my informants in the Church, was on a "short list for nomination" as Pope, before John Paul II was elected. He died in 1980 at the age of seventy. Over the years, I enjoyed his many courtesies in Rome. He was a friend of the Jewish people, even if he did not set Vatican policy regarding the relation of the State of Israel to its own *weltpolitik*. I am convinced that he personally favored the idea of Jerusalem as the capital of Israel.

coming in from Vienna, carrying Russian Jews. These days, they are mostly older people—with their entire families—coming out of Tiflis, the capital city of Georgia.

February 1968

Jerusalem: (Note: While on sabbatical leave from Beth Tzedec Congregation, Toronto, I wrote a series of "Letters from Jerusalem" which appeared every few weeks in my congregational "Bulletin," addressed principally to members of the synagogue. One of these Letters talked about "three phone calls" in Jerusalem. The "Second Call," excerpted from the rest of that Letter, follows. M refers to Meir Rosenne; the "Russian surprise" was Mordechai Chanzin.)

Letter from Jerusalem

"Hello, Stuart. This is M. in Tel Aviv. Now that you've finally come here for a while, I can reciprocate in Israel, at last. Please be our guests at our home, whenever you can. But the sooner the better. I've got an important, special surprise."

A couple of weeks after I put down the phone, we did manage to get to Tel Aviv. And what a surprise he had.

Just seven years ago, in March, 1961, it was my great privilege to represent Canadian Jews to Russian Jews—unofficially, of course—when I went as the first Canadian Rabbi to observe Jewish life in the Soviet Union.

We managed to spend part of every day in Moscow at the Great Synagogue. There, one man, in particular, was extremely helpful and informative. He was the only one there who spoke Hebrew, and thus was in a position to communicate important news in a language others did not understand, with some safety. He had been in solitary confinement in Siberia. Over the years, he had been periodically imprisoned, brainwashed and threatened. But, he told me, and one could plainly see, they would never break his spirit!

His great crime? He was a Zionist, and he read Hebrew books, too!

I confess that when we parted in Moscow I believed that I would never see him again. But miracles do happen. A few days ago, here in Israel, we had a personal re-union. My friend, M., had reason to know all about my contact with this man, in Russia. He also knew that this man was actually allowed to leave Russia—with his wife and daughter—and had arrived in Israel about 18 months ago.

June

Jerusalem: Noted in *Jerusalem Post* stories concerning visit to the United States of Chief Rabbi Yehudah Leib Levin of Moscow. What a mess it appears to be! Very disappointed I couldn't be in New York now, possibly to meet with him. But there—in America—he wouldn't talk much, in any case. He would be as much a captive in the States as he is in Moscow.

Over the next few years, despite the opposition of many official Jewish organizations, I began to urge my congregation, through my columns in the *Beth Tzedec Bulletin*, to send holiday greeting cards to Russian Jews in the Soviet Union. We kept in close contact—as close as possible—with many Russian Jews, both before and after their emigration to Israel. Some of these émigrés even spoke at teach-ins I arranged for my congregation. But men such as Dr. Nahum Goldmann—whom I still respected highly for his important achievements as a Jewish leader—continued to play into the hands of Soviet authorities by denying the existence of any "special Jewish problem" in Russia.

In 1972 I decided that ten years were enough: ten years of trying unsuccessfully to crack the armor-plate of the Jewish establishment in Canada. It was time to set up or work with "dissident groups"—*their* label—to force their hands. Nor was it much different in the United States, save for the greater numbers and the larger possibility for the "critical mass" of non-Establishment groups to make itself felt.

In the United States, the Student Struggle for Soviet Jewry had been set up as early as 1964; it operated out of the bedroom of a recently arrived British Jew, Jacob Birnbaum. He was unhappy with the ostrich-like activities and the snail's pace—two different, but very inhuman models—of the major American Jewish organizations. After several years of trying to goad them into making the Russian problem a major element of their national programs, he and his colleagues came to the conclusion that they would always remain on the "outside"—yet they would be the perennial gadfly. The monied leaders continued to look upon the problem most unseriously.

Here is the way one of Student Struggle leaders viewed their relationship to the organized community, and the games they had to play, in order to win their point: "The Establishment groups are the kingdom and the power—but only up to a point. They have the money, mimeo machines and telephones, it's true, but they don't really have grassroots support. By working in and with communities, SSSJ and others have created independent power bases of *people*, which begin to expose the Establishment organizations as shells without much inside. Over the period of these few years, however, we've evolved to the point where we now have one foot in and one foot out of the 'organized community.' We are in a position of strength, with our 'people power,' to act independently and to get publicity and support, but play with the Establishment to get things as mimeo, phones, mailing lists and the recognition (by some groups, Jewish and non-Jewish; and to a certain extent, by the Russians) only Establishment groups have at this moment."[12]

In Canada, the matter is compounded by the fact that there is a tradition of single-Jewish spokesmanship—through the Canadian Jewish Congress—and not the multiplicity of Jewish

---

[12] Description by Glenn Richter; see William W. Orbach, *The American Movement to Aid Soviet Jews*, University of Massachusetts, Amherst, Massachusetts, 1979, page 29.

The Holocaust and Soviet Jewry 323

organizational voices that pierce the skies in America. By 1971, however, it took the combined effort of two disparate groups—the Jewish university students and a few Jewish women's groups—to help turn the tables on the Congress's inertia. In Toronto, particularly, several younger chapters of the Hadassah Organization and the Federation of Jewish Women's Organizations—and most of all, a group of women of my own Beth Tzedec Congregation—were now ready for the new tasks that were at hand. Phone calls to Jewish activists in Russia, networks for obtaining wanted information about the "refuseniks"—Jews who had applied for exit to Israel, but who were refused, thrown out of work and often jailed and needed medicine or other help—virtually all of these, plus political protest marches, letter-writing to public officials, and media contacts, were taken over by the students and the women. The leaders of Canadian Jewish Congress still remained on the sidelines—whether becalmed, befuddled, or bemused, I can not say.

In November 1971, the women of my own congregation organized a spearheading group, to which I gave the name *Pidyon Shevuyim* Committee—Hebrew for "the redeeming of the captives." They were indefatigable, utterly devoted, and indispensable in helping to create a large community awareness—so much so, in fact, that the Establishment now began to think seriously of its own need to "get into the act." This did not come until well into 1972 when, for the first time, the Congress officially established a National Committee for Soviet Jewry.

When at last that had come to pass I finally put down my "arms" and publicly congratulated my Congress friends who were now showing that they were measuring up, as leaders, to the demands of Jewish history. It was good to know that the repeating history of Jewish passivity of the early Forties would now be put behind us.

Decisionmaking by leaders of the Jewish community of North America remains a crucial test of the vitality of the people at the grassroots—their Rabbis and their congregations, their local U.J.A. groups, their fraternities, lodges, benefit societies and Zionist chapters. Every single Jew, in the last analysis, can and must work hard to assure that community leadership never again returns to the Dark Ages of the Hitler period—the Thirties and the Forties. I remain convinced that the 225,000 Russian Jews who have been set free since 1971 from their dark, never-never land would not have been liberated and allowed to emigrate without the leadership of the grassroots activists in the Jewish world—and particularly in North America—who struggled for over a decade, until the early 1970s, to convince the "Jewish Establishment" to join battle with the Soviets. Goldmann and company had been defeated—and even discredited—by the sheer number of Jews now leaving the Soviet Union—many for Israel.

When Jews began to shout and to stand up to their fullest stature in North America—when *they* no longer remained the "Jews of Silence," look and see what happened:

Year	Number of Jews Granted Permission to Leave the Soviet Union
1968-69	500
1970	1,000
1971	14,000
1972	33,000
1973	35,000
1974	20,000
1975	13,000
1976	15,000
1977	16,000
1978	25,000
1979	50,000
Total	222,500

There is still another haunting statistic that won't go away. Over 400,000 Russian Jews—in 1983—still sought exit permits

The Holocaust and Soviet Jewry

from the Soviet Union. And who knows how many more—in the years and decades still to come? Thus far, in the 1980s, the Soviets have toughened their position and reduced to a virtual trickle the number allowed to leave. But a new day is certain to dawn, and we Jews must continue to clamor for the rights of our people, or no one will.

They are still there, and their whispered words—like the sounds of the ram's horn at Sinai—grow louder and louder as they travel farther and farther across the Jewish world.

I hear those words now, from the lips of a tall, whitebearded, tragic figure, even though he has passed to the great beyond: "*You must never forget us. We will be finished, if you do.*" They are intoned by the sad voice of Rabbi Yehudah Leib Levin, with his even sadder blue eyes.

I will always hear that voice and see those eyes.

PART FOUR:

ISRAEL AND THE JEWS

Chapter 11

A YEAR OF FIRSTS: 1949

Precisely at midnight, on Friday May 14, 1948, Sir Alan Cunningham, the last British High Commissioner for Palestine, sailed out of Haifa harbor aboard a Royal Navy destroyer. The Mandate was over. Even earlier that very day, the moment had been seized. On the eve of the Sabbath, Israel was born, proclaimed as a free and independent Jewish state. That historic proclamation was immediately greeted by an invasion of Arab armies from the south, east and north. Egyptian Spitfires bombed Tel Aviv and the battle for Jerusalem began to rage.

All around the world, Jews danced in the streets. Those heady first hours of statehood were so intoxicating that they turned their minds momentarily from the bloodshed and the fighting. American Jews, especially, had even greater cause for celebrating. Barely ten minutes after the British departed, President Harry S. Truman announced that his government would accept the new provisional government of the Jews and granted it recognition "as the *de facto* authority of the new State of Israel."

In Rochester, the time of his announcement came at exactly 6:11 P.M., as I was walking from my house toward Beth El, to attend Sabbath Services. When the radio news-flash came, some people had spied me passing by their homes, and soon I was heading an instant, impromptu parade of men, women, and children—singing, dancing, and frolicking all the way to the synagogue. There, we sang and danced even more. The President of the United States—our President—had put the tremendous moral weight of the United States of America behind Israel—so swiftly, so unhesitatingly, so unquestionably. We could not lose now. But the problems were only just beginning.

That unusual Truman-Israel connection was fully borne in on me, a few months later, in the Fall of 1948. In September, his Secretary of State, General George Marshall, had suddenly announced what appeared to be a reversal of Truman's commitment to Israel. Marshall made it clear that the Americans now favored the plan submitted by the recently appointed United Nations Mediator of the Arab-Israel conflict, Count Folke Bernadotte. The Bernadotte Plan called for the incorporation of all of Jerusalem, as well as the whole of the Negev, into Transjordan. The Secretary's announcement was regarded as a scandalous betrayal of the pledges of support for Israel's boundaries which had been incorporated into the national platforms of both parties that summer, in anticipation of the Presidential election campaign. Both the Democrats and the Republicans had solemnly committed themselves to support the partition plan of the United Nations, the year before, which guaranteed the Negev to the "Jewish state" that would be established; as for Jerusalem, "the holy city" was to remain open to all as a free international zone.

To give up the Negev was bad enough—but Jerusalem too? Never. This was the word passed along from Zionist leaders in Washington and New York City, to Rabbi Philip Bernstein and myself. The President was making a "whistle-stop" campaign tour of the state, en route to a major and crucial rally to be held that week in New York City. We were asked to meet with him, during his brief Rochester stopover—as were other leaders in upstate communities—to put pressure on him to break openly with his Secretary of State. We were to request that he keep the promise of his "platform" to honor the original boundaries for Israel, as set down in the partition plan, and now overruled by this "Bernadotte Plan" which was endorsed by Marshall.

Philip Bernstein and I met with Truman just as his train rolled into Rochester, late that October. The three of us sat together in his parlor car, at a siding of the train station. We had only a limited time, and came directly to the point in question. In his flat Midwestern speech, but with eyes twinkling through his glasses, Mr. Truman answered: "Rabbis, I was the first to recognize Israel, and I might tell you I did that unilaterally, over the objection of those [Arab experts] in our State Department. I plan to make a statement about the question of 'recognized boundaries' very soon. You will see and you will be pleased. After all, I *am* a Bible-reading Southern Baptist. I want to go down in history as a 'modern Cyrus' who helped the Children of Israel go home again, safe and secure."[1]

He was as good as his word. A few days later, in New York City, he set aside Marshall's endorsement of the Bernadotte Plan and recommitted himself to the boundary lines as indicated in the United States' own partition plan of the previous spring. When he was elected that November in a hair-raising finish over his Republican rival, Governor Thomas E. Dewey, we did not know if he still felt like a "modern Cyrus"—now that the campaign was successfully over. But in late February 1949, even before his inauguration, he nominated James G. McDonald—one of this world's most beloved philo-Semites—a wonderful human being I came to know personally, as

---

[1] Much has been written since, in an effort to understand Truman's motivations in standing by Israel from the first moments of its birth. There are conflicting reports concerning his concern over the "Jewish vote" in New York State, in the 1948 Presidential elections. Whatever his private purposes at the time of recognition of Israel, it is instructive to know that he wanted to be identified religiously with an historic biblical figure, and sought to be regarded in that light. For a political recounting of the events see Zvi Ganin, *Truman, American Jewry, and Israel, 1945-1948*, Holmes and Meier, New York, 1979.

Ambassador to Israel. That act, too, which came a month following Truman's granting of American recognition of Israel *de jure*, and not merely provisionally as before, demonstrated his utter regard for Israel's future and his complete independence from those career "Arab experts" who had long dominated the State Department.

James Grover McDonald retired as Ambassador to Israel in 1951, after a very fruitful, but difficult tenure. He was regarded with suspicion and distrust by the Near Eastern Desk at the State Department because of his long years of pro-Jewish efforts, particularly in the area of refugee resettlement. A native of Indiana, where he first taught government as a university professor, he had also served as National Chairman of the prestigious Foreign Policy Association. As an American member of the Anglo-American Committee of Inquiry of Palestine in 1945, he had advocated the admission of 100,000 displaced Jews into Palestine. This view, which the Committee adopted, infuriated the British, but annoyed the American State Department as well.

He had close family in Rochester, and after his retirement as Ambassador to Israel, he frequently visited them. He looked me up, since I had known him from my student days at the Seminary, when I had invited him to lecture before my congregation in Pleasantdale. On several occasions he repeated his views about Truman and the State Department:

"I was, of course, extremely pleased with my appointment as Ambassador to Israel. But I told Mr. Truman, from the very first, that his sending me—without even consulting the State Department—might do more harm than good for Israel, and I knew that he didn't want that! State knew that *I* was pro-Israel and I knew that *they* were pro-Arab. It wasn't a good situation. I discovered, after getting to Israel in March 1949, that I had not been exaggerating the problem to myself. Some of my key diplomatic messages were simply set aside at the Department; never brought to the President's attention. The old 'experts' there were going to handle Israel 'their' way.

A Year of Firsts: 1949

"I finally got fed up with this maneuvering, and told the President so, on one of my early home leaves. Do you know what he answered? He said something I can never forget. 'Mr. McDonald, I am the Chief Executive of the United States of America, and *I* appointed you Ambassador. You can call me personally, directly, right here in the Oval Office, any time you want to get me to know something about Israel's situation that you're sure those [expletive deleted] at State want to keep from me.' "[2]

The time was nearing for my first visit to Israel. For years, I had been forewarned about all those "Zionist lies" fabricated by Jewish patriots in Palestine. Finally, the day had come to see for myself. I arrived there in June 1949, and almost everywhere I turned I discovered that most of those "lies" were true. When I first set foot on its soil, a short year after it had been established as an independent state, I could still feel most of the vibrations and hear many of the echoes of those "mad" Zionists who had wildly prophesied only fifty years before that a Jewish state would be re-erected in the Land of Israel. For them, Zionism was more than naked nationalism. It was the bearer of a utopian, egalitarian dream.

---

[2] These remarks were made in response to my comments on his book *My Mission in Israel* (Simon and Schuster, New York, 1951), where he delicately referred to the difficulties he had had with the State Department, and pointed to the special understanding of the needs of Israel which President Truman had demonstrated, in spite of his officials in the Department of State. McDonald never wrote what he had told me in private, but a careful reading of his book suggests some of the difficulties he encountered. His letter of resignation as Ambassador, dated November 29, 1950, and Mr. Truman's reply of December 18, 1950 only vaguely hint at the difficulties McDonald had faced. McDonald's reference to Dean Acheson is extremely discreet. But there is every reason to believe that when he suggested to the President that "I feel for *personal reasons* I should return home" (emphasis added) he was clearly saying to the President what he could not spell out then—or in his book, for that matter. There is no doubt in my mind, however, what those "personal reasons" were. McDonald, himself, had described them to me, in these conversations we had, in Rochester, as quoted. (See especially pages xiv; 5; 7; 8; 12; 16-19; 181-189; 235-237 of *My Mission In Israel, idem.*)

These romantics—secular humanists cast in the mold of *fin-de-siècle*, nineteenth-century idealism—conceived of their ambitious program as nothing less than *their* final solution to the perennial and perverse problem of Jewish rootlessness and homelessness. But their brave new world in tiny Palestine would be more than a Jewish Albania; more than just another small, insignificant state, zealously protecting its own identity. It was to be more like Eden.

In their ancestral homeland, they would build a just and humane society, a model for Jews and for the world. Silenced for centuries, destroyed and laid waste by one rapacious empire after another, the land, they were confident, patiently attended their loving return. Never mind that it was filled with malarial swamps and packed with empty deserts. In their mind's eye they beheld a different vision. "The land without a people awaited the people without a land" to come home and make it fruitful again. Only there would the Hebrew prophets speak again, as once they did, as normal, self-respecting people, very much at home with themselves in their own land, yet interlocked with the social hopes of every man, in all lands.

Two men stood out that year—and later—as my faithful reminders of what Israel was originally intended to be: Colonel Meir Batz of the Israel Defense Forces, and Yosef Sprinzak, the first Speaker of the Knesset, Israel's parliament. Slowly, I began to see this new, almost-egalitarian society—so vastly different from what I knew of Jews in America—through their eyes. I identified their Zionist hopes and their Jewish lifestyles with the whole of Israel.

Yet, the country was already being inundated by Jewish refugees from Europe and the Middle East who knew little of their Zionist truths and cared about them even less. All they were seeking were safe harbors and warm shelters from their anti-Jewish masters. Houses, jobs, food, hospitals, schools—these were uppermost in their minds. They did not *come to* Israel, as much as they had *run away from home*; they were not Zionists with a social vision, only insecure Jews in need of a

A Year of Firsts: 1949

haven. Many were physically ill; others in dire need of emotional repair.

I now see more clearly what I was unwilling to understand then. A culture-clash between these two widely differing worlds of Jews would be inevitable. Zionists had come to the land to revolutionize the whole of Jewish life and world history; they wanted to help rebuild the universe, out of Zion. But these hundreds of thousands of refugees now streaming into the country were less "ambitious"; they craved sheer physical security and the creature comforts that usually accompany it.

The year 1949 was not only the occasion of my first visit, it was also a time of contrasts and account-taking in Israel. Was the Zionist dream now finally realized with the establishment of the State? Or was this step only the beginning of a new period of even more serious questions than Zionist theorists—before Hitler—could have possibly foreseen—and for which they therefore had no answers? It was a time that brought to mind the older melodies of Jewish history—full of joyous sounds, yet written in the minor key of sadness and tragedy. And those two remarkable men—Colonel Batz and Yosef Sprinzak—made that music sharper and more understandable to me.

Let me first introduce you to and tell you about my brother-in-law, Batz—Colonel Meir Rabinowitz-Batz, to be exact. If you had been living in Israel since the Thirties, you would need no introduction at all—he was known to almost all the Jews of Palestine of his generation, virtually from the first years after he had landed from Moscow with his parents and younger brother. In 1929, he became Bar Mitzvah aboard ship, one day before it docked at the port of Jaffa after a long journey "home." And when he died in 1979, still virile and youthful at sixty-two, he was on a special mission to Israel's newest, southern Negev port of Elath. He had gone there while working on his life's dream—the building of "his" new canal, linking the Mediterranean and the Dead Seas.

In keeping with ancient Jewish custom, there were no eulogies offered at his funeral, but following a new Israeli tradition, thirty days after the burial, a Day of Remembrance and Study was held in his memory. His old buddies and colleagues came together from all over the country to talk about Batz and his vision. As each rose to the lectern to speak—and these were now the distinguished leaders and luminaries of the country—it was as if chapters from Israel's untold history had sprung themselves loose from hidden memory. What they were telling about Batz was more than personal history. His biography was also their way of portraying a picture of the life and times of the people on the land.

First there was Professor Yigael Yadin, Israel's world-famous archaeologist, then a leader in the government, the Deputy Premier. Many years earlier, he had served with Batz in the Hagana, and then went on to become Commander-in-Chief of the Army—the Israel Defense Force. He recalled earlier days, wistfully:

"Batz was one of the teenagers in Jerusalem who, in the mid-Thirties, devoted their full mental energies and physical strength to a single purpose, and without being told by anyone to do so. Everything they did was devoted to one cause: to build a state and to defend it. In one and the same time, he was a dreamer and a warrior. [In Hebrew, this is a play on the words *lohem*—warrior and *holem*—dreamer.]

"I came to know him beginning with 1933, when he was the leader of a model Boy Scout Troop (*Tzofim*)—called Mattathias—and I was one of his charges. He rigorously put us through our paces, but most of all he forged our character and our love of the land by the many treks he required us to make across a rocky, barren and difficult country—through long stretches of day and night. Mostly, I remember the frequent hikes he led, from Jerusalem to Ein-Gedi, and nearby, to Masada. Those early field exercises made many of us into new men, and taught us more about the Bible than we could learn from reading it. Through him, we came to know every ancient path or road—every clod of earth. There was not a rock in the old-new Land of Israel he did not know and love—not a stream, a hill, a canyon, or a *wadi*.

"He wasn't tall, but wide, and extremely muscular. In our early days in the 'Hagana' he was known as 'Mr. Lance.' I used to call him, jokingly, 'Batz the Terrible,' recalling his own Russian background and the famous 'Ivan' by that name. He taught us how to use the lance in hand-to-hand combat, and even wrote the 'Hagana' manuals for these training courses. These techniques required almost superhuman physical strength. Batz had it, and showed us callow recruits—a year or so younger than his own eighteen years—how to summon the necessary energy for ourselves.

"But his physical might was far overshadowed by the spiritual power within him—he was a sweet dreamer above all, and this was his real strength. This is what brought Batz to the Negev in 1949, and caused him to move to Beersheba from the 'easy life' in Jerusalem, a short time, thereafter. He saw the Negev—as Ben Gurion later saw it, too—as the future of Israel. This is how he came to dream of 'his canal.' With electrical power, fresh water, industry and energy, the Negev could house three million Jews, and become the essential heartland of the country, away from its now-crowded cities and choked streets.

"He raised a generation of disbelievers and made them see with their own eyes, what he could envision with his big heart."

Then followed speaker after speaker—heads of universities, municipalities, *kibbutzim*, and army chiefs. They all knew him well—each from a different angle of vision—from his childhood to maturity. They retold his "tall tales"—*chizbatim*—with relish and quoted his aphorisms and wise sayings. Most of all they also told about his sea-to-sea dream, long kindled in his heart by a seemingly casual reference to the subject first made by the founder of Zionism, Theodor Herzl, at the turn of the century.

That Day of Remembrance was a moving experience for all who were there. And the memory lingered on. I well remember a similar occasion held on his first memorial anniversary, in the summer of 1980, at the Ben Gurion University of the Negev, in Beersheba—a school Batz had helped to found. That whole day was devoted to scientific and technical discussions, in his memory, related to his scheme for the Negev Canal, which by then the Government of Israel had adopted as part of its own official plan. Somehow, I felt that Batz, too, was present at his own "memorial day"—large, blown-up photographs of him in various activities smiled at us from the walls. I even "heard" him say, "*Bi-seder*"—"that's just fine"—*you'll* get there, even if *I* didn't.

Until my first visit to the country in 1949, my own connnections to Jewish Palestine, later Israel, were, of course, the product of a much-blander, pallid Brooklyn-American form of "pro-Jewishness." I thought that I had ached every one of my people's pains and knew all about life there—its hardships and difficulties. After all, wasn't I a "Zionist leader" and hadn't I rallied my fellow Jews to "fight the good fight"? I discovered very soon that I knew precious little, in my sheltered "American hideaway," about the real human gifts Israel had been receiving from people of my own age—gifts of utter devotion, involving the total commitment of their lives and hopes as men and women.

I suddenly realized that there would be a gaping chasm between my American softness and Israeli hardiness, on a morning in May 1949 when I was first "introduced" to Batz. Actually, my introduction came in the form of a letter from my wife Hadassa, who had preceded me to Jerusalem in February. She and our two-year-old daughter, Rachelle (then our only child; Ronni and Elissa Beth, our other daughters, were born in Rochester, several years later), had traveled home to Israel to visit her family. They had bounced around the Atlantic and Mediterranean for seventeen long days, aboard a tiny, jam-packed ship, the S.S. Marine Carp, before arriving in Haifa. Her letter was one of longing and expectation. I was to fly to

Israel in a few weeks to meet her parents for the first time; indeed, I had never met any of her large family living in Israel. Attached to that letter was a clipping she enclosed from the *Jerusalem Post*, about my brother-in-law Batz, who had married her sister, Sara. I must have read the article a dozen times. Somehow, I knew then, that after meeting Batz personally, my "American days" would be over—and I would become more of a Jew than ever before.

We became very close friends, Batz and I—as I knew we would, from the moment he greeted me in the open-air, tumble-down shed at Lydda Airport that served as the "arrival hall" in those days. There he was: with his army jeep and chauffeur—a wild driver in the comely form of a young immigrant Jewess from India, Sherri by name. Together—Batz, Sherri and I—would crisscross the country—up its soft hills, around its stark canyons, and through its scorching deserts—for many weeks of the three months I spent in Israel that summer.

During all that time, we met with many hundreds of Israelis of all kinds: teenage soldiers of *Zahal*—the Israel Defense Force; recent Jewish arrivals from exotic Cochin; swarthy Yemenite Jews, airlifted to Israel from their Arabian subcontinent without having contact with outside civilization for two thousand years; sulking and squabbling Iraqi and Romanian Jewish refugees, living in their squalid *maabarot*—transient tin hutted "cities" waiting restlessly for jobs and permanent housing; black-coated, pious and long-bearded Jews in the old quarter of Jerusalem who had refused to fight, or even defend themselves, against the Arab Legion of Jordan, because they disliked the "godless Zionists" even more than possible Arab captivity. Also not to be forgotten were the Bedouins in the Negev desert; the "Israeli Arabs" in their Galilee villages; and the fierce-looking Druse tribes at the Lebanese borders.

Wherever we traveled, and to whomever he spoke, Batz was looked upon as a special ambassador who could plead their rightful cause. He listened patiently to their problems, took their complaints seriously, and to each was able to offer some measure of hope and comfort. *"Yeheye Tov!"*—"Things will improve; times will be good"—he repeatedly encouraged them. "This is why I am here," he would later explain, when I remained incredulous—and often even impatient—at the long hours he was willing to spend with these armies of grumblers. "To them, I am Israel. I represent authority—the Army—and they have to know that Israel is special. We have our problems—and they won't go away overnight—but we care about people." As a matter of fact, that was *not* why he was officially there, at all—he was then Chief Engineer of the Negev command—but like so many other Israelis of his vintage, he had a "mission": caring about people.

One of our trips, in particular, stands out as a strong editorial statement of the way I came to view Israel in those spirited days of 1949, short months after the War of Independence had ended. This was July, and we were headed for Elath, which was the last point the Israelis had taken from Jordan's crack Arab Legion just four months earlier. Our destination was an army post consisting of about fifty boys, then the sole defenders of what was once King Solomon's port-window to East Africa, which lies on the Gulf of Aqaba at the tip of the southern Negev. (From Elath, with the help of the Phoenician sailors of King Hiram of Tyre, Solomon's ships sailed to Ophir—which scholars today identify as East Africa, possibly Somalia. See II Chronicles 8:17-18.) We were to travel there—through trackless, searing Negev sands—to bring those few score teenaged defenders of Elath "a little comfort," as Batz put it: the chance to cook with, and drink, unsalted water. His jeep was the lead car of a one-lorry "convoy" carrying a rare-for-Israel and hard-to-find portable generator that could desalinate a small amount of sea-water, daily.

We spent five days and nights en route to Elath. Today, there is a good, new highway, and you can get there by bus in less than six hours from Beersheba—or fly from Tel Aviv in about fifty minutes. But these modes of modern travel don't begin to compete with that "modern camel" we had—an Israeli army jeep, as wrecklessly driven by Sherri and carefully navigated by Batz.

We provisioned and made ready for our special "desalination mission" at Qastina, the army camp where Batz was headquartered. It was a former British Barracks, located about 50 kilometers west of Jerusalem and a similar distance northeast of Beersheba. Batz sat up front in our jeep with Sherri, his rifle at the ready. I sat in the back, with a loaded pistol in a holster, though I would hardly have known how to handle it in the event of need. Behind us was a small, open lorry, with its all-important generator securely lashed down, and with two young, armed soldiers seated up front. Before departing, we had been forewarned against the possibility of Arab snipers who were still roaming the Negev, and told to be on the lookout, as well, for Bedouins who might surprise us—merely for the sake of booty. Even before we started out, I was getting a quick introduction to modern Zionism in a way I could never experience in my pulpit back home. This business of "saving Jewish life" was no longer academic; in fact, it wasn't somebody else's Jewish life any more. Fortunately, the trip would be entirely peaceful, and my newfound, borrowed "heroism" never did get a chance to be tested under fire.

We traveled in a southeasterly direction, heading first for Beersheba, which had the audacity to call itself, even then, "the capital of the Negev." Today, it is Israel's fourth largest city—after Tel Aviv, Jerusalem, and Haifa—with a population nudging 135,000. It is the thriving home of Ben Gurion University of the Negev, founded in 1965 as a small institute with a handful of students; it now comprises an undergraduate and graduate body of about 4,000 and faculties exceeding five hundred people. And this is not to speak of its symphony orchestra and its numerous industrial, scientific, and cultural centers. But when we paused briefly in Beersheba that summer of 1949 to take a meal in the soldiers' mess, there were barely 1,000 parched souls living in that dusty and parched village of a city—most of them unemployed, recent immigrants from North Africa, Iraq, India, and Romania, waiting angrily for jobs in their hot, dry, tin hovels.

Moving southeast from Beersheba we began to encounter a world I had never before seen. It is an eerie feeling to come upon scenes so awesome and beautiful—so fierce and weird. These were primordial sights, and to behold them personally was to be catapulted back thousands of years in time—suddenly and instantly. I had thought that what I gazed upon in Jerusalem was biblical, or at least very ancient. But up there, one hundred fifty miles away in the "civilized north"—even in Jerusalem—I had only been confronted with the recent Turkish overlay on a much older city I could not see with my own eyes. There, to discover great antiquity, you had to dig as only archaeologists do, to uncover layer upon layer of the lost empires who had laid waste to the city, after the Children of Israel had been driven from her. Down and down you had to go: from the Ottoman Turks to the Mamelukes of Egypt; to the Crusaders; to the Muslim Arabs; to the Byzantine Christians; to the Romans; to the Greeks; to the Persians—and only then, finally, to the Israelites and Canaanites. Here, you did not need a spade to uncover the Bible. Before your eyes, in these ancient desert badlands, stretched forth the same savage scenery the Israelites lived with, in their forty years' wandering—from their exodus as slaves out of Egypt to their genesis as free men in the promised land.

This territory had remained as it was, unharmed and untouched by "civilizing invaders": the same colorful, uncanny craters and canyons; the same wind-tossed, twitching, scrubby trees; the same winter flash-floods and their *wadi* summer memorials—the gravelly, dry river-beds; the same rugged scarps; the same unyielding, parched loëss soil; the same blazing, scorching days; and the same frosty, milk-starred nights. And through all these sights, Batz was quickened, alive with animation. "Here, in this desert wilderness we became free

A Year of Firsts: 1949

men; learned the meaning of equality and interdependence; saw how hard we'd have to work to make the land yield its promise. Here—in this fierceness—the old Israel was formed, and from here it will be formed again. Here is where the real character of our ancestors was forged. Here, Yahweh himself, who created the world *ex nihilo*—something out of nothing—taught His people to make their world, accordingly. Out of this emptiness and void, we once built—and now, we will rebuild—our land."

I wasn't quite ready for his "sermons." "Batz," I laughingly responded, "I caught you preaching without a license, and as a civil engineer I had expected you to keep your eye on the road and not on the Book." In deadly serious tones, he replied: "But that's my Book too! While you, as a Rabbi, may read it as a theologian, Israelis like me see it as our national history—right here, where it all happened. No, I'm not a religious preacher; I'll leave that to you! But without our Bible as a source of national inspiration, we Jews have no future here, or anywhere else for that matter."

We were now slowly mounting a tortuous, labyrinthine pass, *Maale Akrabim*—the "Ascent of the Scorpions"—and there, strewn on its side, were broken remains of a military transport truck that never made it to the top. "That happened just last week," Batz explained. And then he resumed his role as Bible teacher, quoting from the Book of Numbers, by heart: "'Command the children of Israel and say unto them: When you come into the land of Canaan, this shall be the land that shall fall unto you for an inheritance, even the land of Canaan according to the borders thereof...and the south border shall begin at the end of the Salt [Dead] Sea eastward; and your border shall turn about southward of the wilderness of Zin.' [Numbers 34:3-4.] We are now at the southern boundary of the land promised."

We finally reached the top—even Sherri-the-wild was extremely cautious inching her way up, with the help of four-wheel drive. We jumped out of the jeep and looked southward toward Elath. An amazing and unforgettable view unfolded before us: the arid, desert steppes of the Arava—an almost vertical drop of 400 meters—lay at our feet, confined on the East by the high range of the purple-pink mountains of Edom. To our immediate south, we saw a table-top mountain rising in the midst of the desert plain. Pointing to it, Batz explained that it was Mount Hor, the place where, according to the Bible, Aaron the Priest, brother of Moses, was buried.

"But as for the greater of the two, his brother Moses—Moses our Teacher—the Bible says something altogether different," Batz continued. "It only says that he went up to Mount Nebo, across from Jericho, but not in the land itself; he sees the land from afar, but never gets there himself—and dies. He gets no more than a glimpse. Imagine that! He takes us out of Egypt, struggles with a stiff-necked people, leads them, wandering through *this* wilderness for forty years, and never gets there himself. Doesn't that tell you something about *leadership*? The followers arrive, but he doesn't. But, of course, through us, he got there! It was he who had made it all possible—his dogged, determined leadership. And the Bible has also something to tell us about *Jewish leadership*, in contrast to others. It specifically says that when Moses dies, *somewhere* on that mountain Nebo, 'no man knows of his sepulcher unto this day.' Imagine: no grave to visit, no tomb to adore, no holy place to revere. It's all very clear. Unlike Jesus and other great ones, Moses was never saintly, simon-pure, or worshipped in life—and never sanctified or deified in death. That, too, says something very important about the Jewish people. God is telling us—*your Jewish god*, Shalom—that *we* have got to do it by ourselves: no archangel, no messiah, no savior—not even the United States or the United Nations—can do it for us."

We moved farther south—through the *Arava*—and following us all the way down to our next stopping point were the brilliant Negev mountains—all the colors of the rainbow bouncing softly around them—off to our right, on the west. We were now coming to Timna, a place, Batz advised, that "will one day soon produce thousands of tons of copper each year, just as it did in the days of King Solomon." And he began quoting biblical proof-texts from Deuteronomy which described the area as a "country whose stones are iron, and out of whose hills you can dig copper." (Deut. 8:9.) "King Solomon," his face lit up now, "was, of course, no fool. How do you think he paid for those big expenses of his thousand wives? He sent ships to Ophir and brought from there gold—'four hundred and twenty talents,' the Bible records. With what did he pay—to buy that gold from Ophir? He used his copper ingots, from the smelter I am now going to show you, shipped them out to Africa—and maybe the Far East, too—from the port of Elath, where we'll be arriving later this evening. It's only twenty-five kilometers from here."

We drove up close to those reddish-brown cliffs, "the Pillars of Solomon," which still stand mutely on guard, as defenders of the wise old king's mines and smelter. Then we drove on, jumped out of the jeep, and began climbing a steep path up a rocky hill. At the very top, huffing and puffing, we came upon the remains of a watch-tower that probably guarded the prisoners and slaves who worked in these ancient smelting pits. We could even see the heaps of black slag that still remain on the ground.

(It was only a few years later that Nelson Glueck, the noted American archaeologist, did extensive exploration at that very site. He revealed that the copper smelter built by King Solomon "utilized the principle of the Bessemer blast furnace system. Flues were provided in its wall through which the strong, constant winds from the north were admitted to furnish the draft necessary for the charcoal-fuelled flames in the furnace room."[3] In 1955, the government of Israel erected a modern smelter on this ancient site. By 1966, annual copper production there had exceeded 10,000 tons. Batz was right, once again!)

We got back into our jeep, and moved quickly toward Elath,

---

[3] See Nelson Glueck, *Rivers in the Desert: A History of the Negev*, Grove Press, New York, 1960, p. 36 ff.

making only one brief stop en route. "We're getting off here for some Coca-Cola," Batz announced. "You Americans can't last out the desert trip without one 'Coke' at least." Before I could make my own jocular riposte, he was waving his right hand and pointing to an imaginary signpost: "Welcome to Avrona: population zero, but the drinks are fine!" "Look at those wild Sudan palms!" Now he was no longer imagining—or shall I say hallucinating—but directing my attention to some unusual fruit trees I had not seen anywhere else in Israel. He explained that these trees marked the northerly limit of the zone where this tree can grow. "Now we are entering the tropics," he exclaimed, as we quickly alighted, "the tropical watering-hole of Old Avrona. Mentioned in the Bible, by the way, in case the Rabbi forgot!"[4]

We walked toward a well, fed by the small Avrona spring, just a few hundred yards from the Jordanian border. Batz made sure to take his rifle with him. He took off his worsted army beret—the Israelis copied the British headgear—quickly improvised a long "handle" made of some rope he removed from his pocket, and lowered his "water-cup" into the well. "Here, drink some of this Coca-Cola—no, this nectar of the desert gods—now that it's properly strained and sanitized through the cloth of my beret." I let the drops of water, dripping very slowly through the coarse material, trickle onto my dry lips, then down my cracked, parched throat. It wasn't nectar; nor was it of the gods. But for then and there, in my almost-dehydrated condition, it was much better than the salty, tepid coffee I would be drinking in the Elath military mess that night and the next day.

While we enjoyed our brief "water-break" Batz pointed me back to the areas we had been traversing for the past two days. "You see what real treasures are waiting for us. Just think of the slumbering minerals that have bided their time—just for us Israelis—until we Jews were ready for them. We've got kaolin

---

[4] Numbers 33:34. This was a station in the wanderings of the tribes of Israel through the wilderness.

A Year of Firsts: 1949   347

near Beersheba for a ceramics industry; phosphates at Oron, close to *Machtesh Katan*—the Little Crater; potash, chlorides and bromides all along the Dead Sea 'coast'; glass sand at Yeroham; and gypsum throughout the desert. And you remember the 'Oil Road' we traveled yesterday, near the *Machtesh Gadol*—that bumpy track which nearly threw us out of our seats onto the hot sands. Well, you saw with your own eyes those Texans beginning to take over the rigs of the British petrol company, the I.P.C., and making ready to restart the search for oil and gas, where the geologists have led them."

He took another few droplets of water and, slowly swirling them around his mouth, began again. "Look. We're a rich country, by my reckoning. It's all here, except enough of the right people to work it: The scientists, engineers, industrialists. But they will be here, too. We simply have to get away from that old Zionist custom of *schnorrerei*—of taking handouts from our fellow Jews by crying help all the time. And we've got to mine our own resources and build our own economic and political independence, not allowing either the Americans or the Soviets to keep us in their pockets. Didn't your George Washington tell the first Americans to 'steer clear of entangling alliances'? Well, Israel, too, has to stay out of the way of the two big super-powers, and become the Switzerland of the Middle East. Making it ourselves—without standing on the shoulders of Uncle Sam or of Uncle Sam's Jews—and trying to live in peace with my other Uncle, 'Ivan the Terrible'!"

It was twilight and a small group of Bedouin gathered near the well, watering their black goat herd, now approached us, just as we were about to depart Avrona—in order to make it to Elath before dark. Batz speaks their language. They bowed and scraped before *yahawajah*—Mr. Army—the gentleman-lord from the Israeli forces. It must be his loaded rifle, I told myself. Then, one of their number, a less reticent teenager, answering a question about his age, said that he was "somewhere between ten and fifteen years of age." Bedouin are afraid of the evil eye, Batz whispered to me, they never tell their right age. Now, this youth was asking Batz for *baksheesh*—a gift—before we head on.

My brother-in-law climbed back into the jeep, still holding his rifle, and from his khaki knapsack, scooped up two cans of boiled beef labelled "KOSHER. Food for Israel. A gift from the Chicago District of the Zionist Organization of America." Batz opened one of them with his field-knife and offered it to the young man. He quickly lapped it up, animal-like, while repeatedly asking: "What's this I'm eating?"

"Kosher cow meat from my American brother-in-law," Batz answered, pointing to me, with a straight face.

"Only ate cow meat once before in my life," the boy said, "but didn't like it, then."

"You like it now, I see. That's because it's Kosher," Batz decided. The boy looked at us quizzically. "Here, take this other can to your father for dinner tonight. Tell him that it's a good, Kosher *baksheesh* from the Jews of America." And turning to me, as we hopped into our jeep, Batz laughed mischievously: "See what I've just done to you American Jews! From now on, you'll be running your famous United Jewish Appeal campaigns for the Arabs, too!"

We got into our faithful little vehicle and moved quickly toward our destination, nearby. After a long silence, Batz turned wistfully to me and slowly said: "You know, one day, if we have peace with these Arabs, we'll build a canal connecting the Mediterranean with the Dead Sea and rebuild this wonderful wasteland of a Negev desert and fill it with water, farms, factories, hydroelectrical power—and millions of Jews. And maybe then—or even before—we'll start exporting Kosher 'cow meat' to you Americans—*and thank you very much!*" We both burst out laughing. But he was very serious, inside. I could tell.

Night fell very suddenly just as our "convoy" pulled up to the pre-fab shack which served as headquarters-cum-mess-hall for the tiny military outpost at Elath, hugging the shoreline of the Gulf. The soldier in command was a second lieutenant—*Segen*

Mishneh—and he introduced himsef as "*Segen* Saltzman." I should have known, by that name alone, that then and there something special was brewing for us. We met his *Samal*—sergeant—and I had all to do to keep myself from laughing out loud. His name is "*Samal* Fefferman." So "pepper and salt" were in charge here. And they were, at this briny base. They had never requested a generator from "up north," and they had no need for one, they informed Batz, rather testily. "I know, I know," he apologized, "it was all my own idea. I wanted to bring you guys—the *hevra*—a little comfort, so you wouldn't have to live with the sea in your mouths, too." The "argument" went on and on, and picked up again early on the morning after.

Saltzman and Fefferman were still adamant at breakfast as we took our swigs of "Elath coffee"—the sugar you added only seemed to heighten the undefeatable taste of salt, salt, salt. "If we wanted 'some comfort' we'd have stayed in Tel Aviv, Batz, and would drink the delicious coffee and eat great pastry at Cafe Rowal, with you and the *hevra*. We like things here just the way they are. This is *halutziut*—pioneering—spelled like in the word 'Zionism,' Batz! Thanks, but no thanks. You can take that lousy generator back to Tel Aviv."

They were not ungrateful, just pompously gruff, to make sure that Batz wouldn't force on them that piece of equipment we'd lugged across the desert for three full days.

We spent the day sightseeing, swimming, and hiking. "This is Israel's future Miami," Batz finally announced, with his usual air of prophecy. "They'll come from all over the world—even your Florida—to soak up this tropical paradise." He was dreaming again. The only building there—in all Elath—aside from headquarters, was a small "PX" shed for the soldiers—*Shekem*, as it was called. That was where I had bought two bottles of carbonated orange juice—*Tassas*—the night before, and close to the spot where I had slept, fully clothed on the beach. I had dug a hole at the water's edge and covered over the bottles with coral shells, in order to wake up to "cold orange juice." I was so anxious to get the taste of salt out of my mouth that I drank those two orange bottles shortly after waking, when the sun's early light had pried open my salted, pasty eyelids. This *was* the tropics. Overnight, the sea-water had almost boiled the bottles. I can never forget our trip home, which we began later that day. Boiled orange juice, never take it again, I kept repeating; and if you must—never on an empty stomach!

Nor would I forget that generator which, in the words of Batz, we *schlepped* through the desert for a free roundtrip tour: Qastina-to-Elath-and-return.

Nor would I forget those days. It was still a time when no Israeli was ready to admit that any other—even an army Colonel—could be more of a Zionist than he.

I have another good reason for savoring my salad days in Israel, and his name is Yosef Sprinzak, the founding Speaker of its neophyte parliament, the Knesset. I came to know him and many of his colleagues because of his youngest child, David—still another of my brothers-in-law, who was married to a younger sister of my wife. I could never meet David Sprinzak. Only a few months before my arrival in June 1949, he and his fighter-mate, Matti Yadin—brother of the Commander-in-Chief, Yigael Yadin—were shot dead by the guns of an invading Arab aircraft, and thrown, with their Piper Cub "warplane," into the Sea. The tragic incident saved the lives of many civilians. That fatal dog-fight was played out over the beaches of Tel Aviv, close to the Sprinzaks' home. It was something neither Yosef or his wife, Hanna, ever spoke about. But their eyes always betrayed their silence. They never fully arose from mourning. Neither they, nor thousands of other parents.

In Israel today, the mere mention of the name Yosef Sprinzak conjures up a distinct way of thinking about Jewish life, and of applying it in the new land, that is identified with those unusual Zionist settlers of the Second Aliya—the *olim* who came to the country between 1904 and 1914. They were secular messianists. In its religious, supernatural form, Jewish messianic speculation held that the future would be shaped by the hand of Providence; thus, in principle, it made no room for the fantasies of a material utopia. But in the folk mind, "the messianic age" came to be regarded as a time of Jewish national glory; it became the inverse, in every respect, of the despised exile, where Jews were relegated to the status of an unproductive, pariah people. Second Aliya types would have nothing to do with the exile mentality, everything to do with utopia in Zion.

These hardy and romantic men and women from Eastern Europe numbered a mere 40,000 over the ten-year period of this Aliya, compared to the more than one million Jews from those lands of pogrom and persecution who were then streaming to the fleshpots of "Golden America" to make it in the New World. They could build their Zionist utopia nowhere else but in the ancestral homeland. They deliberately chose the swamps and disease-ridden lands of Palestine to erect their "messianic society." In their fantasy, the desert was waiting for *them* to come, so it could bloom again, in their loving hands.

They laid the foundations for the Jewish labor movement in Palestine, and their leaders became the ruling Mapai Party. They governed the country without interruption, from its founding as a state in 1948 until Menachem Begin's opposition party toppled them in 1977. All of the major institutions identified with pioneering life in Israel emanated from the Second Aliya leaders the mutual-aid and self-help organizations for health and welfare; the earliest *kibbutzim*; the defense system of the Ha-Shomer, and later, the Hagana; the daily Hebrew press; and the flourishing new theater. And, of course, that most unique institution of all—the Histadrut—*the* Labor Union—which continues, to this day, to serve as the canopy organization for most of these activities, but which in pre-state days was really "the government." Some critics regarded it as a "government within a government," even after the State was established.

Its constitution makes clear that the Histadrut is infinitely more than just a labor union. "The organization unites and organizes all workers, without distinction of creed, race, nationality or outlook, who live on the fruits of their labor without exploiting the labor of others, for the purpose of arranging all the communal, economic and cultural affairs of the working class in the country for the building of the labor society in the Land of Israel." When the Histadrut was founded in 1920 by David Ben Gurion, Yitzhak Ben Zvi—Israel's second president, after Weizmann—Yosef Sprinzak, and a few other leading spirits, its guiding principles were to build the land as a socialist-humanist society under the control and management of the workers, whether in the towns or on the communal farms, the *kibbutzim*. Sprinzak never veered from his utopian dream, and throughout all the years preceding his ascent to the chair of Speaker—when he served as chief executive of the Histadrut as its General Secretary—his twinkling eyes and ready wit continued to betray his own warm humanity. Unlike so many others of younger years who followed him to power—inside or outside his party—he never became a bureaucrat, or what is as bad, a technocrat interested only in making the system work without regard to the human dimension. With him, it was man—not the machinery of government—all the way.

It was after our return from Elath, when Batz was required at his Qastina base for a period of about two weeks, that Yosef and Hanna Sprinzak invited me to be their house guest. The house—rather, their two-bedroom walk-up apartment—was located near the Tel Aviv shore at 28 Mapu Street. I slept on a very old, overstuffed sofa in their dining room-living room area, and fell easily into step with their no-frills, almost-Spartan lifestyle. My recent desert trip had served well as a training course. There was only one "luxury" at Yosef's disposal: his official government "limousine"—a pale-blue Chevrolet, the exact shade of the Israel flag. And, of course, Mordechai (Rappoport), his chauffeur-cum-"adviser." In Israel a *nahag*—a driver—of a bus, taxi, or of a Minister of State—is a highly opinionated, highly regarded man.

A Year of Firsts: 1949

(That 1949 Chevrolet, by the way, in contrast to the tiny European cars that were just beginning to find their way onto Israeli roads and highways, did look big enough to me then so that I felt that I was being driven about in a limousine. When I left Rochester to come to Israel, I had sold my 1946 Mercury in order to help finance my trip. When I returned home, in the early Fall, I bought my own "limousine" too—a pale blue, new Chevrolet. It took some time to get that special color, and also, I might add, to arrange for the proper financing. By the time I came home, my bank balance was virtually nil.)

Those were the days of *tzena*—national austerity—and all food was heavily rationed. The minister in charge of Supply and Rationing was a close family friend of the Sprinzaks: Dov Yosef—born in Montreal as Bernard (Barney) Joseph. Barney Joseph had settled in Jerusalem in 1921, and had gone through various chairs in the Mapai Party at the side of my host—his last post had been as Military Governor of Jerusalem during its siege in 1948. I came to know and like him, and his wife Goldie, but Barney was not exactly the most popular person in Israel that summer. Even ingenious housewives whose culinary talents were great could not easily overcome the challenge of "Barney's diet." There were little opportunities to "cook up" anything really interesting from the limited—and rationed—fare: cold-storage eggs from Turkey, dried bakala (cod) fish from Greece, and canned sardines from Portugal. That fairly well exhausted the list of protein-based staples available. The farms were growing very little that year—all their hands had been fighting for many months in the War of Independence—so vegetables too were scarce: a few under-sized potatoes; some blighted, scrawny tomatoes, and since it was summer, some watermelons and grapes for "dessert."

Hanna Sprinzak, of course, was not "allowed" the luxury of blaming poor Barney for all this—as did most other women—but she was not a notoriously good cook in any event. As a result, our meals at 28 Mapu Street were as drab as the rest of the apartment. Potato *purée* laced with some bakala was her usual *pièce de résistance*, and I wouldn't recommend it for serious mention anywhere. Fortunately, there was plenty of bread—mostly *pitta*—and some margarine, or *margarina*. That, plus tea, comprised our daily breakfast menu.

Yet, breakfasts there were always exciting, in spite of the food. The household was up and alive by six each morning, and a half-hour later, Mordechai would arrive with three morning papers, representing three political party groupings: *Davar* (the Mapai labor party); *Al Ha-Mishmar* (the organ of the leftist-Marxist party, Mapam—the United Workers Party); and *Ha-Aretz*—independent, yet spokesman for urban, middle-class-professionals, and then regarded as the voice of the General Zionist party. "How many morning newspapers in this country?" I asked him. "Any others?" He replied: "In this huge country of ours, we support a *huge* paper industry—of course, without any forests of our own. In this *huge* city of Tel Aviv, today, there are over fifteen daily newspapers published every day—except Saturday, thank God—and every one of them represents a *hugely different* political shading; a *huge difference* in *nuance*, you might say. Now you know why Chaim Weizmann claims that in the whole world he is the only President of a country which has no citizens—only presidents. We've got fifteen newspapers, fifteen *huge* political parties—and a million presidents." And looking at Sprinzak, he smiled: "But only one Speaker. Right, Yosef?" To which the latter laconically replied: "Wrong. There are two. *You* and me. And you are the *huge* one!"

Yosef Sprinzak quickly riffled through the sheets of these eight-paged newspapers—there were hardly any advertisements—going first, of course, to his favorite, *Davar*. By this time, the daily ritual was about to begin. The door-bell rang and uninvited "guests" started arriving, one by one. Without exception, they were all new immigrants, barely arrived in Israel, practicing "people's democracy" before my eyes, at the breakfast table. Here was the whole spectrum of that year's crop of *olim*; and all of them had come to Sprinzak personally—right here in the "dining-room"—to complain.

Indian Jews, Romanian Jews, Iraqi Jews, Bulgarian Jews, and so on and on. There was no way, and no one, to stop them. After the fourth day, I asked Sprinzak why he allowed this? And at home? "Why not?" was his answer, and he added: "And what better place than at home?"

(A few years later, after his friend Yitzhak Ben Zvi had become President, he told me this tale, which was intended as an apocryphal story but which I still believe to be true. Certainly, it could be true of *him*. "After Weizmann died and Ben Zvi was called to the Presidency, he and his wife Rachel moved into that small cottage in Jerusalem—the so-called President's House. On the day he was made President, he returned home at night and found a sentry marching up and down in front of his door. He wondered about this. The young serviceman replied that he had been sent by his Chief as an honor guard before the House of the President. Rubbing his head in amazement, Ben Zvi entered the house. The night was cold. After a few minutes, the President came out and said, 'Look here, it is cold tonight. Won't you come in and at least have some hot tea?' The soldier replied, 'I can not leave my post. Orders are orders.' Foiled, Ben Zvi re-entered. After a while, he turned to his wife, Rachel, and bade her make some tea. Then he went out again. He turned to the soldier: 'Look here, I have an idea!' You go in and take some tea, and I will stand outside with your gun and take your post!'")

By nine o'clock we had to leave for the short ride down Yarkon Street—along the Sea—to Allenby Road, the Knesset's temporary headquarters, located in a converted movie theater, which a few months later became the home of the Israeli Opera. (In December, 1949, the seat of government was moved to Jerusalem.) In his tiny, very modest office, there were a few Zionist memorabilia, especially the photograph I most liked— in a simple large, rectangular frame, under glass, hanging on the wall. It was a picture of Chaim Weizmann, standing tall before a very large oil portrait of Theodor Herzl, draped by the banners of the new state, his right hand raised in oath-taking posture, his left hand in his jacket pocket, and Yosef Sprinzak, with his head tilted back, pronouncing the words, as he swears in the first President of Israel—the first internationally recognized head of a Jewish state in more than two thousand years.

The Knesset, I soon discover, sits only on Monday and Tuesday afternoons and evenings, and again on Wednesday mornings: theoretically, this should give its 120 members—ten times the "Twelve Tribes" of ancient Israel—many of whom are *kibbutzniks* scattered across the country, an opportunity also to work at home and to rest on the Sabbath. The plenary never meets on Sundays or Fridays, out of consideration for its Christian and Muslim members' weekly days of rest, but some of the parliamentary committee—where the bulk of the legislative work is accomplished—do meet on Sundays, or other weekdays, except Fridays. Mordechai was told by Sprinzak to escort me to the hall, to sit in the visitors' gallery and attend the plenary. I moved in, with fear and trembling, but soon realized that I was in a parliamentary session as raucous as any in Britain. And with those fifteen or so political parties, and their complicated voting blocs—probably even more so. I marveled at him, Sprinzak, and at the humorous, quick-witted manner he was able to keep the shouting and the interventions under control. Even the spleen-venting Communist group did not faze him—despite their badgering—nor were they offended by the barbs he hurled back at them from the podium. He obviously wielded a light gavel.

Their leader, Shmuel Mikunis, growled at the Chair. Again and again, he demanded "the floor"—and was repeatedly denied—after using up more time than he was allowed. "You are no Speaker, Mr. Speaker," he shouted at Sprinzak, using the English rather than the Hebrew word for his title. "You do not know the first thing about chairing a parliament. Not this parliament, at any rate!" he continued. The presiding officer now turned his "light gavel" into a pummeling, noisy mallet. He looked at Mikunis with all the gravity he can summon; looked and looked, staring him down. The house had fallen speechless. Sprinzak could have him ejected, under the rules, on grounds of personal privilege. The whole parliament was waiting—silently—maybe for the first time in its history—eager to enjoy the spectacle of Mikunis being thrown out. Sprinzak was still motionless, still staring at the offender. Finally, this, spoken in Yiddish, in clear breach of the rules which make Hebrew the Speaker's official parliamentary language: "*Voss vilt ihr fun mir, Mikunis? Mein tatte iz gevehn a Spikker?*" ("What on earth do you want from me, Mikunis? Was my father a Speaker?") With that, he recessed the House, amidst thunderous desk-thumping.

Sprinzak's wit, while sometimes biting in parlimentary debate, was always warm and urbane in private, personal conversation. A few nights later, I had an opportunity to be with him again, and to watch him closely in intimate discussion with his Mapai colleagues. Mordechai drove us from Tel Aviv, a short twenty miles north, along the highway leading to Haifa. We turned westward for a few miles and arrived at Netanya, then a sleepy seaside resort city, where a party conference was being held. That week, the newspapers had been filled with comment by leading government figures suggesting—almost to a man—that since there was a viable state, the long prehistory of Zionism had now come to an end. There was no longer any need, they claimed, to continue the Movement's large apparatus in the Diaspora, or to project the party politics of Israel into the life of Jews in distant lands, who were not intimately connected to the local political scene and all of its nuances. "Zionism is dead," banner headlines had been proclaiming, and this Mapai conference in Netanya—which drew all of the party's heavy guns—was supposed to provide the occasion for its proper burial.

Of course, the featured, keynote speaker at the closing session was to be B.G. himself—the Prime Minister of Israel, David Ben Gurion. Sprinzak had come only for this last evening session, to participate in the debate that was scheduled to follow Ben Gurion's address. Despite Sprinzak's august status, since everybody present was also a "president"—to use Mordechai's well-worn and repeated comment on this subject—we practically had to clamber with our hands and feet through the aisles clogged with "dignitaries," and finally made our way up to the rostrum, where seats had been reserved for us.

It was a pleasant summer evening, and the meeting was being held only a few hundred meters from the shore, in a roofless, outdoor movie house, rented by the party for the three-day conference. All was balmy and light—until Ben Gurion began—and began—and began. He never did quite end. The speech lasted for over three hours, until well past midnight, and there was no opportunity for the planned debate that was to follow.

Most of those on the platform appeared to be—or made out that they were—enraged. They had not come for a "repeat of the old Zionist Congresses," which used to be held in Switzerland and which had sat patiently—for fifty years, it seemed—through one long "Zionist sermon" after another. They wanted "to debate the issues"—especially to give voice to their disparate views on "Zionism is dead," that year's *cause célèbre*. They never had a chance, not that night. Ben Gurion himself, in continuous, crashing crescendos that increased in intensity by the hour, had pronounced the *Kaddish* memorial prayer over Zionism, and all by himself had attended to its last rites. Or so he thought.

Sprinzak differed—but in the only way he knew how—pleasantly and agreeably. After the speech, when most of the others were still livid with anger over what had transpired—"no debate!"—Yosef ambled over to his senior colleague and shook his hand. I was standing by, and overheard his pointed comments.

"Ben Gurion, you were right and you were wrong, tonight. As far as your general thesis is concerned, you were right. It would be better if Israel could disengage the diaspora communities from our own political life here, and dismantle the Zionist party structure there.

A Year of Firsts: 1949

"Parties in the diaspora no longer have any relevant meaning, and can only hurt us here in the long run, because competing Zionist parties will weaken Jewish unity there. We need the diaspora. That's the point on which we disagree. I don't believe that Zionism is dead, which is what, in one way or another, you've been claiming here, all night.

"Let me first prove you wrong by what happened here tonight—by what you yourself did. You gave a *Zionist* speech. Who else can speak for three solid hours except Zionists? And since your audience stayed put, and didn't walk out on you— that proves they are themselves all Zionists, no matter what you, or they, say. *Who else but Zionists are willing to sit through years and years of speeches—including your own tonight?*"

Ben Gurion stood impassively, listening quietly, as Yosef continued: "But there is something much deeper here. The establishment of the State was an act destined to strengthen the Jewish consciousness of diaspora communities. If the only object of Zionism was to achieve statehood, then you are right. Now that we have a state, Zionism's purpose is at an end, as you claim. But there is something larger that Zionism wanted to do. It desired to enhance the awareness of all Jews that they are one; that wherever they are, they belong to a single people. *Am Yisrael*—the People of Israel—is even greater than the State of Israel.

"Re-think, Ben Gurion. The day has not yet come for us to write off the rest of the Jewish world who remain elsewhere. Of course, we will do everything we can to bring them here, to make them want to share their lives with us. Until they come here, let them remain as partners, continuing with us, not a dead and deserted community of Jewish ghosts."

The hour was late. Ben Gurion did not reply. They shook hands once again, and we were soon off into the soft night, with Mordechai at the helm, en route home, to Mapu Street. Yosef knew that I had overheard his remarks to B.G. "No debate, eh? At least he had one from me. Only this time, *he* didn't answer.

And as for you, young man, don't think that you have *my* permission to stay in the Diaspora for the rest of your life."

I returned from my enjoyable visit with the Sprinzaks in Tel Aviv to my Jerusalem base—the home of my parents-in-law, in the Zikhron Moshe section of the city. Zikhron Moshe—Memorial to Moses—was named for Sir Moses Montefiore, the British Jew who had been the grand patron of Palestine, at the end of the nineteenth century; all through the country, you find similar place-names, as constant reminders of his largesse. This quarter of Jerusalem was first established in 1905, as one of the suburbs in the new city, outside the walls of the old. It was a quiet area, populated, in the main, by moderate-Orthodox Jews, whose synagogues and study halls dotted the adjacent landscape.

Hadassa and I were married in New York, five years earlier, and I had never met either of her parents; this visit helped me catch up with the "lost years" in between. Her father, Samuel Agassi, (Hebraized from Birnbaum, meaning "pear tree") was always a delight: scholarly, thoughtful, and studious. There were more valuable books in the small house than articles of clothing, food, or furniture. He had come to Jerusalem from Munkacs, Hungary (now Czechoslovakia) in 1912, at the age of eighteen, after studying for several years at the University of Budapest. Samuel Agassi was as much at home in the classical Greek and Roman worlds as he was in the Jewish universe of discourse—the Bible and commentaries, Talmud, and the writings of the *maskillim* of the nineteenth century, the "enlightened ones," who wrote in modern Hebrew. He was, in fact, an easy rider on the highways and byways of world culture.

He had married my mother-in-law, Fruma (Hasida), daughter of Rabbi Yeshoshua Mayer Reichman, one of the early pioneers in Jerusalem's health and educational circles, head of the Bikkur Cholim Hospital and its religious academy. Fruma Reichman Agassi was a fourth-generation Jerusalemite. She was the great-granddaughter of the fabled Joel Moses

Solomon—for whom popular songs have since been written, and streets named—who had trekked across Europe by foot before reaching the Holy Land in the mid-1800s. What was also unusual about Solomon was that, unlike others of his generation who came to Jerusalem for pious, mystical reasons—they wanted to die there in order to be buried in its sacred soil—he came to help build the country, long before the First Aliya started in 1881. Once arrived in Jerusalem, he resided, as did all other Jews there, in the crowded, medieval Jewish Quarter of the old city. Within a few years—toward the end of the 1860s—he was among the seven families who had the courage to leave that "secure," tight little island of Jews, huddled together in the old city, to venture outside of its walls to found the Nahalat Shiva neighborhood, in an open space to the west. Historians unanimously regard that bold act of those seven families as one of "pioneering and building not only the new Jewish Jerusalem, but of Greater Jerusalem with all its communities and nationalities" that was to come some thirty years later.[5]

Hadassa was the first of her mother's family in five generations not to be born in Jerusalem: She first saw the light in Galilee, however. Her parents had moved to the tiny agricultural village of Yavniel, a few miles from Nazareth, where her father taught school for several years. It was a fairly new agricultural settlement, in a raw part of the country, founded only two decades earlier with monies supplied by Baron Edmund de Rothschild's P.I.C.A.—the Palestine Jewish Colonization Association.

The Depression in Palestine—earlier there than in Europe

---

[5] Joel Moses Solomon was an altogether remarkable man. Not only did he help establish Nahalat Shiva, but in 1863, shortly after he arrived in Jerusalem, he set up and helped edit the first Hebrew newspaper in the history of Palestine, *Ha-Livanon*. Among the settlement programs supported by the paper were Moza, a suburb in the "new" city of Jerusalem, founded in 1859, and the town of Petah Tikvah, seven miles east of Jaffa, which Solomon himself founded as a village, in the 1870s in a malaria-infested area. Today, it is a town of over 100,000—the oldest modern Jewish city in Israel.

and America—soon forced the Agassi family to move to Cairo, Egypt, where Samuel Agassi was a teacher for a short period, before returning—once and for all—to his beloved Jerusalem. Those were difficult and stormy times in the country, not only economically but also from the point of view of security. Arab riots were frequent and often fatal. Jewish homes in Jerusalem and other towns—especially Hebron—were burned, looted, and their occupants massacred.

That summer of 1949, in peaceful and serene Zikhron Moshe, was a far cry from the Jerusalem Hadassa had last seen almost ten years before, when she left as a young teenager to study at New York University, in December 1939. Sitting there in the cool and pleasant courtyard of her parents' home, under the shade of a plum tree, she recalled: "When we used to take the bus to my high school in Beit Ha-kerem, a few miles west of here, every morning, as we passed through the Arab sections of the city, we always knew that we had to lie down prone on the floor, under the seats, to avoid the sniper fire that was sure to come from Arabs lying in wait for us." Now, Jerusalem was alive with new enthusiasm for life. It was a year of firsts—"the first anniversary of the establishment of Israel"—and all the other firsts that flowed naturally from that brand-new fact of Jewish history.

Samuel Agassi's eyes lit up one morning. "Do you realize," he announced, "that tonight, right here in Jerusalem, we are celebrating another first—the First International Bible Contest; a sort of scriptural Olympics. And it will be broadcast over Kol Israel, the state radio, just like they carry those unnecessary soccer matches, each week!" I explained to him that I not only knew about the night's event, but that Yosef Sprinzak had invited Hadassa and me to be his guests at the Hebrew University stadium at Givat Ram, where the Contest was to take place. "Good," he answered. "Only, you will be freezing out there, in the summer night air of Jerusalem, while I drink my hot tea at home, glued to the radio. Don't forget to take a blanket!"

A Year of Firsts: 1949

Mordechai came to Zikhron Moshe, en route to the Eden Hotel, where we were to meet Sprinzak. The Eden was the favorite hostelry for "Mapai-niks" from the rest of the country—principally, their M.K.'s, the Members of Knesset—when they stayed in Jerusalem. Lifschutz, the owner, was a member of the party—the décor was simple, the rooms small, but tidy, and I imagine the "price was right." There really was no other decent hotel in Jerusalem, at the time, except for the King David. But in those days that august place was still seen by Jews as a symbol of the British Army headquarters—used for so many years as a recreation center and "watering hole" by the commanding officers of the despised Mandatory "occupation force." Few Jews ventured near it. At the Eden, besides, things were always lively; it was the center for meetings and political horse-trading. Sprinzak was sure to be found there whenever he came to the city. We met in the crowded, noisy lobby and drove to the Contest.

It was a cool night out there in the stadium, but the festive air warmed up the atmosphere. Israeli flags were flapping slowly in the soft breeze all across a giant, well-lighted outdoor stage. There was music and singing before the contest began, and the huge crowd waited expectantly. On the stage, there were about a half-dozen finalists from many of the world's continents, men and women who had won their "national" runoff competitions back home. These were the giants of the Bible: two or three Israelis, plus a few others, including a Roman Catholic priest from Belgium, and an American Christian Bible student. Sage-looking Israeli Bible scholars were seated in a corner—they were the judges. My father-in-law was right. This was much better then even a championship soccer match—it was the World Cup of the Bible.

Sprinzak was alive to every answer, amazed at the skill and knowledge of the contestants. "How do they do it?" he would exclaim after every superb answer, adding his own vociferous handclapping to the thunderous applause from the crowd. "In Israel," he kept telling me," we have a poor record in world sports. Only our national basketball team, they tell me, has any hope for international success. But you wait and see. One of those Israelis down there on the stage is going to win this match. After all, it's *our book*, and it's *our sport!*"

None of the questions put to the contestants was simple; no "warm-ups" here. They were all tricky and convoluted, relating to singular events or unusual turns of phrase that occurred in the Old Testament. "Where is this mentioned?" "What incident is repeated three times, in three different places in the Bible, but in different ways?" Questions like these led to a seemingly endless round of flawless answers. The crowd hung on every question and warmly cheered every correct answer. At long last, there were only two competitors left—one of them a poor and disabled Jewish caretaker from Jerusalem by the name of Amos Hacham. At night's final end, that name would become a byword throughout the country, and it would be on the tongues of the people for months. He won. "We're going to find him a decent job and give him a better place to live," Sprinzak told me a few days later, when it was discovered how badly he had fared. "'The Bible Champion'—*Aluph Ha-Tanakh*—deserves better from his people than life has dealt him thus far," he said.

There was always that dimension in Israel—the sad, even tragic, dwelling in the midst of euphoria. I saw it in Hanna Sprinzak's unhappy eyes; felt it, even in some of the witty stories her husband told so ebulliently. I heard it over the radio, again and again, in the plaintive army songs of the *Palmach*—the élite commandos—which evoked memories of the dead and the dying. *Hayu Zemanim*, that year's most frequently broadcast ballad, described the "days gone by"—the War of Liberation—just a few months past, when so many of their comrades fell in battle. Was their death too much of a price to pay for what we dreamed about? Would the living remember them? Or would their military regimens of life and their mundane striving to extract a livelihood from an arid, stubborn soil make them forget? And all these new immigrants, from all over the world, with their polyglot languages and cultures—would they, in their own difficult adjustment to the harshness of life here, dismiss from memory the blood spilled *for them*? Over and again, I could see the same large, gnawing question biting away at their inners. Can what was once only a dream—a costly dream—be joyfully realized, when so many young ones lie buried, dead and gone, before their time?

In that vibrant society thoughts such as these had ironically made death an underlying personal and social theme. Memorialism seemed to preoccupy the public and the private conscience. One could understand this in earlier days. Although there is nothing in the biblical tradition to recommend it, European Jews—and later, their Ashkenazic descendants in North America—had improvised a series of memorial practices that emerged out of their frequent encounter with pogroms, persecutions, and country-wide expulsions. Involvement with death was something they *built into* Jewish life: annual visits to the grave of the deceased, the practice of naming children after departed kin, the making of charitable donations in memory of the deceased, and the belief that the dead and the living can intercede for one another, in petition before the Almighty. They consciously shaped Jewish life into a series of "living memories."

Sephardic Jews, living under the influence of Islam, which pays less attention to memorialism, diverged in some basic ways, from their Ashkenazic, European counterparts. They named their children after living rather than deceased descendants, were less preoccupied with rituals surrounding memorial anniversaries, and tended to regard cemeteries with less dread and awe than their compatriots from the West. Yet, in Israel, it seemed, the burden of war and death fell so heavily on the shoulders of all Jews residing there that the European innovations became the norm—and were even added to by state officials and religious authorities.

This was already apparent in 1949, during my visit, but would become even more pronounced over the years, as the wars multiplied and the casualties mounted. Military cemeteries became national shrines, and the landscape was dotted with heroic sculptures erected in memory of the "defenders of," or "the defense of," or the "women and children of," or the "battle of"—one or another military engagement. In August of that year, I was to get a foretaste of a related national theme, when the Government decided to transfer the remains of Theodor Herzl, founder of modern Zionism, from Vienna to Jerusalem. He had died forty-five years earlier, five years after he had written in his diary these words which were later to become magical for Jews: "Today I have founded the Jewish state...perhaps not in my lifetime, but surely, in fifty years." All of the ceremonies surrounding his re-interment were elevated by the authorities—in search of a modern, mythic state hero—into an act of national apotheosis. For a new nation, itself "brought back home," it seemed that the heights of glory had been scaled in bringing Herzl "home" too—to "dwell" among them.

A military honor guard flew to Vienna, where his remains were exhumed and placed in a wooden coffin draped with the flags of Israel. At Lydda Airport, government officials, the Chief Rabbis of both the Ashkenazic and Sephardic communities, and other important persons "met" Herzl. A slow convoy of official vehicles accompanied his coffin as it was driven along the very route—and making the same stops—Herzl had taken some fifty years before—in 1898—when he came to Palestine to meet another important visitor to the country, Kaiser Wilhelm II. (His attempts at persuading the Kaiser then in Jerusalem to grant a charter guaranteeing sovereign status to the Jews of Palestine had failed.) Then, for three days, humble folk from all over the country, came to pass by the ceremonial catafalque that had been erected in the courtyard of the Jewish Agency building, in Jerusalem. This amazed me, since it is a ritual foreign to Judaism, and borders on idolatry, in my view. Yet no one appeared offended. On the contrary. In death, Herzl had now come alive, and the citizens of Israel felt that they had made possible this act of "resurrection." They wanted to participate in his immortal life by coming as close as possible to his mortal remains.

All the country, it seemed, had poured into Jerusalem on the day chosen for the actual re-interment. They walked by foot—as is customary in Jewish tradition—following his remains to the cemetery. Only this time, the place was not yet a cemetery, but a rocky, hilly slope overlooking Jerusalem from the west; it would be re-named Mount Herzl, and would also become "the heroes' cemetery" for Prime Ministers and the like, once this first grave had been put in place. Yosef Sprinzak had asked my wife and me to accompany him to those ceremonies. Thousands of people stood at a distance from the freshly dug grave, waving flags and "enjoying" the solemn national occasion. Near the bier, things were much more serious and earnest. Designated representatives from hundreds of *kibbutzim* and villages across the land came forward in groups, at a signal, to deposit small packages of earth taken from their community. All of the land, not only Jerusalem, was a "Holy Land," and all of the land would receive Herzl. Traditional memorial prayers were chanted, Psalms intoned, and the coffin was slowly lowered to its final resting place.

On the way back from the event, Yosef Sprinzak turned to me and said: "One funeral would have been enough. It breaks my heart that in order for us to live—we have to die again and again—and again."

Chapter 12

THE NEED FOR DIALOGUE

Imperium does not become Israelis. It is not a tradition for which their history has either prepared or trained them, so Jews wear uneasily the crown of military conquest. What is more, their psychological and political burdens as continuing occupiers and annexers of lands taken in bloody battles are becoming increasingly onerous with the passing of each day. They need peace more than they need territory. Jewish life depends on it.

These are second thoughts—thoughts I could not have known or even surmised in 1949.

In 1949, and for years thereafter, Yosef Sprinzak never relented or gave up. Repeatedly and insistently he kept urging me to "come back home and begin life again as a full Jew." He always expected me. Batz, curiously, did not. He had other views.

I can never forget how my brother-in-law would put it, using his tried logistics as a veteran military man. "We Jews are now waging a 'war' with the world," he would proclaim dramatically. "We are engaged in a historic battle to overturn its treatment of us as a cringing, fleeing, uncreative people who they thought had died long ago. We are telling them that we

The Need for Dialogue 369

have returned and intend to stay. We are about to achieve something no other ancient people has done: to come back into history as its natural self."

Invariably, he would zero in on me personally, and indicate his strategic assessment of the way this "war" could be won. "For the foreseeable future, our revolution will remain a two-front battle. We Israelis at the center, on the home front, carrying the essential burden, and showing the flag. But our 'overseas forces' must not fall apart or surrender. They need us for their own self-esteem; we need them for our morale. We need you where you are—and guiltlessly too, or else you're not much use to us. You there, teaching our people that they are also part of this Jewish revolution. We here, opening the doors and building the home. Together one 'army,' one people, one destiny."

His simple, almost-trite analysis has remained with me, even though I would now wish that I could ask him some serious questions. Not why but how? How to open those doors? How to build that Home?

Yet, one thing will always remain clear, despite all the new questions. After the Holocaust, no self-respecting Jew may abandon Israel, or allow her survival to be left to the whims of those who would be pleased to complete Hitler's work.

With the singular exception of Anwar Sadat, Israel's Arab foes remain uniformly implacable: "No peace, no recognition"—this is the bellicose flag still waved in Israeli faces. On the other hand, the world becomes increasingly impatient and wearied with Israel—and with Jews elsewhere, who defend her cause. It is now more than thirty-five years since the Holocaust, and new generations of statesmen have arisen who neither remember nor care to be reminded that Israel was to be the phoenix of the crematoria.

There are recognizable—if unimaginative and even immoral—reasons for the world's growing demand that Israel withdraw from the lines of conquest and adopt a more passive posture in the pursuit of peace. By now, Islamic power threatens world stability—and not only in the Middle East. Moreover, for profoundly psychological reasons that still go largely unnoticed in the Christian West, Muslim hostility toward the State of Israel—as well as toward Jews—has profound religious roots.[1] Khomeini's radical "theology" is not the only ranting anti-Israel voice among the discordant—and often fratricidal—Muslim states. It is not by accident that, despite their own serious separations and divisions, in the view of virtually all devout followers of the Koran, antipathy to the State of Israel is the one thing on which all can agree.

This is so because, to all of these, a Jewish state in their midst is a blasphemous theological insult and scandal. From its earliest days, Islam has had a religious view of itself as an unbeatable, ever-growing *ulammah* (land and people) which was divinely ordained to encircle the whole earth. Thus, for even the tiniest fragment of "Muslim land" to be carved out ("stolen," they would say) of their own expanding patrimony, poses a *religious* challenge to all unreformed Muslims—from the arch-conservative Saudis on the right to the dissident Shiites on the left. In a curious way, the dynamics of their "Jewish problem" work in much the same manner as the theological embarrassment which Judaism's refusal to "recognize its own Messiah" still poses for some benighted Christians. To judge from the history of Christian-Jewish relations, dating back to the first days of the early Church, such religious "embarrassments" can be mortally dangerous to those who are perceived as causing them. In both cases, Jews seem to be "in the way"—the ultimate stumbling block, for both illiberal

---

[1] See D.F. Green, ed., *Arab Theologians on Jews and Israel*, Editions de l'Avenir, Geneva, 1976. These are papers given at the Fourth Conference of the Academy of Islamic Research, held at Al-Azhar University in Cairo in 1970. In the words of a renowned Catholic scholar, these "should open the eyes of anyone who does not realize that Islam, too, has its own 'teaching of contempt' which accuses Jews—as Jews—of every form of depravity short of deicide, and Judaism of being a perverted religion hostile to all humanity." See Rev. Eugene Fisher, "Anti-Semitism: A Contemporary Christian Perspective," in *Judaism*, Summer, 1981, pp. 281-2.

The Need for Dialogue 371

Christians and unemancipated Muslims. It is thus not difficult to understand why Western Christians—even the best-intentioned—are not good candidates for dealing objectively and realistically with this core issue that remains at the heart of the Arab-Israel impasse. Semites, they naively insist, can not be "anti-Semites"; and besides, it is a question Christians should not be called upon to resolve, most especially since Islamic nations are also the big oil-producers. As a result, on the world economic front too, ever since 1973, oil has become the keystone of national policy on Israel throughout the West. It will surely be a long time—if ever—before energy self-sufficiency will permit the non-Arab world to stand up to the oil weaponry imposed upon it by little medieval sheikdoms and kingdoms which repeatedly use Israel as a bargaining chip in their international power games with the weakened, divided, and dependent Free World.

Many thoughtful and sensitive Jews know all these things and realize that, unless Israel remains strong enough to stand up to these overwhelming pressures, she may easily be dismembered and overrun. But they are struggling too, daring to hope that Jerusalem never become Sparta. In their deepest heart they do not wish Jews to be conformed to the "might-makes-right" ethic of others. Yet, they are repeatedly frustrated. The incessant demands the world makes on Israel to be more forthcoming have only succeeded in focussing the spotlight on Israel as the "conqueror"—and have egregiously failed to move Arab-Muslim states a single inch toward the steps taken by Sadat. They also know that a weaker Israel—or one whose strength is steadily diminished by the demands of her "friends"—will not serve the cause of peace, and may only serve the Arabs. But they are deeply pained, too. They fear if Israel remains a fortress state, much that is beautiful in the Zionist dream will either die or grow ugly and unrecognizable to them. Thus it is that in addition to those who worry about the Arabs, the world, and the attitudes of the superpowers, there are some Zionists who are now beginning to have problems with the State of Israel itself. And these are serious moral questions that only members of a family can feel so deeply, when they contemplate the quality of their life, not just its material or physical survival.

From 1967 until the "Yom Kippur War" of October 1973, they had enjoyed an "era of good Jewish feelings"; there was a sense of euphoria during those six years. North American Jews, for the first time in their history, then began emigrating in substantial numbers—relative to other countries. Until the Six-Day War, there were probably less than 15,000 of them living in the country. But in the short period of 1967-1973 alone, well over 25,000 came to settle in Israel, and to join personally in the task of re-building the Jewish national home. And for the first time, young American Jews, many of them previously alienated as Jews—particularly those of the 1960s New Left variety—began arriving in Israel in very large numbers, to spend a few months or a few years on the land, especially as volunteers in *kibbutzim*, in order to partake of Israeli life at first hand.[2] There were also professional Jews, in their many hundreds, who came for a sabbatical year, to "soak up" the Israeli experience or to study or teach at various institutes and universities.

There are good reasons for both the earlier euphoria and the more recent feelings of malaise. I know, for I have shared them both.

Through the months of March to May 1967 the specter of genocide became a real possibility once again, for almost all the Jews of the world. Arab leaders promised to "drive Israel into the sea." The United Nations gratuitously assisted Nasser by removing its force and closing the Straits of Tiran, thus facilitating Egypt's threat to advance on Israel. Israeli leaders nervously flew from capital to capital—from Washington to London, and Paris, many times—criss-crossing the world repeatedly

---

[2] For a fuller description of American immigration to Israel, see Calvin Goldschieder, "American Aliya," in *The Jew In American Society*, ed. by M. Sklare, Behrman House, N.Y., 1974, pp. 355-84. See also Kevin Avruch, *American Immigrants in Israel*, University of Chicago Press, Chicago, 1981.

The Need for Dialogue 373

during those harrowing months, in search of some promise of support to fend off the impending mass Arab invasion from north, south and east. No government was prepared to extend a hand—not even a finger—to help protect Israel from the threat of oncoming war with five Arab armies: Lebanon, Syria, Iraq, Jordan and Egypt. Jews were petrified at what they saw unfolding before their eyes: a replay of the 1940s, with not a single nation willing to come to the aid of their embattled, beleaguered people. Another holocaust stared them squarely in the face and not even "some of our best friends"—Christian churchmen with whom we thought we were "in dialogue"—offered anything more than silence.

Then, just as all seemed lost, all seemed gained. The unexpected and unimagined had happened. Little David had triumphed—in six lightning days of war—against the mighty Goliath. The ecstatic joy that came upon the Jewish world was in sharp contrast to the gloom of just a few days earlier. Then it was going to be Auschwitz and Buchenwald all over again; a mere week later it almost seemed that the Messiah had finally come.

Since 1973—and particularly since Sadat's 1978 peace initiative—the sense of elation that had ruled for six years has slowly been changing into a time of inner tension among Israelis themselves and many diaspora Jews. Some are profoundly concerned with what a "warrior mentality" may do to life in Israel, and with the increasing "hard-line" which the successive governments of Menachem Begin had seemed to cultivate. Perhaps the feelings of disappointment, pain and confusion these days over the future quality of life in part—though not all—of Israel is really the result of the larger-than-life, overindulged ecstasies we Jews allowed ourselves to enjoy after that horrifying genocidal replay of 1967 was miraculously converted into an "eschatological" fulfillment.

On reflection, however, I think not. Those were good and great days, in and of themselves—and they deserve to be remembered as such. What Jews ought do, if they find themselves unhappy with what "is now going on in Israel," is to retrace in their memories, the spirit of the people that emerged immediately after the Six-Day War: the hopes, anticipations, and the dreams. There was exhilaration then—perhaps an over-reaction. But there can yet be fulfillment.

If I now raise questions about the recent reality in Israel, they should be seen in contrast to the 1967 model of Israel in which I exulted. Fortunately, I was there, and lived in Jerusalem for almost a year, with my wife and daughters, while on sabbatical leave from my congregation in Toronto. There was something poetic about the air there, those days. Elated, I tried to capture that mood in a series of "Letters from Jerusalem" that I sent regularly to members of my congregation. My friends told me I was fairly ecstatic—that as they read those published "Letters" they could sense that I was "walking on clouds," living not only in this earthly capital city of Israel, but in the "heavenly Jerusalem," as well.

I ask myself—a decade and more—after those romantic hours of Israel's shining days, whether I feel now as I did then. And even more to the point is the direct question that puts my feelings—and those of others like me—to the real test: Why have I—and they—not made *aliya*? Why have I—and they—remained here in the diaspora of North America, and not responded to that old magnetic tug pulling and drawing me back to Jerusalem, to live and build my life in the new Zion? Why has North American immigration to Israel come close to a halt today, compared to the 1970s? And why have so many of those from this part of the world who did emigrate in those years returned, often saddened and even disheartened, by life in Israel?

What has changed? Is it Israel that is solely at fault? Or have we Western Jews become too conformed to our comfortable "exile"? Is it really more difficult to "get the Exile out of Jews" than to "get the Jews out of Exile"? Or are we overseas "soldiers" who still man our posts loyally, in need of greater reassurance that our love and support will lead to a victory for the Jewish spirit, not just of the Israeli army?

The Need for Dialogue 375

Somehow, as a child, as my grandfather lay dying, I could never picture him dead. He would always be there. Part of my assurance was born, of course, of the blind love all children have of life, and their innate unwillingness, as immature persons, to come to terms with its end. But an equally strong conviction that he would not succumb—not now, at any rate, I felt—was due to his repeated reminders to me of God's goodness. "The Talmud teaches," I can still hear him saying, "that the Almighty provides man with the remedy even before He visits the sickness upon him. Healing will come, my child; it is here already. It waits only for a wise doctor to know how to seize it and use it."

The catalogue of problems facing Israel—inside the country and in the wide world—is long and mean. What it needs are large doses of fearless and imaginative self-criticism and a pragmatic willingness to cast out inflexible ideologies, in order to seize the remedy and help render itself a cure. Healing power for many of its maladies and feelings of malaise is already there—in Israel itself. I know. There is a strange and resilient strength in the depths of many of its people. I speak of those who came there out of love for the land—or were born there, to parents who came to build a new society and a new Jewish people. I am referring to the many who want to live in peace with themselves as Jews, and with their Arab neighbors as well. I am thinking of those for whom "security" is urgent and relevant, but who still refuse to make it into a false god who maddens legions of idolaters into willful self-destruction. I look too to those for whom Zionism is nothing less than it always was: a Jewish liberation movement geared to sharing life, not death. I see it, for example, in a person like A.B. Yehoshua, noted Israeli teacher and internationally acclaimed author, who put it down this way: ·

> "...even in the course of...war it was possible to see how Israeli society tried to soften the impact of the constant presence of death....
>
> "It was a complicated process, for the repression of the

presence of death is highly dangerous for a society in a conflict....

"*We must mourn grievously, deeply. Only thus can we pursue peace with all our strength....*

"We have displayed many fine qualities of spirit in a situation of conflict. Will we also know how to bring forth the best that is within us in lackluster situations?.... I believe that the potential creative forces in Israel in a situation of peace are no less than those which have revealed themselves in the situation of war."[3]

War or peace? Death or life? No other questions run across and through the entire fabric of Israeli society as do these. For most other countries, this issue is regarded as a matter to be handled by their political and diplomatic experts, to be weighed in the scales of national self-interest. Not many members of the United Nations have the same daily worries of unrecognized borders and terrorist incursions, or have been condemned to a state of war for over thirty years with virtually all of their neighbors—even with remote allies of bordering states. All these adamantly refuse to negotiate with, or even recognize, the Jewish state. None of these countries sits in the councils of the world faced with the threats of international blackmail, economic boycott, or political sanctions which Arab nations and their mindless Third World cohorts—in addition to the Communist bloc—regularly hurl at Israel. In the past, Jews have survived the charge of deicide, and more recently the threat of genocide. Now they are confronted daily by the taunts of "politicide"—not only their own death, but the "murder" of their hard-won state as well.

Unfortunately for Israel, the carrying out of preventive or retaliatory measures against Arab terrorist incursions or bombardments, has become a permanent feature of daily life. Thus, war and peace are unavoidably personal, domestic affairs, not

---

[3] A.B. Yehoshua, *Between Right and Right*, Doubleday, New York, 1981, pp. 175-177.

matters of foreign policy as they are elsewhere in the world. The Israel Defense Force consists principally of reservists—up to the age of fifty-five—who are required to spend at least sixty days each year on active duty. As a result, there are virtually no civilians in the country—only soldier-citizens—and the agricultural and industrial economies, as well as schools, universities, small shop-keepers, and cultural or scientific institutions, are all geared to a life of eternal national defense and perpetual military training.

None of these problems, of course, could have been predicted by the early dreamers, those revolutionary Jewish "liberators" called Zionists. The tortuous issues which confront the State of Israel today and tomorrow are the outcome of many unforeseeable factors—like the Holocaust and, later, Arab intransigency. But they are also related to the problems of Zionism itself. There is still great debate as to what Zionism really wanted. What was it trying to do with the Jewish past? What "Jewish reality" was it addressing? What was it anxious to change and correct, in its earnest striving to become the "wave of the Jewish future"? And most important of all, what did it want Jews to be: a normal, "average" people; or a beacon-like nation and a moral force in the world? It is this question—or dilemma—that is at the heart of almost all of Israel's pressing moral issues: Shall we be ordinary or great?

Formula answers to many of these profound political and philosophical questions have already been "ruled on" and distributed (treated like mere resolutions at a party convention: "moved, seconded, and passed") by many leaders of post-State Zionism in Israel. The list of such eminences began with David Ben Gurion, and has since trickled down to other lesser lights and groups, each with its own noisy proclamations. Not to be outdone by the secularists, the religious parties have also added their zealous clamor to the cacophony, in defense of their own Jewish models. But taken altogether, these loudly proclaimed Zionist "answers" sometimes become a further obstacle to the honest problem-solving that is needed. Too often, they are based on a compounding of errors: a warped, politically partisan view of Israeli society built onto a faulty reading of Judaism and Jewish history. Here's a short list of some of their conventional mistakes and inner contradictions which, I believe, need to be openly and honestly confronted. I set them down as a "preface to dialogue" between Israel and the Diaspora:

1. *That the Exile was forced on the Jews against their will, and they have been waiting impatiently to return to the Land.*
2. *That Jews everywhere but in their own land constitute an alien, pariah people, and thus remain eternally doomed in the Diaspora to the frustrations—but especially the persecutions—that flow from anti-Semitism.*
3. *That all Jews who refuse to "make aliya" to their Land, and continue to remain in the Diaspora, will assimilate and be absorbed into their environment.*
4. *That a secular state in Israel—without religious underpinning and the trappings of rabbinical political power—is the true purpose of Zionism.*
5. *That a religiously based state in Israel, centered in Jewish religious law (halaka), is the true purpose of Zionism.*
6. *That a Jewish state would serve as the cultural model, if not the cultural center, of world Jewry.*
7. *That a revived Jewish state would allow Jews to become a normal people—like any other nation on earth.* And the obverse:
8. *That a revived Jewish state would become a "light unto the nations," in the finest, universalist tradition of the ancient Hebrew prophets.*
9. *That Jewish national character has been deformed and misshapen by the perennial minority status of the people in Exile, and only by forming a sovereign majority in their land will Jews become what they once were, in days of ancient glory—a people of students, scholars, and saints.*
10. *That Zionists displaced no one in the land, for they came*

to a barren and deserted country "without inhabitants," and moreover, that Arab-Palestinian nationalism is a hoax, since in any case "a Palestinian nation" does not exist—only "Arabs" who once lived in Palestine.

11. That Israel has a moral right to expect that at least those American Jews who call themselves "Zionists" will settle in the land, to help prevent the country from becominng a small, provincial, Levantine nation.

12. That as aliya—"going up"—to settle in the land is meritorious, so emigrating from the land is yerida—"going down"—and it is to be regarded as a traitorous act.

Without ever forgetting all that I was taught and had felt, first as a child, later as a student, then as a Rabbi—and in the biblical spirit of "love as reproof," my own second thoughts have brought me a different line of responses to the problems accumulating in Israel. Many of them are in no small measure the result of these confusing and contradictory popular Israeli "axioms"—some of which are downright self-deluding. After all, my own Zionist teachers had taught me to question the conventional, accepted "wisdom" of the Jewish establishment of earlier pre-State days, who were then avidly anti-Zionist. My teachers said: Learn to say *Tomar verkert*—seek the truth in different ways; perhaps you will find it is completely different from what you are told to believe. Now there is an *Israeli establishment*. It is not irreverence but hope that prods me to question *it*, as I have been taught. New questions can bring new answers.

The Exile and the Return

Although most Israelis use them interchangeably, scholars would agree that there is a crucial difference between the two terms—"dispersion" (or Diaspora) and "exile." The Hebrew word *galut*—exile—denotes the conception of the conditions and feelings of a nation uprooted from its homeland and subject to alien rule. But only the loss of its political-ethnic center and the accompanying feelings of uprootedness turn *gola*—dispersion—into *galut*—exile. Objective students of Jewish history accept the view that "the residence of a great number of members of the nation, *even the majority*, outside their homeland, is not definable as 'exile,' *so long as the homeland remains in the possession of the nation.*"

Still, from the very outset, the twin phenomena of exile and dispersion demanded some explanation, considering that this terrible fate had been meted out to God's "chosen people." The Talmudic Rabbis had also been preoccupied with this problem, and they put their own question into the mouth of the gentiles: "And His people, what did they do to Him, that He exiled them from their land?" (*Aboth di-Rabbi Nathan*: 1.4.) Understandably, there was no unanimity about the answers they gave to this question, and similar pointed questions, during the next hundreds of years of debate.

Some sages saw Israel's exile as a prerequisite of the divine plan for the ultimate redemption of mankind—as a way of bringing the Torah, His word, to the whole world. Others, like Rav, in Babylonia, thought that it was more a matter of "Jewish merit and demerit." "When Israel merits it, the majority of them will be in the Land of Israel and a minority in Babylonia; but when they are unworthy of it, the majority will be in Babylonia and the minority in the Land of Israel." (*Genesis Rabbah*: 98:9.)

Rav's view seems to have prevailed, certainly throughout the Middle Ages, when "Jewish merit" became linked to a mystical speculation. The longing to return home often assumed the proportions of a messianic movement. Who could have imagined, for example, that a goodly number of sophisticated Middle Eastern Jews should assemble their wives and children on rooftops, expecting to be carried away on "the wings of angels to the Holy Land, aided by their Redeemer" who, they believed, resided in distant Kurdistan? But this strange event actually happened. As late as the twelfth century, David Alroy attempted to establish a Jewish kingdom in Kurdistan, by force

The Need for Dialogue 381

of arms; from there, he announced, he would lead all Jews out of the exile, back to Palestine. Pseudo-messiahs like these—both in the East and in Europe—followed each other in fairly rapid succession, all the way down to the seventeenth century, when the most popular and renowned of all, Sabbatai Zevi, came upon the scene and unsettled almost all of Jewish life.

By and large, from Sabbatai Zevi's time forward, pious Jews determined two positions for themselves that were interconnected. They would *patiently* await the Messiah, and do nothing to "force God's hand" to send Him; they would also remain in their various exiles—difficult though they were—and not return to Palestine until God would send the true Messiah to bring them home again in His good time. Zionists, of course, in the nineteenth century, scoffed at all this as unrealistic, escapist pietism, and turned Jewish messianism into a secular-nationalist movement seeking to regain Palestine by political, not religious, means.

Yet, just as political Zionists had revised the meaning of messianism, so have some contemporary Jewish historians been developing a revisionist theory of exile and dispersion. In a nutshell, here is what one of them has explained to me:

> "A careful reading of history reveals that during the Second Temple period itself (70 C.E.) and thereafter until the present day, generally speaking the Jews seem to have *chosen* to live in exile. It is simply not true that Jews could never have returned to the land of Israel had they indeed wanted to. Emigrating to their ancient homeland would not invariably have constituted a worsening of their conditions; the 'Holy Land' would not have provided a more dangerous, more impoverished, more precarious area in which to live, any more than it would have a more inhospitable or inferior landscape as compared to the locales in which Jews chose to dwell.
>
> "One is tempted to suggest that deep in the 'collective unconscious' of the Jew there seems to have been the idea that somehow the Holy Land was an adverse preserve. Like

the biblical spies sent by Moses, he felt that 'this is a land which consumes its inhabitants.' It was a horrific place; perhaps its very supposed sanctity was the cause of the fear. Whatever the cause or causes be, and no doubt they are multifactorial, the Jew chose every inhabited, quasi-civilized land, from Yemen to Greenland, from Afghanistan to Peru, suffering repression, alienation, marginality and minority status, rather than go to the Holy Land from which he was exiled, and to which, he affirmed continuously, he prayed to be restored through divine intervention and redemption. Instead of seeking to remedy the Jewish condition, the Jews blamed the world, or God's will, and did nothing to end the 'Exile.' "[4]

As to the validity of this attempt at psychologizing history, I have many personal doubts. But I have no uncertainty, whatever, about the current reality. Since 1948, there have been no restraints placed on free Jews in the Western World from "returning home." Why are they not settling in Israel in greater numbers? My own answers to this may be understood from some of what follows, later.

Doomed in the Diaspora by Anti-Semitism?

It is neither by accident or coincidence that the two most crucial ideologues of Zionism were both emancipated, even assimilated Jews, who believed that a single national state for their people—at first, anywhere in the world and not necessarily in Palestine—was the only answer to their impending doom in the diaspora.

Leon Pinsker lived in Russia from 1821 to 1891 and was a zealous patriot, a medical doctor who was honored by Tsar Nicholas I for his outstanding services to Russian soldiers stricken by typhus in the Crimean War. He wrote a daring pamphlet, *Auto-Emancipation*, in 1882.

---

[4] In a personal letter to the author, dated March 31, 1981, from Professor Etan Levine, Haifa University, Israel. For a fuller treatment of this theme see also, A.B. Yehoshua, *op. cit.*, especially the section "The *Golah* as Willed," pp. 26-41.

The Need for Dialogue 383

Dr. Theodor Herzl was born in Budapest in 1860, graduated the law faculty of the University of Vienna, and then became a leading dramatist and well-known Paris correspondent of Vienna's leading newspaper, the *Neue Freie Presse*.

Herzl fathered the Zionist movement when he called together a World Zionist Congress, in Basel, Switzerland, to consider the proposals he had made in his book *The Jewish State*. It was the Dreyfus trial, which he had covered as a Paris correspondent—and the attendant cries all over France of *mort aux juifs*—death to all Jews—which had propelled his theory about the impossibility of Jews to continue to live creatively in the diaspora. If, at the end of the nineteenth century in Paris—the "cultural capital of the world"—Jews had no rest, where else could they find it, save in a state of their own?

It is enough to read their own precise words in order to understand the basic tenets of the Zionism that have since grown up on the foundation of their earlier thought.

In *Auto-Emancipation*, Pinsker summarized his "Appeal to His People By a Russian Jew":

"The Jews are not a living nation; they are everywhere aliens; therefore they are despised.

"The civil and political emancipation of the Jews is not sufficient to raise them in the estimation of the peoples.

"The proper and only remedy would be the creation of a Jewish nationality, of a people living upon its own soil, the auto-emancipation of the Jews; their emancipation as a nation among nations by the acquisition of a home of their own.

"We should not persuade ourselves that humanity and enlightenment will ever be radical remedies for the malady of our people.

"The lack of national self-respect and self-confidence, of political initiative and of unity, is the enemy of our national renaissance.

"In order that we may not be constrained to wander from one exile to another, we must have an extensive and produc-

tive place of refuge, a gathering place which is our own....
"Help yourselves, and God will help you!"[5]

Barely a score of years later, Dr. Theodor Herzl watched in the Paris courtroom as Alfred Dreyfus, an assimilated Jew like himself, was falsely accused of spying for Germany while serving as a captain on the General Staff of the French Army. Emile Zola, the great French writer, was not able to accept this naked anti-Semitism in his own country and he cried out his famous speech beginning with those piercing words, "*J'accuse!*" Herzl did not speak, but wrote, pouring out his shattered heart into a diary he kept while attending the trial. The diary was later rewritten passionately in five feverish days as a pamphlet, and was given the name "Address to the Rothschilds." This was to become his revolutionary book, *The Jewish State*, which could not find a publisher for some time, until it finally appeared in 1896. There, Herzl makes points similar to Pinsker's, although he apparently never even knew about the existence of his Russian-Jewish predecessor at the time he was writing himself. Herzl too underlines anti-Semitism as an eternal presence, one that is the very cause of Jewish nationalism:

> "I referred previously to 'our assimilation.' I do not for one moment wish to imply that I desire such an end. Our national character is too glorious in history and, in spite of every degradation, too noble to make its annihilation desirable. Though perhaps we *could* succeed in vanishing without a trace into the surrounding peoples if they will let us be for just two generations. But they will not let us be. After brief periods of toleration, their hostility erupts again and again. When we prosper, it seems to be unbearably irritating, for the world has for many centuries been accustomed to regarding us as the most degraded of the poor. Thus out of ignorance or ill will they have failed to observe that prosperity

---

[5] Leon Pinsker, *Auto-Emancipation: An Appeal to His People by a Russian Jew*, 1882. May be found in Arthur Hertzberg (ed.), *The Zionist Idea*, Atheneum, New York, 1972, p. 198.

weakens us as Jews and wipes away our differences. Only pressure drives us back to our own; only hostility stamps us ever again as strangers.

"Thus we are now, and shall remain, whether we would or not, a group of unmistakable cohesiveness.

"We are one people—our enemies have made us one whether we will or not, as has repeatedly happened in history. Affliction binds us together, and thus united, we suddenly discover our strength. Yes, we are strong enough to form a State, and, indeed, a model State. We possess all the requisite human and material resources."[6]

Israelis still quote Herzl as their modern prophet and, as we have seen, have elevated him to the top of their national heroes list. Yet, it militates against the facts of Jewish history—not to speak of simple rationality—to insist that Jews can only continue to exist creatively in their own nation-state. What else is the story of Judaism and the Jews but a long and rich chronicle of creativity—often as an alienated people—all across the globe? Perhaps one should add: Alienation is often the mother of vibrant culture—and the Jewish "counter-culture" throughout history is the chief example of this truth.

No. Jewish history refutes this "platform" of modern Zionism. And for Israelis to taunt their brothers who live in free countries of the West, where anti-Semitism surely exists (and must be fought constantly), but where it has not become an instrument of national policy as it had elsewhere, is not helpful to either group—not to Israel itself, not to the Jews of the free diaspora.

It is highly doubtful that Herzl would have gone as far as some of his contemporary Israeli disciples in "luring" American Jews to Israel with downright lurid advertisements, urging them to visit the "Museum of the Potential Holocaust" in Tel Aviv. Week after week, in the Friday magazine supplement of

---

[6] Theodor Herzl, *The Jewish State*: see Arthur Hertzberg, *ibid.*, pp. 219-220.

the English-language *Jerusalem Post* tourists from the United States are assaulted with these terror-tactical admonitions. "Another Holocaust? Not in America? Are you sure? Hate-motivated movements like the American Nazi Party, the Ku Klux Klan, and certain Arab power groups are growing quickly in membership and influence in America. They are gaining the sympathy of many of your neighbors. Hitler is their patron saint. Learn about them. The lesson might save your life.... Visit the authentic, original...Museum of the Potential Holocaust.... Hourly talks for tourists."[7]

This, perhaps, is a mark of the increasing frustration of Israelis with their American brothers, whose emigration from Israel often exceeds the numbers who "make aliya" to the country. But it is also a measure of the hysterical extremism which has overtaken some zealots in Israel. Surely there are better ways to "attract" Jewish settlers than by suggesting to them that they are willfully ignoring the lessons of Hitler's Holocaust by not living in fear of the one that may be awaiting them in America. What can one say to such "Zionists" as these? I find it difficult to engage such people in historical discussion, but somewhere in the hidden recesses of my cerebrum the thought lies firmly imbedded: If American Jewry disappears, what hope that Israel will itself survive?

Doomed in the Diaspora by Assimilation?

The underlying and fundamentally faulty assumption of Herzl and his followers was that there would only be a minority of Jews who would not want to settle in a Jewish state once it was established. This view led them to the conclusion that this relatively small number of Jews could be written off. There, in the Diaspora, they would ultimately assimilate to the majority culture, and thus—in a negative way, of course—their "Jewish problem" would be over. They would cease to live as Jews.

On this question, there is room for honest debate; yet, on the surface at least, it would appear that the second part of this

---

[7] *Jerusalem Post*, March, 12, 1982, Magazine Supplement, p. 6.

"Zionist argument" can be "scientifically" proved to be correct, even if the first part is all wrong. Recent studies by Jewish demographers in the United States point to some startling projections. Says Elihu Bergman, for example: "When the United States celebrates its Tricentennial in 2076, the American Jewish community is likely to number no more than 944,000 persons, and conceivably as few as 10,420. This dramatic decline from a peak Jewish population of nearly 6 million was already in evidence during the Bicentennial. The erosion has two causes: an American Jewish birthrate below the replacement level, which is the level at which the population replenishes itself; *and an increasing rate of attrition among American Jews, which is the rate at which individuals born as Jews lose their Jewish identity.*"[8]

This is not the place to debate Bergman's frightening future statistics, on the basis of his errors of method. Even those other zetetics, however, who may fault his methodology, concede that the Jewish population in America is in decline, and could conceivably fall from its present total of 6 million to only 1.6 million in the year 2070.[9]

Students of American Jewry are generally in agreement, however, that the principal cause—and I would add, the effect as well—of Jewish assimilation is intermarriage. It is reliably reported that in the period of 1966-1972, there was a Jewish intermarriage rate in the United States of 31.7 per cent—an increase of 500 per cent over the rates which prevailed less than ten years earlier. It is not clear, however, how many of the children born to marriages involving a non-Jewish partner were being raised as non-Jews. These numbers vary from community to community—but the range shows that a substantial number of these children are being raised as non-Jews—and thus lost to the Jewish community: from 22 per cent

---

[8] Elihu Bergman, "The American Jewish Population Erosion," in *Midstream*, October, 1977, pp. 9-19.

[9] See, Samuel S. Lieberman and Morton Weinfeld, "Demographic Trends and Jewish Survival," *Midstream*, November, 1978, p. 11.

in Providence, Rhode Island to 70 per cent in Washington, D.C.[10]

However, too little attention is paid to the fact that, not only does Judaism lose adherents in North America by means of apostasy, but also gains adherents by means of converts. According to published surveys, the total numbers, on both sides of the equation, tend to balance each other out. For every million Jews who were born Jewish, 24,000 were said to have become apostates, while, of every million Jews currently considered Jewish, 21,000 had been converted to Judaism. In effect, this means that presently some 125,000 Jews have been lost to other religions (25% to Catholicism; 50% to various Protestant denominations; 25% to sects and cults). On the other side of the scale, however, more than 110,000 of the total present American Jewish population were not born Jewish. Most demographers neglect to take into account the little-noted fact that American Jewry not only has "exports," but "imports" as well. The attrition rate may not be nearly as grave as they have portrayed it to be.[11]

Still, as we have already noted in some detail the portrait of North American Jewry consists of as much light as of shadow. In respect of depth, the predominantly third- or even fourth-generation community in the United States is much less ethnic than were its East-European immigrant grandparents. The Yiddish theater, press, and schools are things of the past, even though they have been replaced by would-be surrogates like Hebrew schools, or Anglo-Jewish weekly periodicals reporting on news of Jewish interest. Most American Jews have become monolingual—speaking only English—something that other Jewries never were.

The so-called "new ethnicity" in the United States helps to paper over some of these losses and gaps. It suggests that the

---

[10] See references in Elihu Bergman, *op.cit.*, p. 9.

[11] See *Journal for the Scientific Study of Religion*, March 1980; also, Allen S. Maller, "Jews, Cults and Apostates," in *Judaism*, Summer, 1981, pp. 306-31.

option of "Jewish survivalism" within a framework of American acculturation is an acceptable and viable alternative, and this is welcome news, especially for secularized Jews. In addition, as some sociologists have already pointed out, the recent "dethronement of America" has helped Jews in that country feel more relaxed in the pursuit of their own separatist lifestyles: no longer must everything "Jewish" be measured against how it conforms to American ways. "The American way of life" is not now seen as the only yardstick even for its own citizens. Since the Vietnam War, a certain debunking of mythic, *wasp*ish America—as the be-all-and-end-all of human hope—has been unleashed, resulting in a more pluralistic society than ever before.

On the other hand—and equally to the point at issue—Israel itself has been succumbing to an increasing "coca-colaization" of its own "Jewish" culture. What Louis Philippe of nineteenth-century France had said of Jewries in Western Europe—that they often mimicked the baser elements of the cultures in whose midst they resided—is ironically true of an Israel which is six thousand miles distant from the United States. It often copies American pop culture with a vengeance: McDonald's hamburgers become "McDavid's"; romantic, pioneering, and work-oriented songs, once created by *kibbutzniks*, have been all but replaced on the state radio by the most vulgar American rock-'n'-roll hits. In the United States and Canada, there are more young people attending the synagogue with some regularity, whereas, despite the many septuagenarians and those older still who do pray devotedly in Israel's synagogues—on Sabbaths, in the spring and summer, the beaches are filled with the middleaged and younger, and they can also be found, in their throngs, in the course of the season, at Saturday soccer contests.

It is far from clear that Israel has not acculturated more to the America it seeks to emulate than have American Jews to the America they no longer adore—as their immigrant parents and grandparents had felt they must. Moreover, since it is

390 THE REAL JEWISH WORLD

living in the midst of an Arab world, and with more and more of its population—by reason of their fecundity—comprised of Oriental, Arabic-speaking Jews, it is highly questionable whether Israel's "Jewish culture" of the future will be, in fact, as Jewish as Zionists had hoped. History is witness to an ironic truth: More than one people has succumbed to a dominant "enemy," not by falling on the field of battle, but by being overthrown by the sheer impact of cultural might and demographic weight. The sociological reality, as much as political considerations, must give Israelis pause when dealing with the desires of some, to annex highly populated Arab areas as part of their ideal of "Greater Israel."

A Secular State without a Religious Base?
Undergirding Zionist theory was the assumption that at the close of the nineteenth century it was now time for Jews to reconstitute themselves as a modern nation, like all others, and to cast off the medieval yoke of rabbinical domination. The glittering humanistic concepts of nationalism, like those which had recently helped to create modern Germany and Italy, were at the heart of this new Jewish political idea. It was, to put it mildly, a radical and revolutionary departure from the previous nineteen centuries of their religious and social history, during which time which Jews had lived as members of self-contained, religious communities, linked together by their religious law (*halaka*), and dominated by their Rabbi-judges.

In order to see the Jewish future "the Zionist way" it was first necessary to create a new Jewish attitude toward the traditional ways of life and belief. Virtually all Zionist thinkers thus found it necessary to abandon the tradition, in order to pave the way to self-acceptance as politically oriented Jewish nationalists. They desired to make possible, here and now, what romantic pietists had left for divine intervention, in some never-never time: a sovereign Zion. In these important respects, Zionism was different from all other Jewish ideologies of the time.

Reform Judaism, a competing modern Jewish movement, had developed principally in Germany a few generations earlier. Like Zionism, it also sought to overthrow traditional religious authority, as well as the medieval corporate structure of communal life. The Reformers saw both of these as stumbling blocks on the road to *their* destination: civic emancipation for Jews and the winning of the right to live as citizens of their own native lands. Jews constitute a "Church" they said, and like other churches, their members should participate in the fullness of the national life of their own country—freely and equally, under the law of the land. "We are," they proudly described themselves, "*Germans* of the Mosaic Confession."

But Zionists went much farther because they were even more radical reformers. The German Reform Jews were emancipated religionists; Zionists surpassed them and became emancipated secularists—they even read the Bible of antiquity as a document of national history, not as the religiously ordained word of God. Zionists would not merely reform the religious tradition, *they would break with it*, and replace it with something they regarded as more vital, necessary, and contemporary—a Jewish brand of the European nationalism of the day. They offered the idea of a rebuilt Jewish nation-state as the welcome substitute for what they saw as outmoded religious structures and institutions.

This explains why, at the start, Zionists were seen as heretics and rebels by the Rabbis and religious laymen of the time. From almost the very beginning of Jewish settlement in Palestine, particularly with the arrival of what is considered today the "cream of Israel," the settlers of the "Second Aliya" who came from 1903 to 1914, Zionism was frowned upon by the Orthodox rabbinate. The religious leaders had only to look out upon the Ben Gurions of that day to see that they were virtually all what were then called "free-thinkers"—secular anti-religionists, social democrats, or socialists. Those early pioneers of the "Second Aliya" had the temerity, the Rabbinate believed, to identify all of Judaism with Zionism, and had made it the only Jewish outlet for their passionate socialist dream of building a better world in the present—without God. To which those *halutzim* responded: We refuse to wait with you and your benighted religious cohorts for your "pie in the sky, bye and bye." We will build the Jewish homeland, with our sweat, blood, and tears, now—with or without God—*and without you too* if need be.

These nationalist sentiments, expressed mainly by Russian Zionists, even by some who preceded Herzl's formal movement, were also the rage among a group known as "Hovevei Zion" (Lovers of Zion), a band of young and romantic intellectual Jews—without the fire of socialism in their bellies—who made up the "First Aliya." They had come from the lands of the Tsar to settle in Turkish Palestine immediately after the bloody pograms of 1881-82. Yet, though the organized Orthodox rabbinate had considered even their "pure" Zionism heretical, there were a few isolated religious voices even then who also saw themselves as "Lovers of Zion," and sought to break the monopoly of these secularists on the idea of a return to the land. The argument, for example, expressed by one leading spokesman, Yechiel Michael Pines, in several essay-pamphlets he published in 1895, is still the basis for the current Orthodox religious challenge to secular Zionism. Today, of course, the Orthodox rabbinate in Israel is strongly entrenched in both the Zionist and the state apparatus. It was clearly not that way at the time of the birth of the movement. Yet, within a few years after Herzl called the first Zionist Congress, in 1897, a new hybrid did come into being: a movement combining Orthodoxy with Zionism, to be called "Mizrachi." These "religious Zionists" followed in the path of thinkers like Pines. To understand how religious traditionalists feel today—now that Zionism has become intertwined with Orthodox Judaism in many sectors of the Jewish universe—we go back to Pines. In one of his pamphlets, titled "Jewish Nationalism Cannot Be Secular," he wrote:

> "I have no sympathy with the currently fashionable idea, with the movement to make the Jewish people a pure secular

nationality in place of the combination of religion with nationality that has enabled us to survive to this day.

"Whatever merit there may be to this theory, it is to be found only in its possible value as applied to the assimilated Jews, that is, to those de-Judaized individuals who have remained members of the Jewish faith in name only and are ready to drop out of the Jewish community. Such Jews may find in the idea of secular Jewish nationality a new bond to reinforce their attachment to their people. But I see a strong tendency these days, one fostered by a well-known school of thought, to impose the idea of secular nationalism on the whole Jewish people, including pious Jews, to try to separate religion from nationality and to make the latter a self-sufficient entity upon which Jewish survival is to depend....

"What, then, is the difference between the Jewish people and all other ethnic groups? The answer to that question is self-evident. The Jewish people did not, at its very beginning, come into the world as a separate entity in the ordinary way, as a result of the combined influences of race and soil, but as a group professing a separate faith and bound in a mutual covenant to observe that faith....

"After the Jewish people acquired a homeland and formed a sovereign state, it still did not look upon its statehood as the essence of its peoplehood; it was generally willing to accept foreign domination with minimal protest and rose in revolt only when its religion was threatened. Conversely, when it was deprived of its homeland and was scattered abroad, and even ceased speaking its national language, the Jewish people continued to live as a national entity only by virtue of the Torah, which accompanied it in all its wanderings and lived with it in every country in which it settled."

That same year he wrote a telling essay whose very title was intended to shock both the Zionists and the Orthodox. It was called "Religion is the Source of Jewish Nationalism." There he wrote:

"Nor have you secularists any monopoly on the Zionist sentiment. I am as much a Lover of Zion as you are, not one whit less. But mine is not the Love of Zion which you have abstracted from the whole Jewish tradition to set it up in a separate existence. Any other people can perhaps have a national aspiration divorced from its religion, but we Jews cannot. Such a nationalism is an abomination to Jews. Moreover, it cannot succeed since it has no roots in our reality.... The nationalism I represent is the nationalism of Rabbi Yehuda Ha-Levi and of Rabbi Moshe ben Nahman, of blessed memory, a national sentiment organically integrated in faith, a nationalism whose soul is the Torah and whose life is in its precepts and commandments."[12]

I value the *saeculum* because I live in it, but I am not a secular Jew. Why then do I sympathize with the so-called "secularist" position in Israel? I have been raised in the modern Jewish world, and am an incurable pluralist. I demand of my Christian neighbors that they recognize my Jewish existence, as a valid expression for me—not for them. I see it as my *Jewish* duty to battle for the rights of all other minorities: I stand at the side of Blacks, Hispanics, women's liberation groups, and other people who have been denied elemental civil rights or political, religious, or social equality. Thousands of Orthodox Jews in North America—though I am not one of them—feel the way I do because, like me, they were also raised in a free society. They too were influenced and taught by their Rabbis and Jewish teachers that we live in a pluralist world, and that

---

[12] Yehuda Ha-Levi was a Jewish poet who lived in Spain in the late eleventh and early twelfth century. He composed many lyrical poems full of longing for Zion. In this connection, his oft-quoted poem begins with the line, "I am in the West, but my heart is in the uttermost parts of the East." Rabbi Moshe ben Nahman (Nahmanides) was also a Spanish Rabbi and philosopher, born in 1195. He left Gerona in 1267 and moved to Jerusalem, where he founded a famous synagogue that year. It was uncovered in the old city of Jerusalem almost intact by archaeologists from the Hebrew University after the Six-Day War. For Pines, see Arthur Hertzberg, *op. cit.*, pp. 411-414.

The Need for Dialogue 395

without devotion to the idea of a multiverse of peoples and cultures, Jews would find it difficult to survive as an identifiable, and equal, group. In this respect, I believe that to be a Jew is to be a member of the most modern of peoples. For over two centuries in the West, Jews have been in the vanguard of those fighting for freedom of expression, religion, and the right to live as equals, in a voluntary society.

What the religious Zionists—and other Orthodox groups in Israel—are doing is of serious concern to anyone raised in the western democratic tradition. Their religious bigotry—inherited from pre-modern Europe—disturbs me. They are willfully excising two centuries of modern Jewish experience and are determined to turn back the clock of time to a Judaism and a Jewish way of life which prevailed in antiquity and the Middle Ages, by insisting that in a modern, Jewish state citizens should be governed by religious law and tradition alone.

For most North American Jews—and other friends of Israel—it comes as a great shock to be told by the officially established Orthodox rabbinate in Israel that all other forms of Judaism—Conservative or Reform, for example—are invalid, save their own brand of rigid Orthodoxy, which is actually closer in spirit to eighteenth-century Poland than to our time. The point is that this is no longer a matter which touches on the life of Israeli citizens alone; what those Rabbis in Israel say and do spills over to the Diaspora too. In effect, the Israeli religious establishment arrogates unto itself the world-rights of Judaism, and performs the un-historical role of a "Jewish Vatican."

This may help explain why it is that in recent years the major source of the small trickles of American Jewish immigration still flowing to Israel comes primarily from young Orthodox families. For some of these, a rigid, authoritarian religious way of life is attractive, and in some ways—for them—more appealing than living as a minority in what they regard as the Christian society of North America. They have even told me that they are really "escaping from the irreligious, non-observant *Jews* of America" even more than from America itself; they do not want their children to be challenged by the existence of plural Judaisms. By the same token, this problem also serves as one good reason why some American Jews have returned, after sincerely trying to start a new life in Israel; and it remains a problem for others who refuse to make the leap of *aliya* to begin with. Most American Jews simply are not Orthodox, and they encounter too much difficulty with the established Judaism of Israel, protected as it is by that disturbing game of "theopolitics" which has been played now ever since the state was founded.

"Theopolitics" is the only word I know that quickly describes the manner in which the Orthodox community in Israel has "taken over"—not only those matters directly related to the religious community, but also issues that clearly affect the entire population, Christians and Muslims as well as Jews. True, it has its roots in the special status the Turks gave to each of the three major religious communities in Palestine under Ottoman rule. Their system, dating back to the nineteenth century, is known as "the millet"—derived from the Turkish word for "religious group," *millah*. The mandatory law of the British continued the "millet system," and so do the Israelis. On the surface, it is a wise and liberal rule—in a country holy to three faiths—which empowers and grants the religious communities complete jurisdiction over such areas as marriage, divorce, alimony, and adoption, and other matters pertaining to "personal status." These are administered under their own separate religious laws, and controlled by the Jewish rabbinical *beth din*—law court, the Muslim *shari'a*—their religious code; and the Christian canon law tribunals.

In practice, however, since Israel was established, what was originally intended to grant freedom of religious expression to these communities has become a pernicious system threatening the basic civil liberties of all citizens. Since the first days of the state, every government has needed the political support of the religious Zionist parties—as well as the "Agudat Israel" group, a bloc of ultra-pious, religious voters who declare themselves as non-Zionists. They adhere to the view that Israel is not a divinely appointed messianic community but merely a secular state with a Jewish government. As a result, political "arrangements" were struck then which have become more convoluted and oppressive as time goes on. In a country where elections based on "proportional representation" have made it impossible for a single party to govern without a coalition of partners, the religious bloc—although it represents a minority of the voters—has managed to bargain for, and win, far greater power than its numbers would warrant.

Theopolitics, for example, disallows Conservative and Reform congregations from obtaining "building permits" without long, often interminable, delays; precludes their spiritual leaders from acting as Rabbis in matters affecting religious law—like marriage and divorce; prohibits ships from arriving or departing on the Sabbath, not to speak of the constant struggle with the national air-carrier, El-Al, to arrange its flight schedules all over the world so as to delete the Jewish Sabbath from its operations. Theopolitics threatens—and has sometimes succeeded—in toppling necessary government coalitions on such issues as: pig-raising in Israel, autopsies, abortions, the demand that major hotels observe the dietary laws and disallow smoking on the Sabbath, and the demand that there be no public transportation on the Sabbath. These and other pressing religious issues have been raised, and they are often the price the government has to pay to keep its Religious Bloc partners in the coalition. Where the rights of others are not destroyed or trampled on, I do believe that it is appropriate in a Jewish state—in the same way as in a country dominated by the Christian heritage—that our own traditions be fostered and preserved. But this valid goal should never be accomplished by refusing the non-religious, or the religiously different, their own options too.

History is witness that Jews were always the bloodied victims of attempts at mixing those two combustibles, religion and politics. What concerns me is that these Jewish aberrations—done for the sake of and in the name of religion—destroy the spiritual character of Judaism since they are coerced and not freely chosen. They are also counter-religious, in many ways, because many Israelis who would, in fact, gladly choose some form of Judaism as their personal way of life are turned off by these "strong-arm" tactics. I worry too that, while the Arab threat still serves as a cementing force for civil unity, if peace should ever break out, a larger battle—the wars of the Jews—may erupt in the form of a *kulturkampf* between the secular and the religious. Perhaps Jewish inventiveness and pragmatic compromise, which even the Talmudic Rabbis had employed, may yet find a home among the pious in Israel. Persuasiveness, not legal coercion, is still the best hope for religious freedom in our time.

Israel: a Model for Jews and the World?

"A political ideal which is not grounded in our national culture is apt to seduce us from loyalty to our own inner spirit and to beget in us a tendency to find the path of glory in the attainment of material power and political dominion, thus breaking the thread that unites us with the past and undermining our historical foundation. Needless to say, if the political ideal is not attained, it will have disastrous consequences, because we shall have lost the old basis without finding a new one. But even if it is attained under present conditions, when we are a scattered people not only in the physical but also in the spiritual sense—even then, Judaism will be in great danger....

" 'Zionism'...begins its work with political propaganda but the 'Love of Zion' (*Hibbat Zion*) begins with national culture, and *for its sake* can a Jewish State be established in such a way as to correspond with the will and the needs of the Jewish people."[13]

The man who said this died more than fifty years ago, and he

---

[13] See Ahad Ha-Am, "The Jewish State and the Jewish Problem," in Hertzberg, *op. cit.*, pp. 268-9.

The Need for Dialogue

wrote these words thirty years earlier still, in 1897. His name was Asher Ginzberg, a native of Russia, and he used the pseudonym "Ahad Ha-Am" (One of the People). He was addressing himself to men like Theodor Herzl, a few months after the first Zionist Congress was convened in Basel. He did not oppose Herzl's political Zionism as much as he went beyond it—or you might say that he came to it from a different perspective, as an Eastern Jew steeped in Jewish culture. He became the father of what came to be called "Cultural Zionism." And there are still many Jews today—in Israel and elsewhere—who repeat his views as their very own. They dream, as he did, of the State as the cultural center of world Jewry—an instrument, not an end in itself. They still speak of the need to transcend even Jewish culture itself, to make of modern Israel a place, like ancient Zion, that can serve as a "light unto the nations." Many of them—and I include myself—could only become "political Zionists" *after* they had accepted his analysis of Jewish nationalism. He saw Zionism as the handmaiden of Judaism, not merely as a tool for building, as he put it, a "puny State tossed about like a ball between its powerful neighbors, and maintaining its existence only by diplomatic shifts and continual truckling to the favored of fortune."[14]

Yet, two major, brutal facts of recent history have changed not only the physical map of Jewry, but also shape the mind and heart of those who have settled in Israel: the post-Holocaust ingathering in that country of Jews, who did not choose to settle there, but who desperately needed a haven; and the outflow of Jews from Arab countries, after 1948, when Israel was established, who found themselves unwanted in countries in which they had lived for more than a millennium. Those who predominate today are these recent refugees—people who remember their brokenness. They are not concerned principally with "culture," but with their own physical and economic security. I do not fault them. Their physical and

---

[14] Ahad Ha-Am, *ibid*, p. 269.

economic needs are primary and, as long as they remain unmet, will serve as an obstacle to the realization of any form of Zionism, not to speak of Ahad Ha-Am's loftier *Jewish* goals.

Considering the volatile problems which have beset Israel, from the days of its founding to the present—both inside the country and all around it—it is hardly likely that the ideals of "cultural Zionism" will soon infuse most of its inhabitants with any of its fervor. Nor should we expect them to behave like angels in a world filled with devils. But this is the "Holy Land," you say. The trouble with being "sanctified," however, is that it traps you; if you don't act like a saint, you are condemned. In the world such as it is, perhaps to try to be a "cultural center," or "a light for the nations," is not a wise or beautiful dream after all. Maybe it is a destructive delusion. It may make you do much less than you should because it asks you to do more than you can.

My own recent sojourns in the country have given me a much more sober view of what can be expected of Israel under the continuing pressures of war—and even the limited prospects of peace. Between 1949 and 1967, I had visited Israel frequently and began to sense a feeling among the people of growing isolation from the world, and of even remoter hope for an early settlement with their Arab neighbors. After the Suez War of 1956, and the forced withdrawal of Israeli troops from the Sinai—owing to pressure from the American Secretary of State, John Foster Dulles—the view of Ben-Gurion became the dominant theme of many. He had said then: What the world thinks of us is not nearly as important as what we do for ourselves in our own self-defense. Israelis, who could not lose a war but could also not win the peace, turned more and more inward, not only from the world but from Diaspora Jewry. Many regarded the Free-World Diaspora, not as a home for Jews, but as a possible future cemetery. There was no secure place for Jews save in Israel—all other domiciles were regarded as exiles doomed to perdition sooner or later. "Zionism" was seen as hypocritical posturing by Jews who refused to recog-

The Need for Dialogue 401

nize, as David Ben Gurion himself would put it, that "Zionists" in the Diaspora who refused to emigrate to Israel were no longer entitled to be called "Zionists" now that there was a state waiting for them to come. Before long, in the argot of the Israeli street, the word "Zionist" itself became an epithet of derision. (Despite later developments, their facile equation of "Zionism" with useless, "high-minded moralism" remains as a serious barrier to sober dialogue with Diaspora Jews like myself who are still nurtured by Zionist teachings. I harbor the hope that the essential humaneness and worldliness of Zionism, which made it a unique liberation movement, may not be "legislated out of existence"—in theory if not in fact—by a provincial Israeli electorate ready to pass its own moral judgments on the motives and aspirations of all non-Israeli Jews merely on the basis of transient political moods.)

But the totally unexpected had come to pass in 1967.

While the world continued to remain aloof from Arab threats to annihilate Israel in the months preceding the Six-Day War in June, the diaspora communities—especially those in North America—had helped the Israelis pull the fat out of the fire. The outpouring of Jewish volunteers from abroad, added to the overwhelming enthusiasm and financial support which those distant communities had lavished on the Jewish state, set some Israelis to rethinking their older, negative attitudes towards "foreign Zionists." They felt that the "Jewish People," not only their own citizen-army, had also won the war.

There were those who were embarrassed by their former dislike for American Jews; they themselves now began looking toward America with new and longing eyes. Their earlier contempt for the free diaspora was changing—perhaps too rapidly and uncritically—and would be replaced by the desire to "try it out for themselves." Soon enough, there were some, especially the young—among them second and third generation natives, or *sabras*—who felt so wearied and burdened by war after war that they went full circle and left their battlefield of a country to breathe the easier air of North America or Britain. To rest up for a while, they said, and to return home "some day."

Many were students who constituted a serious "brain drain" for Israel. And the loss of the young caused Tel Aviv's mayor, Shlomo Lahat, to wince. "The most crucial problem facing Israel is not the enemy or the economy—difficult as these are. It is the problem created by the youngsters who are leaving— the men and women who were born and educated in our country. The greatest danger to Zionist achievements is the loss of our young. The demographics give me pain. The flight of the young leaves me with a greying city: Seventeen percent of Tel Aviv's population is now over sixty-five." By 1983 it was estimated that over 350,000 Israelis had already taken up residence in America. Smaller but significant numbers were also living in Canada—about 25,000—in the United Kingdom and France.[15]

Ironically, just as American Jews began to multiply as new *olim*—"ascenders" or immigrants—so thousands of Israelis were moving out to the new world, as *yordim*, "descenders" or emigrants. Two disparate statistical reports, undertaken without any connection to each other or to the problem of the *yordim*, help put some of the causes for emigration from Israel into a perspective that is often repressed from public discussion. One study reveals that the only developed country in the world where women are relatively short-lived is Israel. The Israeli woman has only 1.7 to two years average life expectancy longer than the man at birth, whereas in the United States she has seven to eight years longer. There were also data showing

---

[15] See Paul Ritterband, *Education, Employment & Immigration: Israel in Comparative Perspective*, Cambridge University Press, New York, 1978. See also Drora Kass and Seymour M. Lipset, "Jewish Immigration to the United States from 1967 to the Present: Israelis and Others," in *Understanding American Jewry*, ed. Marshall Sklare, Transaction Press, New Brunswick, 1982, pp. 279 ff. Indeed, an uneven "exchange of population" seems to be at work: Secular Israelis are emigrating to America in great numbers (but not religious) while a smaller number of *religious* American Jews are now virtually the only serious *olim*.

that people who come to Israel with low disease rates acquire high rates after they live there. The researchers drew the gloomy conclusion that the stress of living in a country which fights for its life, on a daily basis, was a major contributory cause for the debilitations.

The other report, published for the year 1980 by a department of the Israeli government, provides still another clue to the kind of milieu which prevails in the country. Most people, if asked, would undoubtedly reply to the question in accordance with the popular mythology: that Israel is principally an agricultural land and that citrus fruits constitute the bulk of its exports. But this official business report records that far, far ahead of Jaffa oranges are the weapons Israel sells abroad. "Israeli Military Industries"—a company owned and operated by the Army—and several other groups account for the bulk of the country's total exports of $3.7 billion. Indeed, I.M.I.'s Uzi submachine gun has been called "the most respected weapon for close-in fighting in the world and one of Israel's star exports." But what a country like Israel works hard at, it must also think and live. Some Israelis, it seems clear, must find thinking constantly about munitions—imports and exports— disconcerting and jarring to their personal sense of values.

In 1981, a new political party entered the general national elections in Israel, the first to appear with a novel approach to some major problems in years. It called itself *Atzmaut*—the "Independence" Party. In its appeal to the electorate, it offered a series of proposals geared to "make Israel independent of grants from the United States government and gifts from North American Jewry." Among its key points were the following: "In 1979, a total of almost five billion American dollars were channelled to the government from foreign aid, charity grants, and bonds for Israel. These funds assist the political establishment to perpetuate a fairly corrupting system which enslaves Israelis," by reducing their work incentive and lowering their morals. "According to economists, the discontinuation of massive foreign aid, carefully initiated and planned, will force Israel to use its wasted resources, both human and material.... From 1945 to 1981, over 350,000 Jews have left Israel. This means that approximately every tenth Israeli has emigrated, including many who were born, bred and expensively-trained in Israel, creating a brain drain unparallelled in a Western democracy." Once Israel is economically independent, the proclamation averred, emigration—*yerida*—would halt and life would become stable. "When dependence on American aid is stopped, mutual respect in U.S.-Israel relations (between governments and between both communities of Jews) will ensue." I need hardly add that the "Independence Party" failed to gain a single place in the race for the 120 seats in the Knesset, Israel's Parliament.[16]

Apparently Israelis knew very well that such talk was brave but boastful, glorious phrases born of wishful thinking. Without American financial and military aid—not to mention the mammoth donations of its Jewish community—it is clear that Israel could not have survived as a viable economic (and therefore political) entity. Not before, not now, and not for decades to come. A classical love-hate mechanism is at work. Israelis resent benefactions, pretending not to need them when they flex their muscles as "independents." But upon awaking from sweet reveries such as these, despite tough talk about their need and capacity to make their own decisions, they find that they still can not be independent. That discovery, naturally, is most unpleasant; it accounts not only for their ambivalence and confused attitudes towards both America and its Jews, but also for their unwillingness to confront themselves and admit to it. Even if peace, by some miracle, were to break out soon in their region, this problem seems destined to linger on for years to come. A Government report released in Washington in mid-1983 revealed how profoundly dependent on American financial and military aid Israel has been, and seems destined to continue to be well into the 1990s. By then, this official docu-

---

[16] See "An Open Letter to Western Jewry: Israel Can Be Independent," in *Midstream*, May 1981, pp. 22-26.

ment reveals, Israel's accumulated debt to the United States—not taking into account the billions provided as free grants over the years—will amount to more than one billion dollars annually, "and this will produce increasing pressure from Israel for the United States either to increase its direct enonomic support or to provide other forms of financial concessions.... These steps would result in additional costs to the United States."[17] Even if they wanted to do so, Israelis could not reject a positive relationship with America, or with America's Jews.

Not surprisingly, those "descending" emigrants to America were called *Yordim*, which served as a new epithet of disdain. They were regarded as renegades and traitors who sold their souls to Mammon, all the while "Zionists from America," whether as new *olim* or even as mere overseas financial supporters, were gaining increased status and stature in the country—even though they, too, were not without their own serious problems of adjustment and acculturation. The wheels of fortune had turned. Both those *olim* and those *yordim* were to add, in their own special ways, to the growing problems of Israel—inside and outside the country—that began to mount even before the next major hostility, the Yom Kippur War of 1973.

The problems were many even though, on the surface, the country seemed to be thriving. Thanks to monies received from German reparations payments via Bonn; American governmental grants-in-aid; and, of course, the largesse of diaspora Jewish charity gifts, the economy seemed to be expanding in a never-ending, upward spiral. A year after the 1967 war the gross national product jumped by 14 per cent; and it continued to grow, by leaps and bounds, until the eve of the 1973 conflagration. Unemployment by that time had also dropped to an all-time low of 2.7%. The population was also mounting a

[17] Quoted from a Government Accounting Office Report on Israel issued on June 24, 1983. The report also revealed that the military budget of Israel then amounted to about $3.5 billion annually, of which about 40%—or almost $1.5 billion—was spent in the United States. See *New York Times*, June 26, 1983, p. 3.

boom all of its own: In the twenty-four years from the founding of the state until May 1972, the number of Jews in the country had grown by 320%—from 719,100 to 2,074,000.

Nevertheless, a "second Israel" was emerging among the "Oriental Jews" who had come to the country from backward Arab lands. In 1971, they began disrupting public life with street demonstrations and protests under their seemingly weird banner of the "Black Panthers." This was the ironical name they gave themselves to scandalize the rest of the country, a name they lifted from the political life of similarly disadvantaged Americans. Oriental Jews, and Jews of Mediterranean origin, now comprised more than half of the country's population, yet many regarded themselves as part of the "Black Panthers of Israel"—oppressed victims of economic injustice lacking their fair share of the country's growing abundance.

No less than on the economic front, things were muddied on the political scene as well. After twenty-nine years of continuous power—from the state's founding until 1977—the Labor Party lost to Menachem Begin and his right-wing coalition, abetted in the main by that protest vote of the "Orientals." Soon thereafter new Jewish settlements in the disputed occupied "West Bank" area were established with growing rapidity, alarming the American government and even causing grave dissension within Israel itself. Weren't there enough political problems already, many asked? And wouldn't monies expended for these costly new settlement-cum-military outposts be better spent on housing and social assistance programs for the disadvantaged? Or even for young couples who couldn't afford to purchase accommodation (rental housing is virtually nonexistent), considering the skyrocketing inflation which would soon reach an annual rate of 130 per cent?

Ominously—in the eyes of some Israelis and North American Jews—Begin and his government would strike out all references to the "West Bank" (of the Jordan River), and would only countenance calling that area by its biblical names of Judaea and Samaria. Wittingly or otherwise, the invocation

The Need for Dialogue 407

of these two ancient names transformed them into new code words: They smacked of Begin's old opposition party line—the irridentist claim of "both sides of the Jordan" as Jewish territory from biblical days to all eternity.[18] It was assumed that under Begin the Israeli government would become increasingly hawkish and might never yield even a single grain of sand taken in the 1967 war. It was not peace but territory and the sword his government really wanted, the "world" claimed—and many Israelis concurred.

Yet Begin surprised everyone when he warmly encouraged Sadat's journey to Jerusalem in 1978 and the joint peace initiative began. He would even sign a treaty with Egypt at Camp David in which he vowed to return the lion's share of the Sinai to Egypt by April 1982. Yet years have passed since those optimistic Camp David days, and they have not yet brought rest to war-fatigued Israelis. Comprehensive peace with the Arabs seems as illusory as ever.

Non-stop skirmishes, raids and incursions, aimed at defending and protecting Israel's territorial integrity and the security of her citizens have also given birth to veiled and hidden, yet

---

[18] It should be noted that Arabs, too, play their own "games" with the term "West Bank." To the average European or American, "West Bank" clearly refers only to the limited area west of the Jordan River, held by Arab Transjordan from 1948-1967 and occupied since then by Israel. (In 1950, for reasons clearly related to the "West Bank," "Transjordan" suddenly changed its name to "Jordan.") The term "West Bank" is regarded by non-Arabs as a purely political, and not a geographical designation. Arab ideologists, however, manipulate the phrase to combine a dual meaning: not only the 1948-1967 area, but also *all the area between the Jordan River and the Mediterranean*. In this fashion, the "West Bank" has become an Arab code word for virtually the entire State of Israel, except the Negev desert region. Thus, when some Arabs call for a "Palestinian state in the West Bank," they are really asking for the total dismantling of the entire State of Israel. Western audiences almost always understand the name "West Bank" in the limited, conventional sense, yet fail to recognize the destructive, anti-Israel "code meaning" which the name suggests to leaders of the P.L.O., Syria, Libya, Iraq, and more recently, Iran. (See also Michael A. Zimmerman, "What's In A Name?" *Midstream*, November 1982, pp. 7-9.)

serious and real, problems between many North American Jews and the Israeli leadership. Since the United States—besides the Jewish people—is Israel's only ally, a heavy burden of incessant political maneuvering has fallen on the leaders of the established American Jewish national organizations. Israel relies on their total and unswerving rubberstamping of every one of its political and military decisions. Anything less is often considered "treasonous" by the Israeli government—and by many American Jews themselves. Yet there are bound to be severe strains in a relationship that is so completely unilateral, in which "outside Jews," who shoulder neither the military nor security burdens of defending Israel's citizenry, categorically rule themselves out of making, or even questioning, Israeli decisions in these critical areas. Still, they are fully expected to "carry the ball" on the political fields of battle—as American citizens lobbying in behalf of Israel. Official Israel—from government leaders to university presidents and the like—often regards American and Canadian Jews as willing puppets on a string they may manipulate at will.

If this attitude was seen by Israelis as a helpful approach to their problems, they would be proven wrong as time wore on. True dialogue between America's Jews—even its Zionists—and Israel became next to impossible. Jewish policy was not made abroad, only in Jerusalem. Ironically, in war-torn Israel itself, questions of political and military judgment were openly and hotly debated, while in the American lands of the free and homes of the brave, Jewish discussion of these issues was ruled out and virtually squelched—not only by official Israel, but by establishment-type American and Canadian organizations. I am not, of course, arguing that "overseas" Jews should wield a veto over what Israel does in the critical areas of security and military operations, even though not all wars can be regarded as defensive or "just wars" merely because Israeli government leaders of the day say they are. I do contend, however, that if Diaspora Jewish leaders are called upon to serve as "political allies," they can not effectively fulfill policies unless they can also believe in them. They must see them as moral, beneficial, and in the long-term interests of the Jewish family everywhere, and not just as marching orders from sometimes-partisan and highly ideological Israeli governments. If there is no real dialogue on these acutely sensitive *Jewish* issues—which may transcend snap Israeli decisions—there is no telling what future Israeli cabinets may elect to do as long as the Diaspora is counted on forever to remain as a willing, docile and silent partner.

Can all these newer questions which have emerged into clearer consciousness since the Yom Kippur War—and some which emerged even as far back as 1948-9—be simply waved out of view or swept under some rug to be stored away forever? What will become of the grand Zionist vision when on a daily basis there is now grave difficulty finding answers to the accumulated social, economic and political problems that refuse to go away? What will happen to that humane dream now in a restless, peaceless society? Will the euphoria of earlier days lead to no new victories of the spirit, or yield no better memorials to the dead—those of the Holocaust added to those of more recent Israeli battles—other than more tombstones of the fallen in the unfinished wars *of* and *against* the Jews?

The Palestine Irony

Irony is the stuff of which history is made. Nowhere is proof of this more evident than in the simple, ineluctable fact which many Jews find hard to accept. They created "Palestinian Zionism" among the Arabs. And irony of ironies, the success of Zionism in achieving a Jewish State impelled the Palestinians to covet for themselves "a national homeland" too. More than once, Arabs had refused the offer of a sovereign country of their own, since that would legitimate a similar grant to the Jews. But now that there was an Israel, Arabs wanted a "Palestine."

After rejecting a variety of international plans over the years for the partition of the area into two national states—a larger

Arab country and a smaller Jewish one—and after three lost wars, the United Nations Partition Plan of 1947 looked "reasonable" to Arab leaders. As Amos Elon has said: "In 1947, the Arab states had flatly turned it down and had dispatched their armies into Palestine in an abortive attempt to prevent its implementation. After the first war, they might have accepted the armistice lines of 1949. After the second war, they still could have accepted the status quo of 1957, which implied the borders of 1949 plus freedom for Israeli shipping in the Gulf of Aqaba. If they had accepted the status quo of 1957, there would have been no war in 1967, and no Arab defeat."[19]

Still, Israeli arguments over "what could have been" will no longer do. There is a group of Arabs who call themselves "Palestinians"—whether Israel or Jews like it or not—and they will not fold up their tents—or missile-launchers—and simply fade away. It is idle and self-destructive to prolong the argument over the question of "Palestinian nationalism." Too many Israelis derive a certain escapist joy from contending that a single-minded Palestinian Arab nation is the figment of the imagination of Arab leaders who stand to gain by orchestrating the frustrations of refugees they refuse to re-settle or rehabilitate, or that it is merely a ploy for the ultimate destruction of Israel. They may be partially right on both counts—but they are wrong to take any comfort from such an argument. They are surely within their moral and political rights in not according status to the Palestine Liberation Organization as long as it refuses to recognize Israel's right to exist and remains loyal to its own charter, or *mithaq*, which is dedicated to the annihilation of the "Zionist occupiers of Palestine." What must be faced is a different question, how to shape an approach to peace with those who will continue to remain neighbors for centuries to come? *That problem will not go away because the Palestinian Arabs are not going away.* They will still be there, long after Arafat or the P.L.O. is gone.

---

[19] Amos Elon, *The Israelis: Founders and Sons*, Holt, Rinehart, Winston, New York, 1971, pp. 27-28.

It is this crucial fact which Israelis and Jews everywhere must learn to confront, however painful the exercise. Theodor Herzl never faced it, because in typical nineteenth-century liberal European style he believed that Zionism was a progressive, "European-oriented" movement destined to protect the civilized West from the backwardness of the East. Talking expansively to a reporter for the *New York Times* at the opening session of the first World Zionist Congress in Basel, Switzerland in August 1897, "Herzl, the so-called 'New Moses', explained that 'my plan is simple enough. We must obtain sovereignty over Palestine—our never-to-be forgotten, historical home.... The Jews, in exchange for Palestine, would regulate the Sultan's finances and prevent disintegration, while *for Europe we should form a new outpost against Asiatic barbarism and a guard of honor to hold intact the sacred shrines of the Christians'*." (Emphasis added.) If there were Arabs in Palestine, Herzl saw them only as "barbarians" whose threat to European culture Jews would heroically contain.[20]

While years later the Zionist Labor Parties did take note of the existence of the Arabs, they also mistakenly believed that there were no nationalist Palestinian Arabs—only exploited *fellaheen* who would be benefitted by Jewish socialism and economic progress; or a small class of wealthy *effendi*, absentee landlords, who had no nationalist sympathies and whose only interest in the land was to enrich themselves.

There was, of course, the then-relatively uninfluential "revisionist" version of Zionism, fathered by Vladimir Jabotinsky, which came to be viewed by the "official" movement as implacable and strident, an even as outside the historical mainstream of Zionist philosophy. Jabotinsky's militant doctrines of Jewish nationalism were in severe conflict with virtually all other Zionist parties, and as a result, in 1935, he and his followers found it necessary to leave the movement and to establish their own "New Zionist Organization." His views

---

[20] This rarely noticed, remarkable interview appeared in the *New York Times* as a dispatch from Basel, Switzerland on August 31, 1897, p. 7, Col. 3.

concerning Jewish selfhood seemed to appeal to those who could accept his fundamental dictum: "Do not believe anyone; be always on guard; carry your stick always with you." The large majority of Jews had tended to regard him as illiberal. Even more enigmatic—for one who was asking the world to recognize *Jewish* national rights—was Jabotinsky's contemptuous disregard for any form of "Arab nationalism." He was, of course, willing to accord all Arabs who might live in a future Jewish state full equality and civil rights as *individuals*, but not as members of an Arab—or Palestinian—nation. That view can not survive successfully any longer.

It need hardly be added that such a formulation of so-called "Jewish rights" was precisely the target of strong Jewish attacks, when nineteenth century European liberals had offered them what Jabotinsky was later "offering" the Arabs: "To the Palestinian Arabs *as individuals—everything*; to the Palestinian Arabs *as a nation, nothing*." He summarized these views regarding Arab nationalism in clear language when he appeared in the British House of Lords to testify before the Peel Royal Commission on Palestine in 1937: "We maintain unanimously that the economic position of the Palestinian Arabs, under Jewish colonization, has become the object of envy in the surrounding Arab countries.... There is no question of ousting the Arabs. On the contrary...Palestine on both sides of the Jordan should hold the Arabs, their progeny, *and* many millions of Jews. What I do not deny is that in that process the Arabs of Palestine will necesarily become a minority in the country of Palestine. What I do deny is that *that* is a hardship. It is not a hardship on any race, any nation, possessing so many National States now and so many more National States in the future. One fraction, one branch of that race, and not a big one, will have to live in someone else's State. Well, that is the case with all the mightiest nations of the world. I could hardly mention one of the big nations, having their States, mighty and powerful, who had not one branch living in someone else's

State. That is only normal and there is no 'hardship' attached to that."[21]

Under the Begin government Jabotinsky's Revisionist Zionism was to ride high in the saddle. Taken to its ultimate limits, this view had no sympathy whatever for Arab *national aspirations* in Palestine. Indeed, Mr. Begin—whom I knew and admired as a great human being but with whose politics I often disagreed—encouraged an even greater extension of these views by a small but vocal group of super-nationalist religionists who took Jabotinsky's secularist militancy giant steps further by linking it to a divine mandate for holding on to all the biblical lands in which the Children of Israel had ever dwelt. (Some even mean by this not only the "West Bank" but the biblical areas of Jordan, Lebanon, and Syria, as well.) To put their dangerous, simplistic case in a nutshell: The God of Israel promised the Jews—and the Bible is proof enough—both the east and west sides of the Jordan River; the Arabs already have more than their share of states, "awarded" them after the Second World War by Britain and France; and if the Palestinians "need a homeland," they already have one in the Hashemite Kingdom of Jordan, a country the English, in any case, had artificially and arbitrarily created as a free gift to the Palestinians carved out of the older historical land of Israel.

Fortunately, there is still a basic core of humanistic Zionists in Israel who remain outside the sway of these irridentist and strident ideologies, pragmatists willing to seek a comprehensive peace with all the Arab states and who also wish to find a *peaceful accommodation for rising Palestinian aspirations*. They would be satisfied to see Israel negotiate a settlement which would allow for the *national* autonomy of moderate Palestinians—not the vague guarantees of *"personal autonomy,"* à la Jabotinsky, as Menachem Begin and his government saw fit to define the Camp David peace accords. But the

---

[21] See Hertzberg, *op. cit.*, p. 562.

Palestinians have consistently refused to be forthcoming. Though weary of having to live in a "garrison state" until more moderate Palestinians arise, even moderate Israelis will be willing to endure the most severe hardships—and the world's poor opinion of them if need be—and stand fast until all Arabs, especially the Palestinians, follow Anwar Sadat's example and agree to coexist peaceably with a Jewish state. Not necessarily, they add, in a fashion similar to the United States and Canada but, say, like East and West Germany—not exactly the best of friends, yet not about to shoot each other down. I do not disagree.

Nor do I disagree with the Israeli position that the core question still remains the long-standing hardened Arab view that Israel has no right to exist at all. Three basic considerations emerge that are fundamental to any long-term rapprochement. In the first instance, Arab-Israeli relations can best be understood within the context of a vicious circle made up of maximalist behavior and demands by both the Palestinians and the Arab rejectionists leading to war—and then to the inevitable "intransigence" of Israel following each military victory. For anything constructive to happen that circle must be broken. Sadat did just that when he made his historic journey to Jerusalem and Israel was made to respond favorably. This can only be done again if the Palestinians and the states of the Rejectionist Front are willing to make a comparable move. Some cynics have regarded Menachem Begin's concessions to Egypt as a simple trade-off and not as a sign of Israel's willingness to make permanent peace. I do not believe that is so; but in any case, such an argument does not mean very much unless it is tested to the limit.

Second, I am firmly convinced that the real key to the mentality of the average Israeli is the problem of security. To those who live in a beleaguered state surrounded by hostile terrorists and armies, security will always remain paramount. Ideologies will wither when it comes to a choice between security and territory; the former will prevail. I believe that if a

The Need for Dialogue   415

convincing case could be made that territory is standing in the way of security, then annexationist forces in Israel—irridentists of all stripes, religious hard-liners, and assorted "world-be-damned" types—would be defeated. As hard a pill to swallow as was the return of the Sinai to Egypt—and especially the razing and flattening of Yamit, the beautiful desert creation—it could be done, even (perhaps especially) by a government headed by a so-called "hard-liner," Menachem Begin. The bottom line must still seem to be reasonable, and in keeping with Israel's ultimate purpose and interest: peace and security, not war and territory. That is the kind of pragmatic decision Israel should be prepared to make in the future, regardless of what government is in power.

The evacuation and destruction of settlements in northern Sinai in the Spring of 1982 in fulfillment of the Camp David accords had a traumatic effect on Israel's population. It is unlikely that the citizens of the country would ever again agree to dismantle Jewish settlements in the future, certainly not those on the West Bank. Almost all political parties—including some doves in the Labor Party—share the same concerns over the West Bank as a potential base of Palestinian operations against Israel. These fears are unlikely to disappear until the Arab side develops a policy of coexistence with the Jewish state. Despite the bleakness on the horizon, that day must always be hoped for—*and planned for*.

The Israelis are still placed, however, in a constant bind. They cannot be asked to hand over territory without near-certain assurance that it will not jeopardize their security. The argument that Israel is expansionist and intent on sitting on every inch of land its military forces can conquer is not persuasive as long as it remains clear that the Arab world as a whole—including so-called moderate states—is not even close to recognizing the right of Israel to exist. Virtually all Arab and Muslim states remain hostile to Israel, which in their shopworn hyperbole they see as "a thorn in the Arab flesh and a dagger pointed to the Muslim heart." There is no escape: Israeli steadfastness is justified and necessary, in my view, as long as Arabs remain enmeshed in this trap of their own making, or until a new leader like Sadat arises.

Finally, to be realistic, the so-called "Masada Complex" is deeply part of the Israeli psyche, as a result of the unforgettable memories of the Six Million who died while the world—including many Jews—slept peacefully. If the Israelis ever became convinced that their state was fully expendable to others, and left to doom and destruction, I believe that they would not hesitate to inflict unbearable damage on the whole Arab world, even if it threatened to precipitate a world war. *Ultimately, it is this reality that may one day induce neighboring Arab states—and their friends elsewhere—to come to terms with the idea that Israel is in the Middle East to stay.* If this seems like a horrible way to achieve accommodation, think of the "balance of terror" that exists between East and West. Perhaps all that stands in the way of the world's nuclear destruction is the threat of nuclear incineration itself. But little would stand in the way of peace in the Middle East once Arabs accepted Israel's legitimacy. Even the most strident supernationalists in Israel would lose their audience.

There are obviously no easy answers to the profound Arab-Israel conflict, as there are none to many other friction points around the world. Egypt's position after Sadat remains questionable, and the fact that the Camp David treaty is still rejected by all other Arab states can not make one sanguine about the near term in the Middle East. Yet I remain optimistic about the future of Israel once the Arab posture of "no-peace-no-recognition-no negotiation" begins to crack under its own weight, or in the wake of new twists in their *weltpolitik*, or even as a result of true *détente* between America and Russia. Perhaps other problems raised earlier will also fade away as a coefficient of reduced strain from Arab hostility. Still others will also be tackled successfully once Jews—in North America and Israel—have the courage to trust themselves to honest dialogue that looks to the long-range interests of both and not merely to the day-by-day politics Israeli parliamentarians continue to play.

After all, the history of Zionism was no bed of roses, and only when clear-eyed men resolved to meet their challenges "head-on" could they "howl down an Empire," tame the desert, or open gates wide to otherwise-doomed men, women, and children. If those great Zionist tasks could have been achieved in less than half a century—and under implausible and near-disaster conditions—why not these newer challenges too? Israel still contains the largest number of full-time realist-idealist Jews per square foot of all the world's diaspora communities, and therefore continues to remain the best Jewish hope on earth. What we and she need now—both in the Diaspora and the homeland—is not respectful, docile silence towards those in power, or the hallowing of any *status quo*, but something quite different. We need to remember the days of her youth, and not allow short-sighted or over-ideological partisan leaders to make her decadent now—while still young—or ever. Her future, after all, is even more important than her past or present. It will be shared by all Jews—those already there and those who stay close to her, from afar—but only if there is true sharing based on honest respect *for moral differences*.

There is, however, a major caveat. Having returned to the stage of world history, re-encased now in the fragile body politic of a nation-state, and mindful of the fate of the Six Million, Israel is repeatedly tempted to pursue the same path all other states do. All nations go to great lengths to protect their own vulnerable flanks, and act only in terms of what they regard to be their national self-interest. Should anyone reasonably or realistically expect Israel to exceed the norm and do more? Since this is not a rhetorical but a moral question, not surprisingly Jews answer it either "yes" or "no"—depending on what they expect of themselves.

Beginning with Herzl, Zionists had always anticipated that a restored Jewish state would not only be "normal" but also serve as a model community for others. But it is not so easy to fault many world-weary Israelis who tell us that only diaspora Jews can still luxuriate romantically in the "myths" of Zionist idealism propagated decades ago in pre-State days. Outside of Israel's precarious borders, they contend, Jews, even "Zionists," are not constrained to live as they do, in daily confrontation with the guns and missiles of armies and terrorist bands—mortal enemies on all their sides. Accordingly, their argument continues, the real Israel—not the mythic, idealized Zion—must now behave as any *normal*, imperiled state would in similar circumstances. For the moment at least, they urge, the prudent practice of *realpolitik* is the price Israel and Jews everywhere must pay for "normalcy" in an abnormal world, though it creates tension and conflict with the world, and even tension and conflict with the noblest universalist teachings of Judaism.

Nor should anyone expect, they earnestly contend, that Israel's elected leaders should allow themselves to be easily persuaded by outsiders—including overseas Jews—to do otherwise. Even if those others speak as friends, they are wrong to "demand" that Israel behave as "Jews should"—as if any other state in the world even remotely behaves as "Christians" or "Muslims" should. Surely none of a long list of assorted sycophants has any moral right to "preach" to Israel, or to ask for anything of the sort. Not the least, any of these: neither the self-serving Soviets nor their Third World lackeys; or the sensationalist, often misinformed media; or the growing number of double-standard "moralists" at the United Nations; or the shoddy, self-seeking, greedy and grasping petro-politicians and corporations around the world.

Still, the question naggingly persists: Do not Jews have the right—even the need—to expect more of themselves, especially now that their older minority powerlessness has been replaced by their new dominion? Their Book—the covenant from which they escape only at their own spiritual peril—demands that they regard political issues as moral questions. If they had no

Bible—and no vision of Zion—they would not be faced with this unique demand, and politics could be for them what it is for most others—just politics. But then, if they had no Bible, they would have no Israel either. Which is why dogmatic inflexibility must always yield to new openings that may lead to accommodation.

Jews who have lived and studied in the United States know that even "materialistic America," because of a deeply ingrained biblical mentality, repeatedly purges its own excesses by falling back on its own scriptural supports. Indeed, the oft-touted "special relationship" that exists between America and Israel (frequently cited as part of unwavering American foreign policy by successive Presidents) is linked to the biblical heritage—especially of the "Old Testament"—of Protestant, Puritan America. It has often been noted that only that biblical heritage—especially the moral outcries of the Hebrew prophets—has been able to protect America from its own excesses. Vietnam, nuclear proliferation, poverty, racial discrimination, the pollution of the environment—all of these, in an America that still regards itself as a Bible-reverencing nation, ordained by God Himself to live up to the highest human ideals, take on special meanings less related to political doctrine than to moral outrage.

Few outsiders, for example, could understand why millions of Americans were so disturbed by the revelations of Watergate. The reason, I suspect, has to do with a profound irony. Despite its worship of success and power, as a Bible-centered country still spiritually linked to its founding Pilgrim Fathers, the United States has developed a sense of national mission. It is this self-same feeling of special national purpose, rooted in their identification with the higher visions of the Hebrew prophets, that often leads many Americans to feel a corresponding sense of national failure and betrayal. They can, they believe, and should, do better.

I ask myself now: May Jews—givers and keepers of that Book—do any less?

One day, should we not hope, if the world relents, and finally lets us be Jews—as well as Israelis—and mortal fears have fled our hearts, shall we not do even more? Beyond politics, there must still remain for us our vision of humanity. Even in a place where there are no men, must we not strive on to be men?

There is, as my grandfather said, healing power already here. It is deeply imbedded in the unquenched hopes of an old-new nation whose homecoming was always intended to serve as a universal blessing for all mankind.

We require the courage to keep dreaming our utopian dream—and like biblical Jacob to keep building our ladder to the sky now, at last, that it is firmly implanted, even if only on a small piece of our own earth.

We need renewed will to use the spiritual power we have stored for twenty centuries, to be what we have always believed ourselves to be: a covenant nation—a teaching people for all the world.

We need to remember the Book that made us what we are and must remain.

The *real Jewish world* may never fully become *the ideal Jewish world*, but if we do not forget these things, it will always be worth saving. "It is not incumbent upon us," as Rabbi Tarphon said, "to complete the task; but neither are we free to desist from it."[22]

---

[22] *Mishnah Abot*: 2:21.

INDEX

A

Aaron 344
Abella, Irving 278
Abraham 142, 155, 233
Acheson, Dean 333
Adenauer, Konrad 291
Agassi, Fruma Reichman 360
Agassi, Samuel (Birnbaum) 360, 362
Agnon, S.J. 170, 171
Akiba, Rabbi 200
Aleichem, Sholom 14, 289
Alroy, David 380
Aronius, J. 79
Arzt, Max 124, 125, 202
Assembly of Jewish Notables, the 232
Ataxerxes, King of Persia 236
Avruch, Kevin 372
Avtalyon 200

B

Balfour, Arthur James 242
Bar Lev 221
Bar-On, Mordechai 309
Barkley, Alben 269
Baron, Salo W. 158
Bauer, Yehuda 280
Baum, Gregory 207
Begin, Menachem 351, 373, 406, 407, 413, 414, 415

Beit Ha-kerem 362
Bell, Daniel 240
Ben Gurion, David 129, 250, 312, 313, 337, 352, 357, 358, 359, 377, 401
Ben Gurion, Paula 313
Ben Gurion University 341
Ben Gurion(s) 314, 391
ben Nahman, Moshe (Nahmanides) 394
Ben Zvi, Rachel 355
Ben Zvi, Yitzhak 352, 355
Ber, Dov 100
Bergman, Elihu 387, 388
Bergson, Peter 283, 284
Berle, Milton 22
Bernadotte, Folke 330, 331
Bernstein, Philip S. 126, 127, 128, 129, 130, 131, 133, 262, 330, 331
Bikkur Cholim Hospital 360
Birnbaum, Jacob 322
Blau, Zena Smith 145
Bonaparte, Napoleon 232-235
Borowitz, Eugene 138, 140
Brandeis, Louis Dembitz 178, 244, 246, 247, 249
Bratislava 311
Braverman, Joel (Mahr) 4, 5, 9, 26, 34, 59, 151, 218
Bromfield, Louis 285
Bronfman, Sam 300
Buber, Martin 214

421

C

Caesar, Julius 153
Cahan, Abraham 237
Carter, Jimmy 253
Chanzin, Mordechai 293, 295, 320, 321
Cobrin 315
Crow, Jim 122
Cunningham, Alan 329
Cyrus, King of Persia 331

D

Davis, Moshe 202
Dayan, Moshe 292
Dewey, John 78
Dewey, Thomas E. 331
Dinstein, Yoram 315, 316, 317, 319
Donne, John 24
Dreyfus, Alfred 384
Dreyfus Trial 383
Dulles, John Foster 400

E

Eban, Abba 223
Eddy, Nelson 165
Eichmann, Adolph 213, 223
Einstein, Albert 243
Eisenhower, Dwight D. 126
Elazar, Daniel J. 162, 181
Elon, Amos 410
Engels, Jack 317
Epstein, Avraham (Abba Arikha) 5, 9, 229
Eshkol, Levi 319

F

Fefferman 349
Feinstein, Moshe 46, 47, 49
Finkelstein, Louis 201, 202, 205
Fisher, Eugene 370
Ford, Henry 238, 247
Forrest, Al 301
Fosdick, Harry Emerson 73
Frankel 20, 21
French Revolution 234
Freud, Sigmund 214
Friedman, Rabbi 17, 46, 53, 107, 112, 113, 114, 119, 135
Fromm, Erich 212, 214

G

Gamaliel II, Rabbi 166
Ganin, Zvi 331
Gans, Herbert 81
Garber, Michael 289, 300
Gillette, Guy 285
Ginsberg, Harry Louis 202
Ginzberg, Asher (Ahad Ha-Am) 52, 399
Glueck, Nelson 345
Goebbels, Josef 279
Goldberg, Henry 128
Goldfein, Eddie 83, 85, 86, 174
Goldman, Ma 84
Goldmann, Nahum 290, 291, 299, 300, 302, 305, 321, 324
Goldschieder, Calvin 372
Goodman, Percival 176
Gordis, Robert 202
Green, D.F. 370
Greenberg, Simon 202

Grynberg, Henryk 283

H

Ha-Am, Ahad (Asher Ginzberg) 51, 52, 398, 399, 400
Ha-Levi, Yehuda 201, 394
Ha-Livanon 361
Hacham, Amos 364
Hagana 250, 251, 252, 337
Handlin, Oscar 231
Hansen, Marcus Lee 87
Hausner, Gideon 213, 223
Hayes, Saul 289, 301, 304
Hebrew University (at Givat Ram) 362, 394
Hebron 362
Hecht, Ben 275, 276, 283, 284, 285
Heilman, Samuel 101
Helena, Queen of Adiabene 201
Herberg, Will 191
Hertzberg, Arthur 384, 385, 394, 398, 413
Herzl, Theodor 51, 242, 264, 337, 355, 366, 367, 383-386, 392, 399, 417
Herzliah 59, 190
Herzog, Yaacov 213, 319
Heschel, Abraham Joshua 76, 177, 178, 202, 302, 303, 305-309, 315
Hillel 230
Hiram, King of Tyre 340
Histadrut, the 351, 352
Hitler, Adolph 38, 39, 40, 213, 219, 238, 264, 277, 281, 282, 324, 335, 369, 386
Holmes, John Hayes 269

Howe, Irving 164
Hutchins, Robert Maynard 209

I

Ibn Khordadbeh 153
Ibn Shuaib, Joel 117
Ickes, Harold 285
Isaac 155
Isaac, Joseph 100
Israel-Soviet Friendship League 288

J

Jabotinsky, Vladimir 283, 411, 412, 413
Jacob 420
Jassy 7, 8, 14, 18, 291
John XXIII, Pope 318
John Paul II, Pope 319
Johnson, Ed 285
Joseph 44

K

Kahn, Louis 176
Kallen, Horace 211
Kaplan, Mordecai M. 6, 53, 57, 58, 60, 71, 72, 75-78, 87, 91, 102-105, 202, 211, 218
Kass, Drora 402
Katz, Elijah 311
Katz, Mrs. 311
Kayser, Irene 223
Kayser, Stephen S. 218, 219, 221, 223
Kelman, Wolfe 303, 307

Kertzer, Morris 286, 308
Khomeini 370
Khrushchev, Nikita 286, 295
King, Martin Luther 303
Knox, Frank 285
Kook, Abraham Isaac 283

L

Lahat, Shlomo 402
Lamm, Maurice 158
Laqueur, Walter 282
Levin, Yehudah Leib 293, 294, 296, 311, 321, 325
Levine, Etan 382
Lewin, Samuel 305
Lieberman, Samuel S. 387
Lifschutz 363
Lindbergh, Charles 279
Linowitz, Sol M. 253, 254, 255
Linowitz, Toni 253
Lipset, Seymour M. 402
Lochner, Louis P. 279
Lowenthal, Marvin 211
Luther, Martin 97

M

MacDonald, Jeanette 165
Maimonides, Moses 118
Maller, Allen S. 388
Mammon 405
Mann, Horace 26
Mapai Party 353, 357
Margolis, Rabbi 17, 46, 53, 165
Marshall, George C. 330, 331
Marshall, Peter 87
Martin, Paul 314

Marty, Martin E. 93, 95
Massey, Vincent 185
McCormick, "Bertie" 279
McDonald, James Grover 331, 332, 333
Meir, Rabbi 200
Mendelson, Eric 176
Mikunis, Shmuel 356, 357
Mintz, Max 4
Mishneh (Saltzman) 349
Moehlmann, Conrad 203
Montefiore, Moses (Sir) 360
Montor, Henry 128, 130
Moore, George F. 200
Morse, Arthur D. 281
Morse, Wayne 269
Morty (Yeshivah-mate) 256, 260
Moses 16, 112, 155, 344, 382
Moshe Rabbenu 112
Mount Herzl 367
Moza 361

N

Nadya (guide) 293
Nahalat Shiva 361
Napoleon 232, 233, 234, 235
Nasser 269, 372
Nazareth 361
New York University 362
Nicholas I, Tsar 382
Niebuhr, Reinhold 73
Nixon, Justin Wroe 203
Norry, Irving S. 251, 252

O

Ochs, Adolph S. 243, 255

Oesterreicher, John 317
Olan, Levi 308
Orbach, William W. 322

P

Palmach 364
Parkes, James 79
Patton, General 126
Pelzig, Perli 219
Persky, Daniel 46
Petah Tikvah 361
Philippe, Louis 235, 389
Pignedoli, Sergio 318, 319
Pines, Yechiel Michael 392, 394
Pinsker, Leon 382, 383, 384
Popov, A. 305

R

Rabinovich, Itzhak 287, 288
Rabinowitz, Eliyahu 6, 9, 54, 66, 67
Rabinowitz-Batz, Meir 71, 287, 312, 313, 334-350, 352, 368
Rabinowitz-Batz, Sara 339
Rappoport, Mordechai 352, 354, 357, 358, 359, 363
Rav 380
Rebekah 155
Reichman, Yeshoshua Mayer 360
Rembrandt 155
Richter, Glenn 322
Ritterband, Paul 402
Rockefeller, John D. 73
Rogers, Will, Jr. 285
Roosevelt, Franklin D. 32, 33, 44, 255, 273-281, 283, 290, 299

Roosevelt, Theodore 301
Rose, Peter I. 81
Rosenberg, Elissa Beth 338
Rosenberg, Hadassa (Agassi) 47, 253, 310, 315, 338, 360, 361, 362
Rosenberg, Hyman 7
Rosenberg, Joshua Zev 8
Rosenberg, Rachelle 338
Rosenberg, Ronni 338
Rosenne, Meir 291-293, 298, 299, 302, 306, 308-310, 314, 315, 320
Roth, Cecil 219, 220, 222
Roth, Philip 121, 139
Rothschild 384
Rothschild, Lord 242
Rothschild, Edmund de 361

S

Sadat, Anwar 266, 267, 369, 373, 407, 414, 416
Samuel, Maurice 200, 211
Samuel 229
Sanhedrin 233
Schechter, Solomon 141
Schiff, Jacob 98, 230, 231, 239
Schlieffer, Solomon 292
Schneerson, Menahem Mendel 100
Seeley, John 193, 194, 195
Seldon, Harry 285
Shalmaneser 312
Shammai 230
Sharett, Moshe 212, 292
Sharett, Yaacov (Kobi) 292, 296, 297

Shemaya 200
Sherri (chauffeur) 339, 341, 343
Shook, L.K. 317
Shuchat, Wilfred 316, 317
Silver, Abba Hillel 220, 290, 302
Sklare, Marshall 81, 372, 402
Slater, Leonard 252
Solomon, Joel Moses 360, 361
Solomon, King 340, 345
Sonneborn, Rudolph 250, 251, 252
Spiegal, Shalom 202
Sprinzak, David 350
Sprinzak, Hanna 350, 352, 353, 360, 364
Sprinzak, Yosef 334, 335, 350, 352, 354-360, 362, 363, 367, 368
Stalin, Joseph 285, 295
Steinbach, Alexander Allen 43, 44
Strabo 153
Strelsin, Alfred 285

T

Tarphon, Rabbi 420
Thompson, Dorothy 269
Tillich, Paul 73, 214
Toronto Star 288
Toynbee, Arnold J. 199, 201
Traberman, Jake 84
Troper, Harold 278
Truman, Harry S. 329, 331, 332, 333

V

van der Rohe, Mies 178
Van Paasen, Pierre 269
Vatican Congregation for Non-Christians 318, 319

W

Wagner, Richard 162
War of Liberation 364
Warburgs 231
Washington, George 347
Weinfeld, Morton 387
Weisgal, Meyer 244, 269
Weissman, Abraham 8, 12, 15, 178
Weissman family 14
Weissman, Rachel 8
Weizmann, Chaim 242-245, 247, 249, 264, 267, 271, 272, 352, 354, 355
Wiesel, Elie 213, 307-310
Wigoder, Geoffrey 223
Wilf, Alex 285
Wilhelm II, Kaiser 366
Wilson, Joseph 254
Wilson, Woodrow 244
Wise, Stephen S. 53-58, 60, 127, 211, 279, 281, 290
Woocher, Jonathan S. 104
Wright, Frank Lloyd 176
Wyman, David S. 281

Y

Yadin, Matti 350
Yadin, Yigael 213, 336, 350

Yavniel 361
Yehoshua, A.B. 375, 376, 382
Yeshivah (of Flatbush) 190
Yitzhak, Avraham 16
Yosef, Dov (Bernard Joseph) 353
Yosef, Goldie 353
Youngman, Henny 22

Z

Zalman, Shneour 100
Zambrowsky, S. 304, 305
Zevi, Sabbatai 381
Zimmerman, Michael A. 407
Zola, Emile 384